*f*P

Also by Lee Edwards

THE POWER OF IDEAS
The Heritage Foundation at 25 Years

GOLDWATER
The Man Who Made a Revolution

MISSIONARY FOR FREEDOM
The Life and Times of Walter Judd

JOHN PAUL II IN THE NATION'S CAPITAL (ed.)

REBEL PEDDLER

YOU CAN MAKE THE DIFFERENCE

RONALD REAGAN
A Political Biography

The
Conservative
Revolution

The Movement That Remade America

LEE EDWARDS

The Free Press

THE FREE PRESS
A Division of Simon & Schuster Inc.
1230 Avenue of the Americas
New York, NY 10020

THE FREE PRESS and colophon are trademarks
of Simon & Schuster Inc.

Designed by Carla Bolte

Manufactured in the United States of America

10   9   8   7   6   5   4   3   2   1

Library of Congress Cataloging-in-Publication Data

Edwards, Lee.
     The conservative revolution : the movement that remade America /
Lee Edwards.
         p.   cm.
     Includes bibliographical references (p.   ) and index.
     1. United States—Politics and government—1945–1989.   2. United
States—Politics and government—1989–   3. Conservatism—United
States—History—20th century.   4. Republican Party (U.S.)
I. Title.
E743.E23   1999
320.973′09′045—dc21   98-54800
                                                              CIP

To the founders of the American conservative movement, especially Russell Kirk, William F. Buckley, Jr., and Barry Goldwater

Contents

Introduction

WHEN REPUBLICANS IN 1994 CAPTURED THE U.S. HOUSE OF REPRESENTATIVES for the first time in forty years, regained control of the U.S. Senate, and wound up with thirty governorships representing 70 percent of the country's population, stunned Democrats (and not a few analysts) wondered "What happened?"

It was, according to the *New York Times,* "a political upheaval of historic proportions." The change that the American electorate called for, concluded the *Washington Post,* was "almost uniformly in one direction . . . against liberalism and toward the right."[1]

The 1994 elections were, quite simply, the most dramatic manifestation of a conservative revolution in American politics that had been going on for fifty years. It was conservative because it offered an orderly transition to a new form of politics and yet revolutionary because it represented a radical change from the immediate past.

The conservative revolution rested on two epic events, one foreign, one domestic, that have shaped our tumultuous times. The first, and more important, was the waging and winning of the cold war. The second was the American public's rejection, after years of acceptance, of the idea that the federal government should be the primary solver of our major economic and social problems.

Conservatives declared from its emergence that communism was evil and had to be defeated, not just contained. And they saw that the federal government had grown dangerously large and had to be rolled back, not just managed more efficiently.

Because conservatives played a decisive role in ending the cold war and alerting the nation to the perils of a leviathan state, they reaped enormous

1

political rewards, from Ronald Reagan's sweeping presidential victories in 1980 and 1984 to the Republicans' historic capture of Congress in 1994.

But we find little discussion of the conservative revolution in history books. If we seek explanations as to why communism fell, we read that the Soviet Union was much weaker and more extended than we had realized and that history fortuitously produced a Soviet reformer and democrat in Mikhail Gorbachev. These books tell us that the policy of containment worked, although it took several decades longer than its formulator, American diplomat and liberal icon George Kennan, had predicted.[2]

And from such histories we also learn that it was the New Democrat, Bill Clinton, who recognized that "the era of big government is over." He was, they instruct, reacting to the national debt of over $5 trillion produced mostly by the faulty economics of the two previous Republican presidents. It was also Clinton who promised to "end welfare as we know it" and delivered on his promise: The number of welfare recipients across the country declined by 9 percent during the first Clinton administration.[3]

These history books speak of conservatives, it is true, but usually as demagogues, Machiavellians, and simpletons. Accordingly, Senator Joseph McCarthy, a beetle-browed bully, instigated a modern Reign of Terror in the early 1950s. Barry Goldwater, an Arizona cowboy, threatened to destroy social security and start a nuclear war as a presidential candidate in 1964. Ronald Reagan, a one-time B-movie actor, produced a climate of rampant greed with his trickle-down economic policies in the 1980s. And House Speaker Newt Gingrich, reeking of malfeasance, tried to carry out a contract *against* America.

Such an accounting is light-years away from the true political history of America over the past five decades. It glorifies mediocrities and demeans extraordinary men and women. The failure of so many historians, considered eminent in their field, to present an accurate political portrait of the modern conservative movement, and therefore modern American politics, prompted the writing of this book: the political history of a disparate, often fractious group of philosophers, popularizers, and politicians who rose up to challenge the prevailing liberal orthodoxy. And they triumphed over great odds to become the national movement that dominates American politics today.

The conservative revolution that remade America was a long time in the making. Indeed it seemed on the edge of extinction more than once: after the untimely death of Robert A. Taft in 1953, after the crushing defeat of

Barry Goldwater in 1964, after the Iran–contra affair in 1987, and after the demonization of Newt Gingrich in the 1990s. But the conservative revolution not only survived these crises, each time it gained strength and momentum, in large measure because of its principled leaders.

First came the men of ideas: intellectuals and philosophers like Friedrich A. Hayek, the Austrian-born classical liberal; Russell Kirk, the midwestern traditionalist; and Irving Kristol, the New York City Trotskyite-turned-neoconservative. Next came the men of interpretation: the journalists and popularizers like the polymath William F. Buckley, Jr.; the columnist and television commentator George Will; and the radio talkmeister Rush Limbaugh.

Last came the men of action, the politicians and policymakers, led by the Four Misters: "Mr. Republican," Robert A. Taft; "Mr. Conservative," Barry Goldwater; "Mr. President," Ronald Reagan; and "Mr. Speaker," Newt Gingrich. There were also two Republican presidents whose lives and careers were intertwined with the conservative movement from the 1940s through the 1970s: Herbert Hoover and Richard Nixon. Conservatives admired Hoover for refusing to be the passive scapegoat of the Great Depression and for helping to build the conservative movement. And conservatives never forgot that Nixon was the tough young congressman who "got" former Soviet spy Alger Hiss, no matter Nixon's later transgressions such as shaking hands with Mao Zedong in China and using Keynesian methods to deal with the economy.

The conservative revolution was also helped by the decline and fall of American liberalism, which lost its way between the New Deal and the Great Society, between Korea and the Sandinistas, between Harry Truman and Michael Dukakis. Liberals went into free fall, their swift descent marked by a telltale shift from concern for the common man and Middle America to preoccupation with minorities and special interests.

And the conservative revolution was helped by the political maturation of American conservatism itself, as the movement learned how to combine traditionalists, libertarians, and neoconservatives; the South, Midwest, and West; and blue-collar Catholics and Protestant evangelicals into a winning electoral force.

Conservatives triumphed in the 1980s and 1990s when their movement contained all the elements necessary for political success: a clearly defined, consistent philosophy; a broad-based, cohesive national constituency; experienced, charismatic, principled leadership; a sound financial base; and proficiency in the mass media. They were also helped by a sixth factor: an atmosphere of crisis. In 1980, Americans were sharply aware that the nation required leaders who could cope with critical problems like inflation, unemployment, and the Soviet empire, and in 1994, they demanded that something be done about out-of-control government programs like health care and welfare.

And yet electoral politics is one thing and governing politics quite another. Many brilliant political campaigners have been a disappointment or even a disaster in office. Newt Gingrich was a visionary leader in 1994, but after four years as Speaker, he fell under fire from conservatives for compromising too readily on core issues like tax cuts and found himself with too few allies when the 1998 congressional elections produced a loss of five seats for the Republicans rather than the gain of thirty that he had predicted. Three days after the election, he stepped down from the speakership and was replaced by Louisiana's Robert L. Livingston, a more pragmatic conservative. But the chaotic nature of Washington politics was demonstrated yet again when Livingston dramatically resigned five weeks later (admitting marital infidelity), to be succeeded by Dennis Hastert of Illinois, another consensus-seeking conservative.

Conservatives have proved conclusively that they can win elections: even in the so-called disappointing year of 1998, they still retained majorities in the House, the Senate, and among the governorships. But can they build and maintain a governing majority? Or is "a conservative government" an oxymoron, given conservatives' instinctive antipathy toward the state?

Today, conservative ideas reign in the halls and offices of Congress, in the calculations of the Clinton administration, in the statehouses, in national and regional think tanks, in newspaper op-ed and magazine articles, and in daily radio talk shows and Sunday morning television programs. Conservative ideas are even discussed respectfully in a growing number of leading colleges and universities.

But it is the answer to the central question—"Can conservatives govern?"—that will determine whether the conservative revolution has truly remade America or only touched it fleetingly; whether conservatism remains a commanding political movement in America or, like so many other movements, winds up on the ashheap of history.

4

Chapter 1

"Had Enough?"

MORE THAN ANY OTHER EVENT IN THE TWENTIETH CENTURY, WORLD WAR II transformed our nation and our world. Any talk about returning to "normalcy" with the war's end was just that—talk. Indeed, nothing was "normal" in postwar America. The nation's political lodestar, Franklin Delano Roosevelt, was gone, succeeded by Harry S. Truman, a Missouri farmer and judge. Rather than repeating our isolationist impulses following World War I, America happily hosted the founding of the United Nations. Twelve million men and women (more servicemen than had fought in all the previous conflicts in our history) poured back from the war. They wanted a decent job and a nice house, a couple of kids and a new car, quiet nights and lazy Sundays after the shrapnel-riddled fields of Europe and the bloody beaches of the South Pacific. They wanted the American dream, and why not? They had risked their lives to preserve it.

Change was everywhere. Enrollment in colleges and universities doubled as ex-servicemen took advantage of the GI Bill. With government help, home-hungry veterans were able to move into the new suburbs that sprang up outside the cities. Many resettled in the West and the South, creating new constituencies and challenging old electoral alliances.[1]

At war's end in 1945, America had a population of 141 million, but the mustered-out GI Joes and Janes launched a baby boom that continued for eighteen years, producing an America of over 190 million by 1964.

America was the world's number one economic power, and there was no number two. Our 1945 gross national product of $204 billion was about equal to that of the rest of the world combined, although public debt had soared from $49 billion in 1941 to $269 billion by mid-1946. We were a remarkably self-sufficient country. We produced our own food and used our own natural resources for fuel and raw materials. So, too, our automobiles, farm machines, factory tools, electric appliances, and household implements were, by and large, "made in America."[2]

We were a young, optimistic nation with a median age of twenty-nine. Unemployment was less than 4 percent. Immigration was strictly controlled: only 148,954 immigrants came to our shores in all of 1946. Most neighborhoods were able to control crime; as historian James T. Patterson pointed out, "Public disorder was only here and there a major worry."[3]

But there were problems too. Organized labor, representing about one-fifth of the national workforce, was no longer willing to defer raises and other benefits it had set aside during the war. When management did not meet its postwar demands, strikes erupted from Maine to California. There were an astounding 4,750 work stoppages in 1945, the wave of strikes cresting in early 1946 with 1.8 million workers in such major industries as meat-packing, oil refining, electrical appliances, steel, and automobile manufacturing. The year 1946 "became the most contentious in the history of labor-management relations in the United States," according to Patterson: 4,985 stoppages by 4.6 million workers, or about one of every fourteen Americans in the labor force.[4]

Republicans decided to make political capital of the strikes to help gain a congressional majority in the 1946 elections and to prepare the way, they hoped, for their return to the White House in 1948 after a generation in the political wilderness.

World politics had also been changed radically by the world war. America now bestrode the world like a benevolent colossus. Nazi Germany was buried beneath mountains of rubble and occupation armies. Imperial Japan docilely accepted General Douglas MacArthur as its new leader, even allowing him to write a new constitution. Most Americans believed that global peace could be secured through organizations like the United Nations.

But while the United States was demobilizing as quickly as it could, foreign policy experts voiced mounting alarm over the steady encroachment of the Soviet Union. Their concern was intensified by an election address by Premier Joseph Stalin in February 1946. In it, the "candidate" for the Supreme Soviet blamed World War II on "monopoly capitalism," stated that

future conflicts were inevitable because of the "present capitalist development of the world economy," and called for the expansion of heavy industry
in the Soviet Union "and all kinds of scientific research" for the next fifteen
years if necessary. "Only under such conditions," Stalin declared, "will our
country be insured against any eventuality."[5]

Stalin's belligerence disturbed many in Washington, liberals and conservatives alike. Supreme Court associate justice William O. Douglas asserted
that the Soviet leader's speech meant "the declaration of World War III."
Columnist Marquis Childs wrote that "Stalin's speech closed the door" to
U.S.-USSR collaboration. And *Newsweek* magazine referred to the address as
the "most war-like pronouncement uttered by any statesman since V-J
Day."[6]

Three weeks after Stalin's speech, Senator Arthur H. Vandenberg of
Michigan, the leading Republican spokesman on foreign policy, issued an
urgent call for a new policy of firmness toward the Soviet Union. "What is
Russia up to now?" he asked in a Senate speech. Anticipating the rolling
rhetoric of Winston Churchill's famous iron curtain speech, which would be
delivered one week later in Fulton, Missouri, Vandenberg said:

> We ask it in Manchuria. We ask it in Eastern Europe and the Dardanelles.
> . . . We ask it in the Baltic and the Balkans. We ask it in Poland. . . . We ask
> it sometimes even in connection with events in our own United States.
> "What is Russia up to now?" . . . It is a question which must be answered
> before it is too late.[7]

Vandenberg's speech was greeted by a standing ovation from his Senate
colleagues and hailed in much of the American press. The *Omaha World-
Herald* wrote, "This is the voice of responsibility, the voice of statesmanship,
the voice that America has been longing to hear." Arthur Krock of the *New
York Times* correctly interpreted the speech as a criticism of President Truman and Secretary of State James F. Byrnes for their failure to produce a co-
herent foreign policy.[8] This first public criticism of the Soviet Union by a
major American political figure since the end of World War II signaled too
that the Republicans intended to stress foreign policy in the fall elections.

The GOP had already been given several domestic issues to challenge in
Truman's first State of the Union address, delivered in January, in which the
president had asked for another year of wage and price controls. Nor had
Truman backed away from his earlier proposals to nationalize the housing in-

dustry, establish federal control of all unemployment compensation, and pass a strong fair employment practices law. Republicans quickly picked up Truman's gauntlet. House minority leader Joseph Martin of Massachusetts accused the president of "out-dealing the New Deal." And Congressman Charles Halleck of Indiana barked, "This is the kickoff. This begins the campaign of 1946."[9]

Republicans in Congress found important political allies among southern conservative Democrats like Senator Harry Byrd of Virginia and Senators Walter George and Richard Russell of Georgia. The two groups shared a strong distaste for intrusive federal power and a firm commitment to limited government. As *New York Times* correspondent William S. White noted, these southern conservatives were not simply "Democratic rebels lying in wait" to attack their national party. They opposed philosophically the liberal direction of the Roosevelt and Truman administrations and worried about the political impact of such policies back home.[10]

On the Democratic side, many liberals felt that Truman was not going far or fast enough in building on the legacy of FDR. In truth, Truman was a loyal New Dealer, having supported all of Roosevelt's major provisions as a senator in the 1930s. But he was not personally comfortable with liberal ideologues like Henry Wallace and Harold Ickes, preferring the company of his Missouri cronies. When a dissatisfied Ickes resigned as secretary of the interior in February 1946, he publicly charged Truman with collecting "a nondescript band of political Lilliputians" in the White House.[11] The president privately seethed at the criticism but did not respond. Instead, he stuck to his cautious approach. He was dubious about initiating major liberal reforms in the postwar period. "The American people have been through a lot of experiments," Truman told his political aide Clark Clifford. "They want a rest from experiments."[12]

One Republican in particular was exceedingly tired of Democratic "experiments" and was determined to stop them: the brilliant, blunt, indefatigable senior senator from Ohio, Robert A. Taft. Taft was not your ordinary pol. He did not slap backs, he did not twist arms, he did not sip a little "bourbon and branch" with the boys in the backroom. He became the most powerful Republican in the Senate, and in the nation, through his formidable intellect, his huge appetite for hard work and long hours, and his political courage. His bluntness was legendary. A colleague on the Yale Corporation once went to the Senate lobby and called Taft off the floor to check on a pending railroad bill. Asked if the bill would reach the floor that day, Taft replied, "Over my dead body," and stomped back into the Senate chamber.[13]

As partisan as the president, Taft would also bargain if necessary to move legislation important to the nation through Congress. Although Taft "hungered for the White House," in the words of William White, he was first and foremost a man of the Senate and its pragmatic ways.[14]

Taft described himself as "a liberal conservative." By liberal, he meant someone "who is willing to accept change, who believes in freedom for others, and is sufficiently open-minded to be able to consider any proposal that is made to him." By conservative, he meant someone "who knows and appreciates the importance of stability. While I am willing and ready to consider changes, I want to be darned sure—*darned sure*—that they are really better than what we have."[15]

But whatever the label, Taft insisted that the role of the federal government be limited to that of "a keeper of the peace, a referee of controversies, and an adjustor of abuses; not as a regulator of the people, or their business and personal activities."[16] His "guiding principle" as a legislator, he said simply, was whether a policy "increases or decreases the liberty of our people."[17]

He supported "equality of opportunity," whereby all men and women could rise from obscurity. Government, he said, must provide a floor through which no one should be permitted to fall. "This philosophy," wrote Taft biographer Robert Patterson, "was closer to the enlightened noblesse oblige of conservatives like Disraeli and Burke than . . . the probusiness materialism of many of his Republican admirers."[18]

Conservative historian Russell Kirk celebrated Taft's critical contribution to the foundations of modern conservatism in his 1967 book, *The Political Principles of Robert A. Taft*. According to Kirk and his coauthor, James McClellan, Taft recognized that "every right is married to a duty, and that excess of liberty must end in anarchy." He insisted that the rule of law "must not be sacrificed to the vindictive impulse" of the state. He believed, rather, in a "humane economy" founded "upon Christian moral principles and upon the American historical experience." He therefore sponsored legislation favoring federal aid to education, health, and housing, but with the administration of all these programs left in the hands of state and local authorities.[19]

Any proposal for federal action, Taft stated, must be judged by its effect on the liberty of the individual, the family, the community, industry, and labor. "Such liberty," he asserted, "cannot be sacrificed to any theoretical improvement from government control or governmental spending."[20] From the beginning of his career to the end, wrote Kirk, Taft spoke for the "Constitution, self-government, private rights, the rule of law . . . the fabric of civilization." He contended against "ideology, concentrated power, grandiose political schemes . . . economic folly."[21]

The principal conservative leaders who followed Taft—Barry Goldwater, Ronald Reagan, and Newt Gingrich—would contend against the same liberal schemes and make the same commitment to the Constitution and prudential government.

Taft, however, was an activist, not a thinker. He occasionally read political books like Thomas Hewes's *Decentralize for Liberty,* published in 1945, and sometimes inserted quotations from John Stuart Mill's *On Liberty* in his speeches. But when a reporter asked whether he had read Russell Kirk's *The Conservative Mind,* Taft shook his head and chuckled. "You remind me of Thurber's *Let Your Mind Alone,*" he said. "There are some questions that I have not thought very much about, but I'm a politician, not a philosopher."[22]

Taft biographer Caroline Thomas Harsberger has described the senator as tall and balding with "a baywindow stomach."[23] He had gray eyes, sandy eyebrows, and a healthy complexion, and wore old-fashioned shell-rimmed spectacles and "the same dark trousers" morning, afternoon, and night, regardless of the occasion. His Senate office was always piled high with letters, legal briefs, and back issues of the *Congressional Record.* On the mantel stood a small bronze statue of his father, William Howard Taft, the twenty-seventh president and the tenth chief justice of the United States.

Nothing seemed to tire the senator, neither long sessions nor filibusters nor debates with his political opponents. Quite simply, he loved his work.

In 1946, it seemed that Bob Taft was the Senate, and the Senate was Bob Taft. A prime example of Taft's surpassing role came when a national rail strike threatened the nation's major transportation system. On May 25, President Truman appeared before Congress to ask for sweeping powers against the rail workers, in the second day of a walkout. As he was speaking, the president was informed that the rail strike had been settled, and Congress applauded vigorously when told the good news.

But a grim-faced Truman nevertheless requested authority "to declare a state of emergency in case of strikes in vital industries or mines." Sanctions would include allowing the government to operate the struck industries and draft workers into the armed forces. In one stroke, as historian William Manchester expressed it, Truman "alienated the labor movement, the American Civil Liberties Union, the liberal community, and every thoughtful conservative."[24]

Yet so overwhelming was the antiunion mood in Congress, and the country, that the House approved Truman's unprecedented request within two hours by a vote of 306 to 13, and it seemed likely that the Senate would obediently follow suit that same evening—until, that is, Senator Taft rose. He objected to immediate consideration of the bill because the president's proposal "violates every principle of American jurisprudence." There was no excuse, he stated, for such "extreme" and "unconstitutional" demands:

> I am not willing to vote for a measure which provides that the president may be a dictator. It offends not only the Constitution, but every basic principle for which the American Republic was established. Strikes cannot be prohibited without interfering with the basic freedom essential to our form of government.[25]

The GOP Steering Committee, which Taft headed, recommended several amendments, including denying the government the authority to draft strikers—the core of the president's plan. Even administration Democrats acknowledged the inherent dangers of the president's intemperate assault on unions and the Constitution. Only three days after the House had stampeded in favor of the Truman proposal, Taft succeeded in persuading the Senate to defeat it by a decisive vote of 70 to 13.

Some were surprised at Taft's insistence on protecting the right to strike despite the strong national antipathy toward unions. They did not know the man. Taft's stand was a natural consequence of his attachment to principles, his independence of thought, his firm opposition to any expansion of government power, and his devotion to the Constitution. Here in action was Robert Taft, defender of individual rights. Although often labeled probusiness, Taft was committed to the principle of collective bargaining and was far from the "antilabor monster" suggested by some Democratic critics.[26]

The senator was equally opposed to price controls, and was a relentless critic of the Office of Price Administration (OPA), which he charged was preoccupied with curbing profits rather than prices. Here was Robert Taft, the guardian of the American free enterprise system and traditional conservative. Led by Taft and Republican Kenneth Wherry of Nebraska, the Senate passed two amendments to restrict OPA actions. The administration was furious, and Truman attacked Taft by name, calling his efforts the "mainspring" of "an impossible bill" that "provides a sure formula for inflation."[27]

An angry Truman vetoed the bill, killing OPA. But when a surge in prices swiftly followed, another bill was introduced and this one the president eventually signed, although it was very much like a measure he had vetoed a month before. Columnists Stewart and Joseph Alsop observed about Taft's success: "It was a fascinating performance, demonstrating at once the success of [Taft's] legislative methods, the nature of his economic opinions, and the cold-turkey boldness which led Taft . . . to go far out on the limb of a highly controversial issue."[28]

To many Americans in 1946, Truman seemed "inept, uncertain, vulnerable at the polls, a sad successor to Roosevelt."[29] In contrast, the articulate, self-confident Taft caught the public's and the press's eye. *U.S. News and World Report* placed him on its cover in May, *Time* featured him in June, and *Newsweek* gave him a cover story in July. Republicans sensed that they were on the brink of their first great congressional victory since 1928.

The GOP adopted as its slogan "Had Enough? Vote Republican!" An eager Taft went campaigning across the East and the Midwest and did not spare the rhetoric, charging, among other things, that the Democrats "at Tehran, at Yalta, at Potsdam, and at Moscow pursued a policy of appeasing Russia, a policy which has sacrificed throughout Eastern Europe and Asia the freedom of many nations and millions of people." The Democratic party, he said, "is so divided between Communism and Americanism that its foreign policy can only be futile and contradictory and make the United States the laughing stock of the world."[30]

Anticommunism was a major theme in the 1946 campaign. The *Republican News,* the official GOP publication, carried a front-page cartoon of a Russian bear wearing the false ears of the Democratic donkey. And the conservative *Chicago Tribune* reported that pro-Democratic groups like the Congress of Industrial Organizations (CIO) had "openly espoused Russian foreign policies, even at times taking the side of the Russians against American policy."[31]

The Republican charges about communism's spread were corroborated, at least partially, by the nation's top anticommunist, J. Edgar Hoover, the director of the Federal Bureau of Investigation (FBI). In a speech to the American Legion convention in September, Hoover revealed that there were at least 100,000 active communists in America—in "some newspapers, magazines, books, radio and the screen . . . some churches, schools, colleges and even fraternal orders." What most concerned the FBI head was that ten sympathizers stood behind every cardholder "ready to do the party's work"—a veritable army of one million people.[32] Republican candidates immediately began using Hoover's revelations in the campaign, linking them to Democratic accommodation of communism at home and abroad.

However, anticommunism was not manufactured by opportunistic Republicans; it proceeded naturally from the American people, deeply in love with freedom and unswervingly hostile to any force that denied that most precious of possessions. The public's attitude about the Soviet Union had never been more than marginally positive, even during World War II when Moscow was an ally.

In March 1946, eight months after V-J Day, only 7 percent of a Gallup Poll sample approved of "the policy Russia is following in world affairs," while 77 percent disapproved. Sixty percent thought the United States was "too soft" in its relations with Moscow; only 3 percent thought the United States was "too tough." Two months later, 58 percent responded in a Gallup survey that "Russia is trying to build herself up to be the ruling power of the world," while only 29 percent chose the more sympathetic view that Russia is "just building up protection against being attacked in another war"—the argument of the Left. By October 1947, those choosing the phrase "ruling power" in describing the Soviet Union would rise to 76 percent, and those choosing "protection" would fall to 18 percent.[33]

Both political parties aggressively sought the support of a critical voting bloc in the November 1946 elections: the veterans, estimated to number about 8 million. "Every platform and virtually every speech," reported the *Washington Post,* "promises the former serviceman a panacea for his readjustment problems."[34] Many veterans decided they wanted to represent their interests directly and ran for public office. Among those who won were three men who would dictate the course of America's political history.

John F. Kennedy, running for Congress from Massachusetts, frequently referred to his service as a PT boat captain in the Solomons. Richard M. Nixon, seeking to replace Congressman Jerry Voorhis of California, pointed out that while he had been fighting for his country in "the stinking mud and jungles" of the South Pacific, Voorhis had "stayed safely behind the front in

Washington." And the former marine Joseph R. McCarthy, trying to unseat Robert M. La Follette, Jr., of Wisconsin, who had been in the Senate since 1925, distributed several hundred thousand copies of a brochure that trumpeted, "Washington Needs a Tail-Gunner." Displaying his insouciant casualness about numbers, McCarthy accused La Follette of enjoying his Senate salary and "fat rations" while "15,000,000 [sic] Americans were fighting the war."[35]

Most Americans, including veterans, had had enough of strikes, high prices, black markets, rent gougers, and "government by crony." As journalist Joseph C. Goulden put it, Harry Truman woke up the morning after election night 1946 "with a bad cold and a Republican Congress." The new House would have 246 Republicans, 188 Democrats, and 1 independent; the Senate, a 51-to-45 Republican majority. It was a decisive shift in American political power. If the 1946 election had been presidential, analysts estimated, the Republicans would have won 357 electoral votes to Truman's 174.

The anti–New Deal press was ecstatic. The *Chicago Tribune* editorialized that Republicans had "won the greatest victory for the Republic since Appomattox." "The New Deal is kaput," gloated the *New York Daily News.* The more moderate *Washington Daily News* attributed the Republican victory to the "deep American conviction that it is unhealthy in a free government to keep one crowd in power too long."[36]

In the wake of the GOP victory, euphoric Republicans proposed slashing billions of dollars from the budget, lowering income taxes by 20 percent (the pledge of incoming House Speaker Joseph Martin of Massachusetts), abandoning "the philosophy of government interference with business and labor," and even repealing parts of the social and welfare legislation passed since 1932. Senator Styles Bridges of New Hampshire boasted that "the United States is now a Republican country."[37]

Flashing a Cheshire cat smile, Taft declared that the president would have few difficulties with Congress if he accepted the clear verdict of the electorate. "The reason for the controversies during the past two years," he said, "is that the president's proposals always followed the line of increased executive powers." Taft estimated that government spending for fiscal year 1947 could be slashed from the administration's request of $40 billion to as low as $25 billion.[38]

The decisive Republican victory of 1946 was certainly based on conservative themes like cutting taxes, balancing the budget, and containing communism, but these themes were not developed by a conservative movement. Conservatism did not exist in any formal sense in 1940s America. For example, when thirty-nine American and European conservative intellectuals, calling themselves "traditional liberals," decided to form an organization in the spring of 1947, they did not meet in an American city but thousands of miles away in Mont Pelerin, Switzerland. Their mood was somber, for socialism and statism dominated European governments and even seemed to rule in the United States despite the Republican capture of Congress. Declaring that the "central values of civilization are in danger," the free market scholars, led by the London-based economist Friedrich A. Hayek, defined their central goal as "the preservation and improvement of the free society" and named themselves the Mont Pelerin Society. Although their proceedings were not reported on the front page of the *New York Times,* the group demonstrated by their meeting that, in the words of future Nobel laureate Milton Friedman, "we were not alone."[39]

But conservatives were few in number. Conservative publications, for example, could be counted on one hand. The one explicitly conservative journal was *Human Events,* an eight-page weekly newsletter launched in 1944 with the encouragement of four leaders of the Right: former president Herbert Hoover; General Robert Wood, board chairman of Sears, Roebuck; oil executive J. Howard Pew; and Chicago publisher Henry Regnery. Its founding editors were Felix Morley, a distinguished reporter and editor who had won a Pulitzer Prize for editorial writing, foreign policy analyst William Henry Chamberlin, and veteran newspaperman Frank C. Hanighen, whose apartment served as the publication's first office.

Its two-page statement of purpose was cautiously internationalist, calling on America "to develop broader international understanding and to exercise moral leaderhip in accordance with the principles which have made us great."[40] Notwithstanding its august sponsors, the weekly had only a modest circulation of about five thousand by the opening of the Eightieth Congress in January 1947.

Human Events was always firmly anti–New Deal, describing the changes in American government since 1932 as "revolutionary" and resulting in "state socialism." It called on the new Republican Congress to lead a "counter-revolution" and "roll back" the "iron curtain" that separated Washington from the rest of the country.[41]

Radio was then America's primary mass medium, and it is interesting to note, in view of the present-day popularity of personalities like Rush Limbaugh, that the number one radio broadcaster of the 1940s was an unabashed conservative and anticommunist, Fulton Lewis, Jr. Lewis's weekday evening program at seven o'clock was heard by an estimated 16 million Americans over 550 stations of the Mutual Broadcasting System. With a weekly income of $7,000, he was the highest-paid commentator in radio, topping such luminaries as Lowell Thomas and Paul Harvey.

Lewis, who got his start as a reporter on the *Washington Herald,* regularly exposed government inefficiency during and after World War II, producing several congressional investigations. As he put it, "I believe that *Congress* is the bulwark of our republic."[42]

Still, no prominent philosopher, popularizer, or politician called himself a conservative, in part because no one agreed on what "conservatism" was. The traditionalist Russell Kirk, rarely daunted by any intellectual challenge, offered the following:

> "Conservatism" is derived from the Latin verb *conservare,* to keep or preserve. Thus a conservative is a person who, tending to prefer the old and tried to the novel and dubious, endeavors to safeguard the institutions and convictions which his own generation has inherited from previous ages. Generally speaking, the conservative hopes to reconcile what is most important in old customs and in the wisdom of his ancestors with the change that society must undergo if it is to endure.[43]

What is politically important about this definition is the last sentence: that the conservative accepts necessary change. In other words, the conservative is not a reactionary but a reconciler, a fusionist of the best ideas of the old and the most promising of the new. Conservatives know with Edmund Burke, the eighteenth-century British statesman, that healthy "change is the means of our preservation."[44]

Another part of the early intellectual conservative mix was provided by Hayek, who insisted he was not a conservative at all but a "classical" liberal. Hayek argued in *The Road to Serfdom* that "planning leads to dictatorship" and that the "direction of economic activity" inevitably means the "suppression of freedom." He proposed a different road, the road of individualism and classical liberalism, which he insisted was not laissez-faire but was based on a government, carefully limited by law, that encouraged competition and the functioning of a free society.[45] However Hayek and like-minded classical liberals, or libertarians, might protest, this philosophical position placed them squarely in the conservative movement.

The third part of conservatism in these early days was anticommunism, whose most eloquent spokesman was the former *Time* editor and Soviet spy, Whittaker Chambers. His 1952 autobiography, *Witness,* contained three assertions that appealed compellingly to conservatives: one, America faced a transcendent crisis; two, the crisis of the twentieth century was a crisis of faith; and three, secular liberalism was another form of the communist enemy. When he said that the New Deal was not a simple reform movement but "socialist" and "revolutionary," Chambers was hailed by conservatives who had been making the same points for years.[46]

Chapter 2

An Extraordinary Congress

WHILE FRIEDRICH HAYEK WAS PLANNING A MEETING OF CLASSICAL LIBERALS in Switzerland and Whittaker Chambers was debating whether he should testify before the House Committee on Un-American Activities about his old friend and fellow spy, Alger Hiss, Senator Robert Taft and his colleagues were drawing up a Republican agenda for the Eightieth Congress.

The next two years would be a time of significant achievement in domestic policy, elevated bipartisanship in foreign policy, and unrelieved hubris among Republicans who thought the keys to the White House were already in their pockets. "Truman is a gone goose," crowed the sharp-tongued former Republican congresswoman Clare Boothe Luce of Connecticut. Although Democrats fumed, not one publicly challenged her.[1]

To the supremely confident Republicans, the opportunities seemed unlimited. The only question was where to start: reduce the budget, cut taxes, reorganize the executive branch, limit the power of the labor unions, or expose communists in government.

Leaving the area of foreign policy to his more experienced colleague Arthur Vandenberg, Taft began by challenging the Truman administration over its economic policy. To begin, Taft argued, the president ought to cut the proposed federal budget of $37.5 billion by at least $5 billion. Truman, he said, was "like a man tying down the safety valve while he speeds up the stoking under the boiler."[2]

Relying on the research of a new joint congressional committee on the economy, which he headed, Taft kept bombarding the administration with statistics. He opposed increasing the federal minimum wage beyond sixty-five cents an hour despite organized labor's demand for a hike to seventy-five cents. He recommended a $6 billion cut in military spending, unsatisfied with Truman's approval of a decrease from $12.9 billion to $9.5 billion. And he wanted to spend only $1 billion on health, public housing, and federal aid to education. The need for economy, Taft insisted, left the nation no choice.

By the end of the first session, Republicans had succeeded in cutting $2.8 billion from Truman's budget, a reduction of about 7.5 percent. The Eightieth Congress's reductions were a solid accomplishment, although far less than the 20 percent slash some members suggested. Republicans discovered, in political historian James T. Patterson's words, "how economical the administration had tried to be."[3]

At the same time, Taft pushed hard for a tax cut. Federal, state, and local taxes, Taft charged repeatedly, represented 30 percent of the national income. Using a favorite formulation of conservatives, he said, "That means that on the average we are working three days out of ten for the government." Tax reduction, he insisted, was "essential to the welfare of the country, because the present heavy burden of taxation is an evil in itself."[4] For conservatives, then and now, excessive taxes were simply bad economics, discouraging individual initiative and therefore holding down national productivity.

With strong Democratic support, especially among southern conservatives, House Republicans passed tax reform in March 1947, cutting personal income taxes by 30 percent at lower income levels, 20 percent in the middle, and 10.5 percent at the top. The Taft-led Senate passed a slightly more moderate tax reduction in May. The resulting conference bill would have saved American taxpayers about $4 billion.

But Truman quickly vetoed the bill, maintaining that it would encourage consumer spending, stimulate inflation, and deprive the government of $4 billion that should be used to reduce the national debt. And, the president emphasized, the Republican measure favored the wealthy over middle-class and lower-income citizens. It was a classic Democratic argument that pitted class against class, income group against income group, the populist Democrats against the elitist Republicans.

House Republicans picked up enough votes to override the president's veto by delaying the starting date of the reductions until January 1948, but the Senate fell five votes short of the necessary two-thirds. A disappointed Taft consoled himself with the expectation that the people would demand reductions in taxes and Democrats would be forced to "approve a tax cut in the election year of 1948."[5] That, in fact, is what happened.

The Taft plan of reduced government spending and tax cuts—a 1940s version of 1980s supply-side economics—was philosophically prudent and turned out to be economically efficacious as well. Republican pressure forced Truman to cut federal spending more than he would have otherwise. Postwar consumer demand was beginning to decline, and it was reasonable to conclude that tax reduction would not generate out-of-control consumer spending. Indeed, Congress's 1948 tax cut proved to be noninflationary.

From the opening days of the Eightieth Congress, Taft was hard at work on his legislative masterpiece: the Taft-Hartley Labor Act, cosponsored by Congressman Fred Hartley of New Jersey, chairman of the House Education and Labor Committee.

The Wagner Act of 1935 had been called "Labor's Magna Carta" and was arguably the most significant political act of President Roosevelt's first term. It protected organized labor's right to bargain collectively and to accomplish through union action what workers could not do individually. In the intervening twelve years, however, a great depression had ended, a great war had been waged and won, and general prosperity had been achieved. The public's attitude had shifted from a feeling that management was too arrogant and powerful to its opposite: organized labor was now perceived as too strong and overweening, especially in its relations with the people. During the war and afterward, more than one American had caustically commented, "Soldiers in their foxholes don't strike."[6]

Taft was irresistibly attracted to the idea of significant labor reform. It encompassed high national policy, constitutional law, free enterprise, social questions, and electoral politics. He approached what he saw as his mission—"to get rid of at least a good deal of the Wagner Act"—with single-minded yet balanced zeal. His sense of justice compelled him to acknowledge that although strikes might be disorderly and wasteful, they were necessary and constitutional. And management, far from being blameless in all disputes, was often provocative or foolish in its demands. He was interested in reform, not repeal. Accordingly, he would not accept the more punitive provisions of the House version, which included the prohibition of industry-wide bargaining and sharp restrictions on the union shop.

The vote on final passage of the Taft-Hartley bill was 308 to 107 in the

House and 68 to 24 in the Senate. Once again President Truman vetoed the legislation, but this time the House overrode the veto by 331 to 83 and the Senate by 68 to 25. Taft delivered a national radio address in May 1947, right after Senate passage, explaining the proposal's major purpose: "It seems to me that our aim should be to reach the point where, when an employer meets with his employees, they have substantially equal bargaining power, so that neither side feels it can make an unreasonable demand and get away with it."[7]

Under Taft-Hartley, the closed shop was forbidden; union shop agreements were lawful only if a majority of all employees voted for them by secret ballot; jurisdictional strikes and secondary boycotts were made illegal; in any industry in interstate commerce, a sixty-day moratorium had to precede a lawful strike; an eighty-day injunction was provided for in national health-and-safety strikes; and states could outlaw all forms of union security, including the union shop. This last provision, section 14(b), was the controversial right-to-work clause, which had been adopted by twenty-one states by the 1990s. As Edna Lonigan put it in *Human Events,* Taft-Hartley meant that "workers regain the right *not* to join a union." And without the power to compel workers to join or to punish dissent, she wrote, union officials "become answerable to unionists."[8]

Taft and other Republican leaders firmly believed that in passing Taft-Hartley, they had done the right thing legislatively and politically. The new law redressed a labor-management imbalance that had existed for over a decade, and it revised a major plank of the New Deal–Democratic platform. Taft was given full credit, and by all sides, for his masterful steering of Taft-Hartley through Congress, one of the few major works of legislation devised and passed in this century without the help of the executive branch.

But the Democrats were boiling. Angry union leaders referred to the measure as "a slave labor act." Truman agreed and would place Taft-Hartley at the top of his list of Republican "crimes" in his 1948 campaign.

By choice, Taft did not play the same dominant role in foreign policy. He turned over Republican leadership in that area to Arthur H. Vandenberg, the chairman of the Senate Foreign Relations Committee. The senator's son, Arthur, Jr., speaks of a "tacit and informal understanding" between the two men, with Vandenberg deferring to Taft's leadership in domestic policy and Taft reciprocating toward Vandenberg in foreign policy.[9] Writing to Vandenberg in late 1946, Taft noted that a newspaper columnist had tried "to show that I differed with you on foreign policy. I suppose there may be some differences as there always are, but I approve without qualification your whole position as far as I know it."[10]

It fell to Vandenberg to resolve the contradictions within the Eightieth Congress regarding America's relations with the world, especially the Soviet Union. Although most Republican congressmen wanted a tough approach toward Moscow, they were reluctant to pay a high financial price for such a policy. They were politically internationalist but economically isolationist.

They urged President Truman and his administration to take a stronger stand against the Soviets but hesitated when it came time to approve the funds for economic and military programs overseas. Hard-core Republican isolationists like Senator Kenneth S. Wherry of Nebraska and Congressman Clare Hoffman of Michigan took a much simpler view, claiming that the Truman administration was exaggerating Soviet expansionism to secure funds. They questioned whether the Soviet Union was truly a military threat to Western Europe. Foreign aid, they argued, would dangerously strain the American economy and do little for the nations and peoples helped. Other Republicans warned against aiding reactionary regimes in Greece and Turkey.[11] Taft was sympathetic to some of the isolationists' arguments, particularly about endangering the U.S. economy.

Now came one of those catalytic events on which history turns. The combination of one of the worst winters in history and the economic consequences of World War II reduced Great Britain in early 1947 to a state of near bankruptcy. On February 21, 1947, the first secretary of the British embassy in Washington, D.C., delivered two notes to officials in the State Department, stating that Britain could no longer provide economic assistance to Greece and Turkey and would have to halt its aid by no later than April 1.

The thrust of the notes was clear: Since both Greece and Turkey were on the brink of economic collapse and were politically threatened by the continuing success of communist guerrillas, only a firm American commitment could prevent these two countries from being taken over by the Soviets. For the first time since the founding of the Republic, there was no one to protect America's geopolitical interests but America itself. All the other major democratic powers had been rendered impotent. A dangerous bipolar world suddenly loomed.

Undersecretary of State Dean Acheson told Secretary of State George Marshall, "This puts up the most [serious] decision with which we have been faced since the war."[12] The two officials informed President Truman that Greece needed substantial amounts of aid, and quickly. The alternative, Truman recalled in his memoirs, would have been the loss of Greece and the extension of "the iron curtain" across the eastern Mediterranean. If Greece was lost, Turkey would "become an untenable outpost in a sea of communism." The president viewed Greece and Turkey as "free countries being challenged by Communist threats from within and without." America, he felt, had no choice but to help them and thus block Soviet expansionism.[13]

To help these beleaguered countries, Truman needed the support of the Republican Eightieth Congress. Fortunately for Greece, Turkey, and the rest of noncommunist Europe, the president received the bipartisan support of Congress for what came to be called the Truman Doctrine and ultimately the policy of containment. Although Vandenberg was unhappy that he and other congressional leaders had not been consulted earlier, he felt that given the crisis and the president's urgent request, Congress had little choice but to go along or invite future and more serious Soviet aggression.

Still, there were reservations. *Human Events* expressed skepticism about the Truman Doctrine because it concerned itself with the outer "extremities" of Europe. Western Europe, wrote Felix Morley, was like a man "stricken with coronary thrombosis." Greece was "a foot of Europe," while Germany "was the continental heart." Morley accused the Soviets of plotting the "enslavement" of Germany while America had no apparent plan to prevent its collapse, which would inevitably hasten "the decay" of all Western Europe.[14]

Republican opponents of Greek–Turkish aid were heartened when Taft expressed some public skepticism about the Truman plan. But Taft privately told colleagues that he supported the bill, explaining: "I don't like this Greek–Turkish proposition, but I do recognize that perhaps we should maintain the status quo until we can reach some peace accommodation with Russia. I don't like to appear to be backing down." When he formally endorsed the legislation, Taft qualified his support: "I do not regard this as a commitment to any similar policy in any other section of the world."[15] But he accepted the basic premise of the Truman Doctrine: America should assist free nations and peoples threatened by the Soviet Union.

A conference report on Greek–Turkish aid adjusted minor differences in the Senate and House versions and was passed by both houses by a voice vote on May 15, 1947. Approval of the Truman Doctrine was a rite of passage by which once-isolationist America became the leader of the free world. And it helped prepare the way for the next building block of containment: substantial American aid to all of an economically distressed Europe.

The most influential journalist of the postwar period was liberal Walter Lippmann, whose newspaper column, "Today and Tomorrow," was avidly read by everyone interested in foreign affairs, including White House aides, State Department officials, and members of Congress. In today's electronic world, it is difficult to imagine a single newspaper columnist having so great an impact. But by virtue of his formidable intelligence, historical perspective, and sense of timing, Lippmann often helped shape history.

In April 1947, he wrote that "the danger of a European economic collapse is the threat that hangs over us and all the world." He reported that none of the leading nations of Europe—Great Britain, France, Italy, or Germany—was recovering economically from the war and that the collapse of Britain, for example, would force it to withdraw its occupation forces from Germany, leaving the United States "isolated in Europe, face to face with the Russians." To prevent such an ominous prospect, he wrote, "political and economic measures on a scale which no responsible statesman has yet ventured to hint at will be needed in the next year or two."[16]

Billions of dollars had already been channeled into Europe through the United Nations Relief and Rehabilitation Administration (UNRRA), a British loan, and Greek-Turkish aid, but the economic problems left by World War II could not be solved by emergency stopgap relief. So serious was the situation in France, for example, that the State Department privately sent John Foster Dulles, a prominent Republican and future secretary of state, to assess the possibility of a civil war between the communists and supporters of General Charles de Gaulle, who was then making a bid for political power. Finding France torn by strikes, sabotage, and political turmoil, Dulles concluded that prompt economic aid was essential to the future of France and a secure and free Europe.[17]

Other strands of an assistance program began to be drawn together. In mid-May, former prime minister Winston Churchill, speaking in London, described Europe's broken and ravaged condition and declared that only in unity could the Continent achieve security from aggression, economic well-being, and protection of a common culture. About the same time, Undersecretary of State Will Clayton, returning home after six weeks in Europe, wrote an urgent memorandum to President Truman stating that "without further prompt and substantial aid from the United States, economic, social and political disintegration will overwhelm Europe," with "awful implications . . . for the future peace and security of the world."[18]

State Department and other administration officials were agreed that if the United States did not act, and soon, Western Europe would become an overriding economic, political, and strategic problem. And so Secretary of State George Marshall accepted an invitation to speak at Harvard's commencement exercises on June 5, 1947. His brief speech, barely ten minutes long, outlined his proposal for European economic recovery, which committed America to a policy of economic and political solidarity with other nations and thereby saved Western Europe.

Vandenberg described Marshall's Harvard address as a "shot heard 'round the world," but he knew that it fell on many deaf ears in a Republican Congress dedicated to reducing taxes and cutting government spending. There was, for example, strong apprehension among some members that American goods would be removed from the domestic market for foreign consumption and that a successful aid program would serve only to increase foreign competition for American business. It was not as irrational a concern as it might seem to us today. America, and indeed no other nation in history, had ever before attempted so formidable an assistance program to former allies and adversaries. Wisely, the administration did not press for immediate action.

The president knew as well that if the program were named after him, it would not be approved by the Eigthtieth Congress; bipartisanship could be stretched only so far. White House aide George Elsey recalled that Truman was among the first to insist that it be called not the Truman Plan but the *Marshall* Plan, after the widely respected secretary of state. He also urged that the key congressional figures advocating the plan be either Republicans or noncontroversial Democrats. The best politics, the White House decided, was to play no politics.[19]

For their part, congressional Republicans thought that the best politics for them was to deliver on their 1946 campaign promises. But they were puzzled by the lack of public enthusiasm and approval for their record in the first half of the Eightieth Congress. They had reduced spending to a far greater extent than any other Congress in recent history. They had sought a tax cut and would have prevailed in 1947, except for presidential vetoes. And they had passed the historic Taft-Hartley Act in response to the expressed wishes of a majority of the American people. Yet as *Human Events* pointed out, "There has been little evidence of public gratitude."[20] Furthermore, the leader most closely associated with Congress's performance, Robert Taft, saw his popularity as a potential presidential candidate wane steadily as the session went on.

Of particular significance was the tax bill. Until Truman wielded his veto pen, only one president in American history—Franklin D. Roosevelt—had ever vetoed a tax measure. Since the founding of the Republic, taxing power had rested with the legislative branch. Here was a fundamental principle tied to legislation immediately benefiting the American people. "Yet the electorate failed to exert sufficient pressure to obtain the comparatively few additional votes [needed] for repassage over the veto," observed *Human Events.*[21]

Why? Because the mass media of the day—the press and radio—did not urge approval of the tax cut. Because no "Emergency Citizens Committee for Tax Reduction" flooded congressional offices with telegrams and letters. And because Republican congressional leaders, from Taft to House Speaker Joe Martin, failed to go to the people and ask for their help in overriding President Truman's veto.

"The truth," wrote Frank Hanighen in *Human Events,* "is that we have not an effective nongovernmental process here at home to make the public attitude intelligible to its representatives, and vice versa."[22] In other words, no effective national conservative movement existed.

In its absence, Governor Thomas E. Dewey of New York, the favorite of the powerful eastern liberal establishment, rather than Senator Taft of Ohio, the champion of the party's traditional wing, continued to gain as the GOP's likely nominee in 1948. Dewey's strength had grown steadily since his reelection as governor of the most populous state in the Union the previous November. His radio address on election night in 1946, reported *Human Events,* "sent cold shivers down the spines of Taft people. It was smart, modest, well-phrased and . . . well delivered." As of now, concluded the conservative weekly, "Dewey's in the lead."[23]

The most serious threat to the European Recovery Program (as the Marshall Plan was officially known) came from congressional "revisionists" who objected to the size of the authorization ($5.3 billion), the possibility that the Soviet Union and its allies would benefit through the revival of East-West trade, and the support of what they described as "socialist governments" in Western Europe. They centered their hopes on the Taft amendment to cut the first-year authorization to $4 billion. This amendment, rejected 56 to 31 in March 1948, represented the high mark of Senate opposition to foreign aid in the Eightieth Congress.

Republican opponents had also drawn strength from the carefully measured criticism of President Hoover, invited by Vandenberg to be the first witness before the Senate Foreign Relations Committee in January. Acceding to the admonitions of his physician to limit his public appearances, the seventy-four-year-old Hoover instead submitted a memorandum to the Senate committee, which was subsequently released to the press. Hoover began by saying that America should of course aid Western Europe because "the spiritual character of the American people" had always led them to help those in great need, "even to the extent of personal self-denial"; because it was of "vital importance" to stimulate "the economic and political unity of Western Europe" and thereby defeat "Communism in Western Europe"; and because it "builds for peace in the world."[24]

But, the former president conceded, there were inherent "dangers" in the project, including the possible political-economic failure of Western Europe and the acceleration of serious inflationary pressures in America that would "destroy" the one remaining source of aid to "a world in chaos." Since "we must take some risks," however, Hoover suggested certain modifications and safeguards in the proposed legislation on everything from organization and scope to the length of the program and its financing.[25]

The man who had been in charge of aid to war-torn Europe after World War I proposed that the program's administration be bipartisan and not exclusively governmental. And so it was: the first head of the Economic Cooperation Administration (established outside the State Department) was a Republican: Paul Hoffman, president of the Studebaker Corporation and chairman of the board of the Committee for Economic Development. Next, Hoover urged that aid not be limited to Western Europe, arguing that "the front against Communism lies not alone in Europe; it stretches through Latin America and Asia."[26] The result was that the final bill included more than $450 million for China.

Hoover strongly opposed the Truman administration's four-year authorization of $17 billion, suggesting instead that the program be limited to fifteen months. After all, he pointed out, "we cannot even hazard what the export and financial possibilities of the United States will be for more than a year in advance." Even a "moral commitment" to a four-year program was "unwise," Hoover argued. We cannot, he said, "enforce ideas upon other self-governing peoples and we should keep ourselves entirely free to end our efforts without recrimination."[27] Hoover's common sense prevailed: Congress passed a fifteen-month appropriation of $5 billion.

Finally, and almost laconically, the former president suggested that Congress be honest with itself and the American people and distinguish between loans and gifts. The bulk of American assistance, approximately $3 billion in food and other relief over fifteen months, was really a "gift," which neither the recipient nor the donor should expect would be repaid. Gifts, Hoover pointed out, would enable the participating countries "to use their exports to pay for other goods in their programs."[28] So great was Hoover's reputation in the field of relief and so practical his suggestions that Congress made a clear distinction between loans and grants in the European Recovery Program.

Hoover did not limit his role in the Marshall Plan debate to written memoranda. He conducted an extensive correspondence with key members of the Senate and House, including Vandenberg, Taft, Congressman Christian Herter of Connecticut, a key House floor leader, and John Taber, the choleric chairman of the House Appropriations Committee. In March 1948, after two months of congressional hearings and debate, Hoover formally endorsed the program as "a major dam against Russian aggression."[29]

Historian Richard Norton Smith says that the Marshall Plan bore only "a few of [Hoover's] fingerprints." But the plan's final language suggests that Republican leaders used most of Hoover's ideas both to make it more acceptable to skeptics and to secure final passage.

Taking his lead from Hoover, Taft did not oppose the Marshall Plan in toto, but tried to trim its size. His position was not "isolationist," as friends on the Right and critics on the Left claimed, but pragmatic and anticommunist, as can be readily seen in these remarks:

I am in favor of giving aid to the countries of western Europe, but only for specific programs clearly necessary for subsistence, or clearly helpful in increasing their production, especially for export. I am strongly opposed to committing ourselves to any overall global plan to make up some theoretical deficiency in exports and to making any moral commitment beyond the amount authorized for the first year.

I am in favor of extending further aid to the countries of western Europe beyond the demands of charity only because of the effect our aid may have in the battle against communism.[30]

The last sentence rendered the heart of his argument. The program was politically justified because of "the battle against communism."

Vandenberg was also firmly anticommunist, but he regarded the Marshall Plan as a prime product of bipartisanship and American statesmanship. Republicans paid a high political price for their patriotism. By collaborating with the Democrats in approving the European Recovery Program and the largest peacetime foreign aid budget in U.S. history, they deprived themselves of an important campaign issue—Fair Deal spending overseas—and gave the Truman administration its major success in foreign policy.

Taft never shared Vandenberg's enthusiasm for bipartisanship; he was first, last, and always a Republican. Nevertheless, he supported both the Truman Doctrine and the Marshall Plan because America was engaged in an ideological battle of freedom against communism—of justice, equality, and liberty against "a totalitarian state." He anticipated that U.S. aid would "increase the morale" of those fighting communism, and thus supported its adoption without delay.[31]

And he meant it. As the GOP's national convention drew near, House and Senate conferees continued to battle over the specific amount of aid to such an extent that the European Recovery Program seemed to be in jeopardy. At this point, a grim Taft threatened to hold Congress in session until its "moral commitment" had been met and an appropriation passed. Recalcitrant House conferences surrendered, and on June 20, 1948, the European Recovery Program was approved by both houses, a tribute to Vandenberg's legislative skill and Taft's carefully timed bluntness.[32]

Communism closer to home was also on the minds of many members of Congress. In July 1947, the Truman administration admitted to Congress that an estimated 3,181 federal workers were "disloyal" to the government and should be removed from their jobs. These alleged subversives were in addition to the 1,313 already discharged on findings of disloyalty, civil service commissioner Arthur S. Flemming told the House Appropriations

Committee. Flemming based the estimate on his judgment that a loyalty check of 1,466,000 federal employees would discover "derogatory information on loyalty" about 29,000 of them. And about 11 percent of those, or 3,181, he asserted, would warrant an "ineligibility rating."

At about the same time, Congress was also informed that eight hundred disloyal employees had been fired in the nine-month period ending March 31. These people were included in Flemming's figure of 1,313 who had been discharged for disloyalty from July 1, 1940, through March 31, 1947. Committee members, according to the *Chicago Tribune,* noted that Flemming's figures indicated that at least 4,500 "enemies of the United States" were actually in its employ during World War II.

Congressman Frank B. Keefe (R–Wisconsin) recalled that charges by the House Committee on Un-American Activities that "thousands" of communists had penetrated the government had been ridiculed and denounced as "red baiting" by President Roosevelt and his aides.[33] The man in charge of the civil service for the Truman administration had now provided corroboration of the committee's charges. The "red baiting," it appeared, had come from the White House, not Congress.

An emboldened House Committee on Un-American Activities decided to examine the extent of communist influence in the most popular medium in America: the movies. Preliminary investigation revealed that procommunist writers, actors, and directors had reached their greatest power during World War II with the help of a federal government eager to "encourage" Soviet Russia with films depicting communism in the most favorable light, like the 1943 release *Song of Russia,* starring Robert Taylor.[34]

Communists were also interested in controlling those who worked behind the camera: the lighting, sound, editing, and other technicians whose contributions were essential to the completion of a film. One of their favorite tactics was the work stoppage. Indeed, serious strikes had begun in Hollywood even before the end of World War II as procommunist and noncommunist unions fought for jurisdiction over a $5 billion-a-year business. Between 1945 and 1947, half a dozen major strikes hit the film capital.

In October 1947, two prominent producers, Sam Wood and Jack L. Warner, appeared before the House Committee on Un-American Activities and charged that communists had "invaded" the film colony. Wood said bluntly that "these people take their orders from Soviet Russia." He emphasized that "all but a few hundred of the 35,000 workers in the motion picture industry are loyal, patriotic Americans, but their loyalty is being misrepresented and threatened by a tight, disciplined group of Communist party members and party liners who have worked incessantly to gain control of the unions and guilds in Hollywood in the last ten years."[35]

The hearings were held amid the glitter and glare of a Hollywood first night. About five hundred spectators were admitted to seats after one hundred newspapermen, seventy-five motion picture cameramen, photographers, radio announcers, and a television crew had found their places. The efforts of a relatively small group of film writers and directors to propagandize the American people on behalf of communism were carefully detailed.

Film star Gary Cooper, his shy grin and slow drawl both in evidence, revealed that he had refused to act in "quite a few" communist-tainted films. "I remember one," he said, "which had a leading character whose life ambition was to organize an army of soldiers who would never fight to defend their country. That was enough to me to send it back." He recalled remarks at Hollywood parties about the U.S. Constitution's being "150 years out of date" and that "the government would be more efficient without a Congress."[36]

Leo McCarey, who directed the box office successes *Going My Way* and *The Bells of St. Mary's,* was asked if those pictures were also popular in the Soviet Union. "They weren't permitted," responded McCarey. "There was a character in there the Russians don't like." "Who was that—Bing Crosby?" asked Robert Stripling, the committee's staff director. "No," said McCarey simply, "God."[37]

Another witness was the handsome young president of the Screen Actors Guild. Ronald Reagan, resplendent in a cream-colored suit and rust-colored suede shoes, insisted that unlike the writers, Hollywood actors were not dominated by communists. But there was a "dangerous," disciplined minority whose frequent weapon was character assassination. George Murphy, a past president of the actors guild, said that he and Reagan had been labeled "scabs" and "fascists" because of their efforts to settle strikes.[38]

Explaining that many in Hollywood had been lured into communist-front organizations through subterfuge, Reagan told of agreeing to sponsor a meeting supposedly held to raise funds for a hospital. He later learned that the meeting was under the supervision of the Joint Anti-Fascist Refugee Committee, a communist front. Procommunist speakers, including the singer Paul Robeson, made speeches, and a large sum was collected. At least fifty film celebrities had been deceived into lending their names to the affair, Reagan reported.[39]

Fellow Hollywood actor Sterling Hayden, who had briefly been a member of the Communist party, later testified that efforts to persuade a group of film actors and actresses to support a communist-led strike in Hollywood ran into a "one-man battalion named Ronald Reagan." The communists' efforts were defeated.[40]

The House committee also produced as an expert witness Mrs. Frank O'Connor, who, under the pen name of Ayn Rand, wrote *The Fountainhead,* a best-selling novel that had been made into a film starring Gary Cooper. Rand had lived in Russia under the communists until 1926, when her family moved to the United States.

"I have seen and analyzed *Song of Russia,*" said the writer, "and it is communist propaganda so strong that it made me sick. It furnishes an utterly distorted picture of Russian life which could only be designed to deceive the American people. It shows a happy prosperous Russian people when the reality is that of a terror-stricken people constantly wondering where the next meal is coming from."[41]

By the end of the hearings, chairman J. Parnell Thomas (R–New Jersey) announced that the committee had been able to identify ten people prominent in Hollywood as members of the Communist party, a group that quickly became known as the "Hollywood Ten." The battle against domestic communism had been joined.

The White House was also concerned with communist influence, but for its own reasons. On March 21, 1947, President Truman signed Executive Order No. 9835, which established the Federal Employee Loyalty and Security Program. Truman biographer David McCullough states that the president had "misgivings" about the program, saying he wanted "no NKVD [Soviet secret police] or Gestapo in this country."[42] But Truman nevertheless approved the executive order because he had his eye on the 1948 election and did not want any accusations of "administration softness on communism at home" just as he was "calling for a new hard approach to communism abroad." "It was a political problem," Clark Clifford explained to a reporter many years later. "Truman was going to run in '48, and that was it."[43]

But although Clifford and other liberals denied it, there was a serious domestic problem that went far beyond presidential politics. The mother of all congressional investigations into subversion erupted in August 1948 when a portly, graying, rumpled magazine editor revealed to the House Committee on Un-American Activities that he had been an underground agent for the Soviet Union in the 1930s. Among those who belonged to the same Washington communist cell, stated Whittaker Chambers, was Alger Hiss, a former assistant to the secretary of state and the general secretary of the United Nations Conference at San Francisco in 1945, who was now president of the Carnegie Endowment for International Peace.

Chambers had broken with the Communist party in 1937 but remained silent about his espionage activities until the Hitler-Stalin Pact of June 1939. Two days later, he went to Washington and, through the assistance of journalist-biographer Isaac Don Levine, met with Adolph Berle, known as President Roosevelt's "intelligence man." Chambers named six men, including Alger Hiss, as "communist agents."

"Berle was excited," recalled Chambers. "He said, 'We absolutely must have a clean government service—we are faced with the prospect of war.' I was naive enough," admitted Chambers, "to expect that action would be taken right away. A great deal later, I learned that nothing had been done."[44]

With Whittaker Chambers's reluctant appearance before the House Committee on Un-American Activities in the summer of 1948, the lives of all those concerned would be changed irrevocably, as would the politics of America and the conservative movement.

If Hiss was innocent, then anticommunism—and those closely associated with it—would be dealt a deadly and probably fatal blow. If Hiss was guilty, anticommunism would become a permanent part of the national political landscape, and its leaders would be heroes to millions.

In the summer of 1948, one man whose political fate seemed settled, and not happily, was President Truman. Since the Republican victory in 1946, every public opinion poll had come to the same conclusion: If Truman ran for the presidency, he would be soundly defeated. Gallup reported that between October 1947 and March 1948, the percentage of Americans who thought the president was doing a good job had declined steadily and was now down to 36 percent. If he ran, he would lose to every prospective Republican candidate, although not by much: in January 1948, Dewey led Truman by only 46 percent to 41 percent. Many Americans were afraid of an economic turndown, political historian Michael Barone wrote, and were convinced that if it came, "the Democrats would handle the situation better."[45]

While Truman pondered whether he should run (going so far as to suggest to General Dwight Eisenhower that if the wartime hero ran on the Democratic ticket, he would be happy to be his running mate), White House aides Clark Clifford and James Rowe gave their boss a thirty-five-page reelection memorandum. They insisted that Truman had compiled a good liberal record, supporting civil rights for blacks and a Zionist state for Jews and vetoing the Taft-Hartley Act and other "antilabor" bills. In so doing, he had appealed to three key voting blocs of the New Deal coalition that had won four straight presidential elections for FDR. Furthermore, Truman's enlightened proposals for a large housing program and the use of social security for medical care for the aged had been rejected by Republican "reactionaries" like Robert Taft and Joseph Martin. The strategy was clear: Truman could win if he ran as a liberal populist against the elitist Eightieth Congress.

But the president would also have to contend with serious challenges within his own party. Henry Wallace, FDR's former vice president and secretary of agriculture in the Truman administration until the president had been forced to fire him for his pro-Soviet remarks, had announced he would run for the presidency as the candidate of the far-left Progressive party. And a delegation of southern governors, led by Strom Thurmond of South Carolina, prepared to secede from the Democratic party and back a southern candidate, which guaranteed a four-way race in 1948.

Among the influential Democrats vowing to dump Truman were Elliott Roosevelt, FDR's son; Senator Claude Pepper of Florida; President Walter Reuther of the United Auto Workers; and Mayor Hubert Humphrey of Minneapolis. Among those who stuck with Truman was prominent Hollywood Democrat Ronald Reagan, who campaigned vigorously for the president that fall. But the anti-Truman boomlet within the Democratic party collapsed when the CIO took a firm stand against Wallace's third-party candidacy, and General Eisenhower refused to accept the nomination.

Meanwhile, confident Republicans assembled in Philadelphia for their national convention in June so convinced they would win the presidency that they generously left their flags and bunting in place for the cash-strapped Democrats, who would be meeting in the same convention hall in a couple of weeks.[46]

The almost certain GOP candidate was not the bespectacled Ohio senator who had led the Eightieth Congress through two productive years in Washington, but the mustached New York governor who had given Roosevelt a surprisingly close race in 1944. The reasons for the Republican tilt toward Dewey were several.

First, as Taft biographer James T. Patterson points out, the senator's delegate strength was "heavily sectional," concentrated in the Midwest and the South. A more crucial handicap was the widespread feeling among Republicans that Taft "could not match Dewey as a vote getter."[47] (An oft-repeated line among Republicans was "Taft Can't Win.")

Moreover, Taft had little charisma and dismissed almost every effort at image making. Ed Lahey, a *Chicago Daily News* political reporter who had come to admire Taft for his intellectual capacity and political honesty, commented that the senator was "a complete washout in the field of public relations. He won't truckle. He won't explain, he won't polish apples with any group."[48] And at this point, there was no national conservative movement that might have compensated for Taft's lack of personal appeal with organizational muscle to ensure, for example, that conservatives turned out for Taft in key primaries and at local caucuses and state conventions.

Even Taft's widely praised leadership of the Eightieth Congress worked against him. In early June 1948, just weeks before the Republican convention, President Truman took to the rails for an official, "nonpolitical" tour across America. He spent most of his time excoriating the Republicans and their champion Bob Taft for not being interested "in the welfare of the common everyday man." The Eightieth Congress, Truman cried, was "the worst in history." He asked the large, friendly crowds that turned out, "Are the special privilege boys going to run the country, or are the people going to run it?" Over and over he quoted a Taft line that people ought "to eat less" to bring down food prices. At least, went the joke, Marie Antoinette had told the French masses to eat cake, but Taft counseled people to starve.[49]

It was grossly unfair and fiercely partisan, but it foretold what the president would say in the fall if Bob Taft were his opponent. Didn't it make sense, reasoned Republicans, to go with Dewey, who was ahead of Taft and every other Republican in the polls? The general feeling within the party was that Dewey had earned the nomination by reason of his strong showing against the formidable FDR in 1944, when he received almost 46 percent of the popular vote. And Dewey was careful in 1948 to present himself as the candidate of the center between Governor Harold Stassen of Minnesota on the Left and Senator Taft on the Right. Dewey offered a way for Republicans to play it safe.

In the end, Republicans cast their lot with the man who, though he looked like "the little man on the wedding cake" (in Alice Roosevelt Longworth's memorable phrase) was nevertheless beating Truman in all the polls. At the Philadelphia convention, Dewey led Taft by nearly two to one on the first two ballots. On the third ballot, bowing to what he called "simple arithmetic," the senator from Ohio withdrew from the race, and the convention unanimously chose Dewey, who was expected to breeze to victory in November.

But what Taft, Dewey, the Republican party, the press, the pollsters, and almost every other political expert failed to reckon with was the iron will and searing rhetoric of Harry Truman. For thirty-three days, a railroad Pullman car named the *Ferdinand Magellan* served as the campaign headquarters and White House on wheels for Truman and his political team as they engineered the biggest upset in modern American political history. Although historians have made much of Truman's salty speech, his amazing stamina, and his serene conviction that he would win, they downplay a crucial fact: Truman presented to the electorate what can only be described as a deliberately false and mean distortion of the truth about Dewey, Taft, Hoover, Republicans in general, and the so-called do-nothing Eightieth Congress.

He gleefully smeared Dewey, charging that a vote for the New Yorker was "a vote for fascism." He mocked Taft as a "mossback still living back in 1890." He demonized Herbert Hoover, conjuring up "the dark days of 1932" with constant references to "Hoovervilles," "people crying for jobs," and "farmers marching on Washington." From the first day of campaigning, he described Republicans as "gluttons of privilege . . . cold men . . . cunning men," the captives of "big business and the special interests." And he blamed the Eightieth Congress for the high cost of living, for passing a "rich man's tax bill," and for voting against a civil rights bill.[50]

In Chicago, Truman went off the rhetorical chart by comparing the "powerful forces" behind the Republican party to the interests that raised Hitler, Mussolini, and Tojo to power. He said that what happened in Germany, Italy, and Japan "could happen here" if the "evil forces" working through the Republicans triumphed. In Cleveland, he stunned his audience by suggesting that the communists were hoping for a Republican victory: "The Communists believe that a Republican victory means a weak United States, and that is exactly what I think. . . . But I'm going to beat them and there won't be a weak United States."[51]

In New York City, he accused the Hoover administration of making "a complete and ruinous mess of the country. . . . The Democrats saved America." In Boston, he referred to the Republican opposition as "totally un-American," to the Republican platform as the "most hypocritical, deceitful document in history," and to the "unholy alliance" of Republicans and communists.[52]

Taft urged fighting fire with fire. "The only way to handle Truman," he said, "was to hit [him] every time he opened his mouth." But Dewey listened to the reassuring experts around him, talked to confident party operatives across the country, read the polls that had him in the lead, and kept to the high road. He told Taft that over the years he had found that when he got into controversies, he lost votes—"an observation Taft thought disgraceful," according to historian David McCullough.[53]

Had he wanted to, Dewey could have easily exposed Truman's charges. It was the "do-nothing" Eightieth Congress, after all, that had overwhelmingly passed the Truman Doctrine and the Marshall Plan. The much-criticized Taft-Hartley Act had been supported by a majority of Truman's own party in the House. The tax reduction legislation that Truman dismissed as a "rich man's tax bill" had removed 7.5 million people in the lower brackets from the tax rolls. And "Evil Wall Street" was well represented within the Democratic party by such prominent and wealthy figures as Averill Harriman, Robert Lovett, and James Forrestal.

As for the grotesque suggestion that he was a "fascist," Dewey's record proved that he was a moderate Republican who backed aid to Greece and Western Europe, believed in a strong national defense, wanted further progress in civil rights, and had supported the recognition of Israel. Taft held similar positions on these defining issues.

Also at fault was the press, which for the most part simply reported Truman's misrepresentations without comment or context. In those days, the great majority of reporters hewed to a standard of objectivity that precluded editorializing in the news columns. It was up to the opposition, not the press, to set the record straight. And besides, everyone knew Truman was going to lose, so what difference did it make what he said?

Republicans shrugged off the Truman attacks and kept making plans for their first presidential inauguration in twenty years. Although Dewey uneasily noted the large, enthusiastic crowds that turned out at every stop for Truman, he stuck to his mind-numbing message of "constructive change"—and lost.

Truman's victory was the most unexpected electoral triumph in modern political history. The president received 24,105,587 votes (49.5 percent) to Dewey's 21,970,017 votes (45.1 percent). Strom Thurmond and Henry Wallace finished far behind, each garnering fewer than 1.2 million votes. In the electoral college, the tally was Truman 303, Dewey 189, Thurmond 38, and Wallace 0.

Truman carried California, Ohio, and Illinois by less than one percentage point. A shift of thirty thousand votes in those states would have given Dewey an electoral victory. Truman credited organized labor with providing the winning margin. But it was the Republicans' failure to respond to the president's wild campaign charges that prepared the way for the political "miracle." It was also true that times were good: the economy was expanding, employment was high, and inflation was low. As James Reston of the *New York Times* noted, "The people had seldom if ever turned against the administration in power at such a time."[54]

Truman swept in Democratic majorities in both houses of Congress, 54 to 42 in the Senate and 263 to 171 in the House. One defeated Republican, representing a western district that was two-thirds rural and one-third urban, told Frank Hanighen that normally supportive farmers stayed away from the polls in large numbers. They were either "discontented with the Congressman," who had been cool toward price supports and outspoken against the Rural Electrification Administration, or "chilly toward Mr. Dewey."[55]

Would the outcome have been the same if Taft, and not Dewey, had been the Republican presidential candidate? Perhaps, but Taft would have responded quickly and forcefully to every one of Truman's demagogic outbursts. There would have been no free ride for the president in a Truman-Taft race. And Republicans would not have been mesmerized by a false hubris with a Taft-led ticket but would have labored mightily right down to election day. As it was, the GOP turnout was a disappointing 21.9 million, fewer than the 22 million who voted in 1944 and far under the 33.9 million who would back Eisenhower in 1952.

There is also convincing evidence that the Republican candidate the Democrats most feared in 1948 was Taft. Robert Hennegan, chairman of the Democratic National Committee, reportedly said prior to the national conventions, "If the Republicans were smart, they'd run Taft. He'd make a better candidate and would probably be harder for us to beat because he would fight harder. . . . Dewey will be 'me too' all over again."[56]

Even a veteran Democratic strategist like Harold Ickes knew who would have been the more formidable candidate, remarking that the Republicans "sent in a batboy with the bases full and only one run needed. They could have sent in their Babe Ruth—Bob Taft."[57] Taft himself agreed, telling friends, "I could have won the election if nominated."[58]

As disappointed and angry as they were about the outcome, conservatives reassured themselves that certainly the Republican party had learned an important lesson: It would not—it could not—nominate again a candidate who failed to carry the campaign to the opposition or take decisive stands on the issues. There was every reason to believe that Bob Taft would be the presidential nominee in 1952. He had led the fight against big government, and he understood the evil of America's most serious enemy, communism.

The *Chicago Tribune* editorialized: "After this experience, we may hope the Republicans have learned their lesson. If the same forces control the next Republican convention the party is finished and the millions of patriotic men and women who have looked to it for leadership will have to look elsewhere."[59]

Meanwhile, in his first bid for public office, Arizona businessman Barry Goldwater ran for and was easily elected to the Phoenix city council. Ronald Reagan campaigned vigorously for fellow Democrat Truman, whom he called "an outstanding president."[60] William F. Buckley, Jr., was elected chairman of the *Yale Daily News* and began writing about God and man and the spirit of collectivism at Yale. Richard Weaver argued in *Ideas Have Consequences* that seductive ideas like materialism and rationalism had led inexorably to the moral "dissolution" of the West. He offered three reforms to help mankind recover from modernism: defense of private property, respect for language, and piety toward the past.[61]

Russell Kirk was working hard on his doctoral dissertation, which traced the influence of conservatism on America from its founding, although he was not terribly optimistic about its future. Liberal critic Lionel Trilling agreed, making the famous complaint (in 1950) that "liberalism is not only the dominant but even the sole intellectual tradition" in America. Although Trilling conceded that a conservative or reactionary "impulse" did exist here and there, he insisted that it expressed itself only in "irritable mental gestures which seem to resemble ideas."[62]

Chapter 3

We Like Ike

WHATEVER LIBERAL INTELLECTUALS LIKE LIONEL TRILLING MIGHT SAY about the pervasiveness of liberalism, liberal politicians were finding it hard going at home and abroad. Eighteen months after the 1948 election, President Truman's popularity had slumped to the mid-thirties as scandals involving several of his closest associates and Missouri friends, like his military aide Major General Harry H. Vaughn, erupted. In Congress, a bipartisan coalition led by Republican Robert Taft and Democrat Richard Russell prevented passage of most of the Fair Deal, which was not, in any event, generating much public enthusiasm. And although there was general agreement about some form of federal aid to education, Protestants and Catholics were quarreling sharply over whether parochial schools should be included. In the field of civil rights, a majority of Americans favored abolition of the poll tax, but only a third supported a strong fair employment bill. As for the labor question, a solid plurality wanted retention, not abolition, of the Taft-Hartley Act. Finally, the administration's new agricultural program, the Brannan Plan, "could muster little enthusiasm even from the farmers it was supposed to benefit," according to Truman biographer Alonzo Hamby.[1]

For conservatives, all these signs were proof that Truman's victory had indeed been a fluke. The supposedly errant polls had been right: Dewey would have won if he had campaigned like any normal presidential candidate. Instead, he had allowed his opponent to get away with scaring the farmer, the small businessman, and other Republican constituencies into voting Democratic.

So less than two years after the "political upset of the century," Truman's vaunted Fair Deal was a failure. And it was destined to fail, conservatives argued, because it was built on a political aberration: the New Deal. The New Deal had been adopted by the American people because they had lost confidence in themselves and their traditional institutions during the Great Depression. They had reluctantly accepted what seemed to be the only realistic solution: a large helping of big government. In *Reclaiming the American Dream,* published in 1965, libertarian Richard C. Cornuelle wrote:

> That confidence has never been completely restored. Our habit of sending difficult problems to Washington quickly became almost a reflex. A one-way flow of responsibility to the federal government, begun by Depression remedies, has continued and gained speed. In less than thirty years the government has nearly cornered the market for new public responsibility.[2]

The American people had become even more accustomed to big government, big budgets, and big debt during the big war against Germany and Japan. But with FDR's death and the successful conclusion of World War II, Americans decided they wanted less government, not more. Truman misread the 1948 results as an endorsement of liberalism when they were in reality a rejection of me-too Republicanism. Then, too, only Roosevelt, the master politician, could hold together the disparate elements of the New Deal coalition. And everyone, including Truman himself, agreed that Harry Truman was no FDR.

Looking abroad, questions were raised in the late 1940s about the policy of containment as the Soviets exploded an atomic bomb and China fell to Mao Zedong and the communists. In the administration's China White Paper, Secretary of State Acheson laid China's loss squarely on Chiang Kai-shek and his Nationalist government. But congressional Republicans insisted that the U.S. government, led by the State Department, had contributed decisively to China's going communist by, for example, delaying crucial military assistance to the Nationalists.[3]

At home, Alger Hiss was convicted of perjury for denying his pro-Soviet espionage activities and sentenced to four years in jail. Whittaker Chambers, whose testimony about communists in government had been brushed aside by virtually the entire liberal establishment, was vindicated. In March 1949, Winston Churchill delivered a speech in Boston that did much to explain why Americans were so concerned about communists, domestic and foreign. Churchill declared that "it is certain that Europe would have been communized like Czechoslovakia, and London under bombardment some time ago, but for the deterrent of the atomic bomb in the hands of the U.S."[4]

In other words, as William F. Buckley, Jr., and L. Brent Bozell put it in their study of anticommunism, "a single individual could shift the balance of power by delivering to the Soviet Union technological secrets through the use of which they could overcome their strategic disadvantage and proceed to communize Europe." For the first time in history, a traitor could determine the outcome of not just a battle or even a war but "the destiny of the West."[5]

Even most civil libertarians offered little criticism when a group of prominent college presidents, led by James B. Conant of Harvard and Dwight D. Eisenhower of Columbia, declared in June 1949 that communists should be excluded from employment as teachers.[6]

It was in this context of potential treason and at the height of the cold war that Senator Joseph McCarthy of Wisconsin delivered a fateful speech in Wheeling, West Virginia, in February 1950.

Almost fifty years later, it is still being debated whether McCarthy claimed that 205 or 57 or 81 communists were working in the State Department. McCarthy's use of "205" referred to a letter written in 1946 by Secretary of State James Byrnes to Congressman Adolph Sabath of Illinois, in which the secretary stated that adverse security recommendations had been made against 284 employees of the State Department. As of July 1946, some 79 had been discharged, leaving a difference of 205. The other two numbers—57 and 81—referred to individual cases that McCarthy was pulling together, drawing on congressional hearings, State Department sources, and help from the FBI.[7]

Less than two weeks after his Wheeling address, McCarthy was summoned to explain his allegations before a special Senate subcommittee headed by Democrat Millard Tydings of Maryland. After four months of hearings and 1,498 pages of testimony, the Tydings subcommittee issued a report describing McCarthy's charges against the State Department as a "fraud and hoax."[8]

Buckley and Bozell, two of the most uncompromising anticommunists in America, admitted that McCarthy's behavior during the Tydings hearings was "far from exemplary." He "showed himself to be inexperienced, or, worse still, misinformed. Some of his specific charges were exaggerated; a few had no apparent foundation whatever."[9]

But although McCarthy never revealed the names of the "57 card-carrying Communists," he did expose the shockingly lax condition of State Department security. An embarrassed department felt compelled to "reprocess" forty-six of the fifty-nine McCarthy cases still employed. In short order, eighteen of them were gone, and not, we may safely conclude, because they were close to the age of retirement. National security required their departure.

The Wheeling speech and the Tydings aftermath revealed the several faults of Joe McCarthy. He was, in the words of Roy Cohn, his closest aide during this period, "impatient, overly aggressive, overly dramatic. He acted on impulse. He tended to sensationalize the evidence he had. . . . He would neglect to do important homework and consequently would, on occasion, make challengeable assumptions."[10] Cohn attributed McCarthy's carelessness to the fact that he "was a salesman . . . selling the story of America's peril." He may have been wrong in details, Cohn argued, but he "was right in essentials. Certainly few can deny that the Government of the United States had in it enough Communist sympathizers and pro-Soviet advisers to twist and pervert American foreign policy."[11]

Cohn's analysis was echoed decades later by the liberal columnist Nicholas Von Hoffman, who conceded in 1996 that "McCarthy may have exaggerated the scope of the problem but not by much. The government was the workplace of perhaps 100 communist agents in 1943–45. [McCarthy] just didn't know their names."[12] Von Hoffman based his startling admission on Venona, a top-secret program of the National Security Agency during the 1940s that intercepted and then decoded messages between Moscow and its American agents. Venona proved, wrote Von Hoffman, that the Roosevelt and Truman administrations were "rife with communist spies and political operatives" who reported, directly or indirectly, to the Soviet government, just as anticommunists like Joe McCarthy had charged.[13]

A special target of McCarthy was Professor Owen Lattimore of Johns Hopkins University, a noted authority on the Far East and a long-time official of the procommunist think tank, the Institute of Pacific Relations (IPR). The senator declared that he would "stand or fall" on his accusations against Lattimore, whom he described as "one of the principal architects of our Far Eastern policy."[14]

The Tydings Committee investigated McCarthy's charges, heard from Lattimore at length, and found him innocent—the victim of "promiscuous and specious attacks." McCarthy, said the committee, had subjected the respected academic to "ordeal by slander," a phrase that Lattimore used as the title of his subsequent book about his confrontation with the allegedly reckless and irresponsible senator from Wisconsin.[15]

It took more than forty years to establish the truth, but in 1997 the conservative editor-author M. Stanton Evans published a definitive article in *Human Events*. Evans concluded that the evidence was overwhelming that Lattimore was precisely what the Senate Internal Security Subcommittee had concluded he was: "a conscious, articulate instrument of the Soviet conspiracy."[16] The subcommittee, chaired by Democrat Pat McCarran of Nevada, had scrupulously examined Lattimore's influence on U.S. foreign policy. As an example of Lattimore's "disinterested" expertise, Evans quoted from his remarks at a 1949 State Department conference, with the secretary of state present, shortly before the communists seized control of mainland China:

> The type of policy expressed by support for Chiang Kai-shek has done more harm than good to the United States. . . . [Red] China cannot be economically coerced by such measures as cutting off trade. . . . It is not possible to make Japan an instrument of American policy. . . . Japan can keep herself alive by coming to terms economically and politically with her neighbors in Asia, principally China. . . . South Korea is more of a liability than an asset to the interests and policy of the United States.[17]

No wonder we lost China, said conservatives like intelligence expert Robert Morris.[18]

Anticommunism, whether of the undiluted McCarthy brand or the smoother Taft blend, achieved additional acceptability when North Korean forces invaded South Korea on June 25, 1950. Two days later, President Truman condemned North Korea's aggression and ordered American air and sea forces to give South Korean troops "cover and support." Asserting that communism had added "armed invasion and war" to its tactics "to conquer independent nations," Truman ordered the Seventh Fleet to the Taiwan Strait to "prevent any attack on Formosa," an order that laid the foundation for the subsequent Mutual Defense Treaty between the United States and the Republic of China on Taiwan.[19]

Congressman Walter H. Judd of Minnesota, a leading House Republican in foreign affairs, praised Truman's action as "honorable" and having "some chance . . . of stopping this and further Communist aggressions in Asia." But privately he wrote that those in charge of U.S. foreign policies "had steadfastly retreated all these years in Asia" and had placed the United States and its allies "down on our five yard line."[20]

Human Events, abreast as always of communist affairs, had suggested there might be an invasion of South Korea one month before North Korean troops crossed the 38th parallel. In a lead essay published on May 17, Chinese scholar Hsiang Chi-pei described "a strong Communist State" in North Korea, "in direct contact with the Communists of Manchuria and openly preparing to extend its control over the whole peninsula."[21]

Taft blamed the Korean War on the Yalta and Potsdam conferences, where U.S. representatives "handed over Manchuria and North Korea as well as the Kurile Islands and Sakhalin" to the communists. But regardless of the origin of the present crisis, he saw no alternative "except to build up our Armed Forces to a point at least of equality with Russia."[22] This position was in sharp contrast to his strong opposition the previous year to the formation of the North Atlantic Treaty Organization (NATO). Then he had agreed with *Human Events'* Felix Morley, who recalled that twice before Democratic administrations had plunged America into war while "vociferously proclaiming their desire for peace." "The Atlantic Alliance," wrote Morley, "appears as the parallel preliminary for war with Russia."[23] However, congressional Republicans, alarmed by communist advances in Eastern Europe and Asia, had disregarded Taft's and Morley's warnings and endorsed NATO.

Taft had a challenge much closer to home that he had to meet in 1950: his reelection to the U.S. Senate.

Typically, Taft went all out for his reelection, visiting every one of Ohio's eighty-eight counties and spending an estimated $5 million, an astronomical sum for a Senate race at that time. The stakes were raised when the national leaders of organized labor marshaled all their horses and all their men to unseat the author of what they called the "Taft-Hartley Slave Labor Law."

Unlike Dewey two years earlier, Taft went on the offensive—and stayed there. "The general program of the Truman crusade," Taft declared, "is clear—promise everyone everything and hope to back it up with government money. Every American knows in his heart that such a policy will wreck the United States and reduce it to bankruptcy. It will bring first inflation and then depression."[24]

His energy astounded even old friends. Up at dawn, he campaigned until late at night, often driving his car, making three or four major speeches a day, striding through factories to shake the hands of startled union workers who were being told to hate him. What are your main assets as a candidate? he was asked. "A cast-iron stomach and good digestion," he answered dryly.[25] By election day, he later estimated, he had given 873 speeches, spoken 147 times over radio, and toured 334 industrial plants.

In his speeches, Taft called repeatedly for the election of orthodox Republicans. "We need a Congress," he asserted, "which will not hesitate to pass the Mundt-Ferguson bill to require the registration of every Communist organization." And he charged that Truman was seeking "complete and arbitrary power" over the country's economy. Taft had never conceded that government controls would defeat inflation, and he did not intend to start now.[26]

Taft beat his opponent, Joseph Ferguson, by 431,184 votes, one of the greatest margins ever given any candidate in Ohio, and he carried eighty-four of the eighty-eight counties. He was enormously proud that large numbers of people not remotely identifiable as "fat cats" had voted for him along with many thousands of union members. As Taft wrote Herbert Hoover, his reelection showed that "the American workman will not listen to a class appeal, but proposes to vote as an American first. . . . We certainly upset the theory that a heavy vote is necessarily radical."[27] It was the most impressive triumph scored by any Republican senator in 1950, which included victories by Richard Nixon in California and Everett McKinley Dirksen in Illinois.

Taft decided he would again offer himself and all he represented—what he felt was true Republicanism—as a presidential candidate in 1952. "I don't think there is any solution to the present situation," he wrote privately, "except to throw out the present administration at the first opportunity. Their policies have led America into a dangerous situation, and they are utterly incapable of getting us out."[28]

The most dangerous policy of all was Truman's foreign policy, which had produced "a useless war" in Korea and had permitted the conquest of China by communists. "Is it any wonder," Taft asked in a Minneapolis speech, that Americans "pay some attention to charges of pro-communist sympathy in the State Department?" He called for "supreme" U.S. air and sea power but opposed the building of a great land army or the waging of war on the vast land areas of Europe and Asia, "Russia's chosen battle-grounds."[29]

By mid-1951, nearly every political observer agreed that the GOP would probably win the White House in 1952, but conservatives insisted that the party had to nominate the right sort of Republican—Taft or someone very much like him. Pointing to the 1948 debacle, Taft argued that the Republican party could not survive unless it turned away from "the Deweys and the Eastern internationalists in general." The senator was not concerned about the possible defection of easterners if he were the candidate. He was convinced that "millions of *his* kind of Republican had not been voting for years in Presidential elections" because the candidates invariably were Tweedledum and Tweedledee. Taft saw his duty as not to convert the heathen but to bring the faithful back into the fold.[30] But he would discover, yet again, that the Sanhedrin of the GOP still controlled the presidential nominating machinery.

Before formally declaring his candidacy in mid-October 1951, Taft set down on a legal pad the pros and cons of his running:

1. Against—Too old; serious effect on health, and not as good as should be. Job too hard to accomplish anything substantial, and problems insoluble. No relaxation for pleasure.
   Smearing and unpleasantness in the campaign.

2. For—Opportunity to accomplish many things I am deeply interested in. Opportunity to save liberty in U.S.
   Demand of enthusiastic supporters.
   The *duty* to do those things which are imposed on you.[31]

The one word underlined in the memo was *duty*—a principle that drove Taft all his life. There was also the opportunity—one could say obligation—"to save liberty in U.S."

Although there were other candidates (like Harold Stassen, Earl Warren, and Douglas MacArthur), the 1952 presidential nomination race was essentially between Dwight Eisenhower and Robert Taft, between the eastern liberal wing and the midwestern conservative wing, between "modern" Republicans and "regular" Republicans, between pragmatists indifferent to political principle but eager to win and idealists for whom principle was as important as victory.

According to Gallup, Taft was a three-to-one choice over Eisenhower among members of the Republican National Committee and had a three-to-two margin when Republican governors and state chairmen were added to the sample. But Eisenhower was popular with rank-and-file Republicans, and he was the overwhelming choice of Democrats and independents asked to name the Republican they preferred. And despite his impressive senatorial victory in 1950, Taft lacked Eisenhower's broad appeal beyond the party regulars.[32]

Taft pursued his last, best chance for the presidency the only way he knew how—vigorously. Before he finished campaigning in late June, the senator had visited thirty-five of the forty-eight states, had made some 550 speeches, had traveled fifty thousand miles, and had been seen by an estimated 2 million people.

New Hampshire was the first, crucial primary. Taft was the early favorite, but enthusiastic supporters of Eisenhower (who was still in Paris as NATO commander and never set foot in the state) covered every city and hamlet of New Hampshire like a heavy winter snow. They also used dirty tricks. Eisenhower supporter Tex McCrary later admitted that he planted women in every Taft audience who would ask the senator, "I have a son who is being drafted—and he wants to ask you why your voting record is the same as Marcantonio's," referring to a well-known left-wing congressman from New York City.[33] It was a loaded and nonsensical question based on Taft's public skepticism about the conduct of the Korean War. But such questions, which Taft patiently answered, had a harmful impact.

Eisenhower won in New Hampshire, and his supporters followed up by mounting an effective write-in campaign in Minnesota one week later, securing 108,000 write-ins, only 12,000 behind the tally for the state's former governor, Harold Stassen, who was on the ballot. The Minnesota results led Eisenhower to admit that he was "reexamining" his past position against running, and two weeks later, Ike asked President Truman for permission to resign as NATO commander, effective June 1.[34]

Now Taft *had* to win a primary, and he spent twenty-two days in Wisconsin, enduring cold, snowy weather and spending some $100,000, a huge sum for the time. In a large turnout, he received 315,000 votes and captured twenty-four of thirty-six delegates. On the same April day, he also won Nebraska.

Over the next month, Taft showed his strength in the Midwest, the South, and parts of the Plains and Rocky Mountain states. By mid-May, the Associated Press gave Taft a lead of 374 to 337 delegates over Eisenhower, based on his victories in the Illinois, South Dakota, and Ohio primaries and at state conventions in West Virginia, North Dakota, and Wyoming. Just before the opening of the national convention in Chicago, half of the nation's fifty top political reporters thought Taft would win the nomination. But Eisenhower still led the Gallup polls of independent voters by an overwhelming margin and led Taft among Republicans by 44 to 35 percent. Much of Eisenhower's delegate strength was in the populous northern states, while Taft's resided in the southern and border states that since 1932, the Eisenhower people pointed out, had usually voted Democratic.[35]

On Sunday evening, July 6, 1952, the day before the Republican convention opened, Taft held a news conference at the Conrad Hilton Hotel in Chicago. He displayed a large bundle of telegrams—530 of them—from delegates pledged to Taft until hell froze over. "It was perhaps the most impressive display of personal strength," wrote political journalist Richard Rovere, "made by any political leader in American history."[36] Rovere was not the only journalist to note the strong emotions that Taft aroused among his delegates, who saw in the Ohio senator not just a candidate but a political savior.

Taft needed 604 delegates to secure the nomination, which seemed a sure thing, because his organization had apparently covered every possible base. Both the temporary and the permanent convention chairmen were pledged to Taft. He had a majority in the platform committee, the credentials committee, and the national committee. As delegates arrived, they were welcomed by Taft supporters who accompanied them to their hotels and informed them of upcoming events. The Taft people knew what would interest them, for they had compiled detailed notebooks about the delegates, carefully listing political information and personal gossip about each of them. Nothing had been left to chance. They had even picked the music that would be played during the convention.

And they had the warm endorsement of the only living Republican expresident, Herbert Hoover, who praised Taft's forthrightness, integrity, and leadership against "the currents of collectivism in the country." Hoover articulated what every Taft delegate believed in his heart: "This convention meets not only to nominate a candidate but to save America."[37] There did not seem to be any way that Taft could be denied what he had so clearly earned.

But the Eisenhower forces found one by challenging accredited delegates from the South. Since the Civil War, Republican party workers in the South had two responsibilities: to serve as postmasters when there was a Republican president and to vote at the national conventions. These party regulars were 100 percent behind Mr. Republican, Bob Taft.

Regular Texas Republicans had met and selected the delegates who would go to Chicago: thirty for Taft, four for Eisenhower, and four for MacArthur. Eisenhower's managers placed ads in Texas newspapers and mailed thousands of postcards addressed to "Occupant" that invited Democrats to come to Republican party meetings and "vote" for General Eisenhower. The ads stated: "You are not pledged to support the nominee of the Republican Party nor does it prohibit you from voting in the July Democratic Primary nor does it prohibit you from voting for whomever you please in the November election."[38] The ads and the postcards were wrong: Texas law expressly prohibited Democrats who intended to remain Democrats from electing delegates to a national Republican covention.

Nevertheless, Eisenhower "Republicans" convened separately in Texas and picked thirty-three Ike delegates and five Taft delegates. As a result, two Texas delegations showed up in Chicago, each claiming to be the legitimate representative of the Lone Star State.

The convention officials who would decide which would be seated were Taft men, but the Eisenhower people denounced what they called "the Texas steal" and demanded that Taft repudiate such tactics. Masked bandits with guns roamed the Chicago streets carrying placards that read "Taft Steals Votes," while oversized signs appeared proclaiming that "RAT" stood for "Robert A. Taft."[39] Taft replied heatedly, and accurately, that he had never "stolen" anything in his life and that the delegates had been chosen according to accepted party procedures of more than eighty years' standing. Taft was right: The issue was, to use one of Ike's favorite words, tommyrot. The Eisenhower delegates were no more representative of the Texas Republican party than the Taft delegates. At least the Taftites were lifelong Republicans, not Johnny-come-latelies.[40]

But the Eisenhower managers had taken off their gloves. They used the GOP's lust for victory and the general's five-star aura to challenge slates in Georgia and Louisiana as well as Texas. And they persuaded their candidate that fair play was being denied in Chicago. The man with the broad grin who had led America to victory in World War II and was still the idol of a grateful nation vowed to fight "to keep our party clean and fit to lead the nation." He deplored "smoke-filled rooms," "star chamber methods," and "chicanery." He demanded "fair play."[41]

There is little question that the convention delegates wanted to nominate Taft and would have chosen him and later campaigned for him around the clock. So why didn't they? Because the polls showed Ike beating any Democrat by a wide margin. A Gallup Poll showed Eisenhower handily defeating Governor Adlai Stevenson of Illinois, the likely Democratic nominee, by 59 percent to 31 percent. In a similar test between Taft and Stevenson, the Illinois governor held a slim 45-to-44 advantage. Republicans loved Taft, observed William Manchester, but "they loved victory more."[42]

Taft was also badly served by his managers on the convention floor. Governor Arthur B. Langlie of Washington, an Eisenhower man, offered a motion that the contested delegates from Texas, Georgia, and Louisiana remain unseated until their qualifications had been decided by a majority of all the delegates. It was a reversal of long-standing convention rules but was democracy in action. The Taft response came from Ohio congressman Clarence J. Brown, who clumsily offered an amendment that conceded the Eisenhower people almost everything but retained Taftite control of the convention. Brown seemed to be admitting that the Taft forces had indeed been guilty of theft. It was all the convention, eager to embrace Ike, needed. The Brown amendment was defeated 658 to 548, and control of the Republican party passed to Dwight Eisenhower.[43]

Not even Senator Dirksen of Illinois, a renowned orator, could sway the convention when he turned to the New York delegation, leader of the Eisenhower forces, and roared, "When Dewey was the candidate in 1944 and 1948, I went into twenty-three states and fought for him. Reexamine your hearts on this [delegate] issue because we followed you before and you took us down the road to defeat!"[44] Taft believers bellowed their approval, but they did not have the votes to match their emotion.

There were nominating speeches yet to be made and standing ovations for former President Herbert Hoover and Senator Joseph McCarthy, but everyone, including Robert Taft, knew that the nominee had been decided. On the first ballot, the count stood Eisenhower 595, Taft 500, Warren 81, Stassen 20, and MacArthur 10. There was no second ballot: Minnesota asked to be recognized and changed its vote from Stassen to Eisenhower. Senator John Bricker, for Taft, and Senator William Knowland, for Warren, then moved that the nomination be made unanimous.

There were plenty of theories and recriminations as to why Taft lost. Certainly his staff had made mistakes. There had been overconfidence about New Hampshire and a failure to appreciate the importance of the Texas "steal." Clarence Brown, one of Taft's closest advisers for many years, fumbled by first barring television from the deliberations of the national committee and then trying to amend the Langlie resolution at the wrong time and in the wrong way.

And most important, Taft had no conservative movement to help him. As Frank Hanighen wrote in *Human Events* the year before, the "Capitalists" who should have been supporting Taft's ideas were "either stupidly donating money to foundations which oppose his ideas or complacently waiting for his triumph at the polls."[45] One of the few evidences of movement conservatism was the formation, in the spring of 1952, of the Intercollegiate Society of Individualists (ISI), whose organizers argued that the push toward socialism in America began with the Socialist Clubs on college campuses over forty years earlier. ISI's plan was to "foment the organization of campus cells for the study and discussion of Individualistic ideas." Its founding father was libertarian writer Frank Chodorov; its first president was a recent Yale graduate, William F. Buckley, Jr.[46]

But the essential truth about Taft's defeat, as biographer James T. Patterson pointed out, was that the senator carried the burden of being seen as a regional candidate who lacked substantial support in the populous Northeast and Pacific Coast. And it was the eastern states—the eastern establishment— that still ruled the Republican party at convention time.[47]

The easterners, led by Thomas Dewey, did not like Taft because they thought him an isolationist, a small-government Jeffersonian, and a loser. They wanted to win and believed they would win with war hero Eisenhower, a strong internationalist and sympathetic, they thought, to "modern" Republicanism with its belief in efficiently managed government.

But their dreams of victory would have evaporated without the generous public support that Taft, ever the faithful Republican, immediately tendered his rival. Taft supporters were crying and cursing and threatening to walk out when Ike, reversing the usual practice, visited Taft in his Hilton Hotel headquarters. The meeting of the two men, *Human Events* wrote, was "like Grant and Lee at Appomattox."[48] As they stood side by side in the crowded, noisy hall, reporters noted with some surprise that it was Eisenhower who seemed drawn and emotional while Taft was calm and poised.

"I came over to pay a call of friendship on a great American," said the general. "His willingness to cooperate is absolutely necessary to the success of the Republican party in the campaign and the administration to follow." Taft responded in kind: "I want to congratulate General Eisenhower. I shall do everything possible in the campaign to secure his election and to help in his administration."[49] Taft's refusal to display any public bitterness, his quiet acceptance of defeat, awed friend and foe alike. Taft "had no petty jealousy and hatred," journalist Edwin Lahey recalled. "He was freer of them than almost any man I've ever seen in public life."[50]

But many conservatives were not so willing to forgive and forget what had happened in Chicago. Taft was flooded with letters from resentful supporters who vowed, "I will do everything I can to defeat General Eisenhower and I know there are many other men like me." A midwestern politician told *Human Events* that he had never "seen the like" of "the bitterness of the rank and file of Republicans."[51]

Knowing that a divided party spelled defeat, anxious Eisenhower aides contacted Taft and proposed a summit meeting between the two Republican leaders. Taft agreed to a September date but said that Eisenhower would have to agree to "certain assurances" in advance. They included no discrimination against Taft people during or after the campaign; no censorship of Taft's proposals, which included a 15 percent cut in 1954–1955 federal spending and a tax cut; a firm defense of Taft-Hartley; a "reasonably conservative farm policy"; and a sharp attack on Truman's foreign policy as developed at "Yalta, Tehran, Potsdam, and Manchuria."[52] It was strong medicine, but the large spoonful of sugar for the Eisenhower people was Taft's assurance that he would campaign "vigorously" for the ticket.

The long-awaited Eisenhower-Taft meeting took place on September 12 over a two-hour breakfast at Eisenhower's headquarters in Morningside Heights in New York City. There was no joint statement or press conference, but the two smiling men posed for photos. Taft then went across the street to a hotel and warmly endorsed his rival, asserting that the fundamental issue of the campaign, as accepted by Ike, was "liberty against the creeping socialism in every domestic field." It was a triumphant moment for Taft.[53]

Dismayed liberal Republicans dubbed the meeting the "Surrender at Morningside Heights," and Senator Wayne Morse of Oregon, always a maverick, publicly declared his independence from the Republican party.[54] Conservative Republicans, on the other hand, were reassured by Taft's unqualified declaration:

> I am completely satisfied that General Eisenhower will give the country an administration inspired by the Republican principles of continued and expanding liberty for all as against the continued growth of New Deal socialism which we would suffer under Governor Stevenson . . . a representative of the left-wingers if not a left-winger himself.[55]

The Morningside Declaration formed a powerful alliance between two very different men and two very different political wings of a national political party.[56] So long as both sides stood by the declaration, the alliance might last not just for an election but for an administration and even a generation. But as we shall see, for the pragmatists, the declaration was just that: a piece of paper, a commitment to be honored for the moment but not necessarily any longer. After all, who knew what challenges and opportunities might open up in the coming months and years? Surely no one could or should expect a political party, or an administration, to tie itself down to a document composed in the heat of a political campaign.

But for conservatives, the word was all-important. A declaration was a bond to be kept and honored. It was a foundation on which to build an alliance, a party, a movement, a nation. What people said and wrote and promised was important. The Declaration of Independence, the Constitution, and the Gettysburg Address were not just documents but principles and beliefs that constituted an enduring contract between the dead, the living, and the unborn. The Morningside Declaration was in this honorable tradition, at least in the eyes of conservatives.

Although not indifferent to the Burkean sentiment, eastern Republicans were tightly focused on a more immediate "contract" they wanted the American electorate to sign: putting the GOP in the White House after twenty years. Accordingly, their candidate accepted the Morningside Declaration, signaling he would not wage a "me-too" Deweyite campaign. Ike approved a symbol that became the official campaign slogan, K_1C_2—for "Korea, Communism, Corruption." And he campaigned on the 1952 Republican platform, drafted by Taft Republicans, which promised:

> We shall eliminate from the State Department and from every Federal office, all, wherever they may be found, who share responsibility for the needless predicaments and perils in which we find ourselves.
>
> We shall also sever from the public payroll the hordes of loafers, incompetents and unnecessary employees who clutter the administration of our foreign affairs. . . .
>
> We shall see to it that no treaty or agreement with other countries deprives our citizens of the rights guaranteed them by the Federal Constitution. . . .
>
> [There will be] reduction of expenditures by the elimination of waste and extravagance so that the budget will be balanced and a general tax reduction can be made.[57]

A loyal Taft campaigned unstintingly for the nominee and new leader of his GOP, appearing in twenty states of the West and Midwest and rallying, where necessary, his still resentful supporters. He sharply delineated the differences between the two candidates, charging that Stevenson's election "would mean a continuation of the wavering, unstable, pro-Communist philosophy that has almost brought this country to destruction."[58] It was strong stuff, but not a match for the stinging rhetoric of vice presidential candidate Richard Nixon, who invariably described Stevenson as "Adlai the Appeaser" who had received a "Ph.D. from Dean Acheson's Cowardly College of Communist Containment."[59]

And then there was Senator Joseph McCarthy, who, in his travels through ten states campaigning for conservative candidates, referred often to "Alger" Stevenson. The Illinois governor had opened himself up for the gibe by volunteering that Alger Hiss had a "good" reputation so far as he knew. Stevenson's subsequent protest that he had "never doubted the verdict of the jury which convicted him" was ignored by both conservatives and liberals.[60] But it was not only ardent anticommunists like Nixon and McCarthy who sounded the tocsin across the country.

Eisenhower himself took full advantage of the public mood by asserting that a national tolerance of communism had "poisoned two whole decades of our national life" and insinuated itself into our schools, public forums, news channels, labor unions, "and—most terrifyingly—into our government itself." He attributed both the fall of China to Mao Zedong and the "surrender of whole nations" in Eastern Europe to communists in Washington.

"This penetration," Ike declared in a Milwaukee speech, with Joe McCarthy seated behind him on the platform, "meant a domestic policy whose tone was set by men who sneered and scoffed at warnings of the enemy infiltrating our most secret councils." In short, he said, "It meant—in its most ugly triumph—treason itself."[61] Eisenhower went so far as to delete a paragraph praising former Secretary of State George Marshall, a favorite target of McCarthy, who vigorously pumped Ike's hand after his address. Liberals were disgusted at what they called Eisenhower's "cravenness," but conservatives felt vindicated.[62] Ike may not have cared for McCarthy's methods, but he shared the Wisconsin senator's objective: get the communists out of the government. And he wanted to win the election.

Human Events backed Eisenhower in the hope that his victory would mean "the beginning of the end of the Republican Party—and the rise of a new conservative party." It argued that realignment of the parties was inevitable inasmuch as Ike could win only by attracting voters "hitherto outside the Republican Party" whose convictions he would not later be able to disregard. The conservative publication conceded that its "apologia for Ike" was speculative but nevertheless warranted: "Big political changes loom."[63]

The election results did not startle anyone, including the Democrats: Eisenhower captured 33.9 million votes (55.4 percent of the total) to 27.3 million for Stevenson. Ike's impressive vote was almost 12 million more than Dewey had received in his lackluster 1948 campaign. Eisenhower swept the electoral college, 442 to 89, and cracked the so-called Solid South, carrying Florida, Tennessee, Texas, and Virginia. Ike's coattails helped Republicans gain narrow majorities in both houses of Congress: 48 to 47 with 1 independent in the Senate (including a new senator from Arizona, Barry Goldwater) and 221 to 214 in the House. For the first time since 1930, Republicans controlled both the White House and Capitol Hill.

While the Republican triumph was due in large measure to the general's extraordinary personal appeal, other factors were also in play. The Republican party was a united party, thanks to Robert Taft. Many Catholic Democrats, especially those of Irish and Polish background, voted Republican because of K_1C_2 and Joe McCarthy. Arthur Krock of the *New York Times* wrote that "the voting majority indicated approval of the objectives of what the Democrats and independents have assailed as McCarthyism."[64] Ike carried four southern states because he was forced to the right by the Republican platform, the Morningside Declaration, and other conservative pressures. And finally, for all his wit and intelligence, Adlai Stevenson was unable to hold the old FDR coalition together. Political erosion and demographic shifts combined to make the suburbs the new electoral centers of power, and the suburbs were becoming Republican territory, with Democratic strongholds like Levittown, Long Island, and Park Forest, Illinois, voting GOP by two to one.[65]

Stevenson was even challenged in an aspect of campaigning thought to be almost exclusively his: television. While refraining from delivering speeches on television (a Stevenson specialty), Ike did film a number of television commercials. Carefully coached by his advisers (including film actor Robert Montgomery), Eisenhower gave short, simple answers to questions he had encountered in the campaign: "Mr. Eisenhower, can you bring taxes down?" "Yes. We will work to cut billions in Washington spending and bring your taxes down."[66] The campaign spent about $800,000 to air twenty-eight different thirty-second television spots, usually during popular programs. The spots beamed Ike's all-American smile into the living rooms of millions of Americans and were worth every penny. Television had become an indispensable weapon of American politics.

Republicans had begun using visual-sound advertising in the 1950 congressional elections. The technique was developed by Robert Humphreys, a veteran political reporter hired by the Republican Congressional Campaign Committee to be its publicity director. Under Humphreys's direction, the committee provided Republican candidates with color strip films and records containing commentaries on three key issues: the Korean war, the Brannan Plan dealing with agriculture, and "America's Creeping Socialism." Also distributed were material for television appearances, recorded radio spot announcements, newspaper advertisements, and a "speech kit" with data for speeches on more than twenty issues.

Leonard Hall, then a New York congressman and chairman of the Congressional Campaign Committee, reported "an amazing voter response" to the audiovisual presentations, which had never been used before in political campaigns. Republican candidates discovered that people "could be instructed in half the time and were willing to listen twice as long."[67]

By 1952, Humphreys correctly predicted, "television will probably affect every congressional contest in the country." Indeed, and all of American society.[68]

Looking at the 1952 results, a question comes inevitably to mind: What if Taft rather than Eisenhower had headed the ticket? Taft was convinced he too would have won. Although Ike was enormously popular, he needed the Republican vote and the "negative enthusiasm against what had been going on in Washington."[69] Taft believed that the independent vote would have gone—as it did in his 1950 senatorial campaign—to an aggressive, partisan candidate like himself. Political pollster Samuel Lubell agreed, telling a Washington audience several years later that while Taft would not have won by as large a margin as Eisenhower, "still, he would have been elected." According to James T. Patterson, the consensus of analysts was that "Taft would have won, but on nothing like the scale amassed by the beloved Ike."[70]

As to what kind of president he would have made, Taft again had little doubt, writing a friend in December 1952, "I am confident that my administration would have given the people what they want much more than the General's will."[71] That is, a Taft administration would have reduced federal spending, balanced the budget, cut taxes, provided carefully prescribed government services in areas like public housing and education where assistance was demonstrably necessary, cleaned out the State Department, ended the conflict in Korea, and met the Soviet challenge with an expanded air force and navy while keeping American armed forces overseas to an absolute minimum.

Still, as he considered the future in late 1952, Taft had good reason to think that he as head of the legislative branch and Eisenhower as head of the executive branch could be an effective team for their party and their country. Tragically, they would have the opportunity to forge such a relationship for only five short months before Robert A. Taft, the requisite link between regular Republican and modern Republican, Midwest and East, internationalist and nationalist, was dead of cancer.

Chapter 4

Profiles in Courage

THE U.S. GOVERNMENT THAT GREETED DWIGHT EISENHOWER IN JANUARY 1953 was far different from the one the last Republican president had known when he took office in 1929. Herbert Hoover had presided over 630,000 civilian employees; now they numbered more than 2.5 million. Then the annual federal budget had been under $4 billion; now it was $85.4 billion—a twentyfold increase. Then the United States produced and sold most of its goods and services to itself and relied on two great oceans to sustain a splendid isolationism. Now it was the undisputed leader of the free world, engaged in a protracted conflict with the Soviet Union and involved in a hundred crises, large and small, around the globe.

In his inaugural address, Eisenhower repeated the tough, anticommunist themes of the campaign, declaring, "Freedom is pitted against slavery; lightness against dark." In his State of the Union address, he added that the United States would "never acquiesce in the enslavement of any people."[1] Ike was keeping faith with U.S. allies in Western Europe who faced a mighty Soviet phalanx held in check only by American might and will. And he was reassuring congressional conservatives who were watching the White House closely for any sign of foreign policy flinching.

A challenge and an opportunity presented themselves in March when Radio Moscow announced that Joseph Stalin had died. Publicly, the White House sent formal condolences to the Kremlin, but privately, Ike admitted to his favorite speechwriter, John Emmett Hughes, that he was tired "of just plain indictments of the Soviet regime." He lamented the armaments race that would lead "at worse, to atomic warfare. At best, to robbing every people and nation on earth of the fruits of their own toil." He told Hughes he wanted to try a peace offensive.[2]

And so in April, Eisenhower called for a limit on strategic arms and international control of atomic energy. That December, he delivered an "Atoms for Peace" speech to the United Nations, in which he called on the three nuclear powers—the United States, the Soviet Union, and the United Kingdom—to turn over at least some of their fissionable materials to an international agency.[3]

As he promised during his campaign, Eisenhower negotiated an armistice with North Korea, which, however, satisfied no one. After thirty-seven months of fighting and some 2 million dead, 54,000 of them American, Korea was returned to its status quo ante as a peninsula divided north and south, communist and noncommunist. There was not even "a reliable inspection system to prevent Kim [Il Sung] from launching another attack," observed William Manchester. As one Democrat sarcastically remarked, Truman "would have been flayed" for such an agreement, but Eisenhower was praised because he was Ike and the American people were grateful that the fighting had ended, no matter how.[4]

Conservatives like Senator William E. Jenner of Indiana and George W. Malone of Nevada were furious, calling the cease-fire a victory for communism, not for democracy. Senator William Knowland of California predicted bleakly that "we will lose the balance of Asia." General Mark Clark, who had commanded the U.S.-led forces in Korea, said only, "I cannot find it in me to exult in this hour."[5]

There would have been a serious conservative revolt if Taft had led the way. But out of loyalty to the man who had been elected president and was the leader of his party, the senator restricted himself to saying that the prospect of a divided Korea was "extremely distasteful." Although urged by several colleagues, he refused to sow discontent or counsel despair.[6] His overriding interest now was in prudential governing, not in ego-driven politicking. And "he would never contribute to any action that would rupture the [Republican] party," wrote political historian Robert Merry. Besides, as his son noted, Taft felt "a great responsibility" to those who had supported Eisenhower the preceding fall on his recommendation.[7]

While loyal to the president, Taft controlled the Senate, effectively isolating the eastern establishment Dewey forces. Liberals like James Duff of

Pennsylvania and Leverett Saltonstall of Massachusetts were given back-row seats of power. And Taft apparently sought to contain an overeager Joe McCarthy by naming William Jenner of Indiana, every bit as anticommunist as McCarthy, as chairman of the Internal Security Subcommittee of the Senate Judiciary Committee and establishing a guideline that all investigations had to be cleared by the party leadership. McCarthy was given the Government Operations Committee, an important post but normally not concerned with subversion and espionage.[8]

Meanwhile, Eisenhower, no mean politician himself, actively courted his one-time rival and now essential team member. The president initiated weekly meetings with congressional leaders and made it clear that Taft could see him at any time without an appointment. He was careful to involve Taft and other key members of Congress in policy discussions before presidential decisions were made. Yet it took time for the two sides to get used to each other. At one meeting, a White House aide suggested a general to head the Veterans Administration. "No, no!" Taft snapped, looking across the table at the president, "No more generals! No more generals!" The senator, telling the story later, complained ruefully, "The trouble was that nobody laughed."[9]

The two men, so different in temperament and by training, nevertheless began to warm to each other. The president wrote, probably to the consternation of Dewey liberals, "Senator Taft has been the model of cheerful and effective cooperation." Taft responded in kind, telling a friend that the president was "a man of good will."[10]

Taft's motives were as usual a combination of the patriotic and the partisan. He told Herbert Hoover that the stakes were high. If the Eisenhower administration did not succeed and the Republicans lost the White House in 1956, he predicted, "we are going as a nation into a long, long slide."[11] And so would the Republican party.

These were golden days for Taft. He was at the center of policymaking based on conservative principles and the Constitution. He was working with an enormously popular president whom he respected and who returned that respect. He reached a position of legislative power rarely equaled before or since. The *New York Times* Senate correspondent wrote that "no president within twenty years . . . had so effective a Senate leader as Eisenhower had in Taft in the brief months between the Republican return to power in January of 1953 and Taft's death in July." Columnist Walter Lippmann suggested that Taft was acting as a kind of "prime minister" for the president.[12]

Two issues confirmed Taft's critical contribution to the Eisenhower administration's early success: the nomination of career diplomat Charles E. (Chip) Bohlen as ambassador to Moscow and a congressional resolution on the secret agreements between the United States and the Soviet Union at the 1945 Yalta Conference.

Although Bohlen was a Republican, his nomination bothered Taft and aroused McCarthy and other Senate conservatives. Bohlen had accompanied President Roosevelt to Yalta, long described by anticommunists as an American sellout to the Soviets. In his confirmation hearing, Bohlen firmly defended the Yalta outcome (which effectively ceded Poland to Moscow) as having been in the United States' interest at the time. McCarthy led a sharp attack on the Bohlen nomination, demanding that the diplomat take a lie detector test and that Secretary of State John Foster Dulles "testify under oath" on the matter.

Taft moved quickly to settle a dispute that he saw could split Republicans at a critical juncture of the new administration. On the Senate floor, with McCarthy present, Taft called the suggestion that Dulles be placed under oath "ridiculous" and pointed out that FBI director J. Edgar Hoover opposed lie detector tests. He proposed that he and Alabama Democrat John Sparkman inspect summaries of the FBI files that allegedly contained damaging information about the nominee. After several hours of inspection, the two men reported that they had found nothing to indicate that Bohlen was not a loyal American. "There was not any suggestion" in the material, said Taft, "that would in my opinion create even a prima facie case or a prima facie charge of any ill-doing on the part of Mr. Bohlen."[13]

Bohlen was confirmed, 74 to 13. Taft had done his duty by the administration, but he immediately passed the word to the White House: "No more Bohlens!" And he did not allow the press to create a division between himself and the anti-Bohlen conservatives. Asked if the affair signified a "break" with McCarthy, Taft quickly replied, "No, no, no, no."[14] He was committed to exerting every possible effort to keep the Republican coalition together.

A similar furor erupted over a congressional resolution about Yalta, one of the Republicans' favorite proofs of Democratic foreign policy ineptitude. The White House suggested language condemning the Soviets, but not the

Roosevelt administration, for its part in this secret agreement that enslaved the peoples of Eastern Europe. Conservatives rejected the draft as unacceptable, pointing out that the 1952 party platform had repudiated the Yalta agreement without qualification. *Human Events* stated that the president's proposal was "scant nourishment for the . . . peoples behind the Iron Curtain. As a move in psychological warfare, it is a dud."[15]

Taft took the high road by endorsing an amendment stating that in adopting the resolution, Congress was not passing "on the validity or invalidity" of Yalta. This was the equivalent, as William S. White wrote, of saying that Congress doubted President Roosevelt's right to sign the Yalta agreement. "The Democrats at once arose in full cry," followed closely by a number of White House aides.[16] But Taft would not be moved. He would not allow a Republican administration to let a Democratic president off the hook. Nor would he permit the formally approved language of a Republican platform to be ignored so baldly.

The reasons for Taft's different approach to the two issues are instructive. His stance on the Yalta resolution was founded on principle, on which he was inflexible. His position in the Bohlen nomination was based on personality, on which he was willing to bend.

With the Democrats remaining adamant and the Republicans refusing to compromise, the Yalta resolution quietly died in committee. Taft thereby demonstrated "his fealty to principle," avoided a direct confrontation with the president, and scored a subtle but telling political victory against the internationalists.[17]

The Eisenhower-Taft partnership, unique in modern American politics, was often tested in the first few months of the administration, but never more so than on April 30, 1953. Meeting in the Cabinet Room, Ike told the congressional leadership that, contrary to Republican expectations, he would not be able to balance the budget. He could cut the deficit from $9.9 billion to $5.5 billion, but no more without jeopardizing national security. A red-faced Taft exploded in anger and, pounding the table with his fist, yelled, "The one primary thing we promised the American people was reduction of expenditures! With a program like this, we'll never elect a Republican Congress in 1954!" Glaring at Ike, he said, "You're taking us down the same road Truman traveled! It's a repudiation of everything we promised in the campaign!"[18]

It was a deciding moment. If Eisenhower had replied in kind—and his temper was every bit as incendiary as Taft's—Taft might have stalked out of the meeting, and the Republican party would have split asunder there and then. But Ike quietly went over the figures and carefully outlined the strategy he was following to fight the cold war and keep federal spending down. Ever open to logic and the facts, a mollified Taft said he hoped and expected that there would be substantial reductions in next year's budget—and received Eisenhower's assurance on it.[19] (In fact, the 1954 budget would be in deficit too.)

The alliance between the chief executive and the chief legislator held. Who can say what these two political giants might have forged if they had had three or seven more years to work together? But that same month, Taft felt a severe pain in his hip while playing golf with Ike. Less than two months later, he would announce, on crutches, that he was stepping down temporarily as Senate majority leader. He was fatally ill with cancer.

His personally chosen successor was William Knowland of California, whom Taft considered to be an orthodox Republican in his principles and his politics. Taft had been impressed by Knowland's reelection victory in 1952, when he received the largest majority ever given any candidate for any office in California. And Knowland was a West Coast Republican, not an East Coaster—a key distinction for midwesterner Taft. Knowland embodied those personal qualities that Taft had always valued most highly, especially "a very deep sense of responsibility accompanied by . . . political courage."[20]

Knowland was a strong anticommunist (often described as the "Senator from Formosa") and a traditionalist in domestic affairs. More important, Knowland was neither pro-Eisenhower nor anti-Eisenhower; he was pro-Republican. And Taft was determined, above all else, that the Eisenhower administration, a *Republican* administration, should succeed. If anyone beside Taft could manage both the McCarthy conservatives and Dewey liberals, it was Knowland. Taft also knew that Knowland, like himself, was not a mindless compromiser. One reporter later wrote that Taft had said, "I'm going away and I've asked Bill to carry on for me. Nobody can push him around."[21]

It was not a prolonged illness. After naming Knowland as his "acting" successor on June 10, 1953, Taft went to New York City for treatment, which proved ineffective. He spent the next two weeks in Washington reassuring old friends about his health but knowing there was little hope. When President Hoover urged his longtime friend, hobbling about on crutches, to go to the hospital, Taft replied, simply, "I am going to die with my boots on." Somehow he mustered the strength to attend afternoon sessions on the Hill, discuss possible revisions of Taft-Hartley, and attend several White House meetings. He was mellow, "even jocular." When Eisenhower sent him a book on golf entitled *The Laws of the Links,* Taft quipped: "Glancing through the book, I am afraid that a lot of our friends don't follow the rules as they are written, but that seems to be true in politics also."[22]

His last official act in Washington came on July 2 when he attended the swearing in of his old friend, retired Admiral Lewis Strauss, as chairman of the Atomic Energy Commission. When he walked out of his Senate office for the last time, he left behind on his desk a miscellaneous batch of letters, memos, and notes that included the following: "No Indo China—Except in case of emergency invasion by the Chinese."[23]

On July 4, Independence Day, Taft was back in the New York hospital. An operation revealed that the cancer had spread everywhere, and although Taft recovered quickly from surgery, there was no longer any doubt about the outcome. He died quietly on the morning of July 31, 1953. His body, like his father's twenty-three years before, was placed in the Capitol rotunda, where some thirty thousand people paid their last respects to Mr. Republican.

Without Taft, the dynamics of the Republican party shifted dramatically. There was no effective counterweight to the modern Republicanism of the Eisenhower administration, which was never again as conservative as it had been under Taft's guidance in the first half of 1953. And without Taft, there was no one who could challenge Joe McCarthy (as he had done with the Bohlen nomination). Taft would not have given McCarthy free rein to conduct the often careless inquiries in 1953 and 1954 that allowed liberals to transform anticommunism into McCarthyism and hang it around the necks of conservatives for the next thirty years.

Almost single-handedly, Taft had strengthened and shaped the conservative strain in the American character, demonstrating that change was not to be feared but blended and harmonized with the historical experience of the nation. His accomplishments, as conservative historians Russell Kirk and James McClellan wrote, were several and significant:

- He revived the GOP during the postwar period and restored "a conscientious opposition" when parliamentary government had "fallen into decay" throughout most of the world.

- He stood for liberty under law—"the liberties of all classes of citizens, in all circumstances."
- He spoke with effect against "arbitrary power," as when President Truman tried to crush the right of railroad workers to strike.
- He contended for "a humane economy" in which the benefits of American industry might be extended to every citizen.
- He helped restore "the balance between management and [organized] labor" with Taft-Hartley.
- He vigorously and fairly criticized the conduct of American foreign policy, supporting, for example, the Truman Doctrine and the Marshall Plan but opposing NATO.[24]

Four years after his death, Taft was elected to a Senate Hall of Fame, joining John C. Calhoun, Daniel Webster, Henry Clay, and Robert La Follette, Sr. The five men, according to a bipartisan Senate committee headed by Senator John F. Kennedy, had transcended party and state lines and "left a permanent mark on our nation's history and brought distinction to the Senate."[25] Kennedy, the future Democratic president, featured Taft the Republican in his best-selling 1956 book, *Profiles in Courage*.

When Taft died, many conservatives wept for the man who had led them for two decades and seemingly for the end to their chances of nominating one of their own for president. Three times, in 1940, 1948, and 1952, they had put forward Taft, and three times they had collided with the political reality that at convention time, eastern liberals ruled the Republican party.

Conservatives believed with all their heart that Taft should have been nominated in 1952, that he deserved to be nominated, and that if he had been nominated, he too would have defeated Adlai Stevenson and been elected president. Now he was dead and Douglas MacArthur had faded away, and the only champion left was the mercurial, Irish Catholic, Midwest populist, Joe McCarthy.

McCarthy was a conservative backbencher in the Senate when he journeyed to Wheeling, West Virginia, in February 1950 to make the speech in which he declared that a number of communists were still employed by the State Department. From that day until December 1954, when the Senate voted to "condemn" his conduct, McCarthy was at the center of the American political stage. To millions of Americans, he became the preeminent symbol of anticommunism. To many others, he was a reckless character assassin. A new word—*McCarthyism,* the making of baseless accusations—was coined by his enemies. Defiant friends wore that label proudly.

The senator had waged an aggressive, partisan war against President Truman and then criticized President Eisenhower when he felt the head of his own party was not being sufficiently anticommunist. He reached the height of his power in 1953 when Republicans achieved control of Congress, and he became chairman of the Government Operations Committee and its Permanent Subcommittee on Investigations. McCarthy ranged far and wide, even negotiating with Greek shipowners to obtain a pledge they would not send ships behind the iron curtain. Critics accused him of interfering in U.S. foreign policy; he shrugged off the complaint, as he did most criticism.

McCarthy's political power flowed from the circumstances of the day, including the fall of China to the communists, the trials and ultimate conviction of one-time Soviet spy Alger Hiss, the atom spy cases of Julius and Ethel Rosenberg and Klaus Fuchs, and the communist invasion of South Korea. He was backed by a national constituency, many of whom responded to the fact that he was an Irish Roman Catholic (his mail included almost as many rosaries and prayer cards as checks) or responded to him as a midwestern populist whose longshoreman language and careless dress appealed to working-class Americans. Typical of the endorsements by Catholic clergy was that of Francis Cardinal Spellman of New York, who noted that McCarthy "is making America aware of the danger of communism."[26]

As a young Irving Kristol perceptively wrote in the then-liberal journal *Commentary* in 1952, "There is one thing that the American people know about Senator McCarthy: he, like them, is unequivocally anti-Communist. About the spokesmen for American liberalism, they feel they know no such thing."[27]

But McCarthy had a fatal flaw: He rarely listened to anyone, even his closest friends and advisers, particularly when they counseled caution and prudence. Whittaker Chambers constantly expressed his deep concern about McCarthy to Bill Buckley, stating that the senator was "a slugger and a rabble-rouser" who "simply knows that somebody threw a tomato and the general direction from which it came." McCarthy, he said, had only one tactic—"attack"—and that was not sufficient.[28]

McCarthy's decline began in the late summer and fall of 1953 when he took on the Eisenhower administration and the Pentagon by objecting to the promotion of a commissioned army officer named Irving Peress. Peress had invoked the Fifth Amendment when given a loyalty form asking about possible Communist party membership. While McCarthy was investigating the case, Peress was promoted to major and given an honorable discharge, arousing the short-tempered senator.

Brigadier General Ralph W. Zwicker, Peress's commanding officer, was summoned to explain the army's action. Infuriated by the general's somewhat evasive responses, McCarthy lost control and declared that Zwicker, a highly decorated veteran of World War II who had received the Silver Star, the Legion of Merit, the British Distinguished Order, and the French Legion of Honor, was "not fit" to wear his uniform.[29]

McCarthy had gone too far, even for loyal supporters. The conservative *Chicago Tribune* suggested that the senator learn to distinguish between the role of investigator and avenging angel: "We do not believe Senator McCarthy's behavior toward General Zwicker was justified and we expect it has injured his cause of driving the disloyal from the government service."[30]

President Eisenhower, who had publicly commended Zwicker for his wartime service and had never forgotten McCarthy's public attack on his World War II boss, George Marshall, decided that the time had come to take action against the senator from Wisconsin. With White House approval, charges were filed in the Senate alleging that the McCarthy committee had pressured the Pentagon to secure favorable treatment for an army private, G. David Schine, who had served as an unpaid consultant to the committee and was a close personal friend of its chief counsel, Roy Cohn, a McCarthy loyalist. McCarthy and Cohn retorted that the Pentagon was attempting to "blackmail" them into halting inquiries into communist infiltration in the military.

Charges flew back and forth, and a Senate investigation was ordered. The result was the celebrated Army-McCarthy hearings, which were televised live in the spring of 1954 to an estimated daily audience of 20 million people.

McCarthy's enemies had found the key to bring him down: play up the conflict between him and an overwhelmingly popular hero and president. As the televised hearings progressed, punctuated by McCarthy's constant cries of "Point of order, Mr. Chairman!" and the smooth performance of the prosecuting attorney, Joseph N. Welch, opinion polls showed a sharp decline in public approval of the senator. In January, the Gallup Poll had reported that 50 percent of those interviewed held a favorable opinion of McCarthy. Republicans favored him by an overwhelming 62 percent to 19 percent. But by June, 51 percent of Americans disapproved of the senator while only 36 percent approved.[31]

Television accentuated his dark side. As even his chief aide Cohn conceded, "with his easily erupting temper, his menacing monotone, his unsmiling mien, and his perpetual 5-o'clock shadow, [McCarthy] did seem the perfect stock villain."[32]

In July 1954, Senator Ralph Flanders, a liberal Republican from Vermont, proposed senatorial "censure" of McCarthy, presenting a set of charges of misconduct, which he later admitted had been drafted by the National Committee for an Effective Congress, an openly anti-McCarthy organization. After lengthy discussion of the charges, the Senate voted to come back in November after the congressional elections and hold a special "censure session."[33]

McCarthy labeled the session a "lynch party" and predicted that a majority would vote against him. As ever, the senator's loose language was the despair of his supporters, including Senator Price Daniel of Texas, a conservative Democrat, who in November approached freshman Republican Barry Goldwater of Arizona (for whom McCarthy had campaigned in 1952) and told him that if McCarthy would write letters of apology to the two Republican senators (Arthur Watkins of Utah and Robert C. Hendrickson of New Jersey) who felt that he had insulted them, southern senators might well be persuaded to vote against censure.

Goldwater immediately contacted Edward Bennett Williams, McCarthy's lawyer, and the two men drove to Bethesda Naval Hospital where McCarthy was being treated for bursitis. To avoid being seen, they walked up thirteen flights of stairs, slipped past the nurses' station, and entered McCarthy's room. Goldwater gave his friend two letters of apology Williams had drafted, explaining that if Joe signed one of them, he would win valuable support. If he signed both, he had Senator Daniel's word that the southern senators would stand by him. The letters, remembered Goldwater, were "short, mild in their language, and regretted a discourtesy without really conceding any substantive error on McCarthy's part."[34]

Goldwater and Williams warned McCarthy that the other side probably had enough votes to pass the censure resolution. Goldwater recalled that just when they thought they had convinced McCarthy, he suddenly "started to howl and scream at us for being traitors to the cause of anticommunism." He threw a pen across the room and pounded on the table, making so much noise that a nurse came running in, followed shortly by the admiral in charge of the hospital. The admiral declared he was going to call the shore patrol and have the two visitors arrested for trespassing. "You can't do that," Goldwater protested. "I'm a United States senator."

"I don't give a damn who you are," shouted the admiral, "you get out of here."[35]

The two men left, taking with them McCarthy's last chance of avoiding senatorial censure and surviving politically.

Despite the rejection, Goldwater did not stop trying to help McCarthy. Taking the Senate floor, Goldwater attacked those Republicans who wanted to censure one of their own. He accused his colleagues of cannibalism and stated that the Senate ought to concentrate on the key question: "What will happen to America's fight against communism if the efforts of a man who has been active in the fight against this evil are repudiated?" Goldwater emphasized McCarthy's (and his own) antiestablishment stance. McCarthy, he said, had been willing to challenge the powerful men who "were making decisions which were weakening America and strengthening Moscow."[36]

Ignored in the debate was the fact that the key people McCarthy had accused of communist sympathy were guilty as charged. The senator, for example, had asserted that Owen Lattimore of the procommunist Institute of Pacific Relations (IPR) was either "a Soviet agent" or "a member of the Communist Party." A Senate subcommittee headed by Democrat Pat McCarran of Nevada examined back files of the IPR, called some sixty-six witnesses, sifted twenty thousand documents, and compiled more than five thousand pages of hearings. Its blunt conclusion, released in 1952 and unanimously endorsed by all committee members, Republican and Democrat, was that "Lattimore was, from some time beginning in the 1930s, a conscious, articulate instrument of the Soviet conspiracy."[37] The committee was not the first to draw this conclusion; in 1941 the FBI was so concerned about Lattimore's suspicious activities that he was targeted for possible "custodial detention" in the event of a national emergency.[38]

Furthermore, in 1955, after Democrats had resumed control of the Senate, the Permanent Subcommittee on Investigations, now chaired by Senator John McClellan of Arkansas, reviewed the complicated Peress case. The committee concluded that in fact the army security system had been "derelict" and that the Eisenhower administration had withheld "important data" from the Senate.[39] The concession came too late to help McCarthy.

The least publicized phase of McCarthy's accomplishments, according to veteran reporter Willard Edwards, "may constitute his most lasting achievement." His investigations forced changes in military policy that "tightened up" security and made communist infiltration of the army more difficult. President Eisenhower himself admitted (at a March 3, 1954, news conference) that the army had made "serious errors" in handling the case of Major Irving Peress, who was given an honorable discharge although he had been identified as a communist organizer and had taken the Fifth Amendment when asked to answer the charge.[40]

The McCarthy subcommittee was also the first investigative agency to expose the murder, torture, starvation, and inhuman treatment of captured American personnel by North Korean and Chinese communist troops during the Korean War. Twenty-nine witnesses, including twenty-three survivors or eyewitnesses of communist atrocities, added their evidence to affidavits, statements, photographs, and official war records. About two-thirds of the American servicemen taken prisoner died from acts of barbarism, the subcommittee concluded.

Earlier, from 1950 to 1952, McCarthy had been virtually a one-man investigating team, producing a list of eighty-one security risks in the State Department. He named, among others, Owen Lattimore, Philip C. Jessup, John Carter Vincent, Haldore Hanson, John Stewart Service, Oliver E. Clubb, and Edward G. Posniak. Every one of these eighty-one people subsequently left the government by dismissal or resignation.[41]

But in December 1954, few members of the Senate were interested in debating the facts, including McCarthy, who repeatedly said he wanted the vote on censure to take place so he could get back to exposing subversives in government.

The Senate voted by more than two to one to "condemn" McCarthy for contempt and abuse of two Senate committees. All forty-four Democrats present voted for censure, while the Republicans were evenly divided— twenty-two on each side. Goldwater voted against censure. (Independent Wayne Morse of Oregon sided with the majority.) With the Senate's repudiation, McCarthy all but disappeared from public view. He was never again on the front pages until his death less than three years later.

As historian George Nash later wrote, McCarthy's crusade drew many conservatives together in a "common struggle," helping to forge the conservative movement.[42] *Human Events* lamented that so few had explored McCarthy's "crucial" role in the "irrepressible conflict" between the executive and legislative branches. Through his investigations of the wrongdoing in the State Department and other government agencies, said the conservative weekly, the Wisconsin senator had tried to counteract "the tendency of the executive to absorb every function of government and to become a law unto itself. . . . McCarthy . . . was a casualty of that constitutional struggle."[43] William S. Schlamm wrote in *National Review* that McCarthy saw "the central truth of his age . . . his country, his faith, his civilization was at war with communism."[44]

Twenty years after McCarthy's death, Willard Edwards, who had been a confidant of the senator, wrote that even liberal newspapermen who opposed his politics liked Joe McCarthy personally. "One cause of their sometimes reluctant admiration," Edwards reported, "was the way he dared to take on anybody and anything in sight—the entire establishment—without a moment's hesitation. . . . Again and again, he had outfought, outwitted or outrun antagonists stronger than himself, and he had never cried uncle."[45]

Many conservatives in the mid-1950s noticed the same pugnacious, quixotic, antiestablishment air in one of McCarthy's young senatorial supporters: Barry Goldwater. Thus, when those who had supported Joe McCarthy for his anticommunism and Robert Taft for his Republicanism and Douglas MacArthur for his patriotism began looking for another leader, their eyes fell, almost inevitably, on the handsome young senator from Arizona.

Goldwater was a man of plain tastes (a cheeseburger supreme with a slice of raw onion and a chocolate shake for lunch) and old-fashioned virtues (patriotism, hard work, faith in God). Although a college dropout, Goldwater devoured history books about Arizona and the West and had read Hayek's *The Road to Serfdom* as a young businessman. He was quick-witted and self-deprecating in his humor. Once asked how he would respond to a Soviet nuclear attack, he said the first thing he would do would be to circle the wagons.

He never smoked a cigarette or drank a cup of coffee but kept a bottle of Old Crow in the refrigerator of his Senate office for after-five sipping. He was a gifted photographer whose sensitive portraits of Native Americans and scenes of Arizona were hung in galleries around the world. And he was an intrepid pilot who during World War II had ferried a single-engine P-47 Thunderbolt over the Atlantic to Britain and four-engine C-54s over the Himalayas.

He delighted in saying the unexpected and challenging conventional wisdom, but the Constitution was always his guide—which is why the first major legislation that Goldwater cosponsored, along with sixty-three other senators, in January 1953 was the Bricker amendment, which sought to prevent the abuse of presidential power in making treaties and other international agreements.

The tripartite constitutional amendment, authored by Republican senator John W. Bricker of Ohio, was one of the most controversial measures of the Eisenhower period. The first section stated that any part of a treaty that conflicted with the Constitution would be invalid. The second section stated that a treaty could become effective as international law in the United States "only through the enactment of appropriate legislation by the Congress." The third section stated that Congress would have the power to regulate all executive and other agreements with any foreign power or international organization.[46]

The amendment generated a great debate on a question that has challenged policymakers since the founding of the Republic: How much power should the executive branch have in the conduct of American foreign policy?

Among the amendment's supporters were the House of Delegates of the American Bar Association, the American Medical Association, the Committee for Constitutional Government, and the Vigilant Women for the Bricker Amendment, which had delivered petitions signed by a half-million Americans to Capitol Hill. Arrayed against the amendment were the League of Women Voters, Americans for Democratic Action, the American Bar Association's Section on International and Comparative Law, and the American Association for the United Nations.

What the Bricker amendment was really about, historian William Manchester wrote, was Yalta. Conservatives wanted to exorcise that ghost once and for all. Secretary of Defense Charles Wilson agreed, arguing at a cabinet meeting in January 1954 that treaties should not be able to deprive people of their rights and that conventions like Yalta and Potsdam ought to be outlawed. President Eisenhower patiently explained that the Bricker amendment could not have prevented Yalta and Potsdam because they had been "political accords," not treaties or executive agreements.[47]

Conservatives declared that regardless of what technical term was used, Yalta was a "sellout" and must not be allowed to recur. Secretary of State Dulles insisted that the Bricker amendment would alter the nation's traditional treaty-making power, tilting it too far toward Congress, and would hamper the president's constitutional authority to conduct foreign affairs.[48] It was a battle royal between modern-day Hamiltonians and Jeffersonians, advocates of a strong presidency and of a no-less-strong Congress.

Goldwater felt that the Bricker amendment would prudently curb the ability of the president, Republican or Democrat, from committing America to possibly dangerous and unconstitutional agreements. But President Eisenhower strongly opposed the amendment and made the debate personal: a senator was either an Ike man or he wasn't.

In February 1954, needing a two-thirds majority for approval of a constitutional amendment, the Senate mustered only fifty votes for the Bricker amendment, with ninety-two senators voting. But when Democrat Walter George of the Senate Foreign Relations Committee offered a carefully written substitute, omitting Bricker's controversial clause about Congress's regulating executive agreements as well as treaties, there were sixty yeas and thirty-one nays—just one vote short of the required two-thirds. If Taft had been standing in Knowland's place as Senate majority leader, the amendment might well have passed, and American foreign policy over the ensuing decades would have been far different. For example, the 1964 Tonkin Gulf Resolution, authorizing unrestricted U.S. intervention in Vietnam, might well have been rejected as unconstitutional.[49]

For Goldwater, as for most other conservatives, the issue was simple: a president should not make or break a treaty without the approval of Congress.

Chapter 5

"Let's Grow Up, Conservatives!"

THE MID-1950S SEEMED TO BE A TIME OF ECLIPSE FOR THE AMERICAN CON-servative movement. Bob Taft was dead and Joe McCarthy, after his Senate censure, was as good as dead. Eisenhower was offering a "dimestore" New Deal at home, while John Foster Dulles was accused, by some conservatives, of practicing chickenship rather than brinkmanship abroad.[1] When Hungarian freedom fighters rose up in October 1956 (with the encouragment of the U.S.-backed Radio Free Europe) and Soviet forces invaded, the Eisenhower administration declined to help when the Soviets brutally crushed the Hungarian revolution. The GOP rested in the hands of eastern Republicans who tried to remove Vice President Nixon from the 1956 ticket because "he was not a creature of their making" and had ridden to fame as the man who had sent Alger Hiss to jail.[2] Liberals abandoned their anti-Nixon efforts when regular Republicans made it clear that they would rather fight than accept such an unwarranted ouster.

The conservative movement could claim only a few publications, *Human Events* being the most prominent. There were even fewer organizations, the new youth group, the Intercollegiate Society of Individualists (ISI), being a rare exception. Newspaper columnists like John Chamberlain and George Sokolsky and popular radio broadcasters like Fulton Lewis, Jr., plied their trade, but liberals undercut their effectiveness by invariably describing them as part of the "militant right wing." Typical was the comment by CBS's Mike Wallace, who invited television viewers one evening to listen to Fulton Lewis explain "the attraction the far right has for crackpot fascist groups in America."[3]

75

But better times were coming for conservatives. A chorus of articulate critics of the Left was making itself heard. One was Russell Kirk, who was only thirty-five when his seminal work, *The Conservative Mind,* exploded on the American scene in 1953. Liberals smirked that the title was an oxymoron, but they stopped laughing when they read Kirk's brilliant book. It was a 450-page overview of conservative thinking over the previous 150 years and a scathing indictment of every liberal nostrum, from human perfectibility to economic egalitarianism.

The *New York Times* favorably reviewed *The Conservative Mind,* as did *Time,* which referred to the "wonder of conservative intuition and prophecy." Of the first fifty reviews, forty-seven were favorable.[4] There were several reasons for the extraordinary reception of the book. First, it was an impressive feat of scholarship: a synthesis of the ideas of the leading conservative thinkers of the late eighteenth through the early twentieth centuries, including Edmund Burke, John Adams, Alexis de Tocqueville, Benjamin Disraeli, Orestes Brownson, Paul Elmer More, and George Santayana. Second, it was written by a young American who had taught not at Harvard or Yale, but at Michigan State College. Here was no European emigré, no liberal apostate, no southern agrarian, but a midwestern intellectual.

Third, the book established convincingly that there *was* a tradition of American conservatism, one that had existed since the founding. Russell Kirk made conservatism intellectually respectable. In fact, as William Rusher would later point out, he gave the conservative movement its name.[5]

There were other encouraging signs. *Human Events* celebrated its tenth anniversary in February 1954, pointing out modestly that over the years, it had been prescient more than once. In its first issue, William Henry Chamberlin had denounced the Teheran Conference for allowing Stalin to "impose" a Munich-like settlement of the Polish question. In August 1945, Frank Hanighen had warned that by surrendering to Soviet demands, America was risking "the loss of [its] war in the Far East."[6] In mid-1955, the newsletter's circulation reached 13,502, but it had an influence far beyond such modest numbers.

Conservatives also began to get organized. One of the first groups was the Committee of One Million (Against the Admission of Communist China to the United Nations). The committee prevailed as one of the most successful citizen groups in America for nearly twenty years because it reflected the majority opinion of the American people, who did not want a government that played a major adversarial role in the Korean War to be admitted to the United Nations. The committee was strictly bipartisan at the insistence of its chairman, Walter Judd, who understood that if the organization was ever branded as the ideological creature of Republicans and/or conservatives, its effectiveness would be severely impaired.

With President Eisenhower's imprimatur and the backing of the American Federation of Labor, the American Legion, and other citizen groups, the committee set to work collecting signatures. On July 6, 1954, it sent a telegram to the White House announcing that it had received its one millionth signature. In just nine months and with total expenditures of less than $60,000 (most of the contributions were for $10 or $15), the Committee *for* One Million became the Committee *of* One Million and a formidable anticommunist force for the next two decades.[7]

And in Chicago, conservatives of both parties launched a new organization, For America. Clarence Manion, former dean of Notre Dame's law school, along with author John T. Flynn, former Democratic senator Burton K. Wheeler, and former Republican congressman Hamilton Fish of New York, headed its board. Its purpose was to forge a conservative counterpart to the liberal group Americans for Democratic Action and to encourage a "realignment" of parties, with conservatives making up one party and liberals the other.[8]

But in the mid-1950s, the Right by and large lacked focus. Conservative victories, wrote William F. Buckley, Jr., were "uncoordinated and inconclusive" because the philosophy of freedom was not being expounded systematically in the universities and the media. Conservatives decided that a new journal was needed to combat the liberals, compensate for "conservative weakness" in the academy, and "focus the energies" of the conservative movement.[9]

It had seemed, briefly, that the *Freeman* (a title taken from an earlier magazine edited by libertarian Albert Jay Nock in the 1920s) might serve the purpose. Started in 1950 by journalist John Chamberlain, author Henry Hazlitt, and writer Suzanne LaFollette, who had worked with Nock, the *Freeman* declared that it would be a voice for classical liberalism and decentralization as the *New Republic* and the *Nation* had been for the Left and for centralization in past decades. But before long, two factions (one more intellectual, the other more political) began fighting over the *Freeman*'s editorial direction. A final falling-out occurred over whether the journal should endorse Taft over Eisenhower in 1952. When the board endorsed a hands-off policy, Chamberlain, LaFollette, and journalist Forrest Davis, a Taft partisan, resigned in disgust.[10]

Many believed, however, that the right publication would appeal to the three kinds of American conservatives who existed in the mid-fifties: traditionalists, libertarians, and anticommunists. After all, as one historian wrote, there were "no rigid barriers" between them; traditionalists and libertarians were usually anticommunist, and anticommunists generally endorsed the free market and Western traditions.[11]

Conservatives knew who the true conservatives were, although liberals clearly did not. Harvard historian Arthur Schlesinger, Jr., thought that the leaders of an "intelligent conservatism" included Henry Cabot Lodge, Jacob Javits, and Wayne Morse, the most liberal members of the liberal wing of the Republican party. When the *Freeman* first appeared, the left-wing *Nation,* while conceding the need for an intellectual conservative journal, criticized the "sneers and snarls" it found in the first issue. Schlesinger, the apostle of the so-called vital center, added to the distortion, accusing economist F. A. Hayek of adding "luster" to the "homegrown McCarthys" with his thoughtful 1954 work, *Capitalism and the Historians,* and condemned James Burnham's slice of realpolitik, *Containment or Liberation?* as "an absurd book written by an absurd man."[12]

But things were to change dramatically with the appearance in 1955 of the right magazine. The editor and sole owner of the new conservative weekly was the irrepressible William F. Buckley, Jr., a thirty-year-old, six-foot-tall enfant terrible with a flashing smile, a rapier mind, bright blue eyes, and a half-British, half-southern drawl. Buckley had wanted to start his own magazine for a couple of years, first hoping to buy *Human Events* and then corresponding with the conservative Chicago publisher Henry Regnery, who suggested that Buckley edit a monthly magazine along with Russell Kirk. In the summer of 1954, Buckley joined editorial forces with the European emigré and veteran journalist William Schlamm, who had been helping to edit the *Freeman.* As Buckley's biographer John B. Judis observed, Buckley would have founded a magazine eventually, but because of Schlamm, who was obsessed with the idea of starting a journal of conservative opinion, "Buckley threw himself into the project."[13]

Both men believed that the way to change American politics was to challenge the liberal intellectuals who dominated American ideas and that the best vehicle for doing this was a weekly intellectual magazine like the *New Republic.* Their determination was intensified when Leonard Read and the Foundation for Economic Education bought the *Freeman* in 1954 and converted it to a monthly magazine concentrating on economics. To Buckley, this shift accentuated the critical vacuum in conservative ideas. Liberals had eight weekly journals of opinion, ranging from the *New Republic* and the *Nation* to *Commonweal* and the *New Leader.* Conservatives had only *Human Events.*

With a $100,000 pledge from Buckley's father, Buckley and Schlamm wrote a prospectus to attract financial contributors and writers. They declared that the "political climate of an era" was fashioned by serious opinion journals and it was possible to "rout intellectually" the jaded liberal status quo with the "vigor of true convictions."

They described their own convictions as a synthesis of the libertarian, conservative, and anticommunist wings of American conservatism. They sharply attacked the United Nations and the "Social-Democrat" impulses of both parties, but did not mention the Eisenhower administration in order not to offend potential pro-Ike donors. Buckley, however, wrote a letter to former leftist Max Eastman (whom he was trying to recruit as an editor) in which he confided that in an early issue he intended "to read Dwight Eisenhower out of the conservative movement."[14]

Buckley's anti-Eisenhower pledge was significant on two counts: It indicated the uncompromising conservatism he intended to promote in his magazine, and it reflected the growing awareness of conservatives that they did in fact belong to a movement.

In pursuit of funds, Buckley traveled to Texas and southern California. However, oil millionaire H. L. Hunt and other members of the Texas Right found Buckley "too Catholic, too eastern, and too moderate."[15] And they already had their own "opinion journal," *Facts Forum,* edited by former FBI agent Dan Smoot. At one point, a frustrated Buckley wrote to Herbert Hoover, "It is sad that with so much [writing] talent available, there is so little capital. We might as well be living in Somaliland."[16]

The young fund raiser discovered more congenial conservatives in the Golden State. In Beverly Hills, he met several wealthy businessmen through Hollywood writer Morrie Ryskind, an outspoken anticommunist who had written most of the Marx Brothers' movies and had won a Pulitzer Prize for the book of the Gershwins' musical satire, *Of Thee I Sing.* By June 1955, thanks to Ryskind's constant prodding, sympathetic Californians had contributed some $38,000 to the magazine's founding (Buckley figured he needed a total of $450,000 to meet the deficits of the first two years); they continued to help over the next several decades.

But often there were more pats on the back than checks. After being turned down by several of his closest and richest friends, Ryskind wrote Buckley that although it was Rosh Hashanah and he should have been "shouting Happy New Year," it felt more like Yom Kippur, the Day of Atonement.[17] Undeterred, the young entrepreneur pulled out all the stops, including asking Joe McCarthy to approach his financial supporters like the oil-rich Murchisons of Texas.

By September 1955, with the additional help of Yale alumni like South Carolina textile manufacturer Roger Milliken and New York financier Jeremiah Milbank, Jr., Buckley had raised over $300,000. Milliken made the largest single commitment, $20,000, through advertising and future subscriptions to the three thousand members of the Intercollegiate Studies Institute and friends. When the young editor hesitated, Schlamm was adamant that the magazine go ahead. "Willi's point," Buckley recalled, "was that if you get twenty-five thousand readers, your subscribers won't let you die, and that proved almost exactly accurate."[18]

The thirty-page first issue of Buckley's magazine, christened *National Review,* appeared in November 1955, looking, with its blue-bordered front cover, much like the pre-1953 *Freeman.* But the new journal was not a replica of the *Freeman* or any other previous conservative publication; its mission was not just "to renew the attack against the Left" but to consolidate and mobilize the Right.[19] *National Review* was not a journal of opinion but a political act.

Not that the magazine's, or Buckley's, political judgment was infallible. The first issue featured a cover article on foreign policy by Senator Knowland, who, the editors suggested, ought to challenge Vice President Richard Nixon in 1956. The suggestion was unrealistic: Nixon was the solid favorite of regular Taft Republicans who appreciated the vice president's courting of the Right and his anticommunist credentials. As *Human Events* put it, conservatives might prefer Knowland, but they would "rally" behind Nixon because he drove New Dealers "berserk."[20] This sentiment would help Nixon in future crises too.

Buckley's success in welding a broad-based intellectual coalition was impressive. On *National Review*'s masthead and among its writers were traditionalists Russell Kirk and Richard Weaver, libertarians John Chamberlain and Frank Chodorov, and anticommunists James Burnham and Frank Meyer. From the first, the magazine identified the number one enemy as liberalism, with which there could be no accommodation. In their statement of beliefs, the editors declared themselves to be "irrevocably" at war with "satanic" communism; described the central crisis of the era as the conflict between the "Social Engineers" and the "disciples of Truth, who defend the organic moral order"; and joined with the "libertarian side" in the battle against "the growth of government."[21]

In the first issue, Buckley averred that conservatives lived, as did all other Americans, in "a Liberal world" and therefore were "out of place." *National Review* intended to stand "athwart history yelling Stop," confident that "a vigorous and incorruptible journal of conservative opinion" could make a critical difference in the realms of ideas and politics.[22]

Although circulation remained small (fewer than twenty thousand in its first three years, thirty thousand by 1960) and the magazine faced so many financial crises that it converted to a biweekly in 1958, *National Review* became, as Bill Buckley proudly claimed, the voice of American conservatism. The solution to the magazine's perpetual financial deficit was frankly antilibertarian: an annual fund appeal to subscribers who generously made up the difference year after year. When asked why the magazine did not "sink or swim" according to free market principles, William Rusher (who became publisher in 1957) explained that *National Review* was not a commercial enterprise but a "journal of opinion" that combined the qualities of a church, a university, and a political party.[23]

Young activists who would found organizations like Young Americans for Freedom and the New York Conservative party and man the political barricades for Barry Goldwater in the 1960s and then Ronald Reagan in the 1970s and 1980s found in *National Review* "exactly the things I felt I believed," in the words of Patrick J. Buchanan.[24] Young conservatives were inspired by Buckley's willingness to take on and best any liberal, in both the pages of his magazine and public debates on dozens of college campuses.

Future book publisher Jameson Campaigne, Jr., recalls that as a student at Williams College, Massachusetts, in 1960, he invited Bill Buckley to debate one of his deans before almost the entire college. After demolishing the dean during the formal debate, the still fresh Buckley took on most of the

Williams faculty during the question-and-answer period. "Buckley performed like 'Braveheart,'" says Campaigne, "lopping off the heads of one faculty lord and knight after another. . . . It was a devastating performance . . . an inspiration." Campaigne reveals that he still receives letters from Williams graduates recalling that special evening.[25]

H*uman Events* had been the most philosophically dependable and oft-quoted conservative publication since its founding in 1944. Many of its writers now began writing for *National Review*, including Buckley himself, John Chamberlain, William Henry Chamberlin, M. Stanton Evans, and James J. Kilpatrick, and the new magazine quickly superseded its elder in intellectual influence. There was one journalistic area, however, in which *Human Events* was always superior: coverage of Washington politics. Under its new Capitol Hill editor, Allan Ryskind, the weekly became must reading for members of Congress.

It also responded to *National Review*'s intellectual dominance by expanding the space devoted to conservative movement activity. The new activist emphasis was shaped by James L. Wick, a political author and longtime Republican who in mid-1955 became the executive publisher of *Human Events*. In 1956, the weekly began using the ratings of the AFL–CIO's Committee on Political Education (COPE) to rank members of Congress on the basis of their votes on issues. Among the senators who received a zero from COPE and therefore scored 100 percent "conservative" were Republicans Barry Goldwater, Joe McCarthy, Bill Knowland, and Everett Dirksen, and Democrat Harry Byrd.[26]

In the spring of 1963, seeking to expand the publication's influence, Wick converted *Human Events* from a newsletter to a weekly tabloid newspaper. Two years earlier, *Human Events* had begun sponsoring political action conferences in Washington, D.C. The major speakers at the first conference in January 1961 were Senators Barry Goldwater and Strom Thurmond, then still a Democrat. Several hundred enthusiastic conservatives from across the country paid their own way to the meeting, which was intended to "rally those who believe in limited constitutional government, states' rights, private enterprise, and individual freedom."[27]

The *Human Events* meetings were the model for the movement-building Conservative Political Action Conferences (CPACs) of the 1970s and 1980s, cosponsored by the American Conservative Union, Young Americans for Freedom, *National Review,* and *Human Events*. CPAC became the single most important conservative event of the year, affording leaders and workers the opportunity to take the measure of each other and the movement. When President Reagan addressed a CPAC banquet in the 1980s, as many as two thousand conservative activists turned out to salute him.

When Barry Goldwater took to the Senate floor on the afternoon of April 8, 1957, he knew he was crossing a political Rubicon. During his first four years as a U.S. senator, he had been a loyal Republican, voting with President Eisenhower almost all of the time and rarely breaking with the party on issues important to the White House. He had been an effective chairman of the Republican Senate Campaign Committee, raising several million dollars and supporting all Republicans, regardless of their ideology.

But he had been taught that a man should keep his word. And he remembered that in October 1952, presidential candidate Eisenhower had promised to eliminate the federal deficit and lower federal expenditures to $60 billion by fiscal 1955. Goldwater also remembered what Bob Taft had said: "If you permit appeals to unity to bring an end to criticism, we endanger not only the constitutional liberties of our country, but even its future existence."[28]

The Eisenhower administration, in the view of the junior senator from Arizona, warranted serious criticism: it had posted deficits in 1954 and 1955, although it did manage to balance the budget in 1956, an election year. Now Ike had sent to Congress a $71.8 billion budget for fiscal 1957, the largest ever submitted by any president in peacetime.

Nor had modern Republicanism delivered the political goods. Although Eisenhower handily won reelection in 1956, receiving 57.4 percent of the popular vote and 457 electoral votes to Adlai Stevenson's 73, Democrats retained control of both houses of Congress. As *Human Events* put it, in just a decade, liberal Republicans "had changed a substantial GOP majority into a commanding lead for the Democrats."[29] Someone had to take the president and his decisions to task.

Goldwater explained to his Senate colleagues that just as he had campaigned "against waste, extravagance, high taxes, unbalanced budgets, and deficit spending" under a Democratic administration, so he would battle against "the same elements of fiscal irresponsibility in this Republican administration." His criticism, Goldwater made clear, was directed not at the president, but at the policies of his administration that he felt were inconsistent with traditional Republican principles. He would stand or fall on his conservative position when he ran for reelection, adding that if he did not survive 1958, "it will not be because [I have] broken faith with either the American people or the principles of the Republican party in this almost frenzied rush to give away the resources and freedoms of America."[30]

At a presidential news conference two days later, when Eisenhower was asked to comment on Goldwater's characterization of his budget as a "betrayal" of public trust, he responded, "Of course these people have a right to their own opinion." American politics "is a history of the clash of ideas." But, he added, "In this day and time we cannot . . . limit ourselves to the governmental processes that were applicable in 1890"—a none-too-subtle variation of Harry Truman's sarcastic line that Robert Taft was a nineteenth-century mossback.

The president said he believed "profoundly" that the programs he had proposed were "necessary for the country," and there was "no chance of reversing them." He added a few conciliatory words, but there was no mistaking his meaning: big government was here to stay, and it was up to "modern" Republicans to demonstrate they could manage government better than the Democrats.[31] Ike could not have waved a larger red flag at conservatives.

Goldwater and other traditional Republicans from the Midwest and the West were determined to resist the policies of the modern "Me-Too" Republicans: those who trailed in the wake of Democrats as they promised more and fatter giveaways, yelling at the top of their lungs, "Me too, me too!"[32]

It was a measure of Goldwater's growing importance as a Republican leader as well as the spreading influence of the conservative movement that Goldwater's critical remarks sparked strong reaction both within and outside the nation's capital. Newspapers blared that Goldwater, who had just finished a highly praised term as chairman of the Senate Republican Campaign Committee, had "broken" with the president. Taftites and McCarthyites noted that the Arizona senator did not hesitate to stand up for his beliefs. Conservatives needed a leader, wanted a leader, and demanded a leader. And so they wondered, Could Goldwater do what none of their earlier champions had been able to accomplish: capture the presidential nomination and then the White House?

Conservative frustration with Eisenhower and his modern brand of Republicanism manifested itself in different ways, including the formation

of the John Birch Society in 1958 by Robert Welch, a soft-spoken but auto-
cratic Massachusetts businessman. The society took its name from John
Birch, a Protestant missionary to China who had served in the U.S. Army in
the Far East during World War II and had been murdered by the Chinese
communists in 1945. Society members liked to say that Captain Birch was
"the first casualty" of the cold war. From its beginnings, the John Birch Society specialized in shock tactics, with such slogans as "Impeach Earl Warren" and "Get the U.S. out of the U.N. and the U.N. out of the U.S."

An indifferent public speaker but mesmerizing in small, private meetings,
Welch subscribed to the conspiracy theory of history and argued that a small
but powerful group of bankers, industrialists, publishers, and politicians was
responsible for the spread of collectivism in the twentieth century. The conspiracy was everywhere and had ensnared the most unlikely people. Sometimes Robert Welch made Joe McCarthy sound almost like a Harvard
professor. In his book, *The Politician,* for example, Welch asserted that President Eisenhower was either "a mere stooge" for the communist cause or "has
been consciously serving the communist conspiracy for all of his adult life."[33]

As Russell Kirk wisecracked, "Ike's not a communist—he's a golfer!"[34]
But Welch persisted in his extremism. Indeed, it was the key to his success; it
provided a ready explanation to angry, frustrated conservatives as to why
America had lost China, why it had not pursued victory in the Korean War,
how Alger Hiss had risen so high in government, why Castro was able to seize
power in Cuba, and why government continued to grow and taxes to rise.

While not agreeing with all of Welch's conclusions (particularly his
charge that the man in the White House was a communist and therefore a
traitor), Americans by the tens of thousands joined the society, forming local
chapters, opening bookstores, and working "in the political arena on behalf
of candidates deemed worthy of their support," recounted William
Rusher.[35] So seductive was Welch's appeal that in 1962, Buckley and *National Review* were forced to read Welch publicly out of the conservative
movement.

Before he formed the John Birch Society, Welch visited Goldwater in
Phoenix and asked him to read *The Politician.* The senator told Welch that his
notion about Ike's being either a dupe or a conscious communist agent was
inaccurate in the extreme and that the work would harm Welch and the
anticommunist cause. "Welch never sought my advice again," recalled Goldwater.[36]

Once the Birch Society was formed, Goldwater often disagreed with its statements but declined to condemn its members. The last thing conservatives needed when they were building a movement, he said, was "to begin a factional war by reading small minorities or individuals out of our ranks."[37]

A more rational kind of political activity was being contemplated by Bill Buckley—in his words, "right-wing political action in New York State." Meeting in New York City in late January 1957, Buckley, philanthropist Jeremiah Milbank, Jr., lawyer Thomas Bolan, and several other conservatives decided that "the time may have come to attempt to establish a counterpart to the Liberal Party in New York."[38] They believed that such an outside effort could move the Republican party to the right just as the Liberal party had moved the Democratic party to the left and kept it there over the years.

Rather than setting forth "ideological" positions on specific issues like public schools and segregation, argued Buckley and the others, "The Conservative Party" should represent "the right wing of the Republican Party, just as the Liberals represent the left wing of the Democratic Party." Buckley and the others thought that Raymond Moley (a one-time Roosevelt braintruster turned conservative columnist and author) "would make an excellent chairman of the Conservative Party."[39] It would take several years of discussion and planning, but these early meetings would lead to the founding of the New York Conservative party in 1962 by two young, dynamic lawyers— Dan Mahoney and Kieran O'Doherty.

A clear sign of emerging conservatism among younger Americans was the rousing tenth annual convention of the Young Republicans (YRs), held in Washington, D.C., in June 1957. Decisively rejecting modern Republicanism, the YRs adopted a platform that opposed federal aid to education, military aid to communist nations, United Nations membership for communist China, and compulsory union membership as a condition of employment (calling, in effect, for a national right-to-work law). Its favorite senator was Senate Republican leader William Knowland, who was commended for his "vigorous affirmation of the traditional foreign and domestic policies of the Republican Party."[40]

When Professor Philip E. Jacobs of the University of Pennsylvania, author of *Changing Values in College,* was asked whether college students had "radical" political ideas, he replied, "Quite the opposite. This is a conservative generation. . . . They believe that the Government should have a very minimal role in running the economic life of the country."[41]

The same year, Russell Kirk, with the financial help of publisher Henry Regnery, launched the quarterly journal *Modern Age,* which stressed the traditional rather than the libertarian or anticommunist strains of conservatism. Most of the editorial advisers held appointments in universities, and many were Roman Catholic, Anglo-Catholic, or self-described "pre-Reformation Christians."[42] *Modern Age's* circulation never rose above five thousand, but its contributors included such influential thinkers as southern agrarian Richard Weaver, economist Wilhelm Röpke, strategist Gerhart Niemeyer, and newspaper editor James J. Kilpatrick.

Meanwhile, Barry Goldwater's attention was focused on Arizona politics. After one term in the Senate, he was generally described as personable, hardworking, and possessed of strong conservative convictions, and he was often praised for his willingness to attack sacred cows and popular presidents. But few Washington analysts were predicting that this Republican maverick would be reelected from a solidly Democratic state, particularly when he again faced Ernest McFarland, whom he had narrowly defeated in 1952 and who had been a popular governor for the last four years.

But Goldwater had more going for him than the eastern experts realized, for the Arizona Republican party had become a significant political force. Young men and women were attracted by the senator's conservative beliefs and personal charisma. Goldwater's campaign was well financed with donations coming from across the country. The candidate campaigned nonstop, visiting every corner of the state in a twin-engine Beech Bonanza, which he personally piloted. Night and day, he was on television and radio, campaigning the only way he knew how: "Meet the people, tell them how you stand, answer their questions directly. They may not like what you say, but they'll respect you for it. That's what Americans want," he insisted, "somebody that speaks up."[43]

Here was Barry Goldwater, a candidate who would not change his style of campaigning or his beliefs for any man or any office. When all the votes were in, Goldwater had carried eleven of the state's fourteen counties, including the two largest. The final tally showed a decisive 56 to 44 percent victory, making the senator one of the few prominent Republicans to win reelection easily that November.

His impressive showing in a tough year for Republicans (among those who lost was Bill Knowland, who failed in his bid to gain the California governorship and vanished as a national conservative leader) and his willingness to confront President Eisenhower over deviations from conservative principle made Barry Goldwater, two months before his fiftieth birthday, the leading conservative politician in America. Looking ahead to the 1960 Republican National Convention, some conservatives wondered whether he would challenge Vice President Nixon, almost certain to be the nominee.

In May 1959, Clarence Manion, moderator of the popular weekly radio program *The Manion Forum,* and one of the most respected conservatives in the country, called on Goldwater in his Washington office. With him was Hubbard Russell, an old California friend of the senator. They wanted to discuss the formation of a national Goldwater for President organization.

Manion argued that the nomination of either Nixon or Rockefeller would not only lead to defeat in 1960, but would also "shatter the last chance of survival of the Republican Party." The senator repeated his public position that he supported Nixon over Rockefeller but admitted that he was disappointed over the vice president's recent endorsement of the World Court, which Goldwater regarded as a threat to U.S. sovereignty.[44]

Goldwater revealed he had been approached about the presidency by several southerners, including Senator Strom Thurmond of South Carolina, who had run for the presidency as a Dixiecrat in 1948. But Goldwater argued that he had drawbacks, like his name (the senator's forebears had been Jewish, though he had been raised as an Episcopalian), and he felt unqualified for the presidency because of his meager education—about which Manion later wrote in the margin of a confidential memorandum about the meeting, "This may be asset." Undeterred by his objections, the two visitors asked Goldwater not to block their efforts, and Manion noted, "He assured us that he would not at any time repudiate the move."[45]

Manion was elated: the plan to nominate a true conservative as the Republican party's presidential nominee in 1960 had taken a giant step forward. He immediately began writing prominent conservatives, asking them to join a Committee of One Hundred to draft Barry Goldwater for the GOP nomination. Manion argued, "I honestly believe that [Goldwater's] nomination for president by the Republican Party is the *one* thing that will prevent the complete disintegration of that party once and for all in the 1960 election."[46]

The committee's composition was eclectic, including business leader

Herbert Kohler of Wisconsin; Colonel Archibald Roosevelt of New York (a member of the Theodore rather than the Franklin branch of the Roosevelts); businessman Fred Koch of Kansas; former ambassador to Cuba Spruille Braden; Roger Milliken, the South Carolina industrialist who was *National Review*'s top financial supporter; and John Birch Society founder Robert Welch. What they had in common was an unshakable belief in God, country, and capitalism.

To help advance the cause, Manion mentioned the possibility of Goldwater's writing a pamphlet, *What Americanism Means to Me*. Frank Brophy, a longtime Goldwater friend and adviser, suggested Brent Bozell, who was already writing speeches for the senator, as a collaborator. Manion's proposed Americanism pamphlet would become the most widely read political manifesto of modern American politics.

Although Manion tried to keep the Committee of One Hundred confidential, *Human Events* led off its July 1, 1959, issue with an item entitled "Goldwater to the Fore," which reported that Republican professionals were giving serious thought to a Goldwater candidacy. The arguments for the senator included his "smashing" victory the previous fall, his stand on organized labor, and his western heritage, which meant he carried "no taint of New York or Tom Dewey."

GOP pros were impressed, reported *Human Events*, with Goldwater's easy charm and ability to arouse enthusiasm among average citizens. Conceding that the nomination of a candidate from a small state with a limited number of delegates was unprecedented, *Human Events* pointed out that in a time of "political flux and the crumbling of party traditions," precedents could well be broken.[47] There was no similar item about Goldwater's rising political fortunes in *National Review*.

In December 1959, Bozell flew to Phoenix to show the completed manuscript of *The Conscience of a Conservative* (a title suggested by Manion) to Goldwater. The senator, who had seen earlier drafts, read quickly the two-hundred-page manuscript, and then handed it back to his ghostwriter, saying, "Looks fine to me. Let's go with it."[48]

So casually, Goldwater approved a book that would establish him as the leader and the conscience of a political movement. Had he known how the book would change his life, he might have hesitated. But that would not have been Barry Goldwater. However seriously others might take the book, to him *The Conscience of a Conservative* was an "unpretentious introduction to conservative thought."[49] And if there was a high cost to its authorship, so be it. He liked to quote his uncle Morris, who believed that successful people had a moral duty to repay the community that had helped them.[50]

Bozell would have finished the manuscript sooner but was heavily involved in organizing a series of anticommunist demonstrations against the visit of Soviet premier Nikita Khrushchev to the United States. A highlight was a rally at New York City's Carnegie Hall, where Bill Buckley defiantly promised, "In the end, *we* will bury *him*."[51]

Goldwater and Bozell were unlikely literary collaborators: the easygoing westerner and the high-strung midwesterner; the college dropout and the Yale law graduate; the principled politician and the activist intellectual. But they shared a belief that small government is good government. The Constitution was their cornerstone, and they regarded communism as an enemy that had to be defeated. Their book was suffused with a fervor common to all crusades, and there was no denying that American conservatism was a political crusade in 1960.

Like *National Review* before it, *The Conscience of a Conservative* was a skillful fusion of the three major strains of conservatism: traditionalism, classical liberalism or libertarianism, and anticommunism. It presented unequivocal positions on a wide range of issues, from foreign aid to organized labor to education, while always reflecting the need for freedom *and* responsibility. It called for "the prompt and final termination of the farm subsidy program," the enactment of state right-to-work laws, and a flat tax, declaring that "government has a right to claim an equal percentage of each man's wealth, and no more." And it recommended that federal spending on domestic programs be reduced by 10 percent each year.[52]

The final third of the manifesto was devoted to the cold war. America's objective, insisted Goldwater, himself an officer in the air force reserve, "is not to wage a struggle against communism, but to win it."[53] His multifaceted strategy included the maintenance of defense alliances like NATO, the elimination of economic foreign aid, unquestioned military superiority over the Soviet Union, and a drastic reduction in support for the United Nations. In anticipation of the Reagan Doctrine of the 1980s, he urged the U.S. government to recognize that "the captive peoples are our friends and potential allies" and encourage them "to overthrow their captors."[54]

When *The Conscience of a Conservative* was published in April 1960, it was a political sensation, creating a new national spokesman and proclaiming a major new force in national politics: conservatism. In the *Chicago Tribune,* George Morgenstern declared that there was "more harsh fact and hard sense in this slight book than will emerge from all of the chatter of this year's session of Congress [and] this year's campaign for the presidency." *Time* wrote that *The Conscience of a Conservative* served notice that "the Old Guard has new blood, that a hard-working, successful politico has put his stand on the right of the road and intends to shout for all he is worth." And veteran columnist Westbrook Pegler asserted perceptively that "Senator Barry Goldwater of Arizona certainly is now the successor to Senator Taft of Ohio as defender of the Constitution and freedom."[55]

Although most political analysts assert that party platforms are meaningless, both Democrats and Republicans devote significant time and attention every four years to writing one. The platform is particularly important to conservative Republicans because they believe that its rhetoric can determine nominations and elections.

It happened that in 1960, liberal Republicans agreed. Their champion, New York governor Nelson Rockfeller, was demanding bold new policies in such areas as care for the aged, civil rights, foreign affairs, and, most of all, national defense. Echoing Senator John F. Kennedy and the Democrats, Rockefeller declared that America faced a missile gap and urged that at least an additional $3 billion be spent on the construction of missile bases. The governor was, in effect, suggesting the repudiation of the policies of a president who had brought Republicans a national victory eight years before.

Thus, a fierce battle was joined once again between liberals and conservatives. The man in the middle was Nixon, who needed the backing of both groups—not to win the nomination (despite the Goldwater boomlet, nearly everyone was agreed that the vice president would be nominated), but to win the general election. Goldwater made it clear where he stood: as critical as he had been of the administration, he rejected Rockefeller's unqualified criticism and his big-government solutions. And he knew from his military contacts and sources that there was no "missile gap": the United States was far ahead of the Soviet Union in the development and delivery of missiles.[56]

While the Republican platform committee went about its business in Chicago, Nixon met secretly with Rockefeller in the governor's Fifth Avenue apartment to resolve their differences. If Rockefeller had gone to Washington to see Nixon, most Republicans would have approved a Nixon-Rockefeller meeting. But when Nixon went kowtowing to Rockefeller, most Republicans were shocked. Conservatives were furious. As Phyllis Schlafly wrote, "Nixon had paid the price that Taft had been unwilling to pay . . . his independence. . . . Rank and file Republicans knew that this forbode a turn toward the same 'liberal me-tooism' which had twice defeated Dewey."[57]

Goldwater felt betrayed. That spring, as chairman of the Republican Senatorial Campaign Committee, he had called on the vice president. Goldwater told Nixon bluntly that "a number of people I've talked with are disappointed with your failure to take a strong stand on some conservative issues—federal spending, a balanced budget, the growing bureaucracy." Nixon quickly explained that he had remained silent because whatever he said would have been interpreted as criticism of the administration. He assured Goldwater that before long, he would demand a reduction in spending, a balanced budget, and a halt to bureaucratic growth.[58]

The two men then took up the question of the platform committee, which Nixon knew was important to Goldwater. As he did throughout his career, Nixon told his visitor what he thought his visitor wanted to hear: "Rockefeller wants to talk to me [about the platform]. I am treating him very politely, but, I promise, I'm not going to visit with him until after the convention."[59]

That was good enough for Goldwater. The vice president of the United States, his party's future presidential nominee, had promised that he would take a conservative position on key issues like spending and national defense and would not meet with Rockefeller until after he had been nominated.

Now, four months later, a coldly furious Goldwater called the Nixon-Rockefeller meeting "an American Munich" and a "surrender." He insisted that the party's platform should not be "dictated" by two men a thousand miles away.[60] Goldwater suddenly found himself at the center of a Republican rebellion. Because he dared to speak out when others were silent, he became the conscience of a convention.

Amid the political turmoil surrounding the "American Munich," the Texas delegation that had come to Chicago pledged to Nixon began rethinking their commitment and invited Goldwater to address them. Arizona began taking its favorite son candidate more seriously as delegates from several different states in the South and the West demanded to be released from their pledge to Nixon. A group of Young Republicans, led by an energetic young conservative named Robert Croll, staged a lively street parade, carrying signs that read, "Youth for Goldwater for Vice President."[61]

Clarence Manion and other members of the Committee of One Hundred opened an Americans for Goldwater office in downtown Chicago and lent logistical support to Croll and others. Goldwater's suite in the Blackstone Hotel was jammed with enthusiastic friends and frustrated delegates who urged the senator to "get in there and fight." They argued that he could count on the support of 287 delegates—nowhere close to the 666 needed to win the nomination, but far more than enough to show that conservatives were a force that could not be ignored.

Goldwater, like his one-time mentor Bob Taft, could count. He estimated that including the twenty-seven from Arizona and South Carolina, he had perhaps fifty solid delegates and no more. But fervent supporters kept pressuring him so hard that finally he said: "All right, you go out and get those delegates you say are willing to vote for me. I'll sit in this room all night. You bring them in. I want them to sign a paper saying they'll vote for me." Then, he said, we will see what can be done. Goldwater sat patiently, and skeptically, in his hotel suite hour after hour "and not a damned delegate came in."[62] He would never forget that long, fruitless wait.

Despite the lack of a groundswell and despite the fact that the Nixon forces controlled the convention, the South Carolina delegation nevertheless insisted on placing Barry Goldwater's name in nomination. Goldwater opposed such a move, arguing that although it would not affect the outcome, it could hurt his supporters. It was Jay Gordon Hall, the Washington lobbyist for General Motors and sometime speechwriter and adviser to Goldwater, who suggested a way out. He proposed that Arizona nominate Goldwater as a favorite son. After some seconding speeches, Goldwater would take the podium, withdraw his name, and urge all delegates supporting him to vote for Nixon. The nomination would please conservatives, and the withdrawal would satisfy Nixonites.

Goldwater promptly endorsed the idea, pointing out that if everyone handled his part skillfully, "we might unite the party," always a high priority for him, as it had been for Taft. Hall began drafting the senator's speech.[63]

After Nixon was nominated with the usual "spontaneous" fanfare, Governor Paul Fannin of Arizona stepped forward and asked Republicans to pick Goldwater "as the voice of conscience speaking for the conservatives of the nation."[64] Pandemonium broke out as the banners of Arizona, Arkansas,

Louisiana, North Carolina, South Carolina, Texas, Mississippi, Georgia, Washington, Nevada, Wyoming, Utah, Idaho, and Puerto Rico filled the aisles, proclaiming that Goldwater was the favorite of the South and the West and sending shivers down the spines of eastern liberals.

Delegates tooted horns, whistled, and shouted while the band played "Dixie." At last, the silver-haired conservative signaled for quiet and said, "Mr. Chairman, delegates to the convention, and fellow Republicans, I respectfully ask the chairman to withdraw my name from nomination." A cry of "No!" rose from the floor and was echoed by the galleries, "No! No! No!"[65]

That cry was filled with the bitter memories of Taft, Dewey, and Eisenhower, of narrow defeats and public humiliations at previous conventions. It signaled the ongoing struggle between liberal kingmakers and conservative activists for control of the Republican party.

But at this convention, the liberal establishment had the votes, and Goldwater was no kamikaze conservative. He continued, "Please. I release my delegates from their pledge to me, and while I am not a delegate, I would suggest they give these votes to Richard Nixon." The few shouts of "No!" were drowned out by the roar of Nixon supporters.[66] Knowing that many thought he had let them down, Goldwater talked directly to the true believers who had placed his name in nomination: "We are conservatives. This great Republican party is our historical house. This is our home."[67]

Goldwater then laid it on the line to conservatives: Either support the Republican party or let the socialists run the country. Echoing Taft, who had stayed with the party in 1952 despite his deep disappointment over losing to Eisenhower, Goldwater warned what would happen if conservatives walked out of the GOP, as many were threatening to do. "If each segment, each section of our great party," he said, "were to insist on the complete and unqualified acceptance of its views, if each viewpoint were to be enforced by a Russian-type veto, the Republican Party could not long survive."[68]

He concluded with the words that completed the transformation of a junior senator from Arizona into the leader of the American conservative movement:

This country, and its majesty, is too great for any man, be he conservative or liberal, to stay home and not work just because he doesn't agree. Let's grow up, Conservatives! We want to take this party back, and I think some day we can. Let's get to work![69]

Some ultraconservatives refused. Commentator Dan Smoot accused Goldwater of "betraying" conservatism and advancing "the socialist-communist cause" when he endorsed Nixon. Goldwater later commented, "I didn't realize until later there were some conservatives you can never satisfy."[70] Robert Taft had encountered the same cold dismissal from hard-core conservatives when, as Senate majority leader, he accommodated the Eisenhower administration on the Bohlen nomination and other early actions.

The debate within the Republican party also manifested itself in the editorial offices of *National Review.* In May, two months before the Republican convention, senior editor Frank Meyer stressed the sharp difference between the "steady growth of conservative influence on the intellectual level" and the "debacle on the political level." Eight years of a liberal Republican in the White House, he said, had "immensely weakened" the conservative opposition in Congress and the states. Meyer argued that it was therefore the responsibility of conservative leadership, led by *National Review,* to develop and maintain "an independent position" and not endorse Nixon.[71]

Instead, Meyer stated, the magazine should support the nomination of Barry Goldwater, whose emergence as a "principled conservative" gave the conservative movement a powerful "public symbol." Conceding that Goldwater's nomination was improbable, he counseled that in the fall, the magazine could then criticize Nixon and Kennedy on "the basis of the [conservative] standard" that had been established before the conventions.[72]

Bill Rusher argued that conservatives should "oppose Nixon" as a means of "recapturing the Republican Party," seeing opposition as "the first step in breaking away from the Republican Party altogether—toward a third party, to be formed when the moment is ripe." "A vote for Nixon," Rusher added, "merely enhances the power and prestige of the present [liberal] management of the Republican Party."[73]

On the endorse-Nixon side were senior editor James Burnham and managing editor Priscilla Buckley. A conservative, argued Burnham, "has to set his course within the frame of reality." And the reality was that those supporting Kennedy were *National Review*'s "primary targets," including leftist ideologues, appeasers and collaborationists, socialists, fellow travelers, and communists. The only meaningful way to declare against them in the election was to "vote for Nixon." Any "dodge," said Burnham, would be "a mistake, counter to *NR*'s best interests, and perhaps injurious to its future." Priscilla Buckley admitted that although Nixon was "hardly the champion we would choose," he and his advisers were "less apt to play the appeasement game than Kennedy and his advisers."[74] How prophetic were her words when one considers President Kennedy's future inaction with regard to Cuba, Laos, the Berlin Wall, and Vietnam.

Bill Buckley responded that although Burnham's arguments were "compelling," Rusher had made "a very good case" that *National Review* would increase its leverage "by failing to join the parade." Nor did he see how, after five years' sharp critiques of the Eisenhower administration, the magazine could "declare" for Nixon, even "with reservations." He hoped to satisfy Burnham, and Rusher, with a "very diligent disparagement of Kennedy."[75]

In the end, Buckley announced in an editorial that the magazine would neither endorse a candidate nor recommend abstention. He listed the major arguments for each man and then concluded, rather wanly, that "*National Review* was not founded to make practical politics. Our job is to think, and write."[76]

In contrast, *Human Events* endorsed Nixon early and often, publishing, for example, a major article by Goldwater, who argued that conservatives should support Nixon because he was the most "dedicated anti-Communist" on the Eisenhower team and would prove to be "equally sound on domestic issues." In this hour of "Armageddon," said Goldwater, there was "no alternative to Nixon" for conservatives, whether they were Taft Republicans or Jeffersonian Democrats.[77]

As important as the presidency was, it was not all. Conservatives were intent on building a national political movement that would last regardless of who sat in the White House. And there were signs everywhere that America was swinging away from the welfarist ideas that had dominated the country for a generation.

There was, for example, the best-seller status of Barry Goldwater's *The Conscience of a Conservative,* with 400,000 paperback copies in circulation in addition to the original 100,000 hardback copies. The New York publisher of the paperback called the slim Goldwater volume "the biggest political book of my time."[78] There was the continuing success of the Intercollegiate Society of Individualists, which had grown from a mailing list of four hundred students in 1953 to twelve thousand in 1960, including professors.

There was the 1958 launching of Americans for Constitutional Action

(ACA) by Admiral Ben Moreell, a World War II naval hero and past chairman of the Jones and Laughlin Steel Company. ACA's trustees included the former presidents of the American Bar Association, the American Farm Bureau Federation, the American Medical Association, and the Junior Chamber of Commerce.

Herbert Hoover had at first declined Admiral Moreell's invitation to join the ACA board because he was too busy trying to raise funds for the Hoover Institution at Stanford University. But he joined the board in the spring of 1960 after "all the liberal foundations" had turned him down, the Stanford faculty had proclaimed him a "reactionary," and he had still managed to raise $1.25 million for his institution from "righteous foundations." If Moreell still wanted him, said Hoover, "you can add my name to your collection of reactionaries!"[79]

That May, ACA released its "ACA Index," the first analysis of votes by members of Congress ever compiled by a conservative organization. Until then, conservatives had usually reversed the ratings of the AFL-CIO's Committee on Political Education and similar liberal groups, giving a rating of 100 percent to those whom the liberals rated 0 and a rating of 0 to those whom the liberals rated 100 percent. The ACA Index was rightly called a "monumental" effort, because it tabulated and evaluated all the major votes in the Senate from 1955 through 1959 and in the House from 1957 through 1959.

There was no mistaking the sharp differences between the two political parties. Of the 277 Democrats in the House, 200 voted less than 30 percent of the time for "the constitutional principles" embodied in the ACA Index. In contrast, thirteen House Republicans earned a 100 percent rating. Although there were no 100 percent senators, John Williams of Delaware received a 99 percent rating, followed closely by Barry Goldwater (98 percent) and John Marshall Butler of Maryland (93 percent). Harry Byrd was the top Democrat with 92 percent.[80]

All the ingredients of a national political movement were coming together: a charismatic political leader, Barry Goldwater; widely known popularizers both young (Bill Buckley) and old (George Sokolsky); thinkers like Hayek, Kirk, and Milton Friedman in their intellectual prime; and two influential journals of opinion—*National Review* and *Human Events.*

Movement leaders decided that next on the agenda was an organization of energetic young activists who would serve as the ground troops of conservatism. In the fall of 1960, some eighty young conservatives founded Young Americans for Freedom (YAF), with a little help from older Americans for freedom like Bill Buckley, Bill Rusher, and Marvin Liebman. In fact, the young organizers met under the great elm of the Buckley estate in Sharon, Connecticut.

The political action group's beginnings lay in the Student Committee for the Loyalty Oath, created by David Franke and Douglas Caddy in 1958, when both were college students in Washington, D.C. The National Defense Education Act contained a provision that a student had to sign an affidavit stating that he was not a member of any subversive organization and was loyal to the U.S. government from which he was seeking a grant for his higher education. This reasonable stipulation did not sit well with the American Civil Liberties Union and similar groups, and a campaign was launched among liberal-left students to eliminate the provision. The *New York Times* and other establishment publications took up the cry in the name of free speech and civil liberties. Undaunted, Caddy and Franke organized a counter-offensive.

The Student Committee for the Loyalty Oath established campus chapters, collected petitions, testified before congressional committees, wrote articles, distributed literature, and stirred up conservative students. It was the first major manifestation of what author M. Stanton Evans described as a conservative "revolt on the campus."[81]

At Sharon, the young conservatives named themselves Young Americans for Freedom and elected officers, including their first president, the brilliant and irreverent Robert M. Schuchman of Yale, a Jew. Douglas Caddy, a Catholic graduate of Georgetown University, was named executive director. Such ethnic diversity frustrated the attempts of liberals to dismiss YAF as a WASP group. The young conservatives also adopted the magisterial Sharon Statement, drafted by Stan Evans, which affirmed certain eternal truths at "this time of moral and political crisis":

> That foremost among the transcendent values is the individual's use of his God-given free will, whence derives his right to be free from the restrictions of arbitrary force;
>
> That liberty is indivisible, and that political freedom cannot long exist without economic freedom;
>
> That the purposes of government are to protect these freedoms through

the preservation of internal order, the provision of national defense, and the administration of justice. . . .

That the market economy, allocating resources by the free play of supply and demand, is the single economic system compatible with the requirements of personal freedom and constitutional government. . . .

That the forces of international communism are, at present, the greatest single threat to these liberties;

That the United States should stress victory over, rather than coexistence with, this menace.[82]

These are the central themes that have been at the core of modern American conservatism for the past fifty years: Free will and moral authority come from God; political and economic liberty are essential for the preservation of free people and free institutions; government must be strictly and constitutionally limited; the market economy is the system most compatible with freedom; and communism must be defeated, not simply contained.

With this philosophical foundation, YAF members went on to serve the conservative movement throughout the 1960s, providing the National Draft Goldwater Committee with critical manpower in a dozen states; challenging the liberal agenda of the National Student Association on a hundred college campuses; supporting American servicemen in Vietnam through "bleed-ins" (blood donations), debates, and symposia; and picketing the Firestone Tire and Rubber Company when it tried to build a synthetic rubber plant in communist Rumania.

The Kennedy-Nixon presidential race was one of the closest in American politics; Kennedy won by barely 114,000 votes out of more than 68 million votes cast. His electoral margin was respectable, 303 to 219, but depended on razor-thin victories in Illinois and Texas. Chicago Mayor Richard Daley delivered the Democratic vote (living and dead) in Cook County while yellow-dog Democrats provided the margin in the Lone Star State. Despite the loss at the top of the ticket, Republicans were heartened by the gain of twenty-two seats in the House of Representatives and two in the Senate, including such future conservative leaders as Congressman John Ashbrook of Ohio and Senator Peter Dominick of Colorado.

Goldwater, a Republican loyalist like Robert Taft, did not share the satisfaction of some conservatives over Nixon's defeat, although that did not stop him from criticizing the vice president's campaign. He argued that

Nixon and his patrician running mate, Henry Cabot Lodge, failed to give the voters a "clear-cut choice." They did not challenge "the legitimacy of the expanding federal establishment." They lost, in short, "because [they] were not Republican enough."[83]

If he ever ran for president, Goldwater vowed, he would not repeat Nixon's mistakes but would campaign as a traditional Republican and conservative without apology. He quickly added that he had no intention of seeking the presidency; he was content to be a U.S. senator. As he told *Time* when asked about the 1964 presidential race, "I have no staff for it, no program for it, and no ambition for it."[84]

Chapter 6

The Reluctant Champion

FOR CONSERVATIVES, THE SIXTIES WAS THE DECADE NOT OF JOHN F. Kennedy but of Barry Goldwater. Early in the decade, conservatives believed they had found their champion in Goldwater, a true son of the West, where freedom and independence were not simply words but beliefs worth fighting and even dying for. They admired Goldwater's insistence on speaking his mind, regardless of the consequences. They loved his unflinching loyalty to family, friends, and country. And they thought he could go all the way to the White House.

He was certainly doing all the right things to win the presidential nomination. He had twice served as chairman of the Republican Senatorial Campaign Committee, helping dozens of candidates and raising millions of dollars across the country. He was a prominent member of the powerful Senate "Rackets" Committee (chaired by John McClellan of Arkansas) that exposed the illegal activities of power-hungry labor bosses like Dave Beck and Jimmy Hoffa of the Teamsters Union and the wrongdoing of the United Auto Workers against the Kohler Company of Wisconsin. He became a good friend of William J. Baroody, Sr., president of the prestigious American Enterprise Institute (AEI), and was able to draw on AEI's considerable public policy resources. Along the way, he collaborated with a gifted writer, L. Brent Bozell, to produce a best-selling conservative manifesto. And he challenged Vice President Nixon for his party's nomination and transformed himself into a major contender at the next GOP convention.

But none of this was calculated. Barry Goldwater was not engaged in some grand political design but, in each instance, was simply responding to someone else's suggestion or invitation. He was truly a man without ambition for the highest office in the land, but the cumulative effect of all these acts was to make him the leading conservative politician in America and a strong possibility to become president.

Three young but politically experienced conservatives recognized Goldwater's enormous potential and created "the first authentic presidential nomination draft in the history of American political parties."[1] The three—close friends and all former leaders of the Young Republicans—were William A. Rusher, the strategist, who had served in World War II and then graduated from Harvard Law School before becoming a kingmaker (and breaker) in both the Young Republicans and Young Americans for Freedom; F. Clifton White, the tactician, a tall, bow-tied professional politician from New York who had taught politics at Cornell and then worked in the presidential campaigns of Dewey, Eisenhower, and Nixon; and Congressman John M. Ashbrook of Ohio, the ideologue, who represented the same congressional district his father had and was a former chairman of the Young Republican National Federation.

In mid-July 1961, Rusher traveled to Washington to lunch with Ashbrook. Over coffee, Rusher remarked, "If we held a meeting of our old YR crowd today, I'll bet it would be about the third largest faction in the Republican party." Ashbrook quickly agreed, and back in his congressional office displayed the folders of correspondence from across the country that he had accumulated since retiring as YR chairman two years before. The names constituted a national network of one-time YRs who had assumed leadership roles in the party. Rusher was confident that if they were invited to help draft Goldwater for the 1964 Republican nomination, "these old friends of ours would be overjoyed at the chance to work together again."[2]

Back in New York City, Rusher took Clif White to lunch and suggested that the time was ripe for a conservative takeover of the GOP. White revealed that he too had been thinking about the Republican party's future and mentioned his thick files of Young Republicans and other party contacts. They discussed merging the Ashbrook-White material and creating a national organization dedicated "to the nomination of a conservative candidate, or at the very least the drafting of a conservative platform, at the 1964 convention."[3]

Almost exactly three years later—after many months of careful grass-roots organizing, the raising of several million dollars (much of it through five- and ten-dollar contributions), the careful cultivation of key reporters, editors, and columnists, the shocking assassination of a sitting president, the losing and winning of key primaries from New Hampshire to California—Barry Goldwater became, however reluctantly, the first true conservative since 1924 to be nominated for president by a major party.[4]

Goldwater was reluctant because he wanted to remain in the Senate where he was comfortable and effective, because he had real doubts about his intellectual ability to be president (he once told a reporter he did not have "a really first-class brain"), and because all the polls showed him losing to President John F. Kennedy (and later to Lyndon B. Johnson).[5] But he nevertheless accepted the presidential nomination because he wanted to pay back the country that had given him so much, and he was willing to raise high the bright standard of conservatism in 1964.

The process of drafting Goldwater began in October 1961 when some twenty well-connected, conservative Republicans (calling themselves the "hard core") met in Chicago to discuss how they might translate the political passion the senator from Arizona aroused among Republicans into a majority of delegates on the first ballot at the next national convention. White warned that those who had controlled the Republican party for more than two decades, turning back every conservative challenge, "would fight us tooth and nail every inch of the way once they discovered what we were up to."[6]

At a larger meeting in December, a strategy and a budget were adopted. No state, White emphasized, would be overlooked or written off. As Rusher wrote, "We knew that there were conservatives, and therefore potential allies, in the Republican organization of even the most liberal states."[7] While they hoped and expected to gain the support of southern voters, White, Rusher, and the other organizers intended to appeal strongly to voters in the Southwest, the Mountain West, and California. "We could already sense the shifting demographics and politics of these regions," a shift that Kevin Phillips would document seven years later in *The Emerging Republican Majority*.[8]

From the winter of 1961 until the fall of 1963, the indefatigable Clif White traveled more than a million miles on behalf of the Draft Goldwater effort, visiting old political friends, enlisting political neophytes, building an organization in every state and congressional district, and discovering that conservatives (thanks to youth groups like the Young Republicans and Young Americans for Freedom and women's groups like the National Federation of Republican Women) had more political strength than anyone, particularly the media, realized.

Money was another matter. Rusher called the first half of 1962 the "Valley Forge" of the draft movement. The money that Roger Milliken (an original hard-core member) had raised was almost gone, and White was forced to telephone people rather than see them in person. He even dipped into the money he had saved for his son's college education. By September, creditors had become so threatening that a discouraged White and his assistant Rita Bree told Rusher they "would have to fold the tent."[9] But Rusher rallied their spirits and persuaded them to continue for at least one more month.

They were rescued by Robert C. "Randy" Richardson, an heir to the Vicks chemical fortune, who agreed to share the rent of the offices, and by businessmen J. D. "Stets" Coleman and R. Crosby Kemper, who wrote generous checks. J. William Middendorf II and Jeremiah Milbank, Jr., prominent in New York investment circles and Connecticut politics, provided enough money to keep the operation going until after the November elections. Indeed, over the next two years, Middendorf and Milbank became so good at producing cash for the Goldwater campaign whenever it was needed that they were nicknamed "the Brinks Brothers." Rarely has so much been accomplished politically with so little: in its first year of operations in 1962, the draft effort spent a little over $43,000—about what Nelson Rockefeller paid his top speechwriter.[10]

The conservative movement and those seeking to nominate Goldwater were heartened by the astonishing rally of Young Americans for Freedom in March 1962, when more than eighteen thousand enthusiastic conservatives overflowed New York City's Madison Square Garden. Their unmistakable message to the eastern liberal establishment was that conservatism had come of political age.

When the hero of the night, Barry Goldwater, finally appeared, the crowd would not stop chanting "We want Barry!" Finally, an exasperated Goldwater yelled into the microphone, "Well, if you'll shut up, you'll get him!" In his prepared remarks, the senator predicted that a "wave of conservatism" would eventually triumph in America.[11]

While the politicians, led by Clif White, were busy building a national organization to gain the presidential nomination, the popularizers, led by *National Review*, were busily removing counterproductive elements from the movement. In December 1957, Whittaker Chambers had taken up arms against Ayn Rand, the neo-Nietzschean founder of objectivism, and her 1,168-page novel *Atlas Shrugged*. Writing in *National Review*, he declared that its story was preposterous, its characters crude caricatures, its message "dictatorial." Although Rand insisted she was antistatist, argued Chambers, she called for a society run by a "technocratic elite." "Out of a lifetime of reading," he wrote, "I can recall no other book in which a tone of overriding arrogance was so implacably sustained."[12]

Russell Kirk called objectivism a false and detestable "inverted religion." Frank Meyer accused Rand of "calculated cruelties" and the presentation of an "arid subhuman image of man." Garry Wills, then a young classical scholar and favorite of Bill Buckley, called Rand a "fanatic" and said flatly that she was "not conservative."[13] Furious, Rand described *National Review* as "the worst and most dangerous magazine in America."[14]

The casting out of Robert Welch and the extremist positions of the John Birch Society that he headed would prove more difficult but nonetheless necessary.

By mid-1961, it was clear that conservatism was becoming a significant presence in American politics. There were the best-sellerdom of *The Conscience of a Conservative*, the sharp rise in the polls of Barry Goldwater, the increased circulation of *National Review* and *Human Events*, Republican John Tower's upset senatorial victory to fill Lyndon Johnson's Senate seat in Texas, the accelerating activities of Young Americans for Freedom, the possibility of a Conservative party in New York, and the aggressive presence of the John Birch Society in many parts of the nation (its membership of some sixty thousand was concentrated in California and Texas). Liberals had ignored the conservative upsurge but were now driven to denounce and try to bury it. Politicians, academics, columnists, clerics, and even humorists used their various skills, creating what Bill Buckley called "the echo-chamber effect."[15]

They zeroed in on the conservative movement's weakest link: the John Birch Society. President Kennedy delivered a major speech in the fall of 1961 in which he urged Americans to reject "fanatics" who found "treason" everywhere and did not trust the people. Although Kennedy did not name the "fanatics," the *New York Times* helpfully did so in its front-page story about his speech, mentioning the John Birch Society and the paramilitary Minutemen.[16]

The echoes kept coming. Under the title "Thunder Against the Right," *Time* revealed that the president's speech was one that "Kennedy had long wanted to get off his chest." Alan Barth, a prominent *Washington Post* editorial writer, wrote in the *New York Times Sunday Magazine* that members of the "radical right" tended to simplify all issues, believed in the conspiratorial theory of history, and distrusted "deeply" the democratic process and democratic institutions.[17]

Over the objections of Rusher, Frank Meyer, and new senior editor William Rickenbacker, Bill Buckley, supported by his sister Priscilla and James Burnham, wrote a historic editorial reading Robert Welch out of the conservative movement. Although Meyer and others argued that *National Review* should concentrate its fire on communists and liberals, not on other conservatives, Buckley was adamant.

Titled "The Question of Robert Welch," the detailed, six-page editorial declared that Welch was "damaging the cause of anti-Communism." It charged him with consistently failing to make the critical distinction between an "active pro-Communist" and an "ineffectually anti-Communist Liberal." Welch's annual scoreboard, published in the society's *American Opinion,* described the United States of America as "50–70 percent Communist-controlled;" that is, said the editorial scornfully, "the government of the United States is under operational control of the Communist Party."[18]

Noting the criticism of Welch by such staunch anticommunists as Barry Goldwater, Walter Judd, Fulton Lewis, Jr., and Russell Kirk, the *National Review* editorial concluded that a love of truth and country called for the firm rejection of Welch's "false counsels." Anticipating the sharp reaction he knew would come, Buckley wrote, "There are bounds to the dictum: Anyone on my right is my ally."[19]

Welch felt "personally betrayed" by Buckley's attack but declined to respond in kind, affirming his own belief in the maxim that Buckley rejected. "To avoid adding fuel to all of the friction among the anti-Communist forces," wrote Welch in *American Opinion,* "we shall even refrain from defending ourselves against the slings and arrows from the Right."[20]

Senator John Tower was quick to describe the *National Review* editorial as "a courageous and responsible analysis," and Barry Goldwater, in a letter to the editor, described Welch's views as "irresponsible" and called on him to resign as president of the society.[21] They knew that rather than dividing the conservative cause, Buckley's editorial had strengthened it, and they saluted him for his courage and leadership.

As with any other political movement, there has always been a dark side of the Right. In the 1960s, there were conspiracy addicts, like Robert Welch, who believed that communists controlled much of America. There were rabid anti-Semites like Gerald L. K. Smith; Conde McGinley, publisher of the misnamed *Common Sense;* and Willis Carto, the founder of Liberty Lobby, who traced the decline and coming fall of America to Jews. There were racists, usually based in the South, who regarded blacks as less than human. There were armed militants like the Minutemen who lived in remote, isolated places and stockpiled guns, ammunition, canned water, and food in anticipation of the inevitable national collapse. There were fundamentalist preachers who railed against the forces of humanism, liberalism, and secularism and warned of approaching Armageddon. But while all of these doomsayers and paranoiacs were *in* the movement, they were not *the* movement, which as it grew and matured relegated them to the outer reaches of the Right, where most of them withered and eventually died.

There was one other important task that had to be accomplished before the conservative movement could operate effectively in the political realm: It had to be philosophically united. Increasingly, traditionalists and libertarians had been snapping and snarling at each other in the pages of *National Review,* the *New Individualist Review,* and elsewhere. Traditionalist Russell Kirk was accused of being hostile to individualism and laissez-faire economics, while libertarian Friedrich Hayek was faulted for defending freedom on strictly utilitarian grounds rather than according to "the absolute transcendent values upon which its strength is founded."[22]

One conservative in particular was convinced that beneath all the differences lay a true consensus of principle: Frank Meyer, the fast-talking, chain-smoking, ex-communist senior editor of *National Review.* Through articles, books, and endless late-evening telephone calls, Meyer communicated his synthesis of the disparate elements of conservatism, which came to be called fusionism.

The core fundamental was "the freedom of the person, the central and primary end of political society." The state had only three limited functions: national defense, the preservation of domestic order, and the administration of justice between citizens. The "achievement of virtue" was not a political question: indeed, it was not even the state's business. Freedom, Meyer argued, was the indispensable condition for the pursuit of virtue. Freedom was the ultimate *political* end; virtue was the ultimate end of man as man.

And yet Meyer insisted that modern American conservatism was not classical liberalism, which had been significantly weakened by utilitarianism and secularism. Most classical liberals, he charged, were seemingly unable to distinguish between "the *authoritarianism*" of the state and "the *authority* of God and truth." Meyer declared that conservatives were trying to save the Christian understanding of "the nature and destiny of man." To do that, they had to absorb the best of both branches of the divided conservative mainstream. He insisted that he was not creating something new but simply articulating an already existing conservative consensus: "the consensus forged so brilliantly by the Founding Fathers in 1787" at the writing of the Constitution.

Regardless of their philosophical orientation, historian George Nash observed, all conservatives thought that the state should be circumscribed and were deeply suspicious of planning and attempts to centralize power. They defended the Constitution "as originally conceived" and opposed the "messianic" communist threat to "Western civilization."[23]

Although both traditionalists and libertarians often challenged fusionism in the years to come, it prevailed as an effective synthesis until the collapse of communism in Eastern and Central Europe in 1989 and the fall of the Soviet Union in 1991.

And without a united conservative movement behind him, Barry Goldwater would not have been nominated for president in 1964. Indeed, Goldwater was the political personification of fusionism in his presidential campaign, stressing the need for morality in government, lamenting a national decline in law and order, promising less government and more individual freedom, and calling for victory over the Soviet Union in the cold war.

But that was in the future. In the spring of 1961, Goldwater was preoccupied not with his possible presidency, but with the disappointing presidency of John Kennedy, especially abroad. President Kennedy invited his former Senate colleague to the White House in early April 1961, just before the Bay of Pigs invasion in Cuba. Kennedy revealed that the first phase of the Cuban operation had failed to achieve its primary mission: Castro's air force had not been destroyed. Although the anti-Castro exiles were supposed to be given sixteen B-26 bombers, the State Department had persuaded Kennedy to halve the number to make more plausible Washington's denials that the U.S. government was involved.

Goldwater was stunned at Kennedy's indecision. "The president was not a profile in courage," he later wrote. "He did not seem to have the old-fashioned guts to go on."[24] Goldwater argued that there was still time to launch a wave of navy bombers standing by and to destroy Castro's planes. He said heatedly that the action was "moral and legal and would be understandable to the entire free world."[25]

Goldwater left the Oval Office believing that sufficient U.S. air cover would be given the anti-Castro fighters to allow them to land safely at the Bay of Pigs and advance on Havana. But Kennedy approved only one air strike of B-26s and canceled a follow-up attack by U.S. navy jet fighters. Simply put, Kennedy lost his nerve, and three hundred members of the anti-Castro brigade lost their lives. The rest of the fifteen-hundred-man force was imprisoned, and Castro was free to continue his communization of Cuba.

The following year, Republicans began demanding that Kennedy do something about the Soviet program of increased arms aid to Cuba. Led by Senator Kenneth Keating of New York, who was being informed by Cuban exiles about the placement of Soviet missiles in Cuba, Republicans called for a blockade, an invasion, or some other kind of visible action. In late August 1962, Kennedy denounced calls for an invasion of Cuba as "irresponsible" but promised to "watch what happens in Cuba with the closest attention." A week later, he denied there was any provocative Soviet action in Cuba.[26]

Finally, on October 22 (more than two months after Keating had publicly raised the possibility of Soviet missiles in Cuba), President Kennedy delivered a national television address announcing the presence of Soviet offensive missiles in Cuba and the imposition of a U.S. blockade. Republicans and the nation did not learn until years later that Kennedy had pledged to Khrushchev that in exchange for the withdrawal of the Soviet missiles, the United States would not invade Cuba and that other nations of the Western Hemisphere "were prepared to give similar assurances."[27] While it is true that the Kennedy-Khrushchev understanding was never formalized by executive order or treaty, it remains effective U.S. policy to this day. Liberal policymakers consider it a successful application of containment, conservative policy-makers a glaring example of accommodation.

Meanwhile, Goldwater's chances of winning the GOP nomination continued to rise. Rockefeller won reelection as governor of New York in 1962, but by a narrower margin than four years earlier. One major reason was the strong showing of David H. Jaquith, the gubernatorial candidate of the new Conservative party of New York, who received 141,877 votes. Bill Buckley's 1957 memorandum regarding "political action" in New York had paid its first significant political dividend.

While Rockefeller was undoubtedly the leading presidential candidate during the first months of 1963 in the polls and the press, he was not the choice of the Republican rank and file. A survey of delegates to the 1960 Republican convention revealed that their favorite was Goldwater. The senator was also helped by the effective elimination of an otherwise leading 1964 contender, Richard Nixon, who had suffered an embarrassing loss to Governor Edmund G. (Pat) Brown of California in that state's gubernatorial election in 1962.

The conservative cause was also helped by a widely quoted column by veteran political correspondent Lyle Wilson, who pointed out that with "me-too Republicans" in charge, the Republican party had lost three-fourths of the national elections since 1940. What the GOP needed, Wilson suggested, "is a commitment to a set of courageous political principles that clearly distinguish it from the Democratic Party."[28] The hard-core Republicans meeting in December 1962 to finalize plans for a National Draft Goldwater Committee knew where to find those clear-cut principles—in *The Conscience of a Conservative*.

Clif White outlined a Midwest–South–Far West strategy. A key event would be the California primary; its eighty-six delegates would offset any unexpected defections and demonstrate the senator's popularity. White argued that the same focus on the Midwest, the South, and the West would produce a victory over President Kennedy in the general election.[29] An essential element of the strategy was that the South no longer belonged to the Democrats because the national Democratic party had moved so far left. Goldwater could win much if not all of what had long been inviolate Democratic property. At the same time, the money men agreed to pledge a total of $250,000, and the Draft Goldwater movement was truly underway.[30]

Clif White was unanimously elected chairman and instructed to report to Goldwater in January 1963 about their plans. Unbeknownst to him, Goldwater was meeting over the Christmas holidays with Arizona friends and advisers to talk about his political future. The consensus: While Goldwater might be able to win the Republican nomination in 1964, it would be "very difficult" for anyone to defeat President Kennedy. The prudent course for Goldwater was to seek reelection to the Senate.

A wary Goldwater received a smiling White in his Senate office. The New Yorker had hardly begun reporting the "good news" from Chicago when the senator held up a large hand and interrupted, "Clif, I'm not a candidate and I'm not going to be. I have no intention of running for the presidency."

Remembering the last eighteen months of careful planning, hard work, and unremitting travel, White retorted sharply, "Senator . . . You're the leader of the conservative cause in the United States of America, and thousands—millions—of people want you to be their nominee for president."

"Well," responded a stubborn Goldwater, "I'm just not going to run." He added lamely, "My wife loves me, but she'd leave me if I ran for this thing."[31]

A despondent White took the first shuttle flight back to New York City where he bitterly told Rusher, "I'm going to give up politics and go back into business." Even the congenitally upbeat Rusher was discouraged. He agreed with White that "you couldn't take a grown man by the scruff of the neck and force him to run for president of the United States."[32] Or could you?

In mid-February, the hard core gathered in Chicago, seemingly for the last time. They considered and rejected a dozen different ways to persuade Goldwater, the only candidate in the minds of most conservatives, to run. After hours of talk and countless cups of coffee, silence fell, broken at last by an exasperated Robert Hughes of Indiana, who growled, "There's only one thing we *can* do. Let's draft the son of a bitch."[33]

Amid exclamations and an old-fashioned western holler, the small band of conservatives decided that although they could not force a man to seek the presidency, they could draft him in the hope he would accept it for the good of his party and his country. Peter O'Donnell, chairman of the Texas Republican party, agreed to serve as chairman of the National Draft Goldwater Committee, although everyone was agreed that Clif White would steer "the bandwagon we were building right into San Francisco."[34]

Aside from a strong personal distaste for living as a "prisoner" in the White House, Goldwater had valid political reasons for hesitating to run for president. He was, after all, a westerner from a small state with only five electoral votes. He was a conservative in what was still a liberal land. And he could not be certain that his party, for all his many contributions to it, would unite behind him. Furthermore, he was proud of his two senatorial victories and did not want to taint them by losing badly as a presidential candidate. Perhaps most important of all, he worried about what an overwhelming loss would do to the conservative movement. In the end, Goldwater decided that if he campaigned as an unabashed conservative and came within five points of a majority (that is, 45 percent), "that would be really a victory for conservatism."[35]

For the liberal establishment, the possibility that Goldwater might be the Republican nominee seemed remote. The front-runner was still Nelson Rockefeller, despite some grumbling about his personal life. In March 1962, Rockefeller had divorced his wife of thirty-one years and the mother of their five children, and he had been openly involved with a much younger, married woman, Margaretta "Happy" Murphy. The relationship, once much discussed, seemed to have been accepted or at least ignored by the public. Things turned upside down, however, on May 4, 1963, when Rockefeller suddenly married Happy Murphy just one month after she had divorced her husband, who was given custody of their four small children. The affair was thrust back into the news, where voters were reminded of it every time they saw a photo of the beaming New York governor and his new wife.

Rockefeller had been beating Goldwater by about 2 to 1 among Republicans in the Gallup presidential poll. But a month after his remarriage, he sank from 43 to 30 percent while Goldwater surged from 26 to 35 percent—a 22 percent swing. For the first time, the conservative Arizona senator led the liberal New York governor in the Gallup Poll. In a national trial heat between Kennedy and Goldwater, the new GOP front-runner still trailed the president, 60 to 36 percent. But political analysts noted that Goldwater had risen nine points, while Kennedy had dropped seven points since the last survey.[36]

The sharply rising fortunes of the conservative movement and its champion were confirmed by several major events that summer and fall. In mid-July, the Young Republican National Federation elected as its new chairman Donald E. "Buz" Lukens, an ardent Goldwater supporter. Goldwater himself addressed the convention and brought the young men and women cheering to their feet with a slashing attack on "today's liberals" who were "intellectually bankrupt." They had not had "a new idea in thirty years," he declared. "They are dead and finished."[37]

Earlier that same month, eight thousand ecstatic conservatives had jammed Washington's un-air-conditioned National Guard Armory to hold an old-fashioned patriotic Fourth of July rally and help persuade Barry Goldwater to lead a crusade to make America strong and whole and right again. Goldwater was not present, but Senators John Tower of Texas and Carl Curtis of Nebraska and Congressman John Ashbrook of Ohio were there along with Hollywood stars Efrem Zimbalist, Jr., Walter Brennan, and Chill Wills, who crooned in his whiskey baritone to the delighted crowd, "We'll All Be There in San Francisco." A concerned liberal Democrat was quoted as saying, "Last month they were just a faction. But tonight it looks like they've become a political party."[38]

That September, nearly fifty thousand people filled Dodger Stadium in Los Angeles to hear Goldwater deliver a rousing speech. It was the largest Republican rally in Los Angeles since presidential candidate Thomas E. Dewey had campaigned there twenty years earlier. Goldwater was interrupted forty-seven times as he declared that "America needs a change" and "Freedom needs a chance."[39]

These were heady times for Goldwater and the conservative movement, capped by a major article in *Time,* the establishment's favorite magazine, that began:

> Until recently most political observers figured that Democrat John Kennedy was a sure 1964 winner, and that it did not make much difference who the GOP candidate would be. Now, many are changing their minds. . . .
>
> A state-by-state survey of *Time* correspondents indicates that at least Republican Barry Goldwater could give Kennedy a breathlessly close contest.[40]

The weekly reported that while the president could easily beat any other Republican candidate, including Rockefeller and Nixon, he could be rated only even against Goldwater, who could count on carrying states (many of them below the Mason-Dixon Line) with a total of 266 electoral votes, 4 fewer than the total needed to win.[41]

For his part, President Kennedy looked forward to running against Goldwater, with whom he had served in the Senate for eight years. At a November 13 White House meeting about the 1964 campaign, a laughing Kennedy concluded, "Give me Barry. I won't even have to leave the Oval Office."[42]

But apprehensive Democrats were warning Kennedy that he faced reelection problems. Some had already conceded the Deep South if Goldwater were the Republican candidate. And Vice President Johnson pressed the president to visit Texas, where Goldwater was leading the president in the latest poll by 52 to 48 percent.

The contrasts between the two politicians were undeniably stark: Kennedy, the eastern elitist and Harvard graduate, versus Goldwater, the western self-educated cowboy; the cool liberal versus the hot conservative; the new politics versus the old.

As November drew to a close, Barry Goldwater was convinced he could run a strong conservative campaign against an incumbent liberal president. The national polls were encouraging, the organization under the direction of Denison Kitchel was coming together, Clif White and his associates were methodically accumulating delegates, and the money was steadily flowing in.

Everywhere there was abundant evidence that the American conservative movement had come of age and was poised to help him capture the Republican presidential nomination and then, perhaps, the most sought-after prize in American politics—the presidency. What could go wrong?

At 1:32 P.M., Washington time, on Friday, November 22, 1963, the first bulletin came over the wires: "Three shots were fired at President Kennedy's motorcade in downtown Dallas." Thirty minutes later, at Parkland Memorial Hospital, the president was pronounced dead.[43]

The immediate, spontaneous reaction of many conservatives was, "Oh, my God, it must have been one of ours." The majority of Americans were led to the same thoughts by the mass media, which constantly referred to Dallas as the "home of the extreme right wing" and the "heart of Goldwaterland."[44] Television networks ran and reran a film clip of UN ambassador Adlai Stevenson being spat on by "conservatives" in Dallas a month earlier.

Conservatives braced for the worst, and then at 4:23, NBC announced that a suspect had been arrested in Dallas. He was soon identified as Lee Harvey Oswald. All over America, conservative organizations began checking their membership and donor lists.

In Washington, D.C., senior editor Eugene Methvin of *Reader's Digest* said to himself, "I know that name—he's got some communist connection." In less than a minute, his phone rang; it was a very excited Edward S. Butler calling from New Orleans. Butler was almost sputtering. "That's the guy," he kept saying, "that's the guy I debated here in New Orleans—the guy you sent me all the material about."[45]

Methvin had received a telephone call in August from Ed Butler, a young anticommunist organizer with whom he had been corresponding for several years. Butler was going to debate the secretary of the local Fair Play for Cuba Committee, a pro-Castro group, on a New Orleans radio station. He wanted to know whether his opponent had a communist background. Methvin directed Butler to Francis J. McNamara, staff director of the House Committee on Un-American Activities. McNamara agreed to send Butler any material the committee had in its public files about his opponent, whose name was Lee Harvey Oswald.

When Methvin returned from vacation in September, he had found a news release from Ed Butler describing his August 21 radio debate and giv-ing Oswald's background, including his defection to the Soviet Union and his public admission, "I am a Marxist."[46] Methvin had glanced through the material and added it to the growing stack behind his desk. Now he began hurriedly searching and at last found the most important news release he had ever received.

In his shirt sleeves and unwilling to wait for the elevator, Methvin ran down the stairs to the first floor where the Associated Press had its offices. "The place was bedlam." He saw a reporter he knew and asked if he knew who Lee Oswald was. No, replied his friend, "and everyone in the world is trying to find out." "Read this," Methvin urged, handing him Ed Butler's press release and the attached material.[47]

"They put it on the wire," remembered Methvin, "and that's how the nation and the world learned that Lee Harvey Oswald was no right-winger but a one-time defector to the Soviet Union."[48]

Barry Goldwater was devastated by John Kennedy's murder. He told his campaign director Denison Kitchel "to pass the word"—he would not run.[49] The primary reason was his cold contempt for Lyndon Johnson, who would not engage, he was certain, in the issue-oriented campaign that he and Kennedy had envisaged. "Johnson was the epitome of the unprincipled politician," Goldwater said, who would manipulate "Jack's martyrdom" for his own political purposes. He was "treacherous," a "hypocrite," a man "who never cleaned that crap off his boots." Goldwater understood that no Republican, especially a conservative Republican, could win in 1964. As he put it, "the American people were not ready for three presidents in little more than one year."[50]

At Kitchel's insistence, Goldwater called a meeting of his closest friends and advisers. He bluntly stated his position, "Our cause is lost," and then sat silently as his fellow conservatives sought to persuade him to do what he so clearly did not want to do. Despite the assassination, they assured him, the Goldwater delegates were holding firm. He could not let them down.[51]

Goldwater made no response. At last he asked the group of anxious conservatives to let him "sleep on it." Motioning Kitchel to remain, Goldwater sat silently with his old friend and watched darkness fill the room until at last he turned on a light and poured some bourbon for himself and Kitchel. Pacing up and down the room, an uncertain Goldwater asked his friend, "What do you think?" to which Kitchel retorted, "What do *you* think?"

The senator repeated the points that had already been made, returning again and again to the kind of campaign Johnson would conduct. "I wasn't scared of a goddamned thing," he later recalled, "but when you're faced with the fact that black is black, you don't try to change it to white. I knew that running against Johnson you're running against all the controlled political organizations in the country."[52]

Kitchel went to the heart of the matter. "Barry," he said, "I don't think you can back down." What was at stake was not one man's feelings or wishes, but "the millions of conservatives around the country who had made a stand in favor of Barry Goldwater." Goldwater admitted that there was a "virtually unbreakable" bond between himself and conservatives and finally said, with mixed exasperation and resignation, "All right, damn it, I'll do it."[53]

It was an unprecedented act in American politics. Never before had a presidential candidate run knowing beyond any reasonable doubt that he could not win the general election. That hard political reality accounted for his grim face and voice over the next eleven months (no one enjoys committing political suicide), the uncompromising content of his speeches and positions (he would give the voters a *real* choice), and the all-Arizona composition of his campaign team (it was the last wish of the condemned politician to be accompanied by his closest friends as he went before the firing squad).

Yet as he prepared to announce his candidacy, Goldwater could depend on something that heretofore had not existed: a national political movement. Although untested in a national campaign, conservatism did have a clearly defined, consistent philosophy, as articulated by Hayek, Kirk, Weaver, and Chambers; an expanding national constituency, particularly strong in the West and the South; a charismatic, nationally known leader in Barry Goldwater; and a solid financial base, not dependent on a few wealthy individuals but on tens of thousands of grassroots supporters. Only in the mass media was conservatism conspicuously deficient and confronted by a largely skeptical and even hostile constituency.

If he had been able to call on such resources, Bob Taft would probably have been nominated in 1952. Conservatives were determined that Goldwater would not suffer Taft's undeserved fate in 1964.

From the beginning of his presidential campaign on January 3, 1964, Goldwater promised to "offer a choice, not an echo." He would not change his beliefs or tailor his positions "to win votes." Instead, he offered the voters something rare in American politics—"an engagement of principles."[54]

Against the recommendations of Peter O'Donnell, conservative columnist Raymond Moley, and William Loeb, the friendly publisher of the powerful New Hampshire newspaper, the *Manchester Union-Leader,* Goldwater entered the always unpredictable New Hampshire primary. Political amateurs Kitchel and Baroody waved polls showing Goldwater to be the choice of 65 percent of the state's Republicans and independents. Political professionals U.S. senator Norris Cotton and Stuart Lamprey, Speaker of the New Hampshire legislature, assured their fellow conservative that he was a shoo-in.

And so, still healing from an operation on his heel and hampered by a walking cast, Goldwater plunged into twenty-three days of campaigning with as many as eighteen appearances in a single day. As the senator later remarked wryly, "I remember every footstep of that campaign."[55] Nor was he prepared psychologically. He was still looking back at the campaign that might have been against John Kennedy rather than toward the campaign that was against Lyndon Johnson.

Accordingly, he said careless, controversial things—for example, that participation in the social security system might be made optional. "If a person can provide better for himself," he replied when asked for his views about the program, "let him do it. But if he prefers the government to do it, let him." Within hours of the news conference, the pro-Rockefeller *Concord Monitor* ran a banner headline: "Goldwater Sets Goals: End Social Security, Hit Castro." Thus was born the myth of "Goldwater the Destroyer of Social Security."

At another news conference, Goldwater was asked about NATO and the use of nuclear weapons and replied, "The commander should have the ability to use [tactical] nuclear weapons." As the senator knew from briefings as a member of the Senate Armed Services Committee, he was stating long-standing NATO policy in certain situations—when, for example, there was a communications breakdown during an invasion by Warsaw Pact forces. But the Rockefeller propaganda machine suggested that Goldwater wanted to turn over the authority to use theater nuclear weapons to *all* commanders in the field. And so was created the image of "Goldwater the Trigger-Happy Warrior."

While Goldwater and Rockefeller were trying to win over the hard-nosed, tight-spending, balanced-budget Yankees who constituted a majority of New Hampshire Republicans, a Lodge for President headquarters quietly opened in Concord, across from the state capitol. Because Henry Cabot Lodge, the U.S ambassador to South Vietnam, was not on the ballot, his name would have to be written in. There was an intriguing precedent: the upset, write-in victory of General Eisenhower over favored Bob Taft in 1952.

Although the polls showed a tightening race, few observers believed that a write-in candidate halfway around the world could beat the well-organized, well-financed campaigns of Goldwater and Rockefeller.[56] Once again, in an unconventional year, conventional wisdom was proved wrong.

Less than twenty minutes after the polls closed, CBS News projected that Henry Cabot Lodge had won the presidential preference primary in New Hampshire, receiving 33,521 write-in votes, about 35 percent of the total vote. Goldwater trailed with 21,775 votes, 23 percent, and Rockefeller was third with 19,496 votes, about 21 percent. Nixon got 15,752 write-in votes, or 17 percent. Goldwater's 23 percent was embarrassing: one-third of his approval rating the previous October and far less than the 33 percent he had mentioned as a worst-case scenario in February.

What happened? Citizens were literally terrified of Goldwater. Typical was the seventy-two-year-old resident of Concord who told her surprised neighbor she was going to support President Johnson. "But you've voted solid Republican for fifty years," her friend protested. The woman explained that she was "afraid" to vote for Goldwater because "he will take away my TV." "No, no," her friend reassured her, "Goldwater's against the TVA, not *TV.*" "Well," said the concerned woman, "that's good to know . . . but I don't want to take any chances."[57]

With any other candidate, Goldwater's dismal New Hampshire showing would have seriously, even fatally, damaged him. But in 1964, the county and state conventions rather than the primaries were king of the Republican nominating process. Because of the groundwork done by Clif White and the Draft Goldwater Committee, for example, Goldwater picked up forty-eight delegates at conventions in Oklahoma and North Carolina and six delegates at district meetings in Tennessee and Kansas on the same day he lost New Hampshire. White reminded the news media that New Hampshire was only one primary and confidently predicted that the senator would go on to win the nomination in San Francisco.[58]

Most journalists dismissed his remarks as predictable rhetoric (an early version of political "spin") and declared that Lodge was the all-but-certain Republican nominee, harking back to Eisenhower's defeat of Taft in 1952. But Lodge was no war hero, Goldwater was not a senator with only regional appeal and strength, and the conservative movement had come a long way in twelve years.

After admitting over national television, "I goofed," Goldwater reorganized his campaign. He elevated Clif White to codirector of field operations, along with Richard Kleindienst, one of the few members of the Arizona "mafia" with significant political experience. Although they came from far different political worlds, the two professionals shared one objective: nominating Barry Goldwater for president.

A chastened Goldwater returned to his original strategy of focusing on a few selected primaries, particularly California, making major addresses in key cities around the country, and letting the professionals hunt for delegates at state and district conventions. But he did not retreat from his stated intention to offer the American electorate a staunchly conservative platform, although he knew the fury and scorn that liberals would pour on him. He said bluntly, for example, that if the United Nations admitted Red China, the United States should get out. And he reiterated his wish to introduce a voluntary element into the social security system. As *National Review* commented, Goldwater's words and ideas, "the words and ideas of the conservative movement for which he becomes the most conspicuous public spokesman, cannot be ignored or dismissed." His voice would open "many otherwise closed ears and minds."[59]

The California primary between Barry Goldwater and Nelson Rockefeller was the most consequential one in the history of the American conservative movement. It was an epic battle between Goldwater volunteers and Rockefeller mercenaries, the New Right and the old California establishment, the middle class of Los Angeles and the upper class of San Francisco, the man who did not want to be president and the man who wanted only to be president.

Rockefeller gave his campaign organization more than $3 million and carte blanche to win the state and secure the nomination, which now seemed tantalizingly close. Following his solid victory in the Oregon primary (where Goldwater placed third), Rockefeller surged to a 47 to 36 percent lead over Goldwater among California voters, according to Lou Harris's polls.

With less than three weeks remaining before primary day, a fifteen-man Goldwater team headed by Dean Burch accomplished what veteran strategist Steve Shadegg described as "a political miracle" by reversing the Goldwater slide and producing a historic victory, albeit by the slimmest of margins.[60]

Working around the clock, the Goldwater team produced a series of television and radio spots, newspaper ads, and brochures. Heavy emphasis was placed on the photogenic Goldwater family—Barry, Peggy, and their four poised, handsome children—Joanne, Barry, Jr., Michael, and "little" Peggy. The Goldwaters contrasted sharply with the recently divorced Rockefeller and his new, and very pregnant, wife, Happy.

Meanwhile, a Goldwater army of fifty thousand volunteers (the largest number of volunteer workers ever assembled for any primary before or since) was distributing literature, canvassing neighborhoods, and preparing a mammoth effort to get Goldwater voters to the polls. Rockefeller manager Stu Spencer recalled with awe "the number of bodies they kept throwing at us."[61] One of the most effective pieces of literature, according to Rus Walton, head of the conservative United Republicans of California (UROC), was Phyllis Schlafly's antiestablishment book, *A Choice Not an Echo*. An estimated half-million copies of the Schlafly tract were distributed throughout the state.[62]

Sensing that the momentum was shifting, the Rockefeller organization began swinging harder and lower. As Spencer put it, "We had to destroy Barry Goldwater as a member of the human race." A tabloid newspaper was mailed to several hundred thousand California voters linking GOP leaders Lodge, Nixon, Governor George Romney of Michigan, Governor William Scranton of Pennsylvania, and even Harold Stassen to Rockefeller's candidacy. "Which Do You Want," a headline blared. "A Leader? Or a Loner?"[63] But Rockefeller's disinformation ploy backfired: Romney, Nixon, and Scranton all quickly denied being part of any anti-Goldwater or pro-Rockefeller effort.

A final anti-Goldwater bomb was dropped—by Goldwater. Appearing on ABC's *Issues and Answers* nine days before the voting, the senator was asked how communist supply lines along the Laotian border into South Vietnam might be interdicted. In an instant, the candidate who had curbed his tongue since New Hampshire became the careless Goldwater of old and replied:

> There have been several suggestions made. I don't think we would use any of them. But defoliation of the forests by low-yield atomic weapons could well be done.[64]

Goldwater paid heavily for his speculative comment. Both AP and UPI immediately released stories suggesting that the senator had "called" for the "use" of nuclear weapons. Goldwater protested, and the wire services sent out a correction that never caught up with the initial story. An elated Rockefeller branded his opponent a nuclear extremist and approved the mailing of a poisonous brochure entitled "Who Do You Want in the Room with the H-Bomb?" to 3 million registered Republicans in California. But the pamphlet's shrill tone backfired among many California Republicans who knew and admired Goldwater from his many appearances in their state.

Happy was now so close to delivery that Rocky flew home to New York every weekend. When aides pointed out that he was calling attention to an issue that could defeat him, the governor waved their caution aside and wisecracked, "I have a show opening on both sides of the continent the same weekend."[65]

This was too much for the Christian Right of the day. On Thursday,

May 28, sixteen Protestant ministers, representing a wide segment of the Christian community in southern California, held a news conference and suggested that Nelson Rockefeller should withdraw from the race because of his demonstrated inability to handle his own domestic affairs.

The same week, Rockefeller was to appear at Loyola University of Los Angeles at the invitation of its students. R. L. "Dick" Herman, a prominent Roman Catholic layman in Nebraska, was dispatched by the Goldwater team to visit Francis Cardinal McIntyre. The cardinal listened carefully to Herman's argument that Rockefeller's appearance at a prominent Catholic university might be interpreted as a church endorsement but made no promises. However, six hours before Rockefeller was scheduled to speak, Loyola suddenly withdrew its invitation, explaining that the governor's appearance was being "generally interpreted" as an official endorsement of his candidacy. Cardinal McIntyre personally commented that he did not want anyone to think the Catholic church was giving its blessing to a candidate who had been divorced and remarried.[66]

The denouement came at 4:15 P.M., Saturday, May 30, less than three days before the primary polls opened in California, when Happy gave birth to a baby boy in New York Hospital. She named him Nelson Rockefeller, Jr., and gave already critical ministers and pastors throughout California the subject for their Sunday sermon.

On Tuesday, June 2, a red-letter day in the history of the modern conservative movement, tens of thousands of volunteers spread across the state with lists of known Goldwater supporters and made certain they went to the polls. The final count was 1,120,403 votes for Goldwater, 1,052,053 for Rockefeller, a popular margin of 68,350 votes, 51.6 percent of the total. It was not a runaway, but it was enough. The senator received all eighty-six of California's delegates and now had, according to Clif White's private calculations, more than the 655 needed for nomination.

If Goldwater had lost California, he might well have withdrawn from the race. The liberal Republican establishment would have united behind a victorious Rockefeller and done whatever had to be done to defeat conservatives at the national convention (as it had in 1952, 1948, and 1940). But because he won California, Goldwater could assert, justifiably, that he had demonstrated his popular as well as electoral appeal. His nomination was now inevitable.

Barry Goldwater hoped, and wanted, to vote for the Civil Rights Act of 1964 as he had voted for the Civil Rights Acts of 1957 and 1960. As biographer Edwin McDowell wrote, "Few men not deliberately courting minority bloc votes have expressed their sympathy for [blacks]—verbally and through action—more often than Goldwater."[67] As chief of staff for the Arizona Air National Guard, he had pushed for desegregation of the guard two years before President Truman desegregated the U.S. armed forces. He and his brother Robert had hired blacks and served blacks at their Goldwater department store without reservation. He had contributed generously to the Arizona branch of the National Association for the Advancement of Colored People and the Phoenix branch of the Urban League. His first legislative assistant on his Senate staff was a black woman lawyer.

But Goldwater had problems with two sections of the proposed civil rights law: Title II dealing with public accommodations and Title VII on equal employment opportunity. He felt they were unconstitutional and unenforceable. Like Robert Taft, he opposed the idea of a federal Fair Employment Practices Commission, favoring state and local action.

The issue was not job discrimination, Goldwater argued, which was "morally wrong," but the proper role of the federal government in eliminating it. Goldwater argued that if the government "can forbid such discrimination, it is a real possibility that sometime in the future the same government can *require* people to discriminate in hiring on the basis of color or race or religion."[68] Rarely has a politician uttered more prophetic words.

Goldwater explained that he, and all other true conservatives, were for equal opportunity, by which individuals are judged on their qualifications without regard to race, sex, or religion. But he, and all other true conservatives, were opposed to preferential treatment that required individuals to be judged (and hired) on the basis of their race, sex, and religion. "Preferential treatment," of course, is what has come to be known as affirmative action.

Goldwater stated his position on the proposed legislation forthrightly and honestly. Not so the bill's proponents. Senator Hubert Humphrey assured the Senate that the Civil Rights Act of 1964 "does not require an employer to achieve any kind of racial balance in his work force by giving preferential treatment to any individual or group." Democratic senator Harrison Williams of New Jersey insisted that an employer could continue to hire "only the best qualified persons even if they were all white." As black economist Thomas Sowell summed up, "Congress declared itself in favor of equal opportunity and opposed to affirmative action."[69]

But Goldwater and other conservatives were convinced that regardless of the reassuring rhetoric, Title VII would inevitably lead to affirmative action. They were correct. President Johnson quickly formed the Office of Federal Contract Compliance in the U.S. Department of Labor, which by 1968 was referring to "goals and timetables for the prompt achievement of full and equal employment opportunity." But it was under President Nixon that "goals and guidelines" were expressly used to "increase materially the utilization of minorities and women" in jobs. Furthermore, the burden of proof, and remedy, was shifted to the employer rather than the employee. Just eight years after Humphrey and other liberals were adamantly denying any intent to force preferential treatment on the employer, affirmative action in the workforce became the official policy of the federal government.[70]

Goldwater also found serious fault with Title II, because it stated that a landlord could not refuse to rent to anybody. This was absurd to Goldwater, who protested, "I would not rent my home to a lot of whites for many reasons." But he supported the Civil Rights Act's other major provisions that empowered the attorney general to initiate suits or intervene on behalf of complainants in school desegregation and other discrimination cases, and permitted halting funds to federal programs where racial discrimination persisted.[71]

When repeated attempts to remove or modify Titles II and VII failed, Goldwater voted, reluctantly, on June 18 against the Civil Rights Act of 1964, one of twenty-seven senators to do so. Stating that discrimination was "fundamentally a matter of the heart," he argued that it could never be cured by laws alone. Laws, he conceded, could help if they were the right laws— "laws carefully considered and weighed in an atmosphere of dispassion, in the absence of political demagoguery, and in the light of fundamental constitutional principles."[72]

Goldwater did not flinch from the political consequences of his vote. His concern was not with himself or any group but with the nation and "the freedom of all who live in it and all who will be born in it."[73] Goldwater would not surrender to the passion of the moment, no matter how powerful or appropriate it seemed, if it broached the Constitution and endangered freedom.

A quarter of a century later, Goldwater was still defending his vote as consistent with his belief that "more can be accomplished for civil liberties at the local level than by faraway federal fiat." He asserted that many people, black and white, "wanted the 1964 Act passed for their own ends. . . . This was hard-nosed politics based on self-interest."[74]

But it was also a defining moment in American history. Because the leader of the conservative movement voted against major civil rights legislation, albeit for constitutional reasons, conservatives have been tarred ever since as racists and bigots. Jack Kemp, Newt Gingrich, and others have worked hard to build bridges to blacks, whose beliefs in family, church, and community are essentially conservative. In his pre–House Speaker days, for example, Gingrich supported the designation of Martin Luther King, Jr.'s birthday as a national holiday and supported economic sanctions against the apartheid government of South Africa.

But the memory of the Goldwater vote against the Civil Rights Act of 1964 is etched deeply in the minds of most older African Americans. For them, the debate was simple: either you wanted to end segregated luncheon counters and restaurants and boardinghouses and motels or you did not. Either you wanted to enable blacks to move out of the back rooms into the front rooms of factories and businesses or you did not. For African Americans, it was literally a black-and-white issue.

In the six weeks leading up to the Republican National Convention, Pennsylvania governor William Scranton, the Hamlet of the GOP, finally announced his candidacy, declaring the party could not allow "an exclusion-minded minority [to] dominate our platform and choose our candidates."[75]

But his fruitless challenge served only to divide Republicans and gave Democrats the theme of extremism they would use so effectively in the fall.[76] For its part, the Republican establishment thought it could employ the same bully-boy tactics it had in the past and retain its hold on the party. It did not understand that 1964 was not a repeat of 1952. The Goldwater forces had accumulated their rich harvest of delegates as a result of a carefully planned, three-year-long grassroots campaign. They had not stolen them but earned them the old-fashioned way—one at a time. Nor was Goldwater a latter-day Taft. Republicans had respected Taft and thought he had earned the nomination for his many years of service to the party. But conservatives worshiped Goldwater. They were convinced that America, facing socialism, and the world, facing communism, urgently needed Barry Goldwater to stop the former and defeat the latter. As Clif White put it, "Our delegates were a brand-new breed. Nothing could shake them."[77]

When Eisenhower expressed his approval of the Republican platform, adding that if Goldwater campaigned on it, "I don't see how he can go far wrong," the by-now frantic anti-Goldwater cabal produced the "Scranton letter." Addressed to Goldwater and signed by Scranton (who neither saw nor personally signed it before its delivery), the twelve-hundred-word letter called the senator the leader of radical extremists and "Goldwaterism" a collection of "absurd and dangerous positions." The letter summarized the senator's positions as irresponsible, right-wing, extremist, racist, and a "crazy-quilt collection" that would be "soundly repudiated by the American people in November."[78]

The letter failed to shake the steady resolve of an overwhelming majority of the delegates at the 1964 Republican National Convention to nominate Barry Goldwater for president. But it did destroy any possibility of a Goldwater-Scranton ticket (preferred until the last moment by the senator), and it provided Democrats with a ready-made theme for the fall campaign. What Rockefeller had begun in New Hampshire, Theodore White wrote, Scranton finished in San Francisco: the "painting for the American people of a half-crazy leader indifferent to the needs of American society at home and eager to plunge the nation into war abroad."[79]

It also provoked Goldwater into delivering the most quoted and controversial acceptance speech in the history of national conventions. The Goldwater team decided to offer no olive branches to the liberals. They saw Goldwater's nomination as a historic break with the past, an opportunity to signal that conservatives intended to set "a new course in GOP national politics."[80] (The designated speechwriter was Harry Jaffa, a Lincoln scholar and professor of political science at Ohio State University, whose memorandum on extremism, written for the platform hearings, had impressed Goldwater.)[81]

In his speech, Goldwater borrowed from the Old Testament, warning the American people they had been following "false prophets" and exhorting them to return to "proven ways—not because they are old but because they are true." He stated that Americans "must, and we shall, set the tide running again in the cause of freedom."[82]

Eschewing specific policy proposals, Goldwater dedicated his campaign to two basic conservative ideas: (1) individual responsibility and constitutional government are the best guarantors of a free, dynamic society, and (2) peace is possible only through strength, vigilance, and the defeat of those who threaten it. Far more of an active internationalist than Taft, Goldwater argued that "we must look beyond the defense of freedom today to its extension tomorrow."[83]

The content of the speech was eloquent and often moving, but the speaker's tone was frequently harsh and accusing. In truth, Goldwater was still smarting from the Scranton letter and revealing his unhappiness at being a candidate.

As he neared the conclusion of his acceptance address, Goldwater called for a "focused" and "dedicated" Republicanism that rejected "unthinking and stupid labels." The next lines are underlined in the original text:

> I would remind you that extremism in the defense of liberty is no vice!
> And let me remind you also that moderation in the pursuit of justice is no virtue![84]

As conservatives roared their approval, liberals turned red in the face, moderates blanched, and a reporter blurted, "My God, he's going to run as Barry Goldwater."[85]

Indeed he was, knowing that he had as much chance of defeating President Johnson as Billy Graham had of being elected pope. The night before, Goldwater had been given a national survey by his own pollster showing LBJ leading him by nearly three to one, a margin that realistically no politician could be expected to reverse.

But regardless of the outcome in November, everyone now understood that control of the Republican party had passed to the conservatives.

Chapter 7

Landslide

PRESIDENT JOHNSON WAS DETERMINED TO DO WHATEVER WAS NECESSARY to win by "the largest landslide in history."[1] For him, extremism in the pursuit of the presidency was no vice.

Johnson filled his speeches with warnings about the danger of voting for an extremist. He played on the public's fear of nuclear war. He contrasted Goldwater's "intention" to eliminate social security, TVA, and other federal programs with his own commitment to a Great Society in which every American, particularly the underprivileged, would have "a larger share of the growing pie."[2]

He directed his aide Bill Moyers to "remind people of what Barry Goldwater was before he was nominated for president" and began trying to shed "the extremism that surrounded him all of his career."[3] Moyers passed the word to the Democrats' advertising agency, Doyle Dane Bernbach, which disgorged one of the most effective and negative ad campaigns in national politics.

The most controversial ad was the "Daisy" commercial which, slyly, did not mention Goldwater by name or quote anything he ever said.

A little girl standing in a field is picking petals from a daisy when suddenly an ominous voice starts counting down from ten to zero. At "zero," the camera dissolves from the pupil of the child's eye to the mushroom cloud of an exploding atomic bomb. Johnson's voice says solemnly, "These are the stakes—to make a world in which all of God's children can live, or to go into the dark. We must either love each other, or we must die." An announcer repeats the words that appear in white on a black screen, "Vote for President Johnson on November 3. The stakes are too high for you to stay home."[4]

In any other election, these apocalyptic tones might have invoked disbelief or even laughter, but by the fall of 1964, as a result of the unremitting political attacks and the anti-Goldwater bias of the mass media, millions of Americans believed that a President Goldwater would actually bring about a nuclear holocaust.

The Daisy commercial was aired only once, on September 7 during *Monday Night at the Movies,* but once was enough. The White House switchboard was clogged with calls, and Johnson telephoned Moyers to ask excitedly, "Jesus Christ, what in the world happened?" Moyers replied, "You got your point across, that's what." After a pause, a pleased president said, "Well, I guess it did what we goddamned set out to do, didn't it?"[5]

Outraged, Dean Burch filed a complaint with the Fair Campaign Practices Committee and called on Johnson "to halt this smear attack on a United States senator and the candidate of the Republican party for the presidency." To help the electorate understand the reason for the furor, every network news program showed the Daisy ad over and over, transforming it into the most discussed political commercial of the year.[6]

But the Democratic campaign to vilify Goldwater and conservatism had just begun. The same week, viewers of *Saturday Night at the Movies* were treated to an ad featuring a young girl licking an ice cream cone. It turned out that she too was threatened, not by an atomic bomb, but by strontium 90, a radioactive poison. A woman announcer revealed that such poisons had "started to go away" as a result of the nuclear test ban treaty. But Barry Goldwater, she said, "wants to go on testing more bombs" and, the implication was clear, to put poison in little girls' ice cream cones. The ad ended with an authoritative male voice proclaiming, "Vote for President Johnson on November 3. The stakes are too high for you to stay at home."[7]

Like the Daisy spot, the Ice Cream Cone spot appeared only once on network television, but as Moyers later proudly proclaimed, the two Democratic commercials "hung the nuclear noose around Goldwater and finished him off."[8]

A third attack commercial that appeared in September became the most heavily aired Democratic television spot of the campaign. The video showed a pair of large masculine hands going through a stack of photos, IDs, and cards until it reached a social security card. The hands (implicitly Goldwater's) ripped the card in two and dropped the pieces on the table. The announcer said, "President Johnson is working to strengthen Social Security. Vote for him on November 3." The White House also produced a radio commercial that shattered the truth-in-advertising record by asserting, "Barry Goldwater's plan means the end of Social Security, the end of widows' pensions, the end of the dignity that comes with being able to take care of yourself without depending on your children. On November 3, vote for keeping Social Security."[9]

In response to what he called "electronic dirt," Goldwater used every possible medium to assert that, far from wrecking the system, he had voted for every social security measure that had ever come before the Senate. He persuaded Senator Margaret Chase Smith, the fiercely independent Republican from Maine, to attest in a television spot that he had consistently supported social security. The Sunday before election day, full-page ads describing Goldwater's pro–social security position appeared in major papers across the country.

None of it made any difference. Millions of voters, particularly senior citizens and union members, held to their conviction that Goldwater "was a foe of the Social Security system." During the primaries, liberal Republicans had created a cruel caricature, and Democrats reproduced it in every available medium, spurred on by a megalomaniacal president who wanted, he said, to make John F. Kennedy's 118,000 vote victory in 1960 look "like a pathetic peep."[10]

The political impact of the anti-Goldwater campaign continues to this day. Republicans must tread softly in any discussion of social security reform because the minds of so many Americans still retain the image of a social security card being torn in half by the hands of a Republican presidential nominee.

Despite the dispiriting polls, the vicious commercials, and the disdainful conduct of Republican leaders like George Romney and Nelson Rockefeller (who ostentatiously pocketed Goldwater buttons when given them), the senator campaigned aggressively in September, offering his alliterative message of "peace through preparedness, progress through freedom, and purpose through constitutional order." In Chicago, at the annual meeting of the American Political Science Association, he praised the American system of federalism but warned that it was endangered by the Democrats' doctrine that the Constitution meant only "what those who hold power for the moment choose to say that it means."[11]

Wherever he went, Goldwater presented an unabashedly conservative program for America—proposing, for example, a system of unconditional state grants of federal aid rather than the existing programmatic grants; defending the rights of citizens first and criminals second; attacking Secretary of Defense Robert S. McNamara for his conflicting reports about the Vietnam War; advocating education tax credits. For the first time in decades, a presidential candidate was directly challenging the basic premises of the welfare state. As historian Theodore White perceptively wrote, "Here was no ordinary politician pitching for votes; he was on a crusade to free America from [governmental] enslavement."[12]

Although the crowds for Goldwater were large and enthusiastic, the Gallup and other polls still placed the senator only in the low thirties, far below the 45 percent he had once set as a minimum goal. Before Dallas, he had been confident that he could appeal to what he called the Forgotten American, "the man who pays taxes, the man who works, the man who stays out of trouble," and enlist him in his crusade for freedom at home and abroad. Instead, Goldwater ended up running against the cruelly false image of himself created by Republicans in the primaries and magnified by Democrats in the general election. Symptomatic of his problems was how his official theme, "In Your Heart, You Know He's Right," was reversed by opponents to read, "In Your Guts, You Know He's Nuts."

As the days dwindled down, Goldwater resigned himself to a landslide defeat. One reporter described the mood of his campaign plane as "a jolly wake." But to the last, he remained an Old Testament prophet, warning the people to repent and change their ways and at the same time urging the government to let the American people go.

And he continued to offer his vision of a conservative America, "prosperous, free, secure, and progressive" through "the free enterprise and individual liberty upon which this nation was founded." Long ago, he warned, a great, self-governing people had given up their liberty and placed themselves in the hands of their leader, trading their votes for "bread and circuses." The Romans, he said, "lost their nation when they traded away their freedom." He reminded his audiences that there was one freedom, and only one freedom, on which America had been founded: "freedom from government—

from too much, oppressive government."[13] It was to preserve that freedom that he was offering his candidacy.

Goldwater took presidential politics into unexplored waters, listing those people whose votes he did not want. He told an Illinois audience he did not want "the lazy, dole-happy people who want to feed on the fruits of somebody's else labor" or those "who don't care if the Social Security system goes bankrupt as long as it keeps making more and more unkeepable promises" or those "who are willing to believe that communism can be accommodated."[14]

Instead, he sought the support of those Americans who believed in the Declaration of Independence and the Constitution, who rejected promises of something for nothing, whose votes could not be bought. Above all, he wanted the votes of those who knew that "*something must be done*" about an America in which the federal government "will tell you what business you can be in," whether your children can pray in school, and what to charge "for the things you sell." When he snapped, "Let's get our country back!" the faithful cheered, the band played one more chorus of "The Battle Hymn of the Republic," and the journalists began writing the political obituary of Barry Goldwater.

They noted that Goldwater kept doing the unexpected on the campaign trail. They were certain he would discuss cotton and other subsidies in the South, reassure the elderly about social security in Florida, and clarify his stand on TVA in Tennessee. Instead, in Winston-Salem, North Carolina, Goldwater attacked Defense Secretary McNamara and the administration's policy in South Vietnam and never mentioned cotton, peanuts, or tobacco. In St. Petersburg, Florida, he spoke of the rising crime rate, terror in the streets, and the evils of Medicare but uttered not one word about social security. In Knoxville, Tennessee, he appealed for Democratic votes but ignored TVA.

In Texas, he informed his listeners that the TFX airplane contract was "politically motivated" and should have gone to Boeing in Seattle, Washington, because it made a better plane. And at the annual plowing contest in Fargo, North Dakota, Goldwater condemned the Johnson administration's farm program, especially farm subsidies, although he added, "I have no intention of stopping supports overnight."[15] The crowd of 250,000 farmers was so still you could hear the grass growing.

Journalists speculated that such a seemingly perverse strategy must have been devised by rank political amateurs within the campaign. But when Robert Mardian, an old personal friend of the senator, attempted to bring up the subject with Goldwater, the candidate gripped his arm tightly with one of his large hands and said, "You go back and tell your crowd that I'm going to lose this election. I'm probably going to lose it real big. But I'm going to lose my way."[16]

Convinced of Goldwater's certain defeat but concerned about a demoralization of the conservative movement that might ensue, Bill Buckley gave two unusual campaign speeches that fall: one at the annual convention of Young Americans for Freedom in September and the other at the anniversary dinner of the New York Conservative party in mid-October.

YAF leaders wanted to fire up their members for the campaign, but Buckley chose instead to talk about Goldwater's "impending defeat." As students openly wept, Buckley explained that Goldwater's election would "presuppose a sea change in American public opinion" but that the tide was still going in the other direction. The "point" of the campaign, he insisted, was not to gain victory on November 3 but to "win recruits" for "future Novembers."[17] YAF officials were so stunned they did not publish Buckley's address until after the election, but some of them got the message and began laying plans for the future. One important result was the formation of the American Conservative Union less than four weeks after Goldwater's defeat.

At the Conservative party dinner, Buckley hardly mentioned Goldwater but devoted himself to discussing conservatism's future. He confessed his surprise that the conservative movement, confronted as it was by "the contrary tug of history," had advanced as far as it had. But, he said, there was in America a growing "spirit of resistance" to the twentieth century and the fruits of liberalism. The challenge for conservative politics, he argued, was to "mediate between the ideal and the prudential."[18] Coming just two weeks before Goldwater's crushing defeat, any role for conservative politics seemed problematic, but the question of how best to balance the ideal and the prudential would preoccupy conservative leaders for the next thirty years.

The idiosyncratic nature of the Goldwater campaign produced peculiar results like the attempt to cancel what the senator himself called "the best speech of the campaign"—Ronald Reagan's televised address, "A Time for Choosing."

Goldwater and Reagan had known each other since the early 1950s when the film actor had begun visiting his wife Nancy's parents in Phoenix, but they had never been close friends. They shared a passionate love of country and freedom and a no less fervent anticommunism, but their backgrounds, interests, and personalities were strikingly different.

Goldwater's early life was one of privilege; his father was a millionaire. Reagan grew up just this side of poverty; his father was a shoe clerk. Goldwater was outspoken and rebellious, an individualist by instinct. Reagan was thoughtful and reflective, a team player. Reagan wanted others to like him. Goldwater did not care whether they did.

Goldwater worked his way up the political ladder from city council member, to U.S. senator, to presidential candidate. Reagan's only elected office had been as president of the Screen Actors Guild. Goldwater was always a Jeffersonian Republican. Reagan was an FDR Democrat turned conservative Republican.

Despite their personal differences, Reagan admired Goldwater's championing of conservatism and willingly campaigned for him in 1964, speaking at many fund-raising events, mostly in California. In early fall, after one such appearance, several prominent California Republicans asked Reagan whether he would repeat his remarks on national television. "Sure," Reagan replied, "if you think it would do any good." The money was soon raised for a half-hour on NBC, and Reagan filmed his speech, essentially the one he had given from 1954 to 1962 as a spokesman for General Electric.[19]

But two days before the program was to air—on Tuesday, October 27, one week before election day—an "uncomfortable" Goldwater telephoned a puzzled Reagan. Some of his advisers, said the senator, were worried about references in Reagan's address to social security. They wanted to broadcast a different program.

"Barry," Reagan reassured his fellow conservative, "I've been making the speech all over [California] for quite a while and I have to tell you, it's been well received, including whatever remarks I've made about Social Security."

"Well," Goldwater said, "I haven't heard or seen the speech yet. They've got a tape here, so I'll run it and call you back."

After the senator listened to an audiotape (they did not have a filmed version), he looked at everybody and asked, "What the hell's wrong with that?" Reagan's remarks about social security were in fact very close to Goldwater's long-held position, including his suggestion of a voluntary option. Goldwater immediately called Reagan and gave his approval for the thirty-minute speech.[20]

But a persistent William Baroody kept trying to derail the program until three hours before airtime on the evening of October 27 when Walter Knott, chairman of the Goldwater TV Committee, called from California and informed Baroody that he would approve funds only for the Reagan telecast. Reluctantly, Baroody gave the go-ahead for the television program that made political history.[21]

America had come, Reagan argued, to "a time for choosing" between free enterprise and big government—between individual liberty and "the ant heap of totalitarianism." Borrowing language from the Democratic president for whom he had cast his first vote, he concluded:

> You and I have a rendezvous with destiny. We can preserve for our children this the last best hope of man on earth or we can sentence them to take the first step into a thousand years of darkness. If we fail, at least let our children and our children's children say of us we justified our brief moment here. We did all that could be done.[22]

Political analysts David Broder and Stephen Hess called the Reagan speech "the most successful national political debut since William Jennings Bryan electrified the 1896 Democratic convention." Businessman Henry Salvatori said that he and other leading Republicans would not have approached Reagan to run for governor of California had it not been for "A Time for Choosing."[23] It raised several million dollars from constant rebroadcasts in the following week and switched tens of thousands of votes.

But according to Nancy Reagan, Goldwater never wrote her husband a thank-you note for his remarkable speech. Apparently, for one of the few times in his life, Goldwater displayed jealousy, especially when some conservatives, after seeing Reagan on television, suggested that maybe the wrong conservative had been nominated.[24]

On November 3, 1964, President Johnson got his landslide, receiving more than 43 million votes to Goldwater's 27 million. That was more than 61 percent of the popular vote and topped the record set by Franklin Roosevelt in 1936. The president carried forty-four states, for a total of 486 electoral votes. Goldwater won just six states: Alabama, Georgia, Mississippi, Louisiana, South Carolina, and his own Arizona.

Johnson's victory was overwhelming in every region (except the Deep South) and every voting bloc (except among Republicans, and even 20 percent of them defected to LBJ). Republicans lost two seats in the Senate, thirty-seven in the House of Representatives, and 541 in the state legislatures. They added one governor. Of the fifty-four Republican congressmen who had endorsed Goldwater before the convention and then had run for reelection, twenty were defeated.

The biggest winner in the GOP was Richard Nixon, who campaigned hard for Goldwater and defended him after the election, referring to "constant sniping from the rear" and "defectors within his own ranks." Goldwater was so grateful for Nixon's unqualified support that in early 1965 he all but endorsed him for the 1968 nomination.[25]

Liberal commentators quickly and almost unanimously declared that the conservative movement was dead. Columnist Walter Lippmann opined that "the Johnson majority is indisputable proof that the voters are in the center." The *New York Times*'s Tom Wicker wrote that Republicans could win only as a "me-too" party. Richard Rovere argued in *Commentary* that "the election had finished the Goldwater school of political reaction." *Time* declared the conservatives' defeat "was so complete that they will not have another shot at party domination for some time to come." NBC's Chet Huntley dismissed Goldwater voters as "segregationists, Johnson-phobes, desperate conservatives, and radical nuts." And James Reston, Washington bureau chief for the *New York Times,* concluded that "Barry Goldwater not only lost the presidential election yesterday but the conservative cause as well."[26]

Conservatives forcefully disagreed. "A party that polls over 25 million votes," said former Senator Bill Knowland, "is neither bankrupt nor on its deathbed." Two future U.S. presidents seconded that sentiment in *National Review.* Ronald Reagan wrote, "The landslide majority did not vote against the conservative philosophy, they voted against a false image our liberal opponents successfully mounted." George Bush, beaten in his run for a U.S. Senate seat from Texas, urged Republicans to "repackage our philosophy, emphasize the positive, eliminate the negative, warn of the dangers from the Left but do so without questioning the patriotism of those who hold liberal views."[27]

National Review's resilient Frank Meyer pointed out that despite the liberal campaign to make conservatism seem "extremist, radical, nihilist, anarchic," two-fifths of the voters still voted for the conservative alternative. In fact, Meyer insisted, "conservatives stand today nearer to victory than they ever have since Franklin Roosevelt."[28]

Human Events concluded that the Goldwater campaign had accomplished three critical things: "The Republican party is essentially conservative; the South is developing into a major pivot of its power; and a candidate who possesses Goldwater's virtues but lacks some of his handicaps can win the presidency."[29]

It needs to be stressed that no Republican could have defeated Johnson after the assassination of John Kennedy. Denied Camelot, the American people wanted to give the new president a chance to carry out the martyred president's programs. As Bill Buckley wrote, "The Archangel Gabriel running on the Republican ticket probably could not [have won]."[30]

The Johnson White House and the Democrats conducted a highly effective and focused campaign; the inexperienced Goldwater organization did not. Goldwater was always on the defensive, Johnson on the offensive. Determined to stick to principles rather than what he called "personalities," Goldwater ran a nonpolitical campaign against one of the most political candidates in presidential politics.

And unlike 1952, when Taft conservatives supported Eisenhower after losing the nomination, GOP liberals did not unite behind Goldwater. Indeed, they went out of their way not to help the party's nominee. In New York, Goldwater literature was left unpacked and undistributed.[31] The media bias against Goldwater was extensive and conceded, even by the *Washington Post*'s David Broder and the *New York Times*'s James Reston. Ben Bradlee, then Washington bureau chief of *Newsweek* and later executive editor of the *Washington Post*, admitted that "we didn't do justice to Goldwater's run for the presidency."[32]

Perhaps most important, Americans were not yet ready to concede that the New Deal and all the succeeding Democratic "deals" were essentially flawed approaches to government and society. The premise that government could solve just about any problem seemed reasonable in 1964. Years would pass and many billions of dollars would be spent before the Great Society and its utopian ideas would be exposed as failures by social scientist Charles Murray and other scholars.[33]

One of the few liberals who understood that Goldwater was not just another also-ran was historian Theodore White. He wrote that "again
and again in American history it has happened that the losers of the presidency contributed almost as much to the permanent tone and dialogue of
politics as did the winners."[34]

What was so special about Barry Goldwater? He was the first presidential nominee to run openly as a conservative. He was not so much the nominee of a political party as the personification of a political movement.

He was the most important loser in modern presidential politics. His
impact on every important aspect of politics was profound and permanent—
or at least as permanent as anything can be in the world of politics.

With his grassroots appeal, Goldwater helped the Republican party to
broaden its financial base by a factor of thirty to one. Back in 1960, there
were between 40,000 and 50,000 individual contributors to the Nixon campaign. In 1964, the number was estimated to be more than 650,000, nearly
half in response to various television programs, especially the Reagan telecast. Only 28 percent of the Republicans' income, as compared to the Democrats' 69 percent, came in donations of $500 or more.[35] The Goldwater
candidacy gave the Republican party broad-based financial independence
for the first time in its history.

Politics is people, and the Goldwater campaign mobilized unprecedented numbers of volunteer workers. An army of almost 4 million men and
women distributed literature and canvassed neighborhoods, contacting more
than 12 million households. Thousands of young people entered—and
stayed in—politics because of Barry Goldwater. They loved his independence: he would "not be hogtied by anything—not even the conservative
movement."[36]

Today, those young conservatives sit in Congress and on the Supreme
Court, manage campaigns and raise millions of dollars, head think tanks and
write seminal books, edit magazines and run television networks. They include senators, congressmen, Supreme Court justices, and presidential candidates.

Moreover, Goldwater's 1964 campaign built the electoral foundation for
the Reagan-Bush presidential triumphs of the 1980s and the Republican
congressional victories of the 1990s. Former senator William Brock of Tennessee described 1964 as "the salvation of conservatism" because it broke the
hold of the Democrats on the heretofore "Solid South."[37] The Goldwater

campaign also produced significant shifts in the North toward conservatism, particularly among ethnic Catholics. Among Irish and Italian voters in the New York City boroughs of Queens, the Bronx, and Staten Island, Goldwater's support exceeded the vote that Nixon had received in 1960. When social issues like abortion became more intense in the 1970s, a growing number of "Goldwater-Reagan Democrats" helped shift the political balance to the GOP in 1980 and beyond.[38]

Furthermore, rather than setting a "liberal tone" for American politics for a decade and a half, as neoconservative Irving Kristol later charged, the 1964 campaign articulated the major issues—limited government, law and order, and anticommunism—that conservative Republicans used to win election after election starting just two years later.[39] In 1966, Republicans elected forty-six new members to the House of Representatives, most of them Goldwater conservatives, many from the South.

In short, Goldwater addressed in a serious and substantive way the issues that have dominated the national debate for three decades: social security, government subsidies, privatization, law and order, morality in government, and communism. Campaign strategist John Sears argued that Goldwater changed "the rhetoric of politics" by challenging the principles of the New Deal, "something no Democrat or Republican before him had dared to do."[40]

Even on the Left, there were those who strongly disputed the Lippmann-Rovere-Reston thesis that conservatism was dead. In the *Nation*, Hollywood Ten alumnus Dalton Trumbo declared that the Goldwater campaign was "the greatest victory [conservatives] had ever seen." Never before, he pointed out, had "a candidate of the right been so attractive, or aroused such profound devotion." Far from being interred, he lamented, the conservative movement was exhibiting "vigor and variety and burgeoning health."[41] Liberal editor David Danzig concurred, writing in *Commentary* that the Goldwater campaign was a "turning point" in American politics. Conservatives, he said, "have become for the first time an identifiable bloc with demands to make on the *national* scene."[42]

Among the new post-1964 members of this conservative "bloc" were the American Conservative Union, a lobbying organization; the Free Society Association, a think tank; the Conservative Book Club and Arlington House, a publishing house; and the Philadelphia Society, an organization of conservative intellectuals. Reflecting conservatism's growing national character, several of these new organizations were based outside Washington,

D.C. And then there were the foundations that through their funding programs helped create the intellectual climate that made possible, as one foundation official put it, "the first conservative campaign of modern times for the presidency of the United States."[43]

Although the Olin, Bradley, and Scaife foundations are better known and have greater resources, the first, and in many ways the most effective, conservative foundation has been the Relm Foundation (later renamed the Earhart Foundation) of Ann Arbor, Michigan. Indeed, in the 1950s, according to conservative scholar Stephen J. Tonsor, Relm-Earhart together with the Volker Fund were "nearly alone in their patronage of the conservative movement."[44]

Among those supported by Relm-Earhart over the decades were six Nobel laureates in economics: F. A. Hayek, Milton Friedman, George S. Stigler, James M. Buchanan, Ronald H. Coase, and Gary Becker. Starting in the early 1950s, over twenty-five hundred graduate students have received assistance from the foundation as H. B. Earhart fellows. And in 1964, the Relm Foundation joined the Intercollegiate Studies Institute in creating the Richard M. Weaver Fellowships, of which well over three hundred have been awarded. One of those who received an Earhart fellowship in 1960 was Thomas Sowell, today the most influential conservative black intellectual in America.

When Richard Ware retired as president of the Earhart Foundation in 1985, Sowell wrote to him that the foundation's support had made "the difference between my finishing and not finishing my graduate work." In a larger context, added Sowell, Earhart was one of the few institutions "that helped keep alive certain kinds of scholarship that might otherwise have been buried under the prevailing academic orthodoxy and intolerance." In so acting, the foundation "rendered a service not simply to individual scholars but to the nation."[45]

There were several political milestones in the first twenty years of the modern conservative movement: the passage of the Taft-Hartley Act in 1947, the conviction of Alger Hiss in 1950, the defeat of Robert Taft at the 1952 Republican convention, the censure of Joseph McCarthy in December 1954, the founding of *National Review* in 1955, the Soviet crushing of the Hungarian Revolution in 1956, the birth of Young Americans for Freedom in 1960, the building of the Berlin Wall in 1961, the debate over the Civil

Rights Act of 1964. But in lasting political impact, none equals Barry Gold-water's seemingly quixotic run for the White House in 1964. It was, as Patrick Buchanan said, "like a first love" for countless young men and women, never to be forgotten, always to be cherished. It was a beginning rather than an end of conservatism's political ascendancy.[46]

Certainly no other modern politician has been so quickly and completely vindicated. Dismissed as "psychologically unfit" to be president by one publication, Goldwater was overwhelmingly reelected to the U.S. Senate in 1968, while the president who had buried him beneath a historic landslide refused to seek reelection.[47] The major reasons were the disastrous war in Vietnam and the ballooning costs and mixed results of the vainglorious Great Society. Conservatives' feelings were summed up in a giant billboard along the Eisenhower Expressway in Chicago. In the fall of 1964, it read, "In Your Heart, You Know He's Right." For the next eighteen months, it read, "In Time, You Will Know He Was Right." Just before the 1966 elections, it read, "Now You *Know* He Was Right."[48]

Although friends say he was not embittered about 1964, Goldwater never again entertained any idea of running for president, and no one ever tried again to draft him. He happily returned to the Senate in 1968, where he served for the next eighteen years, capping his career in 1986 with his sponsorship of the Goldwater-Nichols Act, which reorganized the Pentagon. Democratic senator Sam Nunn described that legislation as "the most important [military] reform that has occurred since World War II." Six years later, General Colin Powell, then chairman of the Joint Chiefs of Staff, warmly thanked Goldwater for his bill, which helped the United States win the Persian Gulf War in such spectacular fashion.[49]

From his seat in the Senate, Goldwater watched warily, much like an older brother who is not certain that his younger brother is quite ready to take over the family business, as the leadership of the conservative movement passed from him to the man with the golden voice, the warm smile, and a carefully concealed but driving ambition: Ronald Reagan.

Chapter 8

The Citizen Politician

CALIFORNIA IS THE LAST STOP ON THE TREK WEST THAT HAS SHAPED America since discovery. It is truly the Golden State, a place of astonishing beauty, with ocean-lapped beaches, scorching deserts, and snow-capped mountains. It is not only El Dorado, where you seemingly can make your fortune in gold, oil, automobiles, or movies, but Utopia, where seemingly you can be whatever you want to be. The California dream, like the American dream, is founded on freedom. "The customs of California are free," wrote Richard Henry Dana in *Two Years Before the Mast* almost 160 years ago.[1] But times and customs can change.

California in 1965 had a growing economy, a rapidly growing population, and a very rapidly growing budget. If it had been a nation, California's economy would have ranked fifth among Western industrialized nations, behind only the United States, Great Britain, West Germany, and France. Each year, tens of thousands of newcomers flowed across its borders, drawn by its climate, its vitality, and its generosity.

For a quarter of a century, California had been governed by liberal politicians—Republicans Earl Warren and Goodwin Knight, Democrat Edmund "Pat" Brown—who believed that the state was rich enough to pay for a seemingly endless variety of services: parks, welfare, medical aid, unemployment compensation. Need a new highway? Raise gasoline taxes. Running short of water? Build a storage dam that "dwarfed the pyramids" and a water aqueduct that ran almost the length of the state. Governor Brown once

142

boasted that what the Johnson administration called the Great Society, "we just call . . . California."[2]

Ronald Reagan did not want to slow the state's economy, and he was not concerned about the newcomers—he was one himself. But he took a far different view about government spending from that taken by the incumbent governor and his predecessors. Reagan believed that governments, like people, should not spend more than they take in and they should not take in more than was absolutely necessary. He would never forget how, as a movie star in the late 1940s, he had found himself in the 91 percent tax bracket. Why bother to work, he had wondered, if ninety-one cents of every extra dollar he earned went to the government?

Reagan represented the new Republicans—the suburbanites, young managers, and professionals who had done well and wanted to preserve what they had earned. And he reflected the views of the old Democrats—the well-paid blue-collar workers who had joined the middle class and wanted to stay there.

In Washington, LBJ was still basking in the warmth of his historic win over Barry Goldwater and preparing to implement the Great Society. Liberals were busy writing obituaries about American conservatism. But in California, a man who had never run for public office was preparing to offer the people a different kind of society: a "creative society" that would reduce the size and burden of government and make the man in the street feel that he could make a difference in what was going on around him. The Creative Society, Reagan would explain, is "a return to the people of the privilege of self-government, as well as a pledge for more efficient self-government."[3]

In late February 1965, a group of influential California Republicans called on Ronald Reagan at his home in Pacific Palisades overlooking Los Angeles. All were conservatives, all had raised millions of dollars for the GOP, and all were tired of losing to Democrats. They told Reagan that he was the only person around whom Republicans could rally in the 1966 gubernatorial race. They were convinced he could defeat Governor Brown. They urged him to travel around the state, find out for himself whether he was acceptable to the party and the people, "and if you are, please, *run*."[4]

Reagan was skeptical. Nearly twenty years earlier, in the late 1940s, he had rejected a suggestion by Democrats that he seek a seat in the House of

Representatives. Later, he had turned down pleas from Republicans to run for the U.S. Senate in 1962 and again in 1964. But his old Hollywood friend George Murphy had said yes, had proceeded to defeat Democrat Pierre Salinger, and was now in Washington. Reagan had always campaigned for someone else, but now many people, including those whom he respected, were insisting that it was his turn.

"I'm an actor, not a politician," he protested.[5] But he readily admitted that the public reaction to his national telecast for Barry Goldwater had exceeded anything in his movie or television career. The title of his 1963 autobiography (borrowed from his dramatic hospital bed scene in the highly regarded film *King's Row*) was *Where's the Rest of Me?* Was it possible, the fifty-four-year-old actor reflected, that he would find the answer in politics?

In several important ways, Reagan was an ideal candidate for California. He had unquestioned charm and voter appeal. As one Los Angeles magazine stated, "He is one of the rare men whom other men can stomach even while large groups of women are adoring him."[6] He lived in the more populous southern half of the state (nearly 40 percent of the electorate was located in the greater Los Angeles area). He was assured of substantial financial backing from many wealthy Republicans who shared his views.

And he had a ready-made organization: the thousands of dedicated conservatives who had worked for Goldwater in the primary and general elections the year before. As a former Democrat, he would be able to appeal across partisan lines in a state where party loyalty had always been weak. He was an acknowledged master of television, a vital medium in a state with an 840-mile coastline. And according to polls, he was already known to 97 percent of the California electorate.[7]

Finally, Reagan made a deal with the governor makers: if they would underwrite his speaking engagements and travel for six months, he would use the time to find out for himself whether the people—ordinary people, not Republican partisans—really wanted him to run for governor of California. On the last day of 1965, he would tell them whether he would be a candidate. They immediately agreed and hired the best political campaign team in the state—Stuart Spencer and William Roberts—to manage Reagan's unusual journey into the mind of the California electorate. Most politicians are convinced that the people need them desperately; Reagan had to be persuaded that he could help them.

While Reagan was making up his mind whether to run for governor of the second most populous state in the Union, another conservative was mulling over whether to run for mayor of the biggest and most liberal city in America.

There were, in fact, several reasons why William F. Buckley, Jr., was eyeing the New York City mayoralty. First, he wanted to help block the rapid political rise of Congressman John Lindsay, the golden boy of liberal Republicans who planned to move their man up the political ladder from congressman, to mayor, to governor, to president of the United States. That was a prospect devoutly to be resisted by all right-thinking Americans.

Second, the conservative movement could use a political boost after the Goldwater defeat, and a good showing by a conservative candidate in the citadel of liberaldom would do just that.

Third, Buckley had some ideas about the prudential conduct of a large city's affairs (borrowed in part from the Harvard sociologists Daniel Patrick Moynihan and Nathan Glazer) that merited serious public consideration. And where better to do that than in New York City, headquarters of the nation's media?

Finally, running for mayor of New York would be fun and anything but boring, the one thing on God's earth that Bill Buckley could not abide. And he knew he would get a book out of the experience.

Although he insisted at the time and in his witty account of his campaign, *The Unmaking of a Mayor,* that the conservative movement was not a factor in his decision to run, Buckley was being either uncharacteristically disingenuous or unbelievably naive. In the year 1965, you could no more separate Buckley and American conservatism than you could uncouple the pope and Roman Catholicism. Inevitably, Buckley's showing in New York's mayoral race would strengthen or weaken the movement when, following the sinking of the good ship Goldwater the previous November, it was at its most vulnerable.

But first he wanted to prevent John Lindsay from becoming the Republican party's future presidential candidate. Buckley was so adamantly opposed to Lindsay because the New York City congressman was a Republican in name only. Indeed, based on his political pronouncements, Buckley argued, Lindsay was to the "left of the center of the Democratic Party." Far from "revitalizing" the Republican party, as his supporters insisted, Lindsay's election would damage the two-party system and contribute to "the disintegration of New York City."[8]

In early June (and not yet a candidate), Buckley wrote a column jocularly titled "Mayor, Anyone?" that set forth a ten-point platform on which a candidate might run. What strikes one on reading it is how libertarian it is.

Buckley recommended that "anti-narcotic laws for adults" be repealed, gambling be legalized, anyone without a police record be allowed to operate a car as a taxi, and communities be encouraged to finance their own "watchmen," relieving the municipal police force of what he called "an almost impossible job."[9]

He also displayed some impressive prescience. He anticipated the enterprise zone proposal of a decade later by suggesting that state and federal authorities suspend property and income taxes for all "Negro or Puerto Rican entrepreneurs" who established businesses in depressed areas in the inner cities. And he proposed, several years before Governor Reagan offered his hard-nosed welfare reform program in California, that all welfare recipients be required to do "street cleaning and general prettification work" for the city. Here, albeit in a rather crude way, was the first conservative enunciation of the workfare principle or, as Buckley put it, "no workee, no dolee."[10]

Still asserting his nonsuitability (he was, among other things, a resident of Connecticut), Buckley tried and failed, despite the consumption of several bottles of excellent wine over a long evening, to convince his publisher, William A. Rusher, that he should carry the conservative standard that fall. Rusher was a brilliant political organizer and public debater but preferred the back room to the front line. He declined, firmly. The next morning, Buckley telephoned Conservative party chairman Dan Mahoney and asked "whether he wanted me as a candidate."[11] Mahoney immediately and enthusiastically signed up the best-known conservative in America, next to Barry Goldwater.

The *New York Times* was not impressed with Buckley's formal announcement on June 24, dismissing it as an "exercise in futility" and predicting that New York voters would reject Buckley's "kind of Republicanism" as decisively as the nation had repudiated "Goldwaterism" the previous November. Buckley quickly responded with a letter to the editor, listing the reforms for the city that the *Times* had not bothered to mention in its news story about his candidacy: an increase in the police force, lower taxes, workfare, a disavowal of those who "encourage racism, lawlessness, and despair" among blacks, decentralization of city schools, and a reduction of the urban renewal and city planning that were "dehumanizing" New York City.[12] (The parallels with the policies of President Reagan in the 1980s and those claimed by President Clinton in the 1990s are striking.)

As to "repudiation" by the electorate, Buckley concluded that while it was true that "only" 800,000 New Yorkers voted for Barry Goldwater, it was also true that New York continued "to be misgoverned. There may be," he added, "a cause-and-effect relationship here."[13]

A week later, Buckley delivered the most quoted line of the campaign, demonstrating yet again his defiance of political convention. "What would you do if you *were* elected?" a reporter asked. "Demand a recount," Buckley shot back.[14]

By mid-September, no one was dismissing the Buckley campaign, particularly the two other candidates, John Lindsay and Democrat Abe Beame. Lindsay took to picturing himself as "the alternative to Beame, bosses and Buckley." He suggested darkly that Buckley was the "creature" of a right-wing conspiracy whose axis ran "between Arizona and Connecticut."[15]

An alarmed Walter Lippmann accused Buckley of a "strong streak of fanaticism" and declared there was no "precedent in American politics for the kind of wrecking operation that Buckley is conducting." Buckley riposted: at least not since 1964 when Lindsay contributed to the wrecking of the Republican party by refusing to support Barry Goldwater, the Republican presidential nominee.[16]

The widely viewed television debates among the three candidates were devastating for Lindsay, revealing, it was widely acknowledged, his humorlessness, short temper, superficiality, and just plain dullness. Columnist Joseph Alsop, a doyen of the establishment, wrote reluctantly, "Lindsay has hardly proven that he is a man with the toughness, ingenuity, and vision to start a giant, near-bankrupt city on a wholly new course."[17] In contrast, the perpetually poised Buckley always seemed to come up with the right word. In one three-way debate, moderator Morton Dean advised the conservative candidate that he had "another moment if you care to comment," to which Buckley relied, "No, I think I'll just contemplate the great eloquence of my previous remarks."[18]

In between debates and other campaign rituals, Buckley stubbornly offered conservative solutions to societal problems. Borrowing from Moynihan's and Glazer's admirable book, *Beyond the Melting Pot,* he declared that black leaders should stop depending on government and "take on the responsibility of helping their own people." While admitting that the problems of blacks were in part "of our making," he also insisted that they were in part "the making of Negro demagogues and of the Negroes who tolerate them."[19] He advocated a one-year residence requirement for welfare recipients, supported the "neighborhood school system," and opposed a civilian review board that would hamper and harry the police.

In the end, an impressive 13.4 percent of the New York electorate (341,226 voters) voted for Bill Buckley while Lindsay eked out a narrow win, receiving 45.3 percent to Beame's 41.3 percent. Conservatives failed to defeat Lindsay, but they succeeded in their longer-range objective: to prevent the *New York Times* from writing something like "Lindsay's decisive victory catapulted him into a position of national leadership in the Republican Party and established him as a leading Presidential or Vice Presidential possibility in 1968 or 1972."

The Buckley campaign so energized the Conservative party of New York that only five years later, the party would be able to elect his brother, James Buckley, to the U.S. Senate. Buckley's mayoral effort also sketched the outlines of a winning coalition of ethnic, Catholic Democrats, and middle-class Republicans. In his landmark study *The Emerging Republican Majority*, Kevin Phillips cited Buckley's vote in New York's Catholic assembly districts as a "harbinger" of the new majority. As Buckley's biographer, John Judis, says, Buckley's coalition "perfectly anticipated" the northern urban coalition that Ronald Reagan created in 1980 and 1984, enabling him to carry New York City in those elections.[20]

Buckley, however, did not join in the general conservative jubilation over his showing. At the tenth anniversary dinner of *National Review* following the election, he was generous as always in his thanks to colleagues, friends, and supporters but lamented that it was impossible, given the ugly realities of the cold war and the Great Society, to avoid politics—"the preoccupation of the quarter-educated."

In *The Unmaking of a Mayor,* published a year later, he concluded that he could not be optimistic about the future. The conservative doctrine, he said, lacked "mass appeal." Conservatism in America was "a force" rather than "a political movement." The Republican party probably would not survive as "a major party." The New York campaign, he asserted, proved nothing. He greatly regretted the coming decline of the GOP, he said, because the alternative was likely to be "a congeries of third parties, adamantly doctrinaire, inadequately led, insufficiently thoughtful, improvidently angry, self-defeatingly sectarian."[21]

Buckley's lamentation was spectacularly ill timed. Even as he tore at his garments, a brilliant new political star was rising in the West, conservatives were organizing from New York to California, a new mode of political fund raising (direct mail) was emerging, and in the nation's capital an obscure conservative organization, the National Right to Work Committee, was preparing to deny President Johnson, the overwhelmingly Democratic Congress, and the powerful AFL-CIO a legislative victory they thought they had in the bag.

At Robert Taft's insistence, the 1947 Taft-Hartley Act had included section 14(b), authorizing state right-to-work laws, which affirm that no individual may be denied employment because he does or does not belong to a union. In other words, these laws protect the freedom to join a union and the freedom *not* to join a union, leaving the choice with the worker, not union leaders or company management.

Organized labor loathed the principle of right to work and, following Johnson's 1964 landslide victory, set the repeal of section 14(b) as its top legislative objective in the new Congress. In late July 1965, the House of Representatives voted to eliminate right to work from Taft-Hartley. The vote was surprisingly close—221 to 202—but jubilant union officials were confident that their dreams of repeal would be realized in the more liberal Senate.

The one possible impediment was a filibuster. And the only senator who could bring and keep together the conservative Republican–Southern Democrat coalition needed to sustain a filibuster was minority leader Everett McKinley Dirksen of Illinois, who was popular with many Southern Democrats. Under the leadership of Dirksen, a major sponsor of the 1964 Civil Rights Act, the filibuster could not be dismissed as another "Southern filibuster."[22]

Hugh Newton, information director for the National Right to Work Committee, recalled that at the initial meeting with Dirksen, the senator "was not optimistic" about waging a successful battle for section 14(b).[23] Although he had consistently supported the principle of right to work, Dirsken considered it an issue the general public cared little about. The Right to Work Committee knew that this was not true.

One week later, committee officials walked into Senator Dirksen's office with over three thousand pro–right-to-work editorials from fifteen hundred daily newspapers and a thousand weeklies. The newspapers ranged over the political spectrum from the *New York Times* and *Washington Post* to the *Richmond News-Leader* and *Los Angeles Times*. The editorials showed that the majority of Americans were opposed to compulsory unionism and repeal of section 14(b) and would support members of Congress who prevented repeal. "The change in Senator Dirksen's attitude was immediate," Newton recalled. And with his active leadership, "victory had become a definite possibility."[24]

The National Right to Work Committee concentrated on two objectives: to arouse public opinion at the grass roots, which would in turn influence members of Congress, and to provide sympathetic members of Congress with every possible assistance, especially key legislators who would lead the effort to retain section 14(b). Other important members of the right-to-work coalition were the U.S. Chamber of Commerce and the National Association of Manufacturers.

Both sides prepared for battle, and on October 4, 1965, the opening salvos were fired. Senator Wallace Bennett (R–Utah) used the fewest words with the most impact: "Good unions don't need repeal of Section 14(b), and bad unions don't deserve it."[25] One week later, Senate majority leader Mike Mansfield of Montana sought a two-thirds vote to shut off debate and was defeated, 47 to 45.

Talk continued for another two weeks until opponents of section 14(b) reluctantly conceded they did not have the votes and allowed the Senate to adjourn. They went home to try to figure out why they could not dispatch with ease so small a "David" as section 14(b). But the opposition to repeal was even stronger in the next session of Congress.

In January, when Mansfield announced that debate on section 14(b) would soon begin again, Dirksen swiftly replied, in his most Churchillian manner, "We will fight to the end. And there is no amicable compromise possible."[26] By now, other important factors were crystallizing for the right-to-work forces. President Johnson was not pushing as hard as he once had for repeal; he too could measure public opinion. Major strikes around the country, particularly the New York City transit strike, had aroused the public against union leaders and excessive union power. And union officials did not get their members to exert maximum pressure on their senators. This failure was due in large part to the union bosses themselves, who had been so confident of repeal that they had not laid the groundwork for any last-minute push.

On February 8, Mansfield moved again to cut off debate. His motion was decisively rejected by a vote of 51 to 48, far short of the required two-thirds. Two days later, the majority leader tried again to invoke cloture and was again rebuffed. By now, Mansfield had tired of trying to carry organized labor's water up an impossibly steep hill, and he put aside repeal of section 14(b) for the rest of the Eighty-ninth Congress. Since then, for more than thirty years, repeal of right to work has never been seriously attempted by any Congress.

In its campaign, the National Right to Work Committee followed certain basic guidelines that other conservative single-issue organizations would study and copy in succeeding decades: develop dedicated, articulate leadership; do not be distracted from your basic purpose; build a broad-based grassroots membership; and make a long-term commitment.

Among the specific tools the committee employed were establishing a workers' group, Union Members Against Compulsory Unionism; setting up a women's group, WORK—Women for Right to Work; distributing ten thousand information kits to key individuals; providing rapid-response research facilities for members of Congress; underwriting a national advertising program keyed to "doubtful" congressional districts; and holding a series of luncheon meetings with key congressional aides to exchange information and ideas.

No detail was overlooked, even calls of nature. In past filibusters, senators had relied upon "the motorman's friend" (a long tube attached to the waist and running down the inside of a pants leg) when they had to empty their bladder but could not leave the floor. Committee executive vice president Reed Larson was delegated to buy six of the devices at a medical supply house and turned them over to the Dirksen-led coalition. On the opening day of the filibuster, Senator Dirksen wore a "motorman's friend" as a joke but also as a sign of the right-to-work group's commitment. Observers in the galleries wondered why so many senators kept going up to the grinning Dirksen and slapping him so vigorously on the leg.[27]

The National Right to Work Committee's "impossible" victory over President Johnson, Congress, and the AFL-CIO was a defining moment in the history of the conservative movement and convincing proof that conservatism could be an effective political force in the nation's capital, even in the Age of Johnson.

That same year, a young, unknown conservative began experimenting with a new way to raise money and communicate ideas. Richard A. Viguerie was born on September 23, 1933, in Golden Acres, Texas, outside Houston. His parents, of Louisiana French descent, had moved to Texas the day after they were married in September 1929, just before the Great Depression came crashing down. His father started with Shell Oil as a construction worker and worked his way up to top management. His mother, who spoke only French until she started school, worked in a paper mill during World War II. "Our family was thrifty," says Viguerie; "no money was ever wasted."[28]

In college in the early 1950s, young Viguerie's heroes were the two "Macs"—Douglas MacArthur and Joseph McCarthy. "Even when he was inaccurate," Viguerie later wrote, "McCarthy articulated my concern about a very big problem. There *are* communists in this world."[29]

Active in local politics (he was Harris County campaign chairman for John Tower's first Senate try in 1960), Viguerie wanted, above all else, to work in Washington. In the summer of 1961, he answered a classified ad in *National Review* to work as a field man for Americans for Constitutional Action (ACA).

Viguerie flew from Houston to New York City at midnight to save money and arrived at the offices of *National Review* to discover that his interview was not for a field position with ACA but for executive secretary of Young Americans for Freedom. Viguerie knew something of the conservative youth group but had not been invited to its founding meeting the previous September because, as he put it, "none of the organizers had any reason to know who Richard Viguerie was."[30] The energetic, idealistic young Texan hit it off with members of YAF's board of directors and, more important, with conservative impresario Marvin Liebman.

For the next three years, Viguerie learned and practiced the craft of fund raising, particularly direct mail, under Liebman, who was conservatism's leading political organizer during the 1950s and 1960s. Among the major organizations that Liebman helped create and run were the Committee of One Million, Young Americans for Freedom, the American Conservative Union, and the World Youth Crusade for Freedom. He also filled Madison

Square Garden more often than the Ringling Brothers or Barnum and Bailey, and always for conservative causes.

Inspired by Liebman's example, Viguerie decided to start his own direct-mail company in Washington and opened his doors in January 1965 with one employee, less than $4,000 in the bank, and one tangible asset: the names of 12,500 conservative contributors. How he got the names reveals much about Viguerie and the state of the conservative movement in these early days.

Like other young conservatives, Viguerie was shocked by the magnitude of Goldwater's loss, but he saw a golden opportunity in the failed campaign that no one else recognized. He went to the office of the clerk of the House of Representatives, which had on file, as required by law, the names and addresses of all those who had given fifty dollars or more to the Goldwater campaign.

Viguerie copied down their names and addresses by hand "until my fingers were numb." It was then legal to copy such public records and use the names for advertising, but no photocopying was allowed. After two weeks, the finger-weary Viguerie hired several others to do the copying. He wound up with 12,500 conservative donors, the genesis of "my famous list, without which I wouldn't be in business today."[31] Nor, it must be added, would the many conservative groups and organizations that depend on direct mail for a significant part of their income.

At the time, direct mail was a new technique, and most politicians did not understand its potential. One of those who did was Democrat George McGovern, who called Viguerie to ask whether he would like to help him in his 1968 Senate race. The conservative fund raiser politely responded to the liberal candidate that they were "poles apart ideologically" and that he would be better off hiring someone "more akin with [your] philosophy."[32]

McGovern took Viguerie's advice and deepened his appreciation of the power of direct mail when he won in 1968. McGovern began telling liberal organizations and candidates that he wanted to help them raise money. He signed many fund-raising letters, asking for only the names and addresses of those who responded. As a result, when George McGovern announced in January 1971 for president, he had a resource no else had: a mailing list of tens of thousands of liberals who had contributed to left-wing candidates and causes, primarily to end the Vietnam War. Unquestionably, McGovern's long list of liberal donors helped him win the Democratic presidential nomination in 1972.

Viguerie became the king of direct mail. Over the next quarter of a century, he helped finance dozens of political candidates and as many conservative organizations; refined the use of letters as a means of informing and motivating people; trained young men and women in the art of direct mail, many of whom now head their own marketing companies; brought key conservatives together at countless breakfasts, luncheons, and dinners to advance conservatism and confound liberalism; and helped found the New Right. As he puts it, "I'm frustrated on any day when I haven't done something significant to help our country."[33]

Meanwhile, throughout much of 1965, Ronald Reagan was learning how he might help the state of California. He surprised many observers by soon displaying a solid knowledge of state issues. This was no accident. Spencer and Roberts had closeted Reagan with two academics, Dr. Stanley Plog of the University of California at Los Angeles and Dr. Kenneth Holden of San Fernando Valley State College, behavioral scientists who in their spare time ran a small research firm, the Behavior Sciences Corporation of Van Nuys. Plog and Holden set out to provide the prospective candidate with facts and figures that he could absorb and use in a speech or news conference. They did not try to reconstruct Reagan because they discovered that "Reagan knows who he is and what he stands for."[34]

Eventually, some eight briefing books were produced, covering topics from agriculture to redwoods to taxes to water. Reagan used them to write down key facts and phrases on cards, a technique he had developed during his years of speechmaking for General Electric. Reagan had little difficulty keeping up with the cramming. As Bill Roberts said, "Reagan has an extremely retentive mind and is a voracious reader."[35]

He was an unquestioned hit on the precampaign trail, captivating audiences from San Diego to Redding with his charm, his candor, and his intelligence. After every speech, people lined up to shake his hand and invariably asked, "Why don't you run for governor?" He soon realized it was no setup—they really *did* want him to run. When the six months were almost over, Reagan came home one night and asked his wife and closest adviser, Nancy, "How do you say no to all these people?"[36]

They knew that if he agreed, their life would change dramatically, probably forever. But he told Nancy, "I don't think we can run away from it."[37]

Reagan's words, reflecting a willingness to serve and set aside personal desires for a greater good, were remarkably similar to those of Barry Goldwater in December 1963 when he decided, following John Kennedy's assassination, to seek the Republican nomination for president. There was, of course, an enormous difference between the political circumstances facing the two men. Goldwater knew that if he were nominated, the mood of the nation was such that he could not be elected. Reagan realized that if he won the gubernatorial nomination, the mood of Californians was such that he would have an excellent chance of defeating the incumbent, Pat Brown.

After all, taxes were up. Per capita state taxes since 1959, Brown's first year in office, had increased 33 percent. State spending was up. During Brown's tenure, California's population had increased 27 percent while the state budget soared 87 percent. And crime was up: With 9 percent of the nation's population, California accounted for 17 percent of the nation's crime.

Reagan's major primary opponent was liberal Republican George Christopher, the two-term mayor of San Francisco. Christopher, despite his executive and administrative experience, had several flaws. In the words of one reporter, he "looks and talks like a losing television wrestler." Asked why Republicans kept losing elections in California, Christopher replied, "We have straddled the fence with both ears to the ground at the same time too long."[38]

And he was often careless with facts, implying that Reagan was the candidate of the John Birch Society and at the same time pointing out that Reagan had once belonged to three communist-front organizations—without bothering to add that Reagan had broken publicly and vociferously with all three groups when he discovered their affiliations.

Regarding the Birch Society, Reagan released a one-page statement in September 1965 in which he denounced the "reckless and imprudent" statements of Robert Welch but declined to condemn all members of the society. He quoted the 1963 report of a California Senate subcommittee that concluded that although the John Birch Society had attracted "a lunatic fringe of emotionally unstable people," the great majority of its members were not "crackpots or hysterical about the threat of Communist subversion."

Reagan went on to declare that he would not seek the support "of any blocs or groups" because it implied a willingness "to make promises in return for such support." Rather, he intended to persuade individuals "to accept my philosophy, not my accepting theirs." As he would put it more colloquially during the coming campaign, "If anyone chooses to vote for me, they are buying my views, I am not buying theirs."[39]

The conservative's prospective candidacy was aided by the chairman of the California Republican party, Gaylord Parkinson. Tired of losing election after election to Democrats and appalled by the self-destructive infighting that had characterized the Republican primaries of 1958, 1962, and 1964, Parkinson laid down the law, warning the gubernatorial candidates: "Thou shalt not speak ill of another Republican." Dubbed the Eleventh Commandment by cynical journalists, Parkinson's proposal was endorsed unanimously by the state central committee, and every candidate-to-be quickly followed suit.[40]

Reagan was delighted. The Eleventh Commandment effectively blocked Christopher from engaging in ad hominem attacks and guaranteed the united GOP that Reagan needed to win the general election. It also suited Reagan's affable temperament and strong distaste for personal as opposed to programmatic criticism. Reagan often quoted the Eleventh Commandment in the years to come whenever the tempers of his fellow Republicans grew short and nasty.

To no one's surprise, on January 4, 1966, Ronald Reagan formally announced his candidacy for the Republican nomination for governor. He did it with a televised "fireside chat" rather than at the usual formal news conference. The television address was intended to prevent any possible "Goldwaterizing" by the mass media. If Reagan was allowed to speak directly to the people, reasoned his top advisers, without any interpretation by television anchors or newspaper reporters, the people would make the correct decision whether he would make a good governor.

The news media, however, were not ignored. A preview for journalists (the television program had been filmed the day before) was followed by a formal news conference that ended at 5 P.M., just one hour before the announcement aired. More than two hundred reporters filled the ballroom of a downtown Los Angeles hotel. They fired questions at Reagan about the John Birch Society, the riots in Watts, his lack of political experience, the Great Society, the state's most pressing problems and his solutions to them. What was the one issue above all others? one reporter demanded. "To retire Pat Brown," Reagan said, smiling, and the reporters roared with laughter.[41]

Reagan was comfortable on the campaign trail. He had, after all, been campaigning for presidential candidates in California for nearly twenty years, from Harry Truman in 1948 to Barry Goldwater in 1964. He had worked vigorously in 1953 for Mayor Fletcher Bowron of Los Angeles in a hard-fought reelection contest. And nine years later, he was honorary campaign chairman for Lloyd Wright in his try for the GOP nomination for U.S. senator.

But this was the first time that Reagan had ever campaigned for himself, and sometimes he made mistakes—as at the National Negro Republican Assembly's California convention in March 1966. He admitted to the mostly black audience that, although he agreed with the goals of the Civil Rights Act of 1964, he nonetheless felt that it "was a bad piece of legislation" and probably would not have voted for it had he been in Congress. Obviously he had read Goldwater's critique during the Senate debate and agreed that the act was unconstitutional.

The convention delegates did not agree, and both George Christopher and another Republican candidate, businessman William P. Patrick, criticized Reagan, implying that he was a racist and a bigot. Reagan became visibly tenser as the meeting progressed. At last, in the question-and-answer period, a black delegate said bluntly, "It grieves me when a leading Republican candidate says the Civil Rights Act is a bad piece of legislation."

Suddenly Reagan jumped to his feet, threw down some note cards he was holding, and said loudly:

> I resent the implication that there is any bigotry in my nature. Don't anyone ever imply I lack integrity. I will not stand silent and let anyone imply that—in this or any other group.[42]

Reagan stalked out of the hall, leaving behind him an astonished, hushed audience and bewildered aides. It was precisely the kind of emotional outburst a neophyte conservative candidate could not afford. Serious, perhaps irreparable political damage might have been done if Reagan's press aide, Lyn Nofziger, had not followed the candidate to his home in Pacific Palisades and told him bluntly, "We've got to go back. . . . If you don't show they'll think either that you don't like blacks or that you're afraid to face them."[43]

Reagan saw immediately that Nofziger was right and returned to the meeting where, at a cocktail party, he received a generally friendly reception. It helped that neither Christopher nor Patrick stayed for the social event.

Reagan learned from his mistake: He never again walked out of a political debate.

Two major issues emerged in May that Reagan and his team quickly seized on to pull ahead in the race. First, the state's Senate Subcommittee on Un-American Activities accused Clark Kerr, president of the University of California, of having allowed radical students and nonstudents to use the Berkeley campus to become the national "focal point" of the anti–Vietnam War movement.

Reagan called on Governor Brown, in his capacity as president of the university's board of regents, to act immediately "to restore the university to its once high standing." And he accused Brown of a "cover-up" in asking UC's regents, who included Kerr, rather than the state legislature to investigate.[44] Reagan's willingness to criticize campus radicals and support the war in Vietnam was consistent with conservative principles and was good politics, appealing to social conservatives and patriots of both parties.

Second, the state supreme court, by five to two, overturned Proposition 14, which allowed owners of private property to sell or rent their real estate to whomever they wanted, regardless of race, creed, or color. The provision had been approved in a 1964 state referendum by a two-to-one margin. For Reagan, the principle at the heart of Proposition 14 was clear: "the right of a man to dispose of his property or not to dispose of it as he sees fit."[45] Christopher loudly applauded the court's action; Brown was more muted. He was adding up the issues and the votes, and too many of them were ending up on Reagan's side.

Reagan was now rolling along, and on primary day, June 7, he won the GOP nomination for governor by better than two to one, carrying fifty-three of California's fifty-eight counties, and established himself as a favorite to beat Brown in the fall. Analysts used words like *earthquake, landslide,* and *sweeping* as they sought to explain the former actor's political debut. *Newsweek* detected "a new tide of conservatism" in Reagan's startling victory, especially significant now that California was close to passing New York as the most populous state.[46]

Leading Republicans wanted a closer look at the California phenomenon. Former President Eisenhower invited Reagan to have lunch with him in Gettysburg; Ike's warm embrace spelled serious trouble for Pat Brown and his strategy of trying to pin an extremist label on Reagan. Traveling farther east, Reagan gave a witty and deft address at the National Press Club in

Washington, D.C. One columnist wrote that "even President Johnson pricked up his ears when Reagan came to town."[47] Reagan took all the plaudits in stride—he was, after all, used to good "notices"—and returned to California to prepare for the fall campaign.

Republicans of all philosophical hues, sensing a winner, happily clambered aboard the Reagan wagon. Joining the conservatives on his steering committee were Caspar Weinberger, a former state GOP chairman and one of the party's leading liberals (Weinberger would later serve as President Reagan's secretary of defense); state senator John F. McCarthy, a one-time Rockefeller supporter; and liberal Robert T. Monagan, Republican leader in the state assembly.

Nervous Democrats, sensing possible defeat, released what they called a "profound document," entitled "Ronald Reagan, Extremist Collaborator—an Exposé." Among the proofs of Reagan's extremism: he read and quoted from *Human Events,* he was on the national advisory board of Young Americans for Freedom, and he had appeared at a rally with Dr. Fred Schwarz, whose book, *You Can Trust the Communists (to Be Communists),* was widely acknowledged as one of the best primers on communism.[48]

An unruffled Reagan kept hitting the Brown administration about high taxes, uncontrolled spending, the radicals at Berkeley, and the need for morality in government. He called for tuition increases at the University of California, warning that the alternative might be a cutback in the entire higher education program. He asked Democrats to join with him to restore balance to the two-party system in California. And he reiterated his position that a property owner should have the right to sell or rent to whomever he wanted.

Californians listened to what the Democrats were saying about Reagan—puppet, extremist, unstable—and then looked at the calm, controlled, articulate Reagan in person and on television, and decided that somebody was wrong. Just as Rockefeller's people had overplayed their hand against Goldwater in the Republican primary of June 1964, Brown's people went overboard in the fall of 1966.

Reagan appealed to the best in the electorate, suggesting that "we can start a prairie fire that will sweep the nation and prove we are number one in more than size and crime and taxes." Brown played on the people's worst fears in a thirty-minute film telecast one hundred times throughout the state. While talking to a group of black children, Brown said, "You know, I'm running against an actor . . . and you know who it was who shot Abe Lincoln, don't you?"[49] Democrats made a sixty-second television spot of this scene and saturated the state with it in the last week of the campaign.

On November 7, the last day of the campaign, Reagan held airport rallies in six cities. Four days earlier, he had been covered with confetti and cheered by thousands during a parade in San Francisco, Pat Brown's hometown. On that last day, the candidate cautioned the sign-waving crowds against overconfidence and urged them to turn out in full force on the morrow. They did.

The last polls showed Reagan ahead by five to six points, a margin that would translate into a 500,000 plurality. But like his opponents, the pollsters underestimated his strength. With Reagan at the head of the ticket, the Republicans won every major state office but one, reduced the Democratic majorities in the assembly and state senate to razor-thin margins, and picked up three seats in the U.S. House of Representatives.

Reagan trounced Brown by 1 million votes and 15 percentage points— 57 percent to 42 percent. And by the following July, after six months as governor, Reagan was ranked as a serious contender in opinion polls for the Republican presidential nomination, running ahead of Nelson Rockefeller but behind front-runners Richard Nixon and Governor George Romney of Michigan. Asked at a western governors' conference if he would accept the nomination, Reagan replied: "If the Republican Party comes beating at my door, I won't say, 'Get lost, fellows.'" But he immediately added that he did not expect any draft.[50]

Chapter 9

The Real Nixon

RICHARD NIXON ALWAYS KNEW WHERE THE POLITICAL POWER WAS. IN 1960, he cut a deal with Nelson Rockefeller, the leader of the eastern liberal Republicans, to ensure his nomination for president. In 1968, he enlisted the support of prominent conservatives like Barry Goldwater, Strom Thurmond, and John Tower because the power of the GOP had shifted sharply to the right. As he remarked to a friend, "A Republican can't win without the conservatives— 1962 taught me that." He was alluding to his defeat for governor of California after a debilitating primary battle with conservative challenger Joe Shell. But, added Nixon, a Republican "also can't win with the conservatives alone— 1964 showed that." Nixon's 1968 strategy was to "nail down" the conservatives and then move to the center. But Nixon's center tilted to the right.[1]

Goldwater did not need any special persuading to endorse Nixon. In January 1965, the Arizona conservative told reporters that he would support Nixon for his party's presidential nomination three years hence. His early, unqualified endorsement was based on Nixon's enthusiastic campaigning for him in 1964 when other Republican leaders (like Rockefeller) were half-hearted at best in their efforts, and on Nixon's strong anticommunist record and generally conservative position on domestic issues. Often heard in conservative circles was the rationalization, "Nixon's conservative enough."[2]

There was no viable conservative alternative. In the spring of 1968, Reagan had been governor of California for little more than a year and was still largely an unknown quantity, although that did not stop some commentators from speculating about a Reagan candidacy. And while some of his supporters encouraged him to run, Reagan truly believed that "the office seeks the man, the man doesn't seek the office," especially when the office was the highest in the land.[3]

At the same time, Reagan could not help noticing that for a newcomer, he was doing amazingly well in the national polls. A Harris survey in November 1967 disclosed that Reagan was favored over President Johnson by 46 percent to 41 percent, a remarkable showing for someone who had held public office for just ten months. Another Harris poll revealed that the American public, by four to one, thought Reagan was doing "a good job as governor."[4]

And yet Reagan hesitated, as William Rusher has written, because of his feeling that an ex-actor with such limited experience in public office "might not be ready" for the presidency.[5]

Richard Nixon operated under no constraints. He began a systematic wooing of conservatives by hiring Patrick J. Buchanan in January 1966 to serve as a speechwriter and liaison with the conservative movement. As an editorial writer for the *St. Louis Globe-Democrat,* Buchanan had been a fervent supporter of Barry Goldwater in 1964. Nixon also recruited Tom Charles Huston, the former national chairman of Young Americans for Freedom, as a personal assistant. And he later named Arizonan Richard G. Kleindienst, who had shared delegate hunting for Goldwater with Clif White, as his national director of field operations. Kleindienst was the most prominent of many Goldwater political operatives who wound up working for Nixon in 1968.

Next on Nixon's agenda was a series of private meetings with leading conservatives during which views were exchanged and support for his candidacy was subtly invited. In the summer of 1966, Nixon met with about twenty conservative journalists in Washington, D.C., and then with about the same number of conservative youth leaders in Newport, Rhode Island. A set feature of these off-the-record sessions was an hour-long analysis of international affairs (without notes) by Nixon—a global *tour d'horizon* that was also, most attendees agreed, a tour de force.[6]

In January 1967, Nixon arranged a more extended meeting with *National Review*'s William F. Buckley and William Rusher in his New York City apartment. Nixon led a three-hour Sunday afternoon discussion of Washington, London, Moscow, Vietnam, and all points in between. When Reagan's name came up in connection with 1968, Buckley reportedly said that it was "preposterous even to consider Reagan as an alternative. . . . [He's] an ex-actor who has been in office now for less than a month."[7]

Nixon disagreed, arguing that "anyone who is the governor of California is ex officio a candidate for President."[8] But Nixon must have been pleased with Buckley's dismissal of the California conservative: If the GOP nomination came down to a choice between Nixon and Rockefeller, the politician conservatives loved to hate, National Review would surely support Nixon.

Rusher was not converted, but Buckley invited Nixon to appear on his television program, Firing Line, that September and arranged for a profile of Nixon in National Review. Rusher and senior editors Frank Meyer and William Rickenbacker were able to prevent a formal endorsement of Nixon, but Buckley did not try to hide his sympathy for Nixon's candidacy in his public appearances. As a result, conservative opinion makers linked Nixon and National Review.[9] The long Sunday afternoon had paid off handsomely.

Nixon also strengthened the conservative cast of his campaign by enlisting a team of conservative policy analysts to help him frame the issues. They included old-line conservatives like economists Paul McCracken and Arthur Burns and younger conservatives such as economist Martin Anderson of the Hoover Institution, foreign policy expert Richard V. Allen, economist Alan Greenspan, and speechwriter William Gavin. That fall, Anderson was placed in charge of all policy research, with Greenspan responsible for economic policy and Allen for foreign policy. Another conservative who played a small but critical role was William Casey, a New York lawyer, financier, and businessman.

Nixon took full advantage of the growing resources of the conservative movement. Without its fervent grassroots organization, seasoned political operatives, and articulate, persuasive popularizers, Nixon might have been denied the nomination and could have lost what turned out to be a very close election in November.

Nixon formally announced his candidacy for president in February and went on to win ten of eleven primaries, losing to Rockefeller only in Massachusetts. In his stump speech, Nixon took cognizance of what political scientists Richard Scammon and Ben Wattenberg later dubbed "The Social Issue," which covered everything from crime, busing, drugs, quotas, and welfare to draft dodging, capital punishment, and even sexual orientation. Scammon and Wattenberg argued that these issues had gained in salience in the tumultuous year of 1968 and had become dominant in American politics.[10]

Ever sensitive to political trends, Nixon placed the social issue at the center of his campaign, declaring:

> Working Americans have become the forgotten Americans. In a time when the national rostrums and forums are given over to shouters and protestors and demonstrators, they have become the silent Americans. Yet they have a legitimate grievance that should be rectified and a just cause that should prevail.[11]

Although Nixon had what appeared to be a lock on the nomination, the enthusiasm for him among delegates in the South and West was modest to meager. And then Reagan decided, on the eve of the convention, that he wanted to be a bona fide candidate, creating second thoughts about the all-important first ballot. If Nixon could be stopped short of a majority on the first ballot, reasoned Clif White and his fellow Reaganites, his total would shrink on succeeding ballots like "a scoop of ice cream in the sun."[12] The way would then be cleared for a battle between Reagan and Rockefeller, which conservatives were confident their man would win.

But they had not included in their calculations the man still known as "Mr. Conservative." Barry Goldwater made the opening address to the convention and, as in 1960, appealed for party unity. His speech elicited what NBC's David Brinkley called "the most spontaneous, emotional, enthusiastic Republican response of the entire convention."[13] When he returned to his hotel, Goldwater found a note to call Nixon, who, ever the politician, asked the 1964 presidential nominee to remain in Miami and talk to delegates on his behalf.

Goldwater agreed and over the next forty-eight hours met with hundreds of delegates and alternates who were being wooed from the right by Reagan and from the left by Rockefeller. Along with Senators Strom Thurmond and John Tower, Goldwater "shored the Southern dike against Reagan's rising waters,"[14] as Nixon later recalled, adding that the Arizonan's support "made it possible for me to win on the first ballot."[15] At the same time, Nixon kept reassuring restless southern delegates that he opposed school busing, would appoint "strict constitutionalists" to the Supreme Court, and did not favor federal intervention in local school board affairs.

When Wisconsin put Nixon over the top, Reagan made his way to the rostrum to make the nomination unanimous. But Reagan and the conservatives saw to it that Nixon accepted a right-of-center platform; picked a vice presidential candidate, Governor Spiro Agnew of Maryland, who quickly became a conservative favorite; and campaigned in the general election as the leader of the Silent Majority.

That fall, Nixon steered right on most issues. He stated that the United States should "seek a negotiated end to the war" but insisted that "the right of self-determination of the South Vietnamese people" had to be respected by all nations, including North Vietnam. He rejected the idea of strategic "parity" with the Soviet Union. And he described wage and price controls in peacetime as "an abdication of fiscal responsibility."[16]

On a more philosophical note, Nixon declared, in one of several radio addresses, that it was time once again to have "an open administration . . . an administration of open doors, open eyes and open minds." He proposed a commission on government reorganization that would be charged with "searching out every feasible means of decentralizing government" and transferring governmental functions to private enterprise and "the great, vital voluntary sector."[17]

Speaking in Williamsburg, Virginia, Nixon discoursed on "The American Spirit," pointing out that the next president might serve until 1976, the two hundredth anniversary of the birth of America. It would be his duty to lead the American people in a search for a new "spirit of '76" that would bring about a future as glorious as the past.[18]

The New Spirit of '76, Nixon proclaimed, would mean a shift "from federal rule to home rule," from "faceless manipulation to personal participation. . . . If we fail to seize this moment," he warned, "it may never come [again] in our lifetime."[19]

How different the nation and the rest of the world would have been if Nixon had delivered on the limited government, anticommunist promises he made to the American electorate in the fall of 1968, and if he had indeed presided over "an administration of open doors, open eyes and open minds." But instead, from almost his first day in office, Nixon offered a pseudo–New Deal at home and an accommodationist policy abroad. And he closed himself off from the conservatives who had nominated and elected him, preferring the counsel of big-government Democrats like former Texas governor John Connally and Harvard professor Daniel Patrick Moynihan, and practitioners of realpolitik like Henry Kissinger.

The final presidential tally was Nixon, 43.4 percent; Hubert Humphrey, 42.7 percent; and George Wallace, 13.5 percent. Nixon's popular margin over Democrat Humphrey was a slim 510,000 votes. Saddled though he was with the Vietnam War and a fractured Democratic party, Humphrey nearly won because organized labor waged a massive campaign for the vice president, whom it considered a blood brother. Also, a strong majority of blacks, Jews, and big-city Catholics voted for Humphrey, suggesting there was still life in the old FDR coalition. But the coalition could not deliver a vital component, the South. Humphrey received only 31 percent of the vote in the once-solid South, less than either Nixon or Wallace.

A few analysts have suggested Humphrey would have won if Wallace had not run, but most agree with Scammon and Wattenberg that in a Nixon-Humphrey contest, the Wallace voters would have split about seventy to thirty for Nixon. The Wallace vote was essentially a social issue vote, not a racial issue vote, and the social issue was "trending to Nixon," not Humphrey.[20]

One of Nixon's campaign aides, Kevin Phillips, published a seminal work on his victory, titled *The Emerging Republican Majority.* Phillips had been a top assistant to Nixon's campaign manager, John Mitchell, and in what one conservative has called "a dazzling display of erudition and statistics," he showed that the old Democratic coalition was disintegrating and a new Republican coalition was emerging.[21] He predicted that the new Republican majority would be based in the Midwest, the South, and California, while the Democratic minority would be limited to the Northeast and the Pacific Northwest. Rather than appeal to liberal groups in the inner cities and the traditional suburbs, argued Phillips, the GOP should take advantage of the "populist revolt of the American masses who have been elevated by prosperity to middle-class status and conservatism."[22]

It was time, Phillips asserted, for Nixon to "build a new era on the immense middle-class impetus of Sun Belt and Suburbia." His target, said the young Republican analyst, should be fast-growth states like California, Arizona, Texas, and Florida, leaving the Democrats to cope with decline and decay in the no-growth states of New England, as well as union states like Michigan and West Virginia.[23]

That would have meant implementing conservative policies and programs consistent with Nixon's assertion in his inaugural address that "we are approaching the limits of what government alone can do."[24] But the president, faced with large Democratic majorities in both houses, proceeded in an increasingly liberal direction on domestic issues. Nixon approved a five-year extension of the Voting Rights Act of 1965, federal funding for a "war on cancer," and greater government spending for medical training and the National Endowments for the Arts and the Humanities. He also signed Title IX, which banned sex discrimination in higher education.

Although he professed to be bored by environmental issues, Nixon nevertheless signed a slew of bills expanding government regulation of the environment, including landmark legislation like the establishment of the Environmental Protection Agency (EPA). He approved the creation of the Occupational Safety and Health Administration (OSHA), the Clean Air Act, and the Endangered Species Act.

In sum, the president who had promised to shift power from the federal government to the states, the communities, and the people wound up giving far more power to federal bureaucrats through a network of government regulations that enveloped American business and ordinary citizens.

Forgotten was the New Spirit of '76 with its liberating language about encouraging "the great vital voluntary sector." In its stead was a so-called New Federalism that preserved effective federal control of state spending through bureaucratic oversight of billion-dollar grants. Governors happily took the money and kept the welfare state going.

Yet Nixon's domestic program was not a total disappointment to conservatives. He liberalized international trade, ushered in the era of floating currency rates, ended the draft, and instituted the all-volunteer army. Nor was he a big spender. Indeed, at the end of his presidency, economist Herbert Stein wrote, the federal debt as a fraction of gross domestic product "was at [its] lowest point . . . since the beginning of World War II."[25]

And conservatives cheered loudly when Vice President Spiro Agnew took on an institution they deemed an implacable adversary: the national news media. In November 1969, Agnew sharply criticized television network news. No other American institution, the vice president said, had "a more profound influence over public opinion." And yet no other medium had "fewer checks" on its "vast power." Although "the small group of men" who produced and directed the television network news seemed to be well informed, Agnew charged that their views "do not represent the views of America."[26]

The vice president called on the "media men" to examine themselves and their operations and to take steps to improve "the quality and objectivity" of their news presentations.[27] After an initial reflexive denial, the media elite, to their credit, began to include at least some conservative spokesmen on evening newscasts, op-ed pages, and speaking platforms. The year after the Agnew address, PBS's weekly program *The Advocates* had a new advocate, William Rusher, who before long was writing a syndicated column for some one hundred newspapers. He was soon joined in the papers and on the airwaves by conservatives like Patrick J. Buchanan, M. Stanton Evans, and John F. Lofton, Jr. And book publishers, who had been largely unwilling to gamble on conservative authors (both Goldwater's *The Conscience of a Conservative* and Phyllis Schlafly's *A Choice Not an Echo,* two of the most influential political books of 1964, had been published privately), now began to sign up conservatives like Kevin Phillips and Stan Evans.

Although conservatives found much to like in Agnew, Nixon shocked them by instituting wage and price controls. For almost three years, starting in August 1971 and continuing through April 1974, the Nixon administration attempted to suppress the continuing rise in prices by imposing varying degrees of controls. First came a general freeze on prices and wages, followed by the creation of a Price Commission that was directed to disallow all price increases except those justified by rising costs, then by voluntary controls that worked so poorly that a second freeze was ordered, and finally by the imposition of more mandatory price controls.

Yet inflation only worsened. Even Herbert Stein, chairman of Nixon's Council of Economic Advisers, conceded that "the controls were a mistake." Nixon, he explained, considered them to be a "political necessity" because a large part of the country, including congressional Republicans, wanted "some kind" of controls. But, although generally hailed at the time, Nixon's centralizing tactics sparked further disaffection among leading conservatives in and out of Congress. Speaking for many, Milton Friedman called wage and price controls "deeply and inherently immoral" because they threatened "the very foundations of a free society."[28]

Mounting conservative disappointment with Nixon erupted into anger and spilled across the political landscape when the president announced in the spring of 1971 that he was going to Peking. American support of the Republic of China on Taiwan and opposition to the People's Republic of China had been an article of faith with conservatives since Mao Zedong seized control of the mainland in 1949. Public support for the conservative position had been strengthened by China's active role in the Korean War and its subsequent and frequent denunciations of the United States, invariably described as an "imperialist aggressor" surrounded by "running dogs."[29]

Yet from almost his first day in office, Nixon tried to build a bridge to mainland China, which meant dismantling, at least partially, the bridge to Taiwan. For two years, the president and national security adviser Henry Kissinger sent confidential messages to the Chinese communist government, usually through Pakistan and Rumania, on a number of subjects, ranging from U.S.–China trade to a possible Nixon trip to the Middle Kingdom. In mid-April 1971, Premier Chou En-lai sent an unmistakable signal when he publicly received an American Ping-Pong team in Peking.

Nixon responded by suggesting that Kissinger undertake a secret visit to China to arrange an agenda and begin a preliminary exchange of views. Following Kissinger's return, Nixon surprised the world (and stunned conservatives) by announcing on national television in mid-July 1971 that he would visit China. A deeply disappointed Dr. Walter H. Judd, chairman of the Committee of One Million, quoted an old Asian friend: "The United States spends billions to go to the moon. Mao just waits—and the moon comes to him."[30]

Nixon explained in his memoirs that he visited China so that future generations would have "a better chance to live in peace."[31] But the president had his eye on his reelection as well as his place in history. In mid-1971, neither was assured. At the time, the president trailed his chief Democratic opponent, Maine senator Edmund Muskie, by 47 to 39 percent.[32] A presidential visit to China, with all its attendant publicity and television coverage, might lose Nixon some votes on the right but would gain him far more votes from the center. The president carefully calculated that a card-carrying anticommunist like himself could safely visit and do business with a communist country. Most Americans, the president assumed, would rely on the man who had put Alger Hiss in jail and stood up to Nikita Khrushchev in the "kitchen debate" not to give away anything important to the Chinese communists.

If Nixon thought that conservatives had no choice but to vote for him if he were opposed by a liberal Democrat like Muskie or McGovern, he was mistaken. Even before the expulsion of the Republic of China on Taiwan from the United Nations, twelve leading conservatives announced in the August 10, 1971, issue of *National Review* that they were suspending "support of the Administration." What turned them off, literally, was not so much the administration's domestic policy (although they cited "failures" like inflation, excessive taxation, and "inordinate welfarism") but its foreign policy, including the "overtures to Red China" and the "deterioration" of the American military.[33] Military spending by the Nixon administration had fallen in real dollars from $98 billion in fiscal year 1969 to just $70 billion four years later.

The twelve signers of the declaration were Jeffrey Bell, Capitol Hill director of the American Conservative Union (ACU); William F. Buckley, Jr., editor, *National Review;* James Burnham, senior editor, *National Review;* Anthony Harrigan, executive vice president, Southern States Industrial Council; John L. Jones, executive director, ACU; J. Daniel Mahoney, chairman, New York Conservative party; Neil McCaffrey, president, Conservative Book Club; Frank S. Meyer, senior editor, *National Review;* William A. Rusher, publisher, *National Review;* Allan H. Ryskind, associate editor, *Human Events;* Randal C. Teague, executive director, Young Americans for Freedom; and Thomas S. Winter, editor, *Human Events.* M. Stanton Evans, who had been asked to draw up the declaration, declined to sign the final version after Buckley rewrote it to exclude several of the domestic actions the Washington conservatives were most exercised about, like the Family Assistance Plan.

These men were, in a real sense, the executive committee of the American conservative movement, and their joint declaration could not be ignored, certainly not by a president who was running behind his principal Democratic opponent in the polls. The "Manhattan Twelve" (they had met and drafted their statement in New York City) guaranteed the White House's attention by asserting that although they did not plan "at the moment" to encourage any formal primary opposition to Nixon, "we propose to keep all options open . . . in the next months."[34]

The Nixon administration, as Buckley biographer John Judis recounts, "tried to nip the conservative rebellion in the bud." Pat Buchanan was told to pacify the Washington conservatives while Kissinger invited Buckley to the White House for one of their frequent meetings. In the late 1960s and early 1970s, Buckley made about twenty trips to Washington to see Kissinger and often talked with him on the telephone.[35]

Indeed, along with his national security duties, Kissinger was responsible for convincing conservative leaders Buckley, Barry Goldwater, and Ronald Reagan that whenever Nixon moved to the left, (a) he did not really mean it, (b) he was forced to by conditions beyond his control, and (c) he could be counted on to prevent any serious lasting damage to conservative principles or assets. Kissinger was usually successful in his apologias, but it was beyond even Kissinger's considerable powers to persuade Buckley and the rest of the Manhattan Twelve to overlook Nixon's institution of wage and price controls just one week after publication of the Manhattan Declaration; Kissinger's announced visit to Peking; Nixon's statement that he was going to Moscow to negotiate SALT I, the arms control agreement; and the United Nations' double betrayal of admitting China and expelling Taiwan on the same day in late October 1971. A frustrated Rusher summed up the impact of the Manhattan Twelve's get-togethers: "Ever since we've been having these meetings, it has been raining shit."[36]

In early November, *Human Events'* Allan Ryskind, who had enthusiastically supported Nixon in 1968, presented a list of demands from the Manhattan Twelve to White House aide Charles Colson. They included keeping Agnew on the 1972 ticket (Washington was awash with rumors that Treasury Secretary John Connally would replace Agnew—rumors that accurately reflected Nixon's preference, as H. R. Haldeman's White House diaries show); dumping the Family Assistance Plan (a guaranteed annual income program conceived by liberal Democrat Daniel Patrick Moynihan); fully supporting the U.S. defense treaty with Taiwan; and a "demonstration by action" that American foreign policy was not committed to the "illusion of détente."[37]

Agnew aide David Keene has described Nixon as being "paranoid" about primary opposition. But Nixon, still struggling in the polls, was being more practical than paranoid about the Manhattan Twelve. He had needed the conservatives to win the presidential nomination in 1968, and he did not want to arouse their ire and their opposition, if at all possible, in 1972. He pledged (through Buchanan) that in return for the conservatives' support, Agnew would again be his running mate; the Family Assistance Plan would be abandoned (an easy promise because it was tied up in the Senate Finance Committee); and the defense budget would be increased modestly.

But the president's offer was too little, too late, and too obviously a bribe. Led by Rusher and Evans, the Manhattan Twelve endorsed the idea of running a conservative against the president in the Republican primaries. Buckley was concerned that a poor showing would harm the conservative movement he had worked so hard to build, but at last agreed. Buckley's endorsement was essential; without it, the Manhattan Twelve would be eleven conservatives in search of a candidate. As it was, their options were extremely limited.

Just about the only sitting officeholder who would take on the president of the United States was Congressman John Ashbrook of Ohio, chairman of the ACU, an architect of the Draft Goldwater movement, and one of the most principled conservatives in Washington, with a 96 percent rating from the ACU.[38] By mid-1971, the forty-three-year-old Ashbrook shared the growing discontent of many conservatives about Nixon. He had supported Nixon in 1968 because he thought the Republican nominee would turn the country away from the liberal Democratic policies of the Kennedy-Johnson years. He had been mistaken, and he felt betrayed.

As he told New Hampshire voters in February 1972, Americans "have not gotten the change" that President Nixon had promised. In California, Ashbrook argued that "Nixon has followed the policies of the Democrats and has carried us from disaster to disaster."[39] Ashbrook had always been a faithful Republican, but in his own words, he was "an American first, a conservative second, and a Republican third."[40] It was a formulation that Robert Taft could not have made—not only because there was no conservative movement in his time but because of his deep loyalty to the Republican party. But for John Ashbrook, conservative ideas were crucial to his political actions.

Nor did the feisty Ashbrook spare conservative leaders like Barry Goldwater who were insisting that any criticism of Nixon should be made privately, not publicly. The Ohio conservative rejected such a quiet, backroom approach; he wanted his objections out in the open where everyone, especially the president, could hear them. Ashbrook argued that because so many conservatives had nearly pledged they would not "jump ship even when the President engages in the most overt liberal initiatives," Nixon was safe in assuming that he had the "conservatives in his pocket." The supine performance of such conservatives, Ashbrook said bluntly, was responsible in a major way for "the leftward drift of the administration."[41]

Ashbrook insisted that conservatives should stick firmly by their principles under both openly liberal administrations and nominally conservative administrations; otherwise, the political agenda would "continue to be defined by the Left."[42] There was ample precedent for such a principled stance.

Robert Taft had remarked, "If you permit appeals to unity to bring an end to criticism, we endanger not only the constitutional liberties of our country, but even its future existence."[43] And Goldwater had publicly censured the Eisenhower administration in 1957 for submitting the largest federal budget in peacetime. Just as he had opposed "waste, extravagance, high taxes, unbalanced budgets, and deficit spending" under a Democratic administration, Goldwater said he would battle "the same elements of fiscal irresponsibility" in a Republican administration.[44]

The Ashbrook campaign had a galvanizing impact on young conservatives. Ronald Pearson helped coordinate volunteer workers in New Hampshire, especially members of Young Americans for Freedom, which bused in hundreds of students from New England, New York, New Jersey, and Pennsylvania. Neither President Nixon nor the liberal candidate, Congressman Pete McCloskey of California, was able to generate similar enthusiasm among students. Pearson would later become chief of staff for Ashbrook in his congressional office and then campaign manager for Jeffrey Bell when Bell ran for the U.S. Senate in New Jersey in 1978. Charles Black, barely out of his teens, was placed in charge of the Ashbrook campaign in Florida. He would go on to play a prominent role in Reagan's 1976 and 1980 campaigns and is today a partner in one of Washington's top lobbying and campaign management firms.

Almost all of the funds for Ashbrook's cash-starved campaign came from direct mail fund raising, which was coordinated by the Richard A. Viguerie Company. From mid-January through mid-March, the Viguerie Company provided the Ashbrook for President Committee with a basic income of $5,000 a week, a meager sum even then. Viguerie lost an estimated $250,000 trying to raise funds for Ashbrook, but he substantially expanded the direct mail universe of conservative donors. More important for American conservatism, Viguerie resolved, as a result of the Ashbrook experience, to take a more active leadership role in the conservative movement. "I felt isolated and frustrated," he later recalled. "I kept looking for people who could lead, who could make things happen. Finally, reluctantly, I began to call my own meetings."[45] The meetings between Viguerie and other frustrated Washington conservatives over the next two years led to the founding of what came to be called the New Right.

Most conservatives, however, chose to stifle their reservations about Nixon. From Sacramento, Governor Reagan declared that he was in "complete disagreement" with the Ashbrook camp and its sharp criticism of Nixon.[46] One of the few members of Congress to endorse Ashbrook was Congressman John G. Schmitz of California, who would run for president in 1972 on the American party ticket, after George Wallace was shot in May; he would receive over one million votes.

In the eyes of most liberals, the Ashbrook challenge was, as Don Oberdorfer of the *Washington Post* wrote, "particularly feeble" and a "fizzle."[47] After all, in the three states in which he campaigned actively—New Hampshire, Florida, and California—Ashbrook received less than 10 percent of the vote. He did not win a single delegate.

But in the short term, the Ashbrook candidacy almost certainly led to the veto of the Child Development Act, helped keep Agnew on the ticket, and forced Nixon to address the explosive social issue of busing in the Florida primary. White House aides like Kissinger, Buchanan, and Colson were obliged to hold substantive meetings with conservative leaders. Vice President Agnew, the administration's most conspicuous conservative, was ordered to New York City (before Ashbrook entered the race) to try to convince Buckley and Rusher to lay down their arms. The conservative movement experienced a new sense of political power.

In the long term, the Ashbrook campaign "preserved the conscience of the conservative movement" and ensured that there would be "a strong voice of conservative principle" within the Republican party.[48] It demonstrated that conservatives within the Republican party could not be taken for granted. In the caustic words of the *Richmond News Leader,* "Responsible conservatives had not worked hard for Mr. Nixon in 1968 simply so they could eat in the White House dining room or hear André Kostelanetz play 'Hail to the Chief.'"[49]

Like Barry Goldwater in 1964, John Ashbrook ran against President Nixon knowing he could not win. And also like Goldwater, Ashbrook offered a conservative choice to voters, examining aspects of national security and the welfare state that otherwise would have been ignored. Goldwater started a conservative counterrevolution with his stubborn, splendid candidacy. Ashbrook kept the counterrevolution alive—with few workers and little money—when many conservatives were content to go along with a president who, far from being "conservative enough," had turned into an agreeable Keynesian and an avid détentist.

Nixon went on to crush the Democratic candidate, George McGovern, winning forty-nine states and just under 61 percent of the popular vote. His monumental win seemed to suggest all kinds of possibilities, such as a national political realignment. No one, including the Democrats, denied that the Democratic party had been dealt a devastating presidential defeat. Every one of the thirteen states of the formerly solidly Democratic South had supported Nixon, and by a sizable margin. But Democrats were nevertheless able to hold on to their majorities in the House and the Senate, prompting Senator Robert Dole, chairman of the Republican National Committee, to say that the president's reelection was "a personal triumph . . . not a party triumph."[50]

Still, Nixon was one of only four presidential candidates ever to take 60 percent or more of the popular vote. The others were Warren G. Harding in 1920, Franklin D. Roosevelt in 1936, and Lyndon B. Johnson in 1964. William Rusher argued that Nixon's win was based on a "precarious but powerful antiliberal coalition of economic and social conservatives." Nixon himself boasted that his landslide win had been made possible by the support of four previously Democratic groups: "manual workers, Catholics, members of labor union families, and people with only grade-school educations."[51] All were appalled and repelled by the most liberal candidate in their party's history.

Another group of Democrats who began searching for a new political home at about this time were the men and women—urban, intellectual, liberal, mostly Jewish—who had supported Harry Truman, Hubert Humphrey, and Henry (Scoop) Jackson, who believed that the nation, and the rest of the world, faced a clear and present danger in the Soviet Union, and who endorsed the New Deal but had serious doubts about the Great Society. Under the leadership of two brilliant, iconoclastic writers, Irving Kristol and Norman Podhoretz, they would coalesce as the neoconservatives and make a signal intellectual contribution to the Reagan coalition.

The periphery of political history is the domain of runners-up, also-rans, and might-have-beens. Usually they merit only passing attention. But one thing almost happened in the wake of Nixon's triumphant reelection that deserves attention: the reorganization of the House of Representatives by Republican and Democratic conservatives (with, perhaps, Louisiana Democrat Joe Waggonner as Speaker and senior Republicans as committee chairmen).

Historian Godfrey Hodgson provides an excellent description of the serious negotiations between some 40 Democrats and 192 Republicans following the November 1972 elections to run the House of Representatives. With 232 members (218 constituting a majority), the conservative coalition would have had a large enough margin to run the House. No such compromise was possible in the more individualistic Senate, where Democrats had a commanding 57–43 advantage.

The contemplated shift of the mostly southern congressmen was due not merely to the conservative-liberal division in the Democratic party but to the economic and political changes that were transforming the country. "Economic vitality, population, and political influence" were flowing from the traditional power centers of the East and the Midwest toward the Sun Belt—the new electoral giants of Florida, Texas, and California.[52]

As H. R. Haldeman's White House diaries make clear, Nixon talked frequently in 1972 about building a "new" party—an "Independent Conservative Party"—based on a coalition of southern Democrats and conservative Republicans. The aim was to "get control of Congress without an election . . . and make a truly historic change in the entire American political structure."[53]

But the realignment negotiations faltered as Watergate transmogrified from a third-rate burglary into a front-page scandal, and they stopped dead when the Senate Watergate Committee opened its hearings on May 17, 1973. The southerners had no intention of abandoning the *Titanic* for the *Lusitania*.

It is a measure of these tumultuous times that two new branches of conservatism came into being. Hardly anyone anticipated their emergence, paleoconservative historian Paul Gottfried has pointed out, or that they would have so significant an influence on the presidency of Ronald Reagan.[54] The New Right was a reaction to the attempted liberal takeover of the Republican party (epitomized after Nixon's resignation by President Gerald Ford's naming Nelson Rockefeller as his vice president) just as the neoconservatives responded to the liberal seizure of the Democratic party (represented by the nomination of McGovern and the succeeding New Politics). Like Edna St. Vincent Millay's famous candle, both the New Right and the neoconservatives burned with an intense light that neither foe nor friend soon forgot.

Chapter 10

New Right and Old Left

THERE ARE LIARS AND DAMNED LIARS, AND THEN THERE ARE POLITICIANS who tell you what they think you want to hear. Following his landslide victory over George McGovern, President Nixon, oozing hubris, asked Barry Goldwater to Camp David in December 1972 for a confidential talk about his second administration.

Nixon assured his conservative visitor that he intended to implement a conservative agenda. He would sharply reduce government, revitalize federalism by giving the states more authority, and force North Vietnam to come to the peace table. There is evidence, at least in this case, that the president was not just laying down a conservative smokescreen. The previous September, at a Camp David discussion of postelection policy directions, Nixon had told aides that he wanted to move toward "slimming down rather than fattening up the federal government." "The huge colossus of government is a mess," he said flatly. At the end of their lengthy one-on-one conversation, Goldwater was "convinced the second Nixon administration would be vastly different from the first."[1] This time, for sure, Nixon would deliver on his conservative promises.

Goldwater's faith seemed justified when the president ordered twelve days of intense bombing of North Vietnam and the mining of Haiphong Harbor. A month later, on January 23, 1973, representatives of North and South Vietnam, the United States, and the Vietcong signed a treaty ending the longest and most divisive war in modern American history.

Although grateful that the fighting and the dying had stopped, Goldwater could not help reflecting that "those of us who urged an all-out drive to win the war were proved right. . . . Limited war is a brutal, reckless sacrifice of lives and treasures. Once hostilities commence there is no substitute for victory."[2]

But in the area of domestic policy, days became weeks, which became months, and little was done to advance the conservative agenda. The reason was simple: Watergate.

Goldwater, like most other conservatives, accepted the early assertions of the White House that the president and those around him were not involved, because he did not believe that Nixon would lie to him or the American people, and the Watergate break-in was not just unnecessary but amateurish. Why, then, he wondered, didn't Nixon take the necessary steps to clear it up and get on with governing the country?

Never a patient man, the senator from Arizona declared in April 1973 that Watergate was beginning "to be like Teapot Dome. . . . Let's get rid of the smell." He warned that if the incident (not yet a "scandal") was not resolved, it would hurt Republican candidates in 1974. He then repeated his belief that Nixon was not personally involved.[3] His outburst was prompted by the revelation of James W. McCord, one of the seven Watergate burglars, that other people had been involved in the break-in and pressure had been applied on the Watergate Seven to keep quiet about it.

Goldwater was joined by other conservative leaders who expressed their mounting apprehension and anger. Columnist James J. Kilpatrick referred to Watergate as a "squalid, disgraceful and inexcusable affair." Lawrence D. Pratt, executive director of the American Conservative Union, declared that Nixon had been "less than candid. Watergate is going to be an albatross." Ronald Docksai, national chairman of Young Americans for Freedom, urged the president to go public—"all these rumors have to be cleaned up."[4]

Unable to ignore Goldwater and other congressional Republicans or the rising drumbeat of the news media, Nixon reluctantly announced over national television three weeks later that he had accepted the resignations of H. R. Haldeman and John Erlichman and had fired John Dean. He also named Elliot Richardson to replace Richard Kleindienst as attorney general. But the crisis intensified when the Senate Select Committee on Presidential Campaign Activities, starting in mid-May and continuing through early August, received testimony from the top officials of the Nixon administration. In the process, the cover-up cracked wide open.

But conservatives, remembering Nixon's exposure of Alger Hiss's lies and unwilling to follow the lead of the liberal *Washington Post,* refused to abandon Nixon. They continued to accept his word that whatever Mitchell, Haldeman, Erlichman, Dean, and the others had done, the president had not been a party to the planning or the cover-up of the break-in and other dirty tricks.

As the president continued to stonewall, however, his position inexorably deteriorated. John Tower, as strong a Nixon backer as could be found in the Senate, admitted that the "atmosphere of confrontation" that Nixon created had seriously damaged his cause.[5] *Human Events* argued that it would be better for the president to resign, "with Agnew taking over the reins," than to have a politically injured Richard Nixon "offering liberal Democratic programs . . . for the sole purpose of staying in office."[6]

Less than three months later, however, Spiro Agnew stunned the nation by resigning his office after pleading no contest to a charge of income tax evasion as part of an agreement with prosecutors who were about to indict him on bribery charges. Agnew privately admitted to Goldwater that as governor, he had accepted political contributions totaling tens of thousands of dollars from people who did business with the state, and he continued to receive money from them as vice president. His defense was simple and revelatory: every other governor of Maryland had accepted "contributions" from contractors as an income supplement.[7]

It was a measure of the resilience of the conservative movement that Agnew's forced exit from national politics invoked sorrow and regret rather than dismay or panic. As William F. Buckley, Jr., pointed out at the annual dinner of the Conservative party of New York, conservatives should not make the mistake of defending Agnew as liberals had defended Alger Hiss in the 1950s. Rather, they should separate the "valid ideas" that Agnew espoused from the man himself. A stung *Human Events* editorialized that the vice president had "traded away" his many attributes "for a mess of pottage."[8]

When the White House canvassed Republican members of Congress for their recommendation to replace Agnew in the fall of 1973, it offered four names: Treasury Secretary John Connally, Nelson Rockefeller, Ronald Reagan, and House minority leader Gerald Ford. Goldwater warned Nixon that if he appointed either Connally or Rockefeller, "it would provoke a split in the party."[9] Although he was the number two choice of the party according to a Gallup Poll of Republicans, Goldwater was not interested in the job. His personal choice was George Bush, chairman of the Republican National Committee.

In no position to provoke members of his party about anything, Nixon named someone who was acceptable to the left as well as the right of the GOP and who would, he was confident, be overwhelmingly approved by Congress—Gerald Ford. On December 16, 1973, Ford was sworn in as the fortieth vice president of the United States.

But all the while, Nixon sank deeper and deeper in the mire of Watergate. In February 1974, the House, by a nearly unanimous vote of 410 to 4, authorized the House Judiciary Committee to investigate the conduct of President Nixon to determine whether there were grounds for impeachment. The process was a nightmare for the Nixon White House, trying desperately to steer a foundering ship of state, and for Republican conservatives who had helped put Nixon in the White House.

Letters and phone calls poured into congressional offices, entreating members of the House and Senate to do something. Some callers were almost hysterical, Goldwater recalled, warning of "a military coup with possible bloodshed in the streets."[10]

In March, Senator James Buckley provided an answer for his constituents and the country: Nixon should resign to preserve the presidency. Conservatives, however, did not rush to join Buckley publicly. Congressman John Ashbrook stated that he did not consider resignation "practical," while Congressman Philip Crane went further, declaring his "opposition" to the president's resigning.[11] In the Senate, six leading conservatives—Goldwater, John Tower, Strom Thurmond, Jesse Helms, Bill Brock, and Carl Curtis—all declined to endorse their colleague's proposal. But privately, their dismay increased almost daily, fueled by the ever-mounting evidence, albeit still circumstantial, that Nixon was far more involved in Watergate than he had allowed them to believe.

Meanwhile, in response to a subpoena from the House Judiciary Committee, Nixon released in late April edited White House transcripts of tapes of forty-six conversations. While acknowledging that the contents were contradictory and embarrassing, Nixon insisted they would make "the record of my actions [on Watergate] . . . totally clear now, and I still believe it was totally correct then."[12]

But Nixon's once-sensitive political instincts had become—to use a favorite White House word—inoperative. The *Chicago Tribune,* which had enthusiastically endorsed the president in 1968 and 1972, editorialized: "We saw the public man in his first administration and we were impressed. Now in about 300,000 words we have seen the private man and we are appalled."[13]

Following the Supreme Court's July 24 ruling ordering the release of another sixty-four tapes, the House Judiciary Committee approved three articles of impeachment, recommending to the House that Richard Nixon be impeached and removed as president because he had violated his oath of office by (1) "obstruction of justice" in the Watergate cover-up; (2) "abuse of power" through the illegal use of the IRS, the FBI, the Secret Service, the CIA, the Department of Justice, and other executive agencies; and (3) "contempt of Congress" by refusing to comply with the committee's subpoenas.[14] In a bipartisan demonstration, six Republicans joined all twenty-one Democrats, including several from the South, in approving Article I of the impeachment document and seven Republicans, along with every Democrat, in approving Article II.

House debate on the impeachment of President Nixon was scheduled to begin August 19. The vote seemed inevitable to everyone in Washington and the world, except for one lonely man in the White House. Any remaining possibility (slight at best) that Nixon might be able to evade impeachment disappeared with the release, on August 5, 1974, of the "smoking gun" conversations with Haldeman. Now conceding that his impeachment by the House was "virtually a foregone conclusion," Nixon nevertheless stubbornly clung to the mast of the White House and expressed the hope that the Senate would retain its perspective and vote to acquit him.[15]

At this, a distraught Senate Republican leadership met and decided that someone had to tell Nixon that it was time for him to resign. They picked a senator who had never hesitated to do what he thought was right for his party and his country—Barry Goldwater.

In the end, Goldwater agreed to meet Nixon along with Senate Republican leader Hugh Scott of Pennsylvania and House Republican leader John Rhodes of Arizona, but to avoid any direct demand for the president's resignation. On the afternoon of August 7, Goldwater, Scott, and Rhodes walked solemnly into the Oval Office to meet with Nixon. When the president asked how things stood in the Senate, recalled Goldwater, "I told him he could count on about twelve votes, perhaps as many as fifteen. No more."[16] They all knew that thirty-four votes were needed to defeat impeachment charges in the Senate. Scott and Rhodes confirmed Goldwater's stark estimate.

Goldwater observed that a good lawyer might be able to beat Articles I and III (obstruction of justice and defiance of committee subpoenas) in a Senate trial, but Article II (abuse of presidential power) was a different matter. He conceded that he himself was "leaning" toward voting for it.[17] There did not seem much more to be said, and the three members went outside for a brief news conference at which Goldwater soberly stated, "Whatever decision [President Nixon] makes, it will be in the best interest of the country."[18]

Richard Nixon, who liked to boast that when the going got tough, the tough got going, acceded to the inevitable and announced in a national telecast on the evening of August 8 that he was resigning. "It has become evident to me," he said with no apparent irony, "that I no longer have a strong enough political base in the Congress to justify continuing [an] effort" to stay in office.[19]

Meeting prior to his television address with some fifty of his closest congressional friends, including Goldwater, Nixon almost broke down. "I guess what I'm trying to say," he explained, tears in his eyes, "is that I hope I haven't let you down." As the members of Congress filed out of the room, Goldwater stopped and hugged the man who had campaigned unstintingly for him in 1964 when so many Republican leaders had shunned him.[20]

It was a moving scene, but in truth Nixon *had* let down everybody, from the American people to the Republican party to the conservative movement. Goldwater never forgave Nixon for failing to apologize publicly for turning a political scandal into a national tragedy. When President Ford called him in September to reveal that he was pardoning Nixon, Goldwater replied bluntly, "Mr. President, you have no right and no power to do that. Nixon has never been charged or convicted of anything. So what are you pardoning him for? It doesn't make sense."

"The public has the right to know that, in the eyes of the president, Nixon is clear," Ford explained.

"He may be clear in your eyes," Goldwater said coldly, "but he's not clear in mine."[21]

Goldwater was not the only conservative who felt betrayed by Nixon. More than twenty years later, Jon Utley, son of the famed anticommunist writer Freda Utley and a well-known Washington conservative by his own merits, recalled Nixon's imposition of wage and price controls, creation of var-

ious regulatory agencies, and literal embrace of Leonid Brehznev when signing
SALT I and remarked, "They got the right guy for the wrong reasons."[22]

The two men most responsible for the birth of the New Right were Gerald Ford and Nelson Rockefeller.

On the morning of August 20, 1974, conservative fund raiser and activist Richard Viguerie turned on his television set to learn that President
Ford had made his decision regarding his vice president. There had been intense speculation in Washington about his possible choice. Conservatives favored the man that many still thought of as "Mr. Conservative," Barry
Goldwater, although many preferred Ronald Reagan, then in his last year as
governor of California.

Instead, Ford picked as his vice president the man he knew was anath-
ema to conservatives. When he was asked in November to list the achievements of his first hundred days as president, Ford immediately said,
"Number one, nominating Nelson Rockefeller."[23]

Viguerie was dumbfounded. Rockefeller, the liberal whose venomous
misrepresentations about Goldwater during the 1964 primaries had been
used by Democrats to bury the Republican candidate in the general election.
Rockefeller, the liberal who had forced Nixon to sign the infamous Fifth
Avenue Compact in 1960, placing a liberal stamp on the GOP platform that
helped defeat the Republican ticket in the fall. Rockefeller, "the high-fly-
ing, wild-spending leader of the Eastern Liberal Establishment." Viguerie
could not have been more upset "if Ford had selected Teddy Kennedy."[24]

Something had to be done. The following night, Viguerie invited fourteen conservative friends to dinner to discuss how to stop Rockefeller from
becoming vice president. The group included political activists, Capitol Hill
aides, journalists, and a couple of lawyers—but no elected officials. They
came up with several good ideas but realized that they did not have the necessary leadership on or off the Hill to block Rockefeller. Besides, congressional Republicans, although far from enthusiastic about the New York
liberal, "had no stomach for a hard-nosed fight" so soon after Nixon's resignation. As so often in the past, Viguerie recalls, "most Republicans chose to
put party above principle."[25]

Not so these tough-minded young conservatives who were tired of
compromise, accommodation, and losing. Some shared Viguerie's outrage at
the Rockefeller nomination. Others were frustrated by their experiences

with the Nixon administration. Still others had been disillusioned by Spiro Agnew's fall. Although he had stoutly given voice to the Silent Majority, Agnew had turned out to be "all too willing to compromise himself and his office for a few dollars and some groceries."[26]

And some were just impatient, unwilling to wait for older conservatives to start leading. These ambitious, aggressive conservatives had four things in common: technical ability in practical politics, mass media, and direct mail; a willingness to work together; a commitment to put political philosophy before political party; and a conviction that "we had the ability to win and to lead America."[27]

It was political analyst Kevin Phillips who was the first, in 1975, to use the label "New Right" when discussing "social conservatives." And Phillips was the first to use the phrase to describe the collective efforts of Richard Viguerie, Paul Weyrich, Howard Phillips (no relation), and John (Terry) Dolan, the founders of a milestone development in the modern conservative movement. They wanted, wrote Phillips, "to build a new coalition reaching across to what elite conservatives still consider 'the wrong side of the tracks.'" They were, he later added, "a group of anti-establishment, middle-class political rebels more interested in issues like abortion, gun control, busing, ERA, quotas, bureaucracy, and the grassroots tax revolt than in capital gains taxation or natural gas deregulation."[28]

They were a diverse and yet harmonious group: one midwesterner, one East Texan, and two New Englanders; three Christians and one Jew; essentially middle class but a little blue around the collar. Growing up in small towns and big cities, they all attended college, but they were political activists, not intellectuals. They believed in the power of ideas but were committed to putting ideas into action. They were true believers, firmly conservative and fiercely anticommunist. They saw as their enemy the "four bigs" of modern America: Big Government, Big Business, Big Labor, and Big Media.

Each man contributed different talents—long-range strategy, grassroots tactics, fund raising—but all of them were media savvy. They knew how important the front pages and the evening newscasts were to modern politics, and they quickly learned how to wind up on them, usually by attacking the establishment wherever it was to be found, in or out of the Republican party. They were four young men in a hurry to change history—and leaders.

Richard Viguerie declared (in his new magazine, *Conservative Digest*) that conservatives would have to look elsewhere than Barry Goldwater, the man who ignited the conservative counterrevolution in 1964, to lead "the conservative swelling sentiment in America." While conceding that Goldwater had voted right on issues ranging from the Anti-Ballistic Missile Treaty to prayer in public schools, Viguerie charged that Goldwater too often placed party before principle, as with his broad hints that he favored moderate Gerald Ford rather than conservative Ronald Reagan for the GOP's 1976 presidential nomination. Ever the party loyalist, Goldwater viewed Reagan's presidential bid as "divisive."[29]

Equally telling for Viguerie and other New Rightists, Goldwater steadfastly refused to consider, let alone join, their attempt to forge "a conservative coalition between economic and social conservatives." Stating that Goldwater had "more than paid his dues," Viguerie asserted that "we must look for someone else to lead the new majority of the 1970s and 1980s."[30]

Richard Viguerie was rightfully called the Godfather of the New Right because he raised most of its money, but the chief strategist was Paul Weyrich, a working-class German Catholic whose father tended the boilers of a Racine, Wisconsin, Catholic hospital for fifty years. A former newspaper reporter and radio-television journalist, Weyrich came to Washington in 1967 to work as press secretary to Senator Gordon Allott (R–Colorado).

Like the other New Right founders, Weyrich was galvanized by the opposition. During Nixon's first term, he attended a meeting of key liberals planning the enactment of an open housing bill. Present were a White House official, a Washington newspaper columnist, an analyst from the Brookings Institution, representatives from several black lobbying groups, and aides to a dozen senators. Everyone took an assignment.

The Senate aides promised that their bosses would make supporting statements and contact other senators. The White House official said he would keep everyone informed of the administration's strategy. The columnist said he would write a favorable article about the legislation. The Brookings analyst promised to publish a study in time to affect the debate. The black lobbyists agreed to produce public demonstrations at the appropriate time.

"I saw how easily it could be done," recalls Weyrich, "with planning and determination, and decided to try it myself."[31] With funding from Joseph Coors and other conservative businessmen and direct-mail assistance from Viguerie, he became enormously successful, helping to found such key conservative institutions as the Heritage Foundation, the Committee for the Survival of a Free Congress, the Senate Steering Committee, the Moral Majority, and National Empowerment Television (now America's Voice).

The New Right, Weyrich explained, were radicals who were determined to change the existing power structure commanded by liberals. "We are the forces of change," he said, "and if people are sick and tired of things in this country, they had best look to conservative leadership for that change."[32]

Without apology, New Right leaders pointed to liberal groups that served as their models. The Committee for the Survival of a Free Congress was founded to rival the liberal National Committee for an Effective Congress. The Republican Study Committee in the House was started to counter the Democratic Study Group. The Senate Steering Committee was intended to vie with the Wednesday Club, a group of liberal Senate Republicans. The Conservative Caucus was launched to rival the lobbying capabilities of the leftist Common Cause.

"If your enemy has weapons systems working and is killing you with them," explained Weyrich, "you better have weapons systems of your own."[33]

He was referring to "weapons" like the National Conservative Political Action Committee (NCPAC), founded in 1975, which spent over $1 million in cash and in-kind contributions to political races in its first five years. Under its chairman, Terry Dolan, NCPAC specialized in primaries, believing that "a well-placed dollar" had "more clout" in a primary campaign, which is usually poorly organized and underfinanced, than in a general election.[34] The committee also relied heavily on research and polling at the insistence of its pollster, Arthur Finkelstein, who has conducted political research for conservative candidates for a quarter of a century.

Above all, NCPAC pioneered the "independent expenditure campaign," in which a political action committee may legally spend as much as it wants for (or against) a candidate as long as there is no direct contact between the PAC and the candidate and his organization. That is, a PAC called Conservatives for Reagan could spend $1 million for Ronald Reagan—or $1 million against Jimmy Carter—so long as the PAC was not coordinating its actions in any way with Reagan or his campaign staff.

In 1978, NCPAC ran independent expenditure ads in Iowa, Colorado, and Kentucky attacking Democratic senators Dick Clark, Floyd Haskell, and Walter Huddleston for supporting the Panama Canal treaties. Clark and

Haskell were both defeated. In 1980, NCPAC sponsored independent advertising campaigns costing about $700,000 against six of the most liberal Democrats in the Senate: George McGovern of South Dakota, Frank Church of Idaho, John Culver of Iowa, Birch Bayh of Indiana, Thomas Eagleton of Missouri, and Alan Cranston of California. Four out of the six went down to defeat, with only Eagleton and Cranston surviving.

The ads were not subtle. One anti-Church commercial showed an empty missile silo and stated that because they were empty "they won't be of much help in defense of your family or mine. You see, Senator Church has almost always opposed a strong national defense."[35] Accused of being too negative and careless with facts, Dolan responded that he was not after "respectability. . . . The only thing I care about is if we're effective."[36]

While Paul Weyrich was organizing conservatives in Washington, Howard Phillips was organizing conservatives at the grass roots. Phillips, a founder of Young Americans for Freedom, launched the Conservative Caucus in 1975 with a small office and a list of 11,200 names provided by Viguerie. Phillips persuaded antitax Governor Meldrim Thomson of New Hampshire to become his national chairman. By 1980, the caucus had 300,000 contributors, chairmen in about half of the 435 congressional districts, and an annual budget of almost $3 million. "We have three basic jobs," explained Phillips, a tall, burly man who invariably dressed in a dark pin-striped suit: "to recruit and train local leaders, to lobby at the grassroots level, and to help set the agenda for national debate."[37]

Having been born out of Watergate, the New Right channeled its disillusionment with Richard Nixon into a movement independent of the Republican party. In place of "blind Republican partisanship" (Phillips's words) was a conservative movement that flourished with a successful fusion of all elements of conservatism. As Phillips put it, "I think both the New Right—the iron fist—and the Old Right—the velvet glove—are necessary."[38]

The New Right also believed that it was possible to fuse principle and effectiveness. Long-time Reagan aide Lyn Nofziger praised the New Right's emphasis on winning, and grassroots conservatives responded positively to the New Right's can-do approach. In mid-1975, the American Conservative Union, after a decade of hard work, had forty thousand members. The Conservative Caucus had collected almost thirty-seven thousand members in its first eight months of existence. There was inevitable friction between old and new conservatives as they competed for members and money.

Human Events editor Tom Winter, a longtime ACU director, publicly parted with Richard Viguerie about the potential size of the conservative universe. "Richard feels the more groups the better," Winter said. "I disagree. I think that what happens is you get smaller slices of perhaps a slightly expanding pie."[39]

The continuing expansion and effectiveness of the conservative movement over the past twenty years show that Viguerie, not Winter, had the better recipe for political success.

But true believers can get carried away. Infuriated by Ford's selection of Rockefeller as his vice president, New Right leaders began considering other political playing fields, including the Democrats and even a new party.

"I want to strengthen the right wherever I can," Viguerie insisted. So when he was approached about helping George Wallace retire his 1972 presidential campaign debt, he hesitated, but not for long. After all, he and Wallace agreed on about "80 percent of the important issues, social issues like busing and law and order, and the need for a strong national defense."[40]

Viguerie raised an impressive $7 million for Wallace over the next four years, suggesting that the Alabama governor was "the first national candidate since Goldwater" whom many conservatives could get excited about. But Viguerie was roundly criticized by many old-line conservatives for helping a prominent national Democrat and segregationist, and the criticism deepened his disaffection with the established conservative leadership.[41]

Viguerie argued that in the minds of most Americans, "Republican" meant depression, recession, big business, Watergate, and Nixon. "It's easier to sell an Edsel or Typhoid Mary," he declared. He went so far as to predict that "in ten years, there won't be a dozen people in the country calling themselves Republicans."[42]

Far more important to Viguerie than the carping about his anti-Republicanism was his inability to interest Wallace in building a conservative movement. Viguerie found an intellectual ally, though, in William Rusher, whose 1975 book, *The Making of a New Majority Party,* argued not for a "third party" representing some new force or interest on the political scene, but a "new vehicle" for a winning coalition of existing forces—economic and social conservatives. Rusher (and certainly all of the New Right) was frustrated and mystified by the seeming unwillingness of the Republican leadership, "with the important exception of Ronald Reagan," to reach out to Democratic social conservatives.[43]

The key to launching a new party successfully was an "attractive and believable" presidential candidate in 1976. For Rusher, the choice was obvious: Ronald Reagan. Viguerie agreed and promoted a "dream ticket" of Reagan and Wallace in *Conservative Digest*.

The ticket constituted compromise by both Old Right and New Right. While traditional conservatives grimaced at the idea of getting into bed with a once and perhaps future segregationist like Wallace, New Right leaders were not sure that Reagan was conservative enough for them. As governor of California, they pointed out, he had signed the most liberal proabortion state law in the country in 1968, had refused to sign an antihomosexual rights bill, and had allowed the state's annual budget to balloon from $4.6 billion to $10.2 billion. The New Right conceded that Reagan's reforms had reduced the state's welfare rolls by about 350,000, saved some $1 billion in two years, and sparked similar welfare changes in other states, including New York.

And New Rightists readily granted Reagan his considerable charisma. But they wanted Reagan to be more like them, 100 percent philosophically pure, which was impossible. Reagan had deep-rooted principles, but as a practicing politician, he had gained a sense of when to give to get something that would advance liberty and reduce government. When he became president, he complained mildly to aides that conservatives like Senator Jesse Helms seemed to prefer to "go off the cliff with all flags flying" rather than take half and come back for more.[44]

But in February 1975, New Rightists were not sure what they wanted, and so, at the annual Conservative Political Action Conference (CPAC) in Washington, they joined other conservatives in lustily cheering Reagan when he asked, "Is it a third party that we need, or is it a new and revitalized second party, raising a banner of no pale pastels, but bold colors which make it unmistakably clear where we stand on all the issues troubling the people?"[45]

At the same time, in response to the weakened condition of the Republican party following Watergate and the widespread congressional losses in the 1974 elections, CPAC appointed the Committee on Conservative Alternatives (COCA), which assiduously researched the election laws of the fifty states under Rusher's direction.

Operation New Party seemed to be proceeding smoothly. But in April, Reagan informed a disappointed Rusher, at a private dinner at his Pacific Palisades home, that he was not inclined to go "the new-party route." He believed that a coalition of economic and social conservatives could and should be forged "under the aegis of the Republican Party."[46] But Rusher and others did not believe that Reagan could be nominated by a Republican party that had accepted Nelson Rockefeller as its vice president. And so they formed the Committee for the New Majority and set about putting the American Independent party on as many state ballots as possible. They hoped they would be able to persuade Reagan (after he lost the Republican nomination) to carry the AIP's banner. But they soon learned that qualifying a new party was not easy. There were so many different state requirements that they almost abandoned conservative principles and wished for a federal law regulating independent candidacies. And they had a major disability in trying to raise money, even with the help of the king of direct mail, Richard Viguerie: They had no candidate.

In their drive to get on as many state ballots as possible, Rusher concedes, he and other New Rightists often allied themselves with people and groups whose motives differed widely from theirs. The resulting coalition was thus part New Right Republican, part southern Democrat, and part kook. The tone of the 1976 AIP convention in Chicago was set by keynote speaker John M. Couture of Wisconsin, who declared that "atheistic political Zionism is . . . the most insidious, far-reaching murderous force the world has ever known, which plotted two world wars, undermined countless governments, [and] dictates the policy of numerous others."[47] His words brought cheers and flag waving from many of the three hundred delegates and plunged Rusher, Viguerie, and the other attending New Rightists into despair.

They had hoped to use the AIP to forge a new party that would attract a "new majority" of conservative Republicans and Democrats who no longer had an allegiance to their parties. But their hopes were dashed by the anti-Semitic atmosphere of the convention and the conspiratorial suspicions of the delegates, who put forward the racist former Georgia governor, Lester Maddox, for president. Bitterly disappointed at their failure, Rusher and other New Rightists deliberately left the convention before Maddox was nominated.

Rusher declared that Reagan had "missed a historic opportunity . . . to lead a true conservative movement."[48] But in truth, the New Right had been saved from an exercise in futility that would have drained away enormous amounts of time, money, and energy. With their failed experiment in

utopian politics, exercise in personal ego, and faulty political judgment behind them, the New Rightists reset their sights on more attainable goals.
"The only way for conservatives to win," declared Howard Phillips, "is to
shift the focus from the national battlefield to the grassroots where single
conservative issues can win."[49]

On Thursday evening, March 22, 1979, more than fourteen hundred
high-spirited people filled the ballroom of the Shoreham Americana
Hotel in Washington, D.C., to celebrate a death: the death of the equal rights
amendment.

The U.S. Constitution guarantees the same rights to men and women
while permitting some laws to extend special rights, benefits, and exemptions to women in divorce and the military, reflecting the obvious sexual differences between men and women. In 1923, feminists drafted the equal
rights amendment, which would have legally negated those differences.

For fifty years, Congress allowed ERA to lie buried in committees. It
was supported by almost no one of national importance in or out of Congress. But in the late 1960s, the women's movement seized on ERA as the
vehicle to bring about their goal of a gender-blind society. They removed
the amendment's qualifying clauses (which would have permitted exceptions
such as military combat duty for women) and eliminated reference in section
2 to "the several states" in order to require federal enforcement.

Determined feminists began to lobby Congress and encountered little
opposition. Most legislators saw ERA as innocuous, with little legal impact
and an easy way to gain favor with women voters. Thus, despite the valiant
opposition of Senators Sam Ervin and Barry Goldwater, Congress passed the
equal rights amendment by an overwhelming majority on March 22, 1972.
The amendment declared, innocently enough:

> Equality of rights under the law shall not be denied or abridged by the
> United States or by any State on account of sex.
>
> The Congress shall have the power to enforce, by appropriate legislation,
> the provisions of this article.[50]

Thirty-eight states had to ratify ERA within seven years to make it the
law of the land. By its first anniversary in 1973, thirty states had ratified
ERA, most of them without study, hearings, or debate. Ratification seemed
on schedule, but the pro-ERA establishment did not pay sufficient attention

to two small clouds in the sky: the legislatures of both Oklahoma and Illinois had voted against ratification as a result of the tireless efforts of Phyllis Schlafly, the conservative activist who had written *A Choice Not an Echo* in 1964.

Schlafly had organized STOP ERA in the fall of 1972. She devised a simple but effective strategy: concentrate the organization's limited resources (STOP ERA's annual budget was a paltry $50,000) on key legislators in key states. Schlafly instructed housewives and mothers on how to appear on radio and television, how to testify before a legislative committee, how to answer a question from a television reporter in fifteen seconds so he could not edit it, and how to organize a letter-writing campaign.

They soon became a formidable political force. One Illinois state senator, for example, was so pro-ERA that he would not talk to representatives of STOP ERA. But after he received five thousand personalized letters from his constituents opposing the equal rights amendment, "he became a firm friend," noted Schlafly with satisfaction.[51]

Although STOP ERA was very much a conservative cause in the beginning, it attracted many nonideological allies as ERA proponents revealed their true colors. The amendment, Schlafly argued, would not "broaden" women's rights but would take away the legal rights women already had in divorce. And its enactment, she argued, would be used to achieve the goals of the radical feminists: government-financed abortion, state nurseries, same-sex marriages, and even changing school textbooks to eliminate "what they call the stereotype of women in the home as wife and mother."[52]

As the word spread, more and more profamily groups and organizations declared their opposition to ERA. Then came the churches, including the Mormons, the Lutheran church (Missouri Synod), Orthodox Jews, the Southern Baptist Association, and the Catholic Daughters of America. STOP ERA evolved into a classic single-issue movement, an unprecedented coalition of conservatives, liberals, Republicans, Democrats, independents, Protestants, Catholics, and Jews. Their cause was helped by gatherings like the International Women's Year (IWY) Conference in Houston in November 1977, financed by American taxpayers to the tune of $5 million.

At the IWY conference, a spokeswoman of Black Women for Wages for Housework demanded that housewives be paid $20,000 a year. Conservative columnist John F. Lofton, Jr., pointed out that this would mean an annual expenditure of $800 billion (there being 40 million housewives) and asked who would pay all these salaries. Pushing hard for the legalization of prostitution was Margo St. James, head of COYOTE (Call Off Your Old Tired Ethics).

Standing at the podium, feminist leader Betty Friedan exulted, "I have never seen anything like this," inspiring Lofton's response, "I agree. And I hope I never do again. But, if I do, I at least hope I'm not helping pay for it."[53]

Schlafly predicted that the International Women's Year convention would mark the "death knell" of the drive for ERA because the radical character of its supporters was at last revealed. And indeed, churchwomen, appalled by what they saw and heard and read, began turning out by the thousands at anti-ERA rallies. The following year, Kentucky voted to rescind its approval of the amendment, and Nevada and Florida voters passed anti-ERA referenda.

By mid-1978, it was clear to everyone, pro and con, that ERA could not be ratified before the end of the seven-year deadline, which would fall the following spring. Under intense pressure from the Carter White House and the liberal establishment, Congress extended the ratification deadline an extra three years, to June 30, 1982. But it made no difference: ERA was unable to obtain the ratification of the required thirty-eight states and dropped out of sight in the summer of 1982.

Another New Right leader who combined iron and velvet in his operations was Louisiana-reared Morton Blackwell, who argued that the conservative movement was still reacting to liberal initiatives. He suggested that conservatives were at a stage of growth comparable to that of liberals in the 1920s, before the New Deal. "Until we take one of the houses of Congress," he said, "the actual formation of the agenda is going to be out of our hands."[54] That seemed a distant and unattainable goal to most conservatives, but not to a freshman congressman from Georgia named Newt Gingrich, who was elected to the House of Representatives in 1978 with the help of the New Right.

Looking around him in 1979, Blackwell perceived "a galaxy" of conservative organizations at the national and local levels, but no leader around whom they could coalesce.

A series of events in the late 1960s and early 1970s jolted a small but influential group of old-fashioned liberals and forced them to move out of their no-longer-comfortable Democratic digs. These cataclysmic happenings included the Democratic presidential candidacy of George McGovern; the seeming willingness of modern liberals to let Vietnam and any other nation under siege fall into the hands of the communists; the refusal of prominent Democrats to fault the UN for its virulent anti-Israel rhetoric; and the revolution in sexual and social relations that produced what liberal critic Lionel Trilling called the "adversary culture."

Another precipitating occurrence for these liberal intellectuals was the radicalization of the institution that had meant so much in their lives and to their elevated position in politics and society, the American university. Although a *Fortune* poll reported that only 12.8 percent of college students were "revolutionary" or "radically dissident," this militant minority disrupted and paralyzed institutions from coast to coast in 1968 and 1969—and got away with it.[55]

San Francisco State University was closed for three weeks. A student-faculty rally forced the resignation of Rice University's president. At the University of Wisconsin, the Black People's Alliance called a strike. When blows were exchanged, the governor called out nineteen hundred National Guardsmen, and tear gas spread across the campus like early morning fog. At Harvard, undergraduates invaded University Hall, evicted the deans, and began rifling confidential files. Radicals urinated on the carpet in the office of Columbia University president Grayson Kirk.

Robert Bork, then a professor of law at Yale University, admitted that he and his faculty colleagues "had no understanding of what it was about, where it came from, or how long the misery would last."[56] But some liberals, like Irving Kristol and Norman Podhoretz, *did* understand what was happening. Kristol had once been a man of the Far Left, a fervent Trotskyite at City College of New York in 1940. But gradually he had moved away from the Left, becoming, in the 1940s and 1950s, a staunch cold war liberal. Indeed, he shocked fellow liberals in 1952 when he excoriated the anti-anti-communists for denying the existence of slave labor camps in the Soviet Union, blessing the murder of kulaks, and approving the fraudulent Moscow trials.

The polarization of the 1960s hardened Kristol's perspective about the Left and softened his attitude about the Right. Nineteen sixty-eight was a milestone year, filled with one convulsion after another: the anti-Vietnam campaigns of Eugene McCarthy and Robert Kennedy; LBJ's unexpected decision not to seek reelection; the barricading of buildings and clashes with police at Columbia University; the assassinations of Martin Luther King, Jr., and Robert F. Kennedy; the televised street violence during the Democratic convention in Chicago and Mayor Richard Daley's famously rigid third finger; a teachers' strike in New York City that produced charges of racism among mostly Jewish teachers and anti-Semitism among black activists; Nixon's narrow presidential win over Hubert Humprhey.

"Mugged by reality" (Kristol's phrase), the neoconservatives attacked the radicals as despoilers of the liberal tradition. Nathan Glazer, the coeditor of *The Public Interest,* explained his evolution from a "mild radical" to a "mild conservative":

> I, for one, indeed, have by now come to feel that this radicalism is so beset with error and confusion that our task, if we are ever to mount a successful assault on our problems, must be to argue with it and to strip it ultimately of the pretension that it understands the causes of our ills and how to set them right.[57]

In place of liberal radicalism, Kristol called for a return to the "republican virtue" of the founding fathers and invoked the idea of a good society. He endorsed the notion of a "moral and political order" and conceded that the idea of a "hidden hand" has its uses in the marketplace.[58] The founder of the neoconservatives was not just endorsing but embracing conservative principles and practices. And conservatives welcomed him warmly. William F. Buckley, Jr., set the tone by declaring that the New York neoconservative was "writing more sense in the public interest these days than anybody I can think of."[59]

Another salient forum for the emerging neoconservatives was *Commentary,* the monthly magazine edited by Norman Podhoretz and underwritten by the American Jewish Committee. If Kristol was the grand strategist, calm in person and magisterial in his prose, then Podhoretz was the neoconservatives' main tactician, passionate in temperament and ever polemical in his essays and books. By 1971 and 1972, virtually every issue of *Commentary* crackled with at least one antiliberal analysis of social issues—articles with explicit titles like "The Limits of Social Policy," "Is Busing Necessary?" and "Liberalism vs. Liberal Education." Other articles criticized the radical bias of the American Civil Liberties Union and the efforts of the Department of Health, Education and Welfare to compel universities to hire equal numbers of men and women or lose federal aid, an early version of affirmative action.[60]

Kristol and Podhoretz, however, were not the first refugees from the Left to cross over to the Right. Former communists like Whittaker Chambers, Frank Meyer, and James Burnham (who always insisted he had been a Trotskyist, never a Stalinist) had helped to shape the conservative revival in the 1950s and 1960s.[61]

The neoconservatives had such an extraordinary impact on conservatism and American politics because they were not simply a small group of New York–based thinkers and writers. Rather, they were, as Theodore H. White put it, "action intellectuals" with connections to America's leading universities and the more important mass media, direct access to officeholders and the political elite, good relations with "major elements of the labor movement," and strong roots in influential foundations and think tanks with multimillion-dollar budgets.[62] They were uniquely able to carry the conservative message where no conservative had dared go before.

Kristol and Podhoretz helped to spawn almost as many institutions as Paul Weyrich and Richard Viguerie did on the New Right. These included influential journals like *The Public Interest, The National Interest,* and *The New Criterion,* and organizations like the Coalition for a Democratic Majority (founded in the wake of McGovern's intraparty victory in 1972) and the foreign policy–oriented Committee on the Present Danger (launched in 1976). And just as Weyrich forged a close relationship with wealthy businessman Joseph Coors, Kristol found a generous benefactor in William E. Simon, former secretary of the treasury and president of the John M. Olin Foundation, who put up $600,000 to start *The National Interest* and $100,000 to found *The New Criterion.*

Yet throughout the 1970s, the neoconservatives refused to break irrevocably with the Democratic party, although the presidential nomination of Jimmy Carter in 1976 did make them pause. In the meantime, the neoconservatives continued building an intellectual and cultural counterestablishment. Although they never said so publicly, they agreed with traditional conservative scholar Stephen Tonsor, who affirmed that "New Deal liberals are as dead as a dodo. The only problem is they don't know it."[63]

Finally, in 1978, while the New Right was battling to save the Panama Canal and targeting liberal Democrats in the fall elections, Irving Kristol and William Simon launched the Institute for Educational Affairs to provide funds for the "war of ideas" against the "adversary culture." As Simon explained, "We wanted to persuade businessmen to make the commitment to compete and win on the battlefield of ideas as well as support their friends rather than their foes in this battle."[64] Like Richard Viguerie on the New Right, Kristol came to be known among neoconservatives as "the Godfather" for his ability to provide generous grants and fellowships. "Irving," said supply-sider Jude Wanniski, author of the influential supply-side economics book, *The Way the World Works,* "is the invisible hand."[65]

The contrasts between the New Right and the neoconservatives, at least in the beginning, were stark. The New Right was religious in objective, language, and membership, with its eye ultimately on the City of God. The neoconservatives were secular in outlook and rhetoric, concerned primarily with the City of Man.

The New Right was deeply suspicious of government, while the neoconservatives embraced it. The New Right liked the mechanics of politics, while the neoconservatives preferred the higher plane of public policy.

But both hated communism and despised liberals—the New Right for what they had always been, the neoconservatives for what they had become.

In the end, it was the neoconservatives' fierce anticommunism and equally determined resistance to the raging counterculture of the 1960s and 1970s that won the favor of conservatives of all stripes and led to a marriage of necessity in 1980. The minister who presided over their nuptials was Ronald Reagan.

To get elected, Reagan needed the brainpower of the neoconservatives and the manpower of the New Right, especially their most powerful constituency, the Christian Right. Ironically, there would have been no Christian Right if President Jimmy Carter, a born-again Christian, had not alienated the fundamentalist Christians who had supported his election with notable fervor.

In August 1978, Carter's director of the Internal Revenue Service stated that any private school started after 1953 was presumed to be discriminatory and would lose its tax-deductible status. Because the great majority of private schools in the South are Christian, the Southern Baptists and other fundamentalist Protestants rightly viewed the IRS ruling as a deadly threat. The crisis forced them to do something they had resisted throughout their history: organize politically. They did so in order to protect their constitutional right to practice not discrimination (many of their schools were integrated) but their faith.

The National Christian Action Coalition, headed by fundamentalist activist Dr. Bob Billings, led the campaign that defeated the IRS attempt to tax Christian schools that refused to set racial quotas for their student bodies. The IRS received nearly 200,000 letters protesting its ruling, more than it had ever received on any other proposed change. The White House and Congress were flooded by another several hundred thousand letters, cards, and telegrams, enabling conservative members of Congress to hold hearings and pass legislation blocking application of the new IRS guidelines. In short, the IRS ruling was "a political disaster" for Democrats and liberalism, for it gave birth to the Moral Majority.[66]

It was Howard Phillips, a Jew, and Paul Weyrich, a Melkite Catholic, who persuaded Jerry Falwell, an ordained Baptist minister, to get into politics and launch what has come to be called the Christian Right. They found a willing convert, for in early 1979, Falwell suddenly felt that God was calling him to bring "the good people of America" together to fight permissiveness and moral decay.[67] As historian Godfrey Hodgson pointed out, Falwell had not always felt that way. In 1964, when discussing the civil rights ministry of Martin Luther King, Jr., Falwell had insisted that "preachers are not called to be politicians, but soul-winners."[68] The New Right picked Falwell because he was one of the most influential Christians in America, reaching 15 million Americans weekly with his *Old Time Gospel Hour* television and radio program.

The man who brought Phillips, Weyrich, and Falwell together in early 1979 was Ed McAteer, a business executive and lifelong Christian lay leader who had worked for Phillips's Conservative Caucus. Weyrich was giving a briefing to Falwell on the current state of American politics when he remarked, "Out there is what you might call a moral majority. They are politically and socially conservative. If we could get these people active in politics there is no limit to what we could do."

McAteer interrupted and asked Weyrich to repeat himself. "A 'moral majority,'" McAteer mused; "that's a great name."[69] Falwell too was struck by it: "That's it. That's the phrase I've been looking for."[70] And thus the Moral Majority was born.

With the energetic Falwell as its chairman, the organization quickly involved itself in domestic policy issues like abortion, school prayer, the equal rights amendment, and gay rights, and foreign policy issues like SALT II, soon becoming a formidable political force. Evangelists like Falwell; Pat Robertson, who had started the Christian Broadcasting Network (CBN) in the early 1960s; and Jim Robison of Dallas reached an estimated 20 million viewers each week with their televised programs. Separation of church and state, they frequently reminded their audiences, did not mean separation of God and government.

Once committed, Falwell, Robertson, and the other television evangelicals set about organizing their followers. From the end of November 1979 through July 1980, the Moral Majority and other Christian organizations registered 2.5 million new voters. They would become to the Republican party what blacks have been to the Democrats: an indispensable part of a winning coalition.

Chapter 11

Winning Conservative

THE PRESIDENCY OF JIMMY CARTER WAS A TIME OF ECONOMIC MISERY FOR the American people and of communist gains around the world. But they were golden days for conservatives. Following Watergate, Republicans had been told—and many believed—that their party was finished. But in the 1978 off-year elections, after just two years of Carter, the GOP gained three seats in the Senate and thirteen seats in the House of Representatives, almost all of them conservatives. America was not interested in abandoning its two-party system.

Because of Carter's ineffectiveness, things got even better for conservatives in the next two years. By the end of 1979, the inflation rate stood at 13.3 percent—the highest since the Korean War and nearly double the 7.2 percent that Carter had inherited from Gerald Ford on his election in 1976. Confronted by mounting economic woes, Carter refused to blame himself or his administration's maladroit decisions. Instead, he faulted the American people, who, he said, were deep in the throes of a spiritual "crisis of confidence."[1] They were also being slowly strangled by "stagflation"—double-digit inflation coupled with zero economic growth.

Things were no better abroad. The pro-West shah of Iran was ousted, Marxist regimes were established in Angola and Mozambique, and the Soviets invaded Afghanistan. Casting about for an explanation of communism's global aggression, Andrew Young, Carter's ambassador to the United Nations, went Orwellian, asserting that the thirty thousand Cuban troops in Angola brought "a certain stability and order" to the country.[2]

What better time for a conservative to run for president?

Ronald Reagan was eager to declare his candidacy in 1980, in contrast to his more cautious course in 1975. Then he had hesitated to challenge incumbent President Ford. A turning point for Reagan was Ford's refusal in July 1975 to meet with famed Russian dissident and author Alexander Solzhenitsyn. In his syndicated column, Reagan ridiculed the reasons given: the president had to attend a party for his daughter; the Russian writer had not formally requested a meeting; it was not clear "what [the president] would gain by a meeting with Solzhenitsyn." Reagan made it clear that a President Reagan would have been honored to sit down with the famed survivor and chronicler of the Gulag Archipelago.[3]

Formally announcing that he was a presidential candidate in November 1975, Reagan soon headed north to New Hampshire, site of the first primary. He was the early favorite with the enthusiastic backing of Governor Meldrim Thomson, publisher William Loeb of the *Manchester Union-Leader,* and other key conservatives in the state.

But the Ford people shrewdly zeroed in on a Reagan proposal to transfer some $90 billion worth of federal programs to the states, including education, public housing and community development, revenue sharing, and certain health and welfare programs. Ford operatives charged that state and local tax rates would have to be hiked to cover the cost of the transferred programs. At the same time, there were suggestions (echoing the anti-Goldwater, anticonservative rhetoric of 1964) that if he were elected president, Reagan would slash social security, veterans' benefits, and other welfare programs.

Reagan was placed on the defensive and was kept there by an overly protective campaign staff headed by campaign manager John Sears, a Nixon pragmatist who constantly sought to mute Reagan's conservatism. Fearful of further missteps, Sears pulled Reagan out of New Hampshire the weekend before the primary election, neglecting to tell the candidate that his once-comfortable lead had disappeared.

On primary day, a disappointed Reagan received 48 percent of the popular vote to Ford's 49.4 percent and lost New Hampshire by a wafer-thin 1,587 votes. Reagan's showing against a sitting president was undoubtedly impressive but could not erase the fact that he had been expected to win. Temporarily eclipsed by the New Hampshire defeat and the $90 billion flap was Reagan's substantial record as governor of California—a major selling point of Reagan's delegate hunters.

When he had taken office in Sacramento in 1967, Reagan discovered that California was spending a million dollars a day more than it was taking in. When he left office eight years later, he turned over to his successor a surplus of $554 million. Editorialized the *San Francisco Examiner,* "We exaggerate very little when we say that [Reagan] has saved the state from bankruptcy."[4]

Most analysts agree that the most significant and far-reaching achievement of Reagan's governorship was welfare reform. The California legislature, dominated by liberal Democrats beholden to the welfare bureaucracy, fiercely resisted the governor's proposed changes. But Reagan asked the people of California, through a series of television and radio programs, to let their legislators know how they felt about reducing the number of people on welfare but increasing the support for those who truly needed help. One day, Assembly Speaker Robert Moretti appeared at Reagan's office door and, holding up his hands, said, "Stop the cards and letters. I'm ready to negotiate a welfare reform act."[5]

California's balanced approach to welfare reform was so effective that even Governor Nelson Rockefeller adopted it for New York.

Following his narrow New Hampshire win, President Ford won succeeding primaries in Massachusetts, Vermont, Illinois (Reagan's native state), and Florida, establishing himself as the undisputed front-runner. Contributions to the Reagan campaign dried up, and conservative spirits sagged across the country. Just about everyone was ready to give up, including Nancy Reagan, who was convinced that her husband would "embarrass" himself if he kept campaigning and losing.[6]

Reagan's campaign chairman, Senator Paul Laxalt, left the gloomy Washington headquarters and flew to Raleigh, North Carolina, expecting to find the candidate as despondent as his strategists. Instead, Laxalt found a determined, combative Reagan with "his back up because of all the demands that he get out" and "campaigning better than I ever saw him campaign before."[7]

Reagan abandoned John Sears's "nice guy" strategy and, stung by Ford's personal attacks on him as extremist and misinformed, went after the president hard. He focused on gut issues like the Panama Canal, détente, and deficit spending. With the guidance of Senator Jesse Helms and his astute campaign aide, Tom Ellis, Reagan campaigned twelve full days in North Carolina.

Conservative analyst M. Stanton Evans has described the March 23 primary in the Tarheel State as "the second most important primary in modern conservative politics," the first being the epic Goldwater-Rockefeller California primary in 1964.[8] If Reagan had failed in North Carolina, it would have been his sixth straight primary loss. In all likelihood, he would have been forced to withdraw from the race and head home to California and political obscurity.

Instead, Reagan won North Carolina by a solid 52 percent to 46 percent and took a majority of the delegates. He achieved a political resurrection largely of his own making and posed the most serious challenge to an incumbent Republican president since Theodore Roosevelt had taken on William Howard Taft sixty-four years earlier.

Noting that thousands of Democrats and independents voted in the Texas Republican primary in May as well as the Indiana, Georgia, and Alabama GOP primaries, all of which Reagan won, some analysts suggested that these voters had jumped into the Republican battle because that was "where the action was."[9] It was a shallow explanation of a seismic shift occurring in American politics.

What was really happening was that the former Democrat Reagan was forging a new majority of Republicans, Democrats, and independents under the Republican banner. A special target was the Wallace Democrats to whom Reagan offered "something to vote for, not against."[10] Both Reagan and Carter were doing well, wrote conservative author Richard Whalen, because they were "perceived as unsullied by Watergate, untainted by Vietnam, and uncorrupted by a Washington system that isn't working."[11]

By the end of May, Reagan and Ford were in a virtual deadlock for the nomination. The climax came with the June 8 primaries in California, Ohio, and New Jersey. Reagan thought he was well ahead in his home state until "we let ourselves be scared by a Field Poll" that had him running behind Ford. Two days before the primary, and after extensive campaigning in California, "we realized the poll was as phony as a three-dollar bill." Reagan immediately headed for Ohio, where he campaigned hard but only for one day. "I'm convinced," he later said, "we could have won Ohio."[12]

The conservative challenger received 40 percent of the popular vote in Ohio, a respectable showing given his circumscribed effort, but took only six of the ninety-seven delegates. Even an easy win in California could not erase the Reagan camp's feeling that the advantage had shifted to the incumbent president.

Believing that something dramatic had to be done, Sears persuaded Reagan to announce his running mate before the convention. The politician chosen was Senator Richard Schweiker of Pennsylvania, a sometime conservative Republican who nevertheless had a 90 percent rating from the AFL-CIO. Schweiker assured Reagan and his aides that he could pry loose delegates from Pennsylvania and other Northeast states.

But the Schweiker gambit failed. The senator persuaded only one Pennsylvania delegate to switch to Reagan, while Clarke Reed, the conservative chairman of the Mississippi delegation, moved across the line to Ford. Equally ineffective was a roll call vote at the convention to force Ford to name *his* vice president in advance, which was rejected by a vote of 1,180 to 1,069, an indication of things to come. Not even an emotion-charged, hour-long demonstration for Reagan on nomination night changed the numbers.

The ballot was heartbreakingly close: Ford, 1,187, and Reagan, 1,070—one of the closest nomination votes in any national convention in this century. Conservatives speculated that Ford might well have been denied the nomination if Barry Goldwater had not formally endorsed him some six weeks before the convention. Goldwater's backing was all the more crucial because it tended to negate the commitment of prominent conservatives like Senators Paul Laxalt and Strom Thurmond to Reagan.

Although Goldwater's endorsement of Ford surprised grassroots conservatives, it had been anticipated by Washington insiders. Both Goldwater and Reagan were conservative in their beliefs, but they had little else in common. Goldwater was an individualist, a maverick, an antihero; Reagan was a communitarian, a team player, a Hollywood hero. Goldwater liked to use the Protestant "I," Reagan the Catholic "we." Goldwater hated what he called "phonies"; Reagan was not so judgmental. Goldwater was Arizona adamantine, Reagan was California mellow. The two men never connected personally.

Although Goldwater did not think that Reagan was ready to succeed him as the leader of American conservatism, most conservatives emphatically disagreed. *Human Events* editor Thomas Winter says that 1976 was the year "when Goldwater and the conservative movement parted."[13]

Following his acceptance speech, Ford generously invited Reagan to the platform and invited him to say a few words. Reagan gave a rapt convention and tens of millions of viewers a taste of what they would have heard if he had been nominated. He delivered, without notes or a TelePrompTer, the rhetorical highlight of the 1976 convention. Reagan wondered how Americans one hundred years from now would look back at this time. Would they say, "Thank God for those people in 1976 who headed off that loss of freedom; who kept us now a hundred years later free; who kept our world from nuclear destruction?" That was this generation's challenge, Reagan declared. "Whether [the Americans of 2076] have the freedom that we have known up until now will depend on what we do here."[14]

The following day, in what was widely interpreted as his farewell to national politics, Reagan thanked his campaign advisers and workers, many of whom were weeping. "We lost," he acknowledged, "but the cause—the cause goes on." And then he added a couple of lines from an old Scottish ballad, "I'll lay me down and bleed awhile; though I am wounded, I am not slain. I shall rise and fight again."[15]

They were inspiring words and movingly delivered, liberals conceded, but they were obviously the final curtain speech of a defeated and aged candidate. After all, Ronald Reagan would be *sixty-nine years old* if he chose to run again in 1980, four years past retirement. The experts overlooked the import of Reagan's other words that morning: "Nancy and I," he emphasized, "we aren't going to go back and sit in a rocking chair and say, 'Well, that's all for us.'"[16]

Dismayed by the Carter presidency and convinced that he could do in Washington, D.C., what he had done in Sacramento, Reagan prepared for another presidential run. In early March 1979, Senator Paul Laxalt announced the official formation of the Reagan for President Committee in Washington, D.C. In 1976, Laxalt had been a lonely Washington voice for Reagan—one of only two members of Congress to support the former California governor. This time, he was joined by a dozen senators and congressmen and over 365 prominent Republicans as founding members of the exploratory committee. Included were former Ford administration officeholders like Treasury Secretary William Simon and Health, Education and Welfare Secretary Caspar Weinberger.

Reagan and his supporters knew that their first and most important task was to win New Hampshire. And to do that, the candidate would have to overcome the opinion held by some voters and many journalists that he was too old, too conservative, and too dumb to be president. With regard to the first point, conservatives readily admitted that if elected, Reagan would be, at sixty-nine, the oldest man ever to assume the presidency, but they reminded voters that the post–World War II world had been dominated by old lions like Winston Churchill, Charles de Gaulle, Konrad Adenauer, and Dwight Eisenhower, all of whom were older than Reagan when in office. Asked about his age, Reagan characteristically replied with humor. "You know, I was in the Orient last year," he told one audience. "They thought I was too young."[17]

But nothing would be more convincing than cold, hard facts. And so in October 1979, the six-foot, two-inch Reagan underwent a complete physical examination, including a treadmill stress test, and received a glowing report. He weighed 185 pounds, almost the same as in his college football days. He exercised every day, even when on the road. And he did all the tough chores at Rancho del Cielo, the Reagan ranch located in the hills thirty miles from Santa Barbara. Almost single-handedly, he remodeled the simple two-bedroom Spanish-style home in which he and Nancy spent their weekends and vacations. He built a fence around their home out of old telephone poles and constructed a rock patio.

As for being too conservative, a Harris poll revealed that the majority of Americans liked Reagan's right-of-center philosophy. More than half disagreed that he was "too conservative," and nearly 60 percent felt that he "has a highly attractive personality and would inspire confidence as President." A solid majority also agreed that Reagan "is right to want to get government out of business so that free enterprise can operate freely."[18]

No one has ever reported his IQ, but Reagan was smart enough as governor of California to earn the praise of an establishment magazine like *Newsweek,* which pointed out that during his eight years he "balanced a deep-red budget, held down employment by the state, pared the welfare rolls, and in other ways demonstrated his competence to govern." The *Los Angeles Times* agreed, stating that Reagan had left office as "an accomplished practitioner in the art of government, a proven administrator and a polished and potent force in conservative national politics."[19]

Determined not to concede any part of the nation in his presidential quest, Reagan flew to New York City and there, on November 13, 1979, announced his candidacy. He delivered his remarks to a packed hotel ballroom and over a special network of television stations that reached an estimated 79 percent of the electorate. All three major networks—CBS, NBC, and ABC—had refused to sell him time for a half-hour program.

He pledged a 30 percent tax cut along the lines of the bill introduced by Congressman Jack Kemp of New York and Senator William Roth of Delaware; an orderly transfer of federal programs to the state and local levels along with the funds to pay for them (no $90 billion gaffe this time); a revitalized energy program based on increased production of oil, natural gas, and coal through deregulation; the development of a long-range diplomatic and military strategy to meet the challenge of the Soviet Union; and a North American economic accord among the United States, Canada, and Mexico.

He concluded with words familiar to old Reagan watchers but more appealing than ever before to a people wondering whether their best days were behind them:

> A troubled and afflicted mankind looks to us, pleading for us to keep our rendezvous with destiny; that we will uphold the principles of self-reliance, self-discipline, morality and—above all—responsible liberty for every individual; that we will become that shining city on a hill.
>
> I believe that you and I together can keep this rendezvous with destiny.[20]

Vying with Reagan for the Republican presidential nomination were six of the GOP's brightest and best: Howard Baker of Tennessee, Senate Republican leader and former co-chairman of the Senate Watergate Committee; John Connally of Texas, treasury secretary under Nixon; Senator Bob Dole of Kansas, the 1976 vice presidential nominee; Congressman Phil Crane, chairman of the American Conservative Union; Congressman John Anderson of Illinois, the only liberal; and George Bush, former Texas congressman, U.S. envoy to China, and chairman of the Republican National Committee. Seldom has a major political party had a more impressive lineup of candidates for the nation's highest office.

Reagan was the front-runner, routinely receiving 40 to 50 percent in Republican polls. Baker had been campaigning hard but still trailed far behind Reagan. Despite his undeniable speaking and fund-raising abilities, Connally was not catching on with Republicans, who viewed the one-time Democrat as something of a turncoat. Dole was poorly organized and often abrasive on the stump. Crane's slim chances depended on Reagan's faltering. Anderson was too liberal for about three-fourths of the party he wanted to lead. Bush had put together a good campaign organization but still nestled near the bottom of the challengers with about 3 percent; he had not won an election since 1968 when he was reelected to Congress from Houston.

The first test came on January 21, 1980, with the Iowa precinct caucuses. Reagan hardly campaigned in the state (forty-one hours in all), even declining to participate in a Des Moines debate two weeks before the caucus vote. He was following a "Rose Garden" strategy carefully plotted by campaign manager John Sears, seeking to protect Reagan from his opponents and himself. "It wouldn't do any good to have him going to coffees and shaking hands like the others," explained Sears haughtily. "People will get the idea he's an ordinary man, like the rest of us."[21]

But Iowa Republicans were not interested in having a monarch in the White House and, like most other voters, wanted to feel wanted. Thousands of them turned out for Bush, who spent thirty-one grueling days in Iowa. Bush narrowly defeated Reagan by 31.5 percent to 29.4 percent and immediately became the front-runner. Political analysts, recalling Reagan's 1976 stumbles in New Hampshire and Florida, wondered whether Reagan, for all his star power, was capable of winning a presidential nomination.

Understanding that everything now depended on his capturing New Hampshire, Reagan doubled his schedule of speeches and barnstormed all over the state in a bus for almost three weeks. Gerald Carmen, the former chairman of the state Republican party, built a network of Reagan volunteers, including members of single-issue groups like right-to-life and antigun control, and directed it from a crowded, chaotic office in downtown Manchester. Columnist Mark Shields, contrasting Carmen's working-class background with the tweedy liberal Republican past of Bush manager Susan McLane, argued that the race was "between Schlitz and sherry, between citizenship papers and collected papers, between night school and graduate school."[22]

And once again, the state's largest and most influential newspaper, the *Manchester Union-Leader*, was strongly backing Reagan with publisher William Loeb penning vitriolic front-page editorials that painted George Bush as a closet liberal and a willing tool of the eastern establishment.

Having learned from the voters' rebuff in Iowa, Reagan agreed to debate not once but twice in New Hampshire. After the first debate among all the contenders, his polls told him that he had done well but was still only slightly ahead of Bush. The second debate was the turning point in New

Hampshire and, indeed, in the entire primary season. It was a telling example of high-stakes politics, with one candidate conducting himself flawlessly and another committing one blunder after another.

Reagan agreed to a one-on-one debate with Bush in Nashua, sponsored by the local newspaper, the *Nashua Telegraph*. But two days before the debate, the Federal Election Commission ruled that the paper's sponsorship constituted an illegal campaign contribution because it benefited only Reagan and Bush. Reagan suggested that he and Bush split the $3,500 cost of the debate. Bush refused because his campaign was close to its spending limit (Bush Mistake #1), so Reagan sent a check for the whole cost.

When the other candidates began complaining that they had been excluded, Reagan (at Sears's suggestion) invited them to participate. Anderson, Baker, Dole, and Crane showed up in Nashua (John Connally was campaigning in South Carolina) and joined Reagan in a classroom across the hall from the Nashua High School gym. Bush arrived separately with his campaign manager, James A. Baker, and other aides and was invited to join the others. He declined. (Bush Mistake #2.) Reagan was disturbed at Bush's rude treatment of fellow Republicans.

Bush strode into the gym and seated himself in one of the two chairs on the stage. Reagan then marched onto the stage with the four other candidates, his mouth set in a thin straight line. It was High Noon in Nashua on a Saturday night. While Reagan sat in the other reserved chair at the front of the platform, Anderson, Baker, Dole, and Crane lined up behind him like so many wooden Indians but all dressed in dark blue suits. People in the audience began shouting, "Get them chairs, get them chairs!"[23]

Bush sat stiffly with his back to the four standing men, and refused to acknowledge them. (Bush Mistake #3.) It was, as Frank van der Linden wrote, "an incredible scene," created by Bush's boneheadedness: Four prominent Republicans vying for the presidency were treated as interlopers and expected to remain silent.

When Reagan began trying to explain the situation, Jon Breen, the debate moderator and *Telegraph* editor, shouted, "Will the sound man please turn Mr. Reagan's mike off?" The audience burst into loud boos. A red-faced Reagan seized his microphone and shouted in raw anger, "I'm paying for this microphone, Mr. Green!"[24]

Although Reagan got the moderator's name wrong, his passionate outburst won the cheers of the audience. It was featured in every New Hampshire newspaper and television and radio report for the next forty-eight hours. Meanwhile, Bush sat shaken and silent but at last said confusedly, "I was invited here by the editors of the Nashua newspaper. I am their guest. I will play by the rules, and I'm glad to be here."[25] (Bush Mistake #4.) The explanation of why George Bush, a genuine hero of World War II, could be called a "wimp" by the media and political opponents begins with his feeble performance at the Nashua debate.

Not appreciating the measure of his miscalculation, Bush flew home to Houston that weekend and was pictured jogging in his shirtsleeves in the Texas sun while Reagan slogged through the snow all weekend and right up to primary day. No one was now saying that the former California governor was too old to run for president. And the two debates convinced a majority of New Hampshire Republicans that Reagan had, in the words of his pollster Richard Wirthlin, the "mental agility" to compete with any of his opponents and to be president.[26] In what had once been regarded as a close contest, Reagan buried Bush by more than two to one, collecting as many votes as his six rivals combined.

The political momentum had now shifted. By the end of March, Baker, Connally, and Dole had withdrawn from the nomination race, followed in April by Crane and Anderson. But Anderson, who had not won any of the nine Republican primaries he entered, declared himself an "independent" and announced that a committee would study whether he could get his name on enough state ballots to win and whether sufficient money could be raised for a national campaign.[27]

Reagan beat Bush in Texas, his home state; in New York, the capital of the Eastern liberal establishment; in Michigan, the center of organized labor; and in Oregon, the most liberal of the Western states. Finally, on May 26, Bush acknowledged the inevitable and conceded the 1980 Republican presidential nomination to Ronald Reagan. Bush's decision not to continue was realistic and politic; he was soon widely mentioned as a possible running mate for Reagan.

The principal on-site architects of the 1980 Republican platform were Senator Jesse Helms of North Carolina and Congressman Jack Kemp of New York. They were an odd conservative couple, but each represented a powerful section of the Republican party. Helms was a traditional conservative, a former Jeffersonian Democrat, who liked his government like his steak—lean and rare. Kemp was an economic conservative, an enthusiastic follower of F. A. Hayek and Milton Friedman, who never met a tax he didn't want to cut. Together they produced a conservative platform that called for a 30 percent tax cut in accord with the Kemp-Roth plan; the systematic reduction of federal rules and regulations over business and industry; the decentralization of social welfare and public assistance programs; free enterprise zones in the inner cities to attract capital, entrepreneurs, and jobs (an idea first advanced by the Heritage Foundation's Stuart Butler and adopted by Kemp); a constitutional amendment banning abortion on demand; the support of equal rights for women but not the the Equal Rights Amendment; the building of new weapons systems to help the United States achieve military superiority over the Soviet Union; strong support for Israel and the Republic of China on Taiwan; and a North American economic accord among the United States, Canada, and Mexico.

At the same time, Reagan went out of his way to reassure special interest groups that he was aware of their goals and aspirations. He told a group of woman delegates that he would fight discrimination based on sex and would promote equality of opportunity if he were elected president. He pledged to black delegates that he would deliver American blacks from the "bondage" of welfare and sponsor measures to build up the black community economically. Reagan was determined that no one would pin an "extremist" label on him as they had done to his conservative colleague and mentor, Barry Goldwater.

Accordingly, when Henry Kissinger, arch-architect of détente, addressed the convention, he was greeted with polite applause, in contrast to the angry booing that had inundated Nelson Rockefeller at the 1964 GOP convention. And when Benjamin Hooks of the NAACP met privately with black delegates, convention organizers quickly altered the schedule to allow him to speak to the convention. His call for a "laundry list of social spending programs" was politely received and quietly ignored.[28]

The Detroit convention now experienced one of those intense outbursts of irrationality that, like sudden summer storms, sometimes sweep across mass political meetings. The catalyst was an unexpectedly dynamic speech on Monday night, July 15, by former President Ford, who declared, "This country means too much for me to comfortably park on the park bench. So, when this convention fields the team for Governor Reagan, count me in."[29]

Maybe, the delegates began saying to themselves and then to each other, we ought to field a Reagan-Ford team. Top Republicans—conservative, moderate, and liberal—tried to make it happen. Reagan and several of his advisers (like Paul Laxalt and William Casey) already favored the former president as a running mate. Richard Wirthlin's polls showed that Ford measurably strengthened the ticket.

And so on Tuesday afternoon, following numerous meetings with party leaders, Reagan met with the former president. "I would like you to serve on the ticket with me," he said to the man whom he had nearly defeated for the nomination four years earlier, "to run against and hopefully defeat Carter. I know it's a difficult decision for you. Likely, it will involve some sacrifices. I think a lot's at stake as far as our country is concerned. Would you give it some consideration?"[30]

The language provides revealing insights into Reagan's negotiating style: direct but not confrontational, simple and yet subtle, deferential but not fawning. He was as persuasive as he could be, feeling strongly that Ford was important to his winning the presidency.

Ford raised three questions: whether a former president could fit comfortably into the vice presidency; whether the staffs of the two men could work together effectively; and whether such a ticket would run afoul of the Twelfth Amendment, which says that if the candidates for president and vice president come from the same state, the electors from that state may not vote for both. (Ford was then living most of the year in California.) Reagan advised Ford of his lawyers' opinion that Ford could move his legal residence to Vail, Colorado, where he had a vacation home, or even back to Michigan, where he had been born. Ford agreed to consider Reagan's offer but stressed that he did not think it would work. Think it over, replied his persistent suitor, refusing to take an answer just then.[31]

Aides to both men met in almost continuous session trying to arrive at an acceptable arrangement. The Reagan side presented a two-page memorandum, prepared by Meese, that outlined Ford's responsibilities, including daily supervisory authority but not veto power over the National Security Council, the Office of Management and Budget, and the Council of Economic Advisers—the president's most important advisory groups. In effect, the vice president would become a deputy president, drawing extensively on Ford's experience in national security, the appropriations process, and Congress.

Ford called the proposal a "reasonable effort" but still expressed doubt. Alan Greenspan, an economic adviser to both men, recalled thinking that they were trying to resolve in just twenty-four hours some of the most difficult organizational problems of the U.S. government.[32]

While the two sides were trying to rewrite the Constitution and balance political forces and egos, Reagan met with a New Right delegation that subjected him to an hour of emotional protests against the selection of Ford, George Bush, or Howard Baker. Reagan-Ford was not a dream but a nightmare to these conservatives. Howard Phillips warned that Reagan risked losing the South to Carter if he allowed "media and other liberal power brokers" to influence his choice of a running mate. Senator Gordon Humphrey of New Hampshire recalled that he had helped Reagan win his first primary and pleaded with him not to let "the Ford-Bush Republican hierarchy" dictate the other half of his ticket.[33]

Phyllis Schlafly, who had been fighting the liberal establishment's dominance of the GOP since 1952, cautioned Reagan against disillusioning the "pro-family" voters who held deep convictions against the ERA, abortion, and the drafting of women. Nellie Gray, the founder and leader of the annual March for Life in Washington, argued that the anti-abortion movement was a powerful political force that should not be ignored, to which Reagan quickly agreed.[34]

Reverend Jerry Falwell warned that the 72,000 Protestant pastors in the Moral Majority would "surely lose some of their enthusiasm" for Reagan if he disappointed them with his vice presidential choice.[35]

Reagan listened patiently and sympathetically to every one of the conservatives' warnings. He revealed that Baker was no longer on the vice presidential list but that Bush was acceptable to such stalwart conservatives as Strom Thurmond and John Tower. Why couldn't the New Right accept him too? He did not mention the intense negotiations with Ford, which were still confidential.

The visitors left "downhearted," convinced that their appeal had failed. But Reagan had met with them and had given them an opportunity to voice their opinion. By including them in the selection process, he had demonstrated his respect for the New Right and its prominent place in the majority coalition he was trying to forge.

Ford and Reagan met briefly at 5:15 P.M., at Ford's request. The former president mentioned Henry Kissinger and Alan Greenspan as the kind of people he would like to see in the cabinet. Reagan responded, "Jerry, I know all of Kissinger's strong points, and there's no question that he should play a role . . . but not as secretary of state. I couldn't accept that."[36] It was a revelation for Ford. For all his smiling affability, Reagan could be as unyielding as stone.

The turning point came, as happens so often in our age of media politics, over national television. In a CBS interview with Walter Cronkite two hours later, Ford revealed to millions of viewers and the delegates to the Republican convention that he was seriously considering the vice presidency. After some probing, Cronkite asked a direct question: "It's got to be something like a co-presidency?" Although it was not his word, Ford did not reject it, simply replying, "That's something Governor Reagan really ought to consider."[37]

Watching in his hotel, Reagan was dismayed. He had scrupulously kept the discussions behind closed doors, and yet there was Ford discussing them live with Cronkite and then with Barbara Walters on ABC. And "co-presidency"? No one had suggested that there ought to be *two* presidents in the White House. Ford and his wife, Betty, also raised the political temperature by mentioning their strong support of the equal rights amendment, which was opposed by the 1980 GOP platform and by Ronald Reagan.

As aides continued to wrestle with language, Reagan realized that a decision had to be made that night, or he would appear to be weak and indecisive. He called Ford, who responded, "My gut instinct is that I shouldn't do it," but refused to give a flat no. Suddenly, at 10:30 P.M., in the middle of the voting for the Republican presidential nomination, Ford turned to his wife and said, "I'm going down to tell him that I'm not going to do it." In Reagan's suite, the once and future presidents talked for only ten minutes, but with no tension or bitterness, about the collapse of the "dream ticket."[38]

Eager to assert his command of the convention and to prevent the television networks from rumor-mongering throughout the night and into the morning, Reagan telephoned a surprised George Bush, who thought along with most of the rest of America that Reagan-Ford was a done deal. "I plan to go over to the convention," revealed Reagan, "and tell them you are my first choice for the nomination." An elated Bush responded, "I can campaign enthusiastically for your election and the platform."[39]

A few minutes later, from the podium of Joe Louis Arena, Reagan revealed to a hushed convention that former President Ford felt he could be "of more value" campaigning for the ticket than being on it. He was therefore recommending the nomination of George Bush. The delegates, who earlier had overwhelmingly picked Reagan as their presidential nominee, roared their approval.

Reagan's avid pursuit of Ford is illustrative of his pragmatism, inventiveness, and quick reflexes. To implement his conservative ideas, he had to get elected, and if Jerry Ford would help him achieve that end, he was willing to run with someone he once critized for allowing America to become "dangerously weak." And it did not bother him that picking a former president as his running mate was an unprecedented action; he was not bound to the past, only respectful of it. When the proposed merger collapsed, he acted quickly to line up a replacement almost as acceptable to all parts of the Republican party, particularly the eastern wing.

Reagan's acceptance address sought to bind together all the elements of the GOP, while also reaching out to independents and disillusioned Democrats. It articulated the traditional sources of American thought from the Mayflower Compact to the founding fathers to Lincoln's Gettysburg Address, and ended with a quotation from Franklin D. Roosevelt attacking excessive government spending, followed by a silent moment of prayer for the American hostages in Iran. Its central theme was summed up in five words—family, work, neighborhood, peace, freedom—that would serve as guideposts for his administration.

Behind Reagan's nomination and ready to help him as he began his presidential campaign were dozens of conservative organizations involving thousands of people and spending millions of dollars annually—a counterestablishment only dreamed of by the most optimistic conservatives a decade before.

Among them was the Washington-based American Conservative Union, sponsor of the annual Conservative Political Action Conference (CPAC). In 1979, ACU's annual budget was nearly $3 million, up from $350,000 just five years before. Much of the organization's growth had come about through its leadership in the fight against ratification of the Panama Canal treaties. ACU affiliates included the Conservative Victory Fund, one of the first conservative political action committees, and the ACU Education and Research Institute, which, under M. Stanton Evans, would create the National Journalism Center. The center trained about sixty young journalists a year.

The National Taxpayers Union (NTU), founded by tax specialist James Dale Davidson, helped create a receptive climate for Reagan's fiscal policies. By the late 1970s, NTU had 220 affiliated chapters across the country. Its main objective was to convene a constitutional convention for an amendment requiring the federal government to balance the budget. By 1979, thirty states had passed resolutions calling for such a balanced budget convention—three short of the required thirty-three.

With a membership of 300,000 and an annual budget of about $5 million in 1980, the National Tax Limitation Committee, started by former Reagan aide Lewis B. Uhler, worked in both the nation's capital and state capitals to limit taxes and spending. The committee's strategy, Uhler explained, was to keep building up the grassroots pressure on the federal government, "where we all recognized the big culprit was located."[40] In November 1979, NTLC won an impressive victory when California voters approved Proposition 4, drafted by Uhler, which put a tight lid on state spending. The first state to adopt a constitutional spending limit in 1978 was Tennessee. By 1980, almost one hundred members of Congress were cosponsors of NTLC's constitutional amendment, which limited federal spending to a declining share of the gross national product.

For years, anyone who wanted free legal aid had to talk to the American Civil Liberties Union or some part of Ralph Nader's citizen rights complex. In the 1970s, conservative public interest law firms sprang up, led by the Pacific Legal Foundation, with offices in Washington, D.C., Sacramento, and Seattle. PLF was founded by Ronald A. Zumbrun, an architect of Reagan's welfare reform program in California, and Roy Green, a former president of the Sacramento Chamber of Commerce. With an annual budget of $2 million, the foundation scored several impressive victories, such as getting California's nuclear moratorium declared unconstitutional. Director Raymond Momboisse frequently asked, "Who is more unrepresented than the silent, hard-working taxpayer? The little man who foots the bills of the great social experiments of the bloated bureaucracy—we represent him."[41]

Other conservative public interest firms included the Washington Legal Foundation, headed by twenty-nine-year-old Daniel Popeo, often described as the "Ralph Nader of the Right." By the late 1970s, Popeo had brought cases against President Jimmy Carter, the Democratic National Committee, the General Services Administration, and the Federal Mine Safety Commission. WLF represented Senator Barry Goldwater in his historic case against

Carter's canceling, without Senate approval, the mutual defense treaty between the United States and the Republic of China on Taiwan. Goldwater went all the way to the Supreme Court before losing on a technicality.

Think tanks like the American Enterprise Institute (AEI), the Heritage Foundation, and the Cato Institute helped to place conservative ideas at the center of the public policy debate. AEI, in 1979, was by far the largest and most influential, with an annual budget of $7 million, just behind the $8 million level of the liberal Brookings Institution. Among the prominent public officials and scholars whom AEI recruited in the 1970s were former president Gerald Ford, former solicitor general Robert Bork, former treasury secretary William Simon, former Federal Reserve Board chairman Arthur Burns, and such thinkers and academics as Irving Kristol, Herbert Stein, and Jeane Kirkpatrick.

Conservative efforts on Capitol Hill were significantly strengthened by two in-house groups: the Republican Study Committee, organized in 1973 by veteran Congressman Ed Derwinski of Illinois, and the Senate Steering Committee, brought to life in 1974 through the determined efforts of Republican senators Carl Curtis of Nebraska and James McClure of Idaho. With a membership approaching ninety House members by 1980, the Republican Study Committee helped produce conservative victories on campaign reform, OSHA, land use, and East-West trade.

Throughout the late 1970s, the fourteen members of the Senate Steering Committee met regularly over lunch each Wednesday to discuss conservative strategy, politics, and legislation. Among the issues the group tackled were the Panama Canal treaties, SALT, labor law "reform," Rhodesia, campaign financing, and balancing the federal budget. Margo Carlisle, the committee's executive director and one of the most quietly effective conservatives on the Hill, explained, "We work hard and we work with the staffs of the other senators." Conservative activist Paul Weyrich commented that comparing conservative effectiveness in the Senate before and after the steering committee was "like comparing night and day. Without their orchestration, we'd have lost constantly."[42]

By 1980, after three decades of unending trial and frequent error, conservatives had learned several critical lessons they would soon put to effective use:

- It is not enough to be philosophically right. You must also be technologically proficient. That is, conservatives must be expert in the tools of politics such as precinct organization, communications, canvassing, direct mail, and polling.

- Conservatives must work together with other conservatives. There is not just safety but strength and victory in numbers.
- Conservatives should be realistic about their goals, and patient. Like the Fabians in Great Britain and the Progressives in America, conservatives were in politics for the long haul.
- Conservatives should be optimistic, trusting in the ultimate good sense of the American people to make the right political decisions.

Although all the national polls placed Reagan far ahead of Carter right after the Republican convention, the president got a bump from his own convention in August, and the two men were about even by Labor Day.

From the first day of campaigning, President Carter brought out the usual anticonservative arsenal of charges, portraying Reagan as a right-wing extremist opposed to peace, arms control, and working people—a man who would divide the country. Carter appealed to traditional Democratic groups like blacks and organized labor and played on doubts about Reagan's expertise in the vital area of war and peace.

The president played the race card early and often, accusing Reagan of injecting hatred and racism into the campaign by using "code words like 'states' rights.'" Appearing at Martin Luther King, Jr.'s church in Atlanta, Carter grinned and shook the hand of Congressman Parren Mitchell of Maryland, who had just said of Reagan, "I'm going to talk about a man . . . who seeks the presidency of the United States with the endorsement of the Ku Klux Klan."[43] It did not matter to Mitchell, or to Carter apparently, that Reagan had immediately repudiated the Klan's endorsement.

But Carter's tactics sparked immediate and widespread condemnation. Liberal columnists Jack Germond and Jules Witcover wrote that the president had brought the campaign "down to a new level" and such accusations had no "pertinence" in the politics of 1980. In an editorial entitled "Running Mean," the *Washington Post* said, "Jimmy Carter . . . seems to have few limits beyond which he will not go in the abuse of opponents and reconstruction of history." Reagan called Carter's attack "shameful, because whether we're on the opposite side or not, we ought to be trying to pull the country together."[44]

The president insisted stubbornly at a news conference that he did not "indulge in attacking personally the integrity of my opponents" and complained that "the press appeared to be obsessed with the race issue." But the Carter-Mondale Re-Election Committee showed its true colors by launching a national advertising campaign in black newspapers that claimed that Republicans were out to beat Carter because he had appointed thirty-seven blacks to judgeships and had cracked down on job discrimination.[45]

Refusing to be thrown off-course, Reagan went on courting the blue-collar, ethnic Catholic vote, concentrated on Carter's sorry economic record, and endeavored to reassure the voters that he could handle the weighty duties of the presidency. The strategy was based on the Black Book, a remarkable 176-page document written by Richard Wirthlin, Reagan's longtime pollster and president of Decision Making Information. The Black Book listed four target groups: southern white Protestants, blue-collar workers in industrial states, urban ethnics, and rural voters, especially in upstate New York, Ohio, and Pennsylvania.

When the president refused to participate in a three-way debate with Reagan and John Anderson, Reagan readily agreed to appear with his independent opponent. The 55 million Americans who watched the Reagan-Anderson debate on Sunday evening, September 21, were treated to an impressive political demonstration. The answers pointed up the sharp differences between the two men, with Reagan urging smaller government and less spending and Anderson proposing billion-dollar government solutions for the problems of energy and the inner city. Reagan repeated his call for a 10 percent tax cut for each of the next three years, noting with satisfaction that his proposal "has been called inflationary by my opponent, by the man who isn't here tonight."[46]

An immediate ABC–Lou Harris Poll reported that viewers believed that Anderson had "outplayed" Reagan by 36 percent to 30 percent, with 17 percent calling it a tie. But according to a *New York Times*/CBS poll, Reagan was the true beneficiary because an increased number of people believed that Reagan understood the complicated problems facing a president, had a clear position on the issues, offered a clear vision of where he wanted to lead the country, and would exercise good judgment under pressure. The debate dispelled the concerns of many voters that Reagan was incompetent or reckless. The poll also reported that Reagan now led Carter by five points.[47]

Reagan was now campaigning smoothly, presenting specialized messages to key constituencies in the communities he visited. In Miami, he denounced Fidel Castro and promised that America would remain a refuge for those fleeing tyranny. In Springfield, Missouri, he criticized Carter for hesitating to declare the state a disaster area following a severe drought. In Tyler, Texas, he charged that Carter was afraid to debate energy policy with him. And in Grand Junction, Colorado, he declared that westerners knew how to manage their water resources better than the federal bureaucracy did. The content of his speeches was traditional Republican—cut taxes, limit government—but his style was traditional Democratic, with constant references to family, neighborhood, work, and peace.

With three weeks left in the campaign, Reagan held a narrow lead of five points in the popular vote and a comfortable margin in the electoral vote. Republicans were organized and united as they had not been for years, and there was sufficient money for a final advertising blitz. The candidate was ready for intensive final campaigning in key states like Pennsylvania, Michigan, and Ohio.

The Reagan organization *was* concerned about one issue over which it had no control: the American hostages in Iran. Washington was alive with rumors about their imminent release. If they were freed at the eleventh hour, how would the public react? Would the American people be caught up in the euphoria of the moment and reelect Carter? Or would they dismiss the release as October politics and vote their pocketbooks? Reagan and his advisers concluded that they could not afford to sit on a safe but slim lead and played their last card: they agreed to a debate with Jimmy Carter one on one. A national debate would enable Reagan to reassure the public, personally and directly, where he stood on war and peace. The announcement of a debate would "freeze" the campaign where it then stood, with Reagan ahead. And Reagan and his people were confident that he would best Carter.

After all, Reagan had won every debate in his political career, starting with former San Francisco mayor George Christopher and Governor Pat Brown of California in 1966 and right up to George Bush and John Anderson in 1980. Undoubtedly Carter would have more facts and figures at his command, but television had been Reagan's medium for almost thirty years, and he had just the message for the 100 million Americans who would be watching: "Are you better off than you were four years ago? If not, vote Republican."

Indeed, the news was bad almost everywhere for Carter and his administration. Inflation stood at 12.7 percent. Interest rates were beginning a rapid rise that would see them double within six months. *National Review's* Richard Brookhiser wrote that "interest rates were kissing President Carter's popularity levels."[48] Unemployment was spreading across the Northeast. The crime rate was accelerating to the point where New York City reported two thousand murders in a single year. Abroad, Western Europe wondered whether the United States had the will to lead the free world; West German chancellor Helmut Schmidt was openly contemptuous of Carter. Iran, Nicaragua, Afghanistan, Angola: the list of crisis spots stretched around the globe.

On Tuesday evening, October 28, one week before election day, Ronald Reagan and Jimmy Carter stood behind specially constructed rostrums on the stage of Cleveland's Music Hall for their first and only debate of the 1980 presidential campaign. Their audience was an estimated 105 million Americans. Both men wore dark suits and muted ties. The similarities ended there.

Carter was grim-lipped and stood rigid, rarely looking at his opponent. He was "pinched, acidulous, aggressive," in the words of ABC journalist Jeff Greenfield. He immediately went on the attack and stayed there for ninety minutes. He debated by the numbers: seven mentions of his being a Democratic president, seven mentions of lonely, life-and-death decisions, ten mentions of the Oval Office, and no fewer than fourteen mentions of his running against a challenger whose ideas and positions were "dangerous," "disturbing," and "radical."[49]

Reagan was calm, cool, ever presidential. He occasionally gestured with his hands and tilted his body to make a point. He smiled. He seemed to be enjoying himself. He spent much of his time patiently explaining where Carter had misquoted or misrepresented him, much like a professor pointing out the errors of an overzealous student.

The climax of the debate—and the effective end of the campaign—came when Carter tried to link Reagan with the idea of making social security voluntary and argued that Reagan had opposed Medicare. That familiar crooked grin appeared on Reagan's face, and with a rueful shake of his head, he looked at Carter and said, "There you go again."[50] The Carter campaign of fear collapsed in an instant.

Reagan sealed Carter's defeat and his victory with his closing remarks when he looked straight into the camera and quietly asked the viewer:

Are you better off than you were four years ago? Is it easier for you to go and buy things in the stores than it was four years ago? . . . Is America as respected throughout the world as it was? Do you feel our security is as safe, that we're as strong as we were four years ago?[51]

After briefly defending his record as governor of California, Reagan ended by promising a crusade "to take government off the back of the great people of this country and turn you loose again to do those things that I know you can do so well, because you . . . made this country great."[52]

An Associated Press poll found that 46 percent of those who watched the debate thought Reagan did the better job, with 34 percent saying Carter did. And a CBS survey revealed Reagan the winner over Carter by 44 percent to 36 percent. Significantly, the same survey also showed that undecided voters were moving toward Reagan by a two-to-one margin.[53]

It seemed that it was all over but the voting. Then on Sunday, November 2, forty-eight hours before election day, the Iranian parliament announced its terms for freeing the fifty-two American hostages. Carter dramatically interrupted his campaigning to fly home to Washington to confer with his top security advisers. He went on national television Sunday afternoon to say that the conditions "appear to offer a positive basis" for an acceptable agreement. But he refused to predict when the hostages might come home and pledged that "my decisions on this crucial matter will not be affected by the calendar."[54]

But the October surprise on which the Carter campaign had been heavily depending turned out to be a November insult. Iran made impossible demands that would require extended negotiations. There would be no triumphal return of the hostages before the voters went to the polls.

Although most of the national polls said it would be a close election, Reagan won by an electoral landslide and more than 8 million popular votes. The conservative Republican carried forty-four states with a total of 489 electoral votes. His 43.9 million votes were the second largest total on record, behind only Richard Nixon's 47.2 million in 1972—a victory across the board and across the country.

Just as important, Reagan's political coattails were long and wide, helping the GOP to pick up twelve seats in the Senate, giving it majority control for the first time in a quarter of a century. Without exception, the Democrats who were defeated—George McGovern, Frank Church, Birch Bayh,

John Culver, Gaylord Nelson—were liberals. Not since 1955 had there been a Republican president and a Republican Senate at the same time. In the House, Republicans registered a gain of thirty-three seats, almost all of them conservatives.

Pundits and politicians agreed that the results constituted an overwhelming rejection of Carter's leadership and policies and a broad mandate for Reagan to change the direction of American politics. Former presidential candidate George McGovern said flatly that the voters had "abandoned American liberalism." In an editorial titled "Tidal Wave," the *Washington Post* acknowledged that 1980 was not an ordinary election: "Nothing of that size and force and sweep could have been created over a weekend or even a week or two by the assorted mullahs and miseries of our times." Pollster Louis Harris concluded that Reagan had won "his stunning victory" because the conservatives, particularly the Moral Majority, "gave him such massive support."[55]

And Reagan won because he dominated the five key elements of every political campaign: organization, money, candidates, issues, and the media. Organizationally, the Republican party was united behind the Reagan-Bush ticket. Even Gerald Ford campaigned widely and effectively for his former rival. The Democrats, still divided after a bitter primary struggle between Carter and Senator Edward Kennedy, were unable to mount a similar organizational effort.

Under federal law, both candidates were restricted to spending the $29.4 million provided by the federal treasury. But Reagan was helped by his national party, which spent $7.5 million on a national television campaign with the theme "Vote Republican for a Change." And there were the independent campaign committees, which spent more than $6 million on pro-Reagan and anti-Carter television and radio advertising. Carter had no such financial help from the Democratic party or independent committees.

As to issues, there were two major ones in 1980: Carter's record and Reagan's ability to govern. Once the focus shifted from the latter to the former, as it did following the presidential debate, Carter was doomed.

As to personal appeal, Carter was one of the poorest public speakers to occupy the White House in the twentieth century. Although he tried to present himself as humble and open-minded, he came off as what he was: arrogant, condescending, and self-righteous. And he was matched against one of the most effective and likable communicators in modern politics. Carter's challenging Reagan to a national televised debate was like Leslie Howard's daring Clark Gable to step into the ring.

As to the news media, most journalists, particularly members of the Washington press corps, did not like Carter, who had shown as much disdain for them as he had for the rest of official Washington. Carter thought he did not need them, and he rarely went out of his way to court them, as had John Kennedy. By contrast, many journalists were taken by Reagan's personal warmth and charm even though they disagreed, often sharply, with his policies. ABC's Sam Donaldson recalled that when he and other veteran political reporters got together, they talked most about Ronald Reagan.[56]

In the final analysis, Ronald Reagan won because he was a man with an idea whose time had come. The idea was that government had grown too big and should be reduced, and America's military had grown too weak and ought to be strengthened. The American people liked the sound of that and elected him president. At last, as *Human Events* put it, conservatives were in a position to govern. "If we fail, we have only ourselves to blame."[57]

Chapter 12

Golden Years

RONALD REAGAN CAME TO THE PRESIDENCY WITH SEVERAL IMPORTANT political advantages. He had an express mandate from the American people who knew what he intended to do: cut income taxes from top to bottom, reduce the size of the federal government for the first time since the New Deal, and make the U.S. military number one in the world. To help him in this revolutionary task, he had a Republican Senate and a feisty Republican minority in the House determined to avoid legislative gridlock.

And he had something else—something that neither Robert Taft nor Barry Goldwater could have counted on if either of them had been elected president: a vital, committed conservative movement. Reagan could turn to the Heritage Foundation, the American Enterprise Institute, the Center for Strategic and International Studies, and other think tanks for ideas.

He could call on groups like the Committee for the Survival of a Free Congress, the American Conservative Union, the National Rifle Association, and the National Tax Limitation Committee for political muscle.

He could staff his administration with professionals who had gotten their start in the movement. In the White House alone, there were conservatives Ed Meese, Richard V. Allen, Martin Anderson, Robert Carleson, Lyn Nofziger, Tony Dolan, and Kenneth Cribb, all in senior positions. And he could draw on the neoconservatives for respected foreign policy experts such as Jeane Kirkpatrick, Max Kampelman, Richard Perle, Kenneth Adelman, and Elliott Abrams.

Outside his administration, Reagan could depend on the support of opinion molders like columnists George Will, Patrick J. Buchanan, William F. Buckley, Jr., James J. Kilpatrick, and John Chamberlain. Will and Buchanan would become major television commentators before the end of the decade; Buckley had always been a major television presence. Reagan could rely for guidance on the analytical skills of the editors and writers of a wide range of journals like *National Review, Human Events, American Spectator, Commentary, The Public Interest,* and *The National Interest,* and the editorial pages of the *Wall Street Journal.*

And thanks to direct mail, there was money to fund the activities of the conservative movement—and those of the Republican party, especially when Reagan signed the letter.

Reagan needed every bit of this help. Internally, the nation faced a multitude of serious economic problems: double-digit inflation, high unemployment, and a prime interest rate of 21.5 percent, the highest since the Civil War. Overseas problems had also proliferated: the energy crisis, the red-tinged Sandinistas in Nicaragua, the unbalanced SALT II treaty, the brutal Soviet invasion of Afghanistan, falling dominos in Africa, the American hostages in Iran. The Vietnam syndrome that permeated and obstructed U.S. foreign policy was reinforced by Carter's maladroit actions and the malaise that he, not the American people, produced.

The new president and his top advisers were well aware that they had to act, and quickly. In presidential politics, as in the 100-yard dash, a quick start is everything.

Richard Wirthlin, the president's pollster, had developed "a strategic outline of initial actions" to be taken during the administration's first 180 days—from the inauguration until early August, when Congress usually recessed for a summer vacation.[1] The plan was based in large part on an address that Reagan had delivered the previous September before the International Business Council of Chicago. The candidate had proposed strictly controlling the rate of growth of government spending, reducing personal income tax rates, revising government regulations, establishing a stable monetary policy, and following a consistent national economic policy.

Democrats attacked it with abandon, and, predictably, big business mouthpieces like the National Association of Manufacturers complained because the plan did not cut business taxes enough. But research director Martin Anderson and the other numbers crunchers were content: they had produced a document (with projections through 1985) showing that Reagan could cut taxes, balance the budget, and increase domestic growth if given the right kind of cooperation by Congress.[2] The *Wall Street Journal* agreed, commenting that Reagan had "spelled out a prudent, gradual, responsible reordering of economic priorities."[3]

The first and most decisive step was tax reform. The top marginal rate on individual income was 70 percent, and Reagan, who had majored in economics in college and had read extensively in the field since the 1950s, concluded that if you reduced tax rates and allowed people to spend or save more of what they earned, "they'll be more industrious, they'll have more incentive to work hard, and money they earn will add fuel to the great economic machine that energizes our national progress." Some economists called this approach supply-side economics; "I call it common sense," Reagan wrote in his 1990 autobiography.[4]

As early as 1964 in his famous television speech for Barry Goldwater, Reagan had sharply criticized the high taxes and large subsidies demanded by America's welfare state and warned, "No nation in history has ever survived a tax burden that reached one-third of its national income." As governor of California, he had striven to reduce taxes, even sponsoring a tax limitation amendment to the state constitution, which had been narrowly defeated. Reagan was a supply-sider, wrote Ed Meese, his long-time colleague, "long before the term was invented."[5]

The conviction "that the size of the economic pie must be increased, not simply sliced differently," was fundamental to supply-siders. For Jack Kemp and others, this was a far more appealing message than the "balance the budget" imperative usually associated with Republicans. The "bibles" of this new economic gospel were Jude Wanniski's *The Way the World Works,* published in 1978, and George Gilder's *Wealth and Poverty,* published in 1981. It had first been proposed legislatively in 1977 by Kemp and Senator William Roth of Delaware with their 30 percent tax cut. But supply-side economics was far more than tax cuts; it envisioned a world "stripped of the tax preferences, subsidies and economic regulations" that were "strangling" the economy.[6]

It would take fireside chats with the American people, deals with boll-weevil Democrats in the House of Representatives, pep talks with discouraged aides, and recovery from an attempted assassination, but on August 17, 1981, President Reagan signed the Economic Recovery Tax Act (ERTA) into law. It was the tax reform he had been urging for decades. *Newsweek* called it a "second New Deal potentially as profound in its import as the first was a half century ago."[7]

The measure cut *all* income tax rates by 25 percent, with a 5 percent cut coming that October, the next 10 percent in July 1982, and the final 10 percent in July 1983. The law reduced the top income tax rate from 70 percent to 50 percent, indexed tax rates to offset the impact of inflation, and increased the tax exemption on estates and gifts. Conservatives have consistently argued that ERTA was a prime factor in the economic growth that prevailed throughout the 1980s and into the 1990s.

There followed sixty straight months of economic growth, the longest uninterrupted period of expansion since the government began keeping such statistics in 1854. Nearly 15 million new jobs were created—a total of 18 million by the time Reagan left office. Just under $20 trillion worth of goods and services, measured in actual dollars, was produced from 1982 to 1987. To give some notion of how much that is, by the end of 1987, America was producing about seven and one-half times more every year than it produced in John Kennedy's last year as president.[8]

The expansion was felt everywhere, as conservative economists had predicted, including in the government's own income. Total federal receipts in 1982 were $618 billion. Five years later, federal receipts were just over $1 trillion, an increase of $398 billion—more than enough, one would have thought, to satisfy all but the most eager advocates of the welfare state.

And as Reagan had promised, the military benefited the most from the economic growth. In President Carter's last budget, America spent just under $160 billion on national defense. In 1987, the Reagan administration spent $282 billion, including more than twice as much on military hardware. During Reagan's first seven years, he was able to expend over $1.5 trillion on national defense, "a staggering amount by anyone's standards."[9]

Although Reagan promised deep cuts in domestic spending, that did not turn out to be the case. Indeed, overall welfare spending increased during the Reagan presidency, primarily because Reagan could not overcome, even with vetos and the bully pulpit of the White House, the spending impulses of Congress, which, after all, signed the checks. Throughout his two terms, he was confronted by Democrats still enthralled by the New Deal, as well as Republicans (particularly in the Senate) still mesmerized by its political appeal.

When the administration proposed to abolish the Department of Education in 1981, Howard Baker, the first Republican Senate majority leader since 1954, actively opposed abolition.[10] Baker wanted to remain majority leader and was worried that getting rid of the department would alienate too many voters.

Reagan was not discouraged. He understood he had to proceed prudently with cuts, one billion dollars at a time; he could not just pull the plug on the federal government. Over the past fifty years, millions of people had grown dependent on it.

Many people remember Reagan saying in his inaugural address that "government is not the solution to our problems; government is the problem." But the new president also said:

> It is not my intention to do away with government. It is rather to make it work—work with us, not over us; to stand by our side, not ride on our back. Government can and must provide opportunity, not smother it; foster productivity, not stifle it.[11]

Here was no radical libertarian with a copy of *Atlas Shrugged* in his back pocket but a traditional conservative guided by the prudential arguments of *The Federalist*. Reagan was a modern federalist, echoing James Madison's call for a balance between the authority of the national and state governments. He also shared Madison's concern about "the abridgement of the freedom of the people" by the "gradual and silent encroachment of those in power." As he later said in his 1990 autobiography, "We had strayed a great distance from our founding fathers' vision of America."[12]

He was determined to recapture that lost vision. As he stated in his inaugural, he would begin by seeking to "curb the size and influence of the federal establishment." Revealing his pragmatism, his immediate target was the welfare excesses of Lyndon B. Johnson, not the long-established social programs of Franklin D. Roosevelt. As he wrote in his diary in January 1982, "The press is trying to paint me as trying to undo the New Deal. I'm trying to undo the Great Society."[13]

It was a slow, uneven process, always made more difficult by a Democratic House of Representatives. Reagan was obliged to allow federal spending for welfare—work programs, education and training, social services, medicine, food, and housing—to rise sharply; expenditures almost doubled from $106.1 billion (in real or nominal dollars) in 1980 to $173 billion in

1988.[14] Nor did Reagan's own cabinet secretaries protest when the increases benefited their agency or department.

Conservative critics like the Heritage Foundation's Stuart Butler did not try to hide their disappointment and frustration. Six years into the Reagan presidency, Butler wrote that "the basic structure of the Great Society is still firmly intact. . . . Virtually no program has been eliminated."[15]

But Reagan reduced federal outlays in some welfare areas—such as regional development, commerce, and housing credit—from $63 billion in 1980 to just over $49 billion in 1987, a decrease of about 22 percent. And the size of the federal civilian workforce declined by about 5 percent, much of it traceable to conservatives like Gerald Carmen at the General Services Administration, Raymond Donovan at Labor, and the Office of Personnel Management's Donald Devine, described by the *Washington Post* as "Reagan's terrible swift sword of the civil service."[16] The agencies that led the personnel downsizing were Education, down 24 percent; Housing and Urban Development, down 22 percent; Office of Personnel Management, down 19 percent; and General Services Administration and Labor, both down 15 percent.

Five principles guided the Reagan welfare cuts: The growth of government should be curbed; federal benefits should be focused primarily on the poor; benefits should be contingent on an individual's effort to leave welfare; decisions on social programs should be returned to the states and localities; and programs that do not work should be eliminated. At the heart of all these principles was a simple proposition: Entitlements as the "underlying principle of American social policy" should be replaced by "benefits contingent on responsible behavior."[17]

But in practice these principles were sometimes shunted aside, as in the case of the politically popular Medicare program. The "most serious policy error of the Reagan administration," conservative analyst Ronald F. Docksai asserted, was its support for the expansion of Medicare to provide catastrophic acute care protection for the elderly. Reagan believed, correctly, that senior citizens should not be impoverished by a serious or persistent illness. But instead of seeking legislation to give private insurance companies an incentive to offer catastrophic hospital and long-term-care insurance, the president was "persuaded by administration officials and Republican lawmakers" to endorse an expansion of Medicare and the federal government. Conservative congressmen who favored a private sector approach to provide quality care and constrain federal spending were undercut by the White House and labeled "anti-elderly" by liberal Democrats.[18]

Reagan's personal feelings about social security had not changed since his 1964 televised address for Barry Goldwater, when he had suggested the introduction of "voluntary features" into the system so that "those who can make better provisions for themselves" be allowed to do so.[19] But he had come to accept, reluctantly, that social security was an issue that Republicans could not touch without getting badly burned. Two months into his presidency, biographer Lou Cannon wrote, the White House was given a congressional initiative that would have sharply slowed the growth of social security and reduced the budget deficit. The device was a freeze or severe reduction in automatic cost-of-living allowances, which had increased social security payments so much that the program now accounted for 21 percent of the total budget.

Reagan was tempted, but as he told Senator Peter Domenici of New Mexico, the author of the amendment and chairman of the Senate Budget Committee, "I made a commitment during the campaign not to cut Social Security, and . . . I don't want to go back on my word."[20] Other senators, including John Tower and William Armstrong of Colorado, endorsed Domenici's approach, but Reagan would not be moved. And regardless of the modest bipartisan support in the Senate, liberal House Democrats would have relished an opportunity to charge that Republicans were once again trying to reduce the size of the monthly social security checks on which millions of senior Americans depended.

There is no denying that American indebtedness increased significantly during the Reagan years. Reagan borrowed $1 for every $5 he spent, increasing the national debt by $1.5 trillion through 1988. He did not have to worry too much about where to get the money; America was still such a good credit risk that people around the world "pressed money on us, and we obliged, borrowing easily, quickly, and almost guiltlessly," in Cannon's words.[21] But Reagan did feel guilty about the accumulated debt—as much as anyone with his unassailable optimism could feel guilty. He admitted that his failures to cut federal spending absolutely and to balance the federal budget were his "biggest disappointments" as president.[22]

But it is a little-remembered fact, as Cato Institute economist Stephen Moore has emphasized, that by the end of the Reagan era, the federal deficit as a share of gross domestic product was falling, and rapidly—from 6 percent in 1985 to 3 percent in 1989. As Reagan left office, the Democrat-controlled Congressional Budget Office projected that "deficits were on a path to fall to about one percent of GDP by 1993" without any action by future presidents.[23]

Reagan never ignored the deficit; he just had more important things on his mind. As he said in 1981, "I did not come here to balance the budget—not at the expense of my tax-cutting program and my defense program."[24] Still, every budget he submitted to Congress outlined spending reductions that would have reduced the cumulative deficit during the 1980s by several hundred billion dollars. But Congress nullified this possibility with a succession of "continuing resolutions" that enabled the government to keep operating and keep spending at the same level.

The persistent deficits had an unintended impact on Congress, which for the first time in the postwar era began to "impose limits on the growth of government." Of all the measures we know, Milton Friedman wrote, "the deficit has been the only effective restraint on congressional spending."[25]

President Reagan devoted most of his time in the spring and early summer of 1981 (after he had recovered from the March 30 shooting by would-be assassin John Hinckley) building a consensus for his economic recovery program. *Time*'s Lawrence Barrett described the president's strategy as initial "seduction" followed by a "blitzkrieg."[26] Reagan began by showing the Washington establishment that he was not a dangerous man or a "political freak." He had drinks with House Speaker Tip O'Neill, a meeting with Senator Edward Kennedy, and a chat with publisher Katharine Graham of the *Washington Post*. Quite a charmer, they agreed, but certainly no real threat to the way Washington works.

O'Neill was so deceived that he condescendingly offered some advice to the new fellow in town. "You were governor of a state," he told Reagan, "but a governor plays in the minor leagues. Now you're in the big leagues. Things might not move as quickly as you would like." Just eight months later, the House of Representatives passed Reagan's economic recovery plan, 238–195, with the cross-over help of forty-eight Democrats who did not mind going against their Speaker when it was in the best interests of their constituents.

Reagan called Congress's passage of the bill "the greatest political victory in half a century." Jubilant conservatives hailed it as a "new economic beginning." David Broder of the *Washington Post* proclaimed Reagan's tax victory as "one of the most remarkable demonstrations of presidential leadership in modern history."[27] The $162 billion tax cut dwarfed any previous one in the postwar period; Ford's $22.8 billion reduction in 1975 was a distant second.

The cuts in personal income taxes "had a permanency unlike that of any [previous] tax bill" because of the indexing provision. In the past, individuals were pushed into higher tax brackets whenever their income rose along with inflation. ERTA did away with "bracket creep" and prevented political leaders from "solving" fiscal deficits by waiting for inflation to increase revenues each year. From now on, Congress had to pass and the president had to sign any tax increase out in the open. How to collect government revenues "became the dominating political issue of the 1980s."[28]

"People are policy," Ed Feulner of the Heritage Foundation has often remarked, and nowhere was this truer than in the Reagan administration. There was a constant struggle between the Reaganauts, who wanted to transform the government, and the pragmatists, who were content with change at the margin. Between them was the president himself, who sometimes aligned himself with the Reaganauts and sometimes with the pragmatists, instinctively seeking a golden mean between the two camps. He was willing to accept less than 100 percent if that was all he could get and if the agreement moved him toward his basic goal of minimizing government and maximizing individual freedom. As he once said of his landmark welfare reforms in California, "If I can get seventy percent of what I want from a legislature controlled by the opposition, I'll take my chances on getting the other thirty when they see how well it works."[29]

Sometimes Reagan went along with a pragmatist like chief of staff James Baker, who persuaded the president to accept the Tax Equity and Fiscal Responsibility Act of 1982 (TEFRA), which turned out to be the great tax increase of 1982—$98 billion over the next three years. That was too much for eighty-nine House Republicans (including second-term congressman Newt Gingrich of Georgia) or for prominent conservative organizations from the American Conservative Union and the Conservative Caucus to the U.S. Chamber of Commerce, which all opposed the measure.

Baker assured his boss that Congress would approve three dollars in spending cuts for every dollar of tax increase. To Reagan, TEFRA looked like a pretty good "70 percent" deal. But Congress wound up cutting less than twenty-seven cents for every new tax dollar. What had seemed to be an acceptable 70–30 compromise turned out to be a 30–70 surrender. Ed Meese described TEFRA as "the greatest domestic error of the Reagan administration," although it did leave untouched the individual tax rate reductions approved the previous year. (TEFRA was built on a series of business and excise taxes plus the removal of business tax deductions.)[30]

The basic problem was that Reagan believed, as Lyn Nofziger put it, that members of Congress "wouldn't lie to him when he should have known better."[31] As a result of TEFRA, Reagan learned to "trust but verify" whether he was dealing with a Speaker of the House or a president of the Soviet Union.

Sometimes the president sided with reformers as when, after a year of hard work, he signed the Tax Reform Act of 1986 into law. In his 1985 State of the Union address, Reagan had signaled his intention "to simplify the tax code so all taxpayers would be treated more fairly."[32] An unusual coalition formed around the president's initiative, including Democrats Richard Gephardt and Dan Rostenkowski in the House and budget chairman Pete Domenici and Democrat Bill Bradley in the Senate. A bipartisan deal was ultimately struck, with Reagan agreeing to close existing tax loopholes if the Democrats would agree to lower marginal rates for individuals and families.

Reagan was deadly serious about the measure. In mid-December 1985, for example, he made an unusual personal visit to Capitol Hill to lobby members of Congress for his tax reform. A few days later, he telephoned House Speaker O'Neill to report that he had rounded up at least fifty Republican votes for final passage of the legislation. O'Neill had set the fifty-vote requirement for bringing the bill to the floor.

Describing his plan as a "Second American Revolution," Reagan promised that it would make taxes lower, fairer, simpler, and more productive. And it did, lowering the top marginal rate from 50 percent to 33 percent, simplifying the number of tax brackets, and increasing personal deductions so much that an estimated 4.3 million low-income families were removed from the tax rolls. At the same time, a minimum tax was established to ensure that wealthy taxpayers would not escape paying at least some income tax. And hundreds of special interest provisions, such as deductible "three martini luncheons," were eliminated.

Reagan described his tax reform initiative as one of the proudest achievements of his administration. He called his tax reform act "the best anti-poverty bill, the best pro-family measure and the best job-creation program ever to come out of the Congress of the United States."[33]

However, whichever way he tacked, Reagan often found himself being roundly criticized by leaders of the New Right, eager as always to find fault with a conservative for not being conservative enough. Richard Viguerie and others pointed out that regardless of Reagan's successful battles to reduce income tax rates, the average American's total tax payments had actually gone up in Reagan's second year if you included increases in social security withholding. As for Reagan's spending cuts, the New Rightists stressed, they were not absolute reductions but merely reductions in the rate of increase.

"We constantly hear nonsense about how conservatives are running everything," remarked Terry Dolan, head of the National Conservative Political Action Committee (NCPAC). "If that were true, we wouldn't have the biggest budget deficits in history."[34]

Even the Heritage Foundation, as good a friend of the Reagan administration as there was in Washington, concluded after one year that although headed in the right direction, the administration "should and could have accomplished more." The foundation estimated that of two thousand recommendations made in its monumental *Mandate for Leadership: Policy Management in a Conservative Administration,* published in late 1980 just before Reagan took office, about 1,270 suggestions—"only" 60 percent—had been implemented or initiated. The "only" seemed gratuitous: Even the fabled Ted Williams of the Boston Red Sox would have been satisfied with a .600 batting average. But conservatives, out of power for decades, were impatient and demanding of results.

Certainly the Reagan administration achieved much in the domestic field in its first term: reducing inflation, lowering unemployment, cutting the prime interest rate in half, and producing economic growth of 6 percent in 1983. But it did not solve all the old problems and indeed failed even to tackle some, such as the federal deficit and intrusive federal departments like the Department of Education. After chalking up a series of impressive budget victories in their first year and maintaining the policy initiative, Reagan officials, according to Heritage's Stuart M. Butler, "appeared to lose their edge."[35]

There were several reasons for the slowdown. The federal bureaucracy, protective of its power, began to dig in and practice its well-honed delaying tactics. The Democratic opposition in Congress, led by the wily House Speaker, Tip O'Neill, organized more effectively. Pragmatic Reagan aides like Jim Baker kept resisting bold initiatives. And the complicated budget process (authorization, appropriation, conference committees, etc.) allowed liberal legislators to block White House proposals and whittle away at the president's early antispending victories. All the while, the mounting federal deficits made conservatives in Congress increasingly nervous.

Contrary to conservative hopes, Reagan was not able to cut overall government spending, which remained at roughly 22 percent of GNP during his eight years in office. But the change in priorities was significant, with defense spending increasing from 5.0 to 6.5 percent of GNP, thus enabling the president to deal with the Soviets from a position of strength. Even so, Heritage analysts Robert Rector and Michael Sanera pointed out, the Reagan buildup, measured in constant dollars, was "about half the size of Eisenhower's peacetime military increases,"[36] which suggests, ironically, that Ike himself might have been responsible, at least partially, for the creation of the military-industrial complex that he warned America about in his farewell address.

Still, if one examines the economic report cards of American presidents from Truman through Reagan, Reagan easily finishes first. Using the change each year in inflation, unemployment, interest rates, and growth in gross national product, Harvard economist Robert Barro ranked Reagan number one. Among other things, Reagan engineered the largest reduction in the misery index (the total of inflation and unemployment) in history: 50 percent. In fact, sums up economist Richard B. McKenzie, the 1980s were, up to then, "the most prosperous decade in American history."[37]

The more than 350 federal judges that Reagan appointed during his eight years in office also constitute an important legacy. He named close to half of all lower-court federal judges, more than any other president. He also elevated conservative William H. Rehnquist to chief justice of the United States and appointed three associate justices, including the first woman, Sandra Day O'Connor, a moderate conservative. Almost as important as the Rehnquist nomination was that of Antonin Scalia, a U.S. Court of Appeals judge and a former scholar at the American Enterprise Institute. Scalia has been unwavering in his opposition to affirmative action, abortion, and what he has called the "liberal jurisprudence" that undergirds judicial activism.[38]

As Reagan stated in 1986, his goal was a federal judiciary "made up of judges who believe in law and order and a strict interpretation of the Constitution."[39] The man in charge of the selection process, Attorney General Edwin Meese III, emphasized that the administration aimed "to institutionalize the Reagan revolution so it can't be set aside no matter what happens in future presidential elections."[40]

The president persuaded the Senate to approve his judicial nominations because he was able to forge a broad coalition among traditional conservatives like Strom Thurmond, chairman of the Senate Judiciary Committee; New Right conservatives like John East of North Carolina and Jeremiah Denton of Alabama; and moderate law-and-order Republicans like Arlen Specter of Pennsylvania. That changed abruptly when Democrats regained control of the Senate in 1986 and named Joseph Biden of Delaware chairman of the Judiciary Committee.

Reagan's most dramatic defeat came in 1987 when he nominated Judge Robert Bork to the Supreme Court.[41] Bork's confirmation became an ugly battle against liberal organizations like the American Civil Liberties Union, the AFL–CIO, and People for the American Way. One analyst put the cost of the anti-Bork media campaign at $15 million.[42]

Although the American Bar Association rated Bork "well qualified," the ACLU called him "unfit." Senator Edward Kennedy, who led the Senate fight against the conservative jurist, charged that Bork's nomination would lead to an America where

> women would be forced into back-alley abortions, blacks would sit at segregated lunch counters, rogue police would break down citizens' doors in midnight raids, school children would not be taught about evolution, writers and authors could be censored at the whim of government and the doors of the federal courts would be shut on the fingers of millions of citizens.[43]

Not since 1964 and LBJ's anticampaign against Barry Goldwater had a conservative been subjected to so fierce and unfair an attack. The *Boston Globe*'s Supreme Court correspondent wrote that Kennedy "shamelessly twisted Bork's world view."[44]

Bork's nomination dominated the political agenda in the late summer and early fall of 1987. His five days of testimony before the Senate Judiciary Committee were nationally televised. Former president Gerald Ford personally introduced the nominee to the committee. Former president Jimmy Carter then sent a letter stating his opposition. One hundred and ten witnesses appeared for and against Bork during two weeks of hearings. Finally, the Democrat-controlled Judiciary Committee refused by a vote of 9 to 5 to recommend Bork's nomination. The Senate then voted 58 to 42 against confirmation: 6 moderate Republicans broke party ranks and voted with 52 Democrats against Bork, while 2 Democrats voted for Bork. Liberals loudly celebrated their victory; soon after, Reagan nominated and won confirmation of a low-key moderate, Anthony M. Kennedy.

Several factors combined to deny Robert Bork a seat on the Supreme Court: a strongly partisan Democratic Senate, a president weakened by the Iran-contra affair, a White House that did not launch its nomination campaign early enough, a liberal opposition that was better organized and financed than the conservative support, and a nominee who was often contentious and contradictory in his testimony. But ultimately Bork was rejected because of his view that the Constitution was "the Founders' Constitution" bound by original intent and not a "living document" susceptible to the interpretation of current justices.[45] Today, however, Bork's traditional view of the Constitution is increasingly articulated by a majority of the Supreme Court.

Although Bork's defeat was a major setback for the Reagan administration, it could not negate Reagan's significant legal legacy of a conservative federal judiciary from top to bottom. "Reagan's success lies not simply in quantity but quality," concluded conservative author Terry Eastland, who worked in the administration's Justice Department. Indeed, Reagan's judges, according to biographer Lou Cannon, "ranked above [those of] Carter, Ford, Nixon and Johnson."[46]

The Reagan years were paradoxical ones for the conservative movement, with some conservative organizations rising to new heights of influence and affluence and others fading and falling from sight. In 1974, the Heritage Foundation could fit all eight of its employees into a couple of rented offices and had a tiny budget of $250,000, almost all of it provided by one generous businessman, Colorado brewer Joseph Coors. A decade later, Heritage had a staff of more than one hundred people—analysts, academics, and support personnel—and an annual operating budget of about $10.5 million based on the contributions of over 100,000 individuals, foundations, and corporations.

In contrast, several New Right groups were in near free fall. The Moral

Majority was damaged by the financial misdeeds of Jim Bakker and the sexual misconduct of fellow television evangelist Jimmy Swaggart, although neither was a conservative activist. Many Americans simply did not or could not distinguish between Bakker and Swaggart on the one hand and Jerry Falwell, Pat Robertson, and other ministers of the Religious Right on the other. Also, many of the Religious Right's people shifted their allegiance and financial support to conservative organizations based in Washington, D.C.[47]

Despite a continuing high media profile, the National Conservative Political Action Committee was in serious financial trouble, with millions of dollars of unpaid bills. Its problems were compounded by the ill health of its articulate, aggressive chairman, Terry Dolan, who died in January 1987.

Howard Phillips found organizing at the grass roots more and more difficult. Many conservatives were convinced that with Reagan in the White House, the political war had been won. Phillips thought differently and kept searching for the right issues to motivate people, from limiting taxes to supporting freedom fighters in Angola. And he became increasingly critical of Reagan, which won him attention in the news media but earned him the enmity of the administration.

Appalled by the treaty banning medium-range missiles from Europe, Phillips scorned President Reagan as "a useful idiot for Kremlin propaganda."[48] The Conservative Caucus leader and similar hard-core conservatives seemed to think that arms control negotiations had only one purpose: to prevent arms control agreements. But Reagan, as the *Chicago Tribune* stressed, "always said he would sign a treaty that served America's interests."[49] Phillips later summed up Reagan as "a superb chief of state and a deficient chief executive."[50]

Frustrated by the New Right's decline, Richard Viguerie became more sharply populist during the Reagan years, attacking Big Government, Big Labor, Big Business, and Big Media in a new book, *The Establishment vs. the People.* He charged that both the Democratic and Republican parties had "come to defend a privileged elite against the will and interests of the majority." He faulted President Reagan for raising taxes, hiring "5,200 additional IRS agents," and failing to veto "unnecessary" government spending. "Who will speak for the little guy?" Viguerie demanded.[51] Writing in *National Review,* Viguerie claimed both Thomas Jefferson and William F. Buckley, Jr., as inspirations for his antielitism, amusing Jefferson scholars and startling the patrician Buckley.[52]

With all his many activities and connections, Paul Weyrich should have been a contented man. He was head of Coalitions for America, which through its three divisions—the Kingston Group, the Library Court Group, and the Stanton Group—served as a central forum for nearly 120 different conservative organizations concerned with domestic policy and economics, profamily issues (particularly abortion), and national defense and international affairs. A frequent participant and sometimes co-chairman in the weekly meetings of the Kingston Group was Congressman Newt Gingrich, who appreciated its political clout.

Weyrich was acknowledged by experts on the Left and the Right as one of the shrewdest politicians in Washington. An AFL–CIO publication grudgingly credited the New Right and Weyrich's Committee for the Survival of a Free Congress for "a whole passel of persons sitting in the U.S. House and Senate."[53]

But Weyrich was concerned that conservatives were still reacting to the Left and not framing their own agenda. "We need more bills like the Family Protection Act," he said—the omnibus bill setting forth a profamily agenda including school vouchers and larger tax exemptions for children.[54] Weyrich drafted the bill, which was first introduced by Senator Paul Laxalt of Nevada, President Reagan's closest friend in the Senate.

More of a pragmatist than Howard Phillips, Weyrich believed that it was important to keep lines open to Congress and the Reagan White House. He became somewhat alarmed at the anti-Republican, populist rhetoric of his old friend and colleague, Viguerie. Certainly the New Right had demonstrated in the 1978 and 1980 congressional elections that it could defeat liberal Democrats, but could it build an effective conservative coalition?

By 1986, Weyrich was promoting what he and coauthor William S. Lind called "cultural conservatism," whose philosophical antecedents could be found in Russell Kirk's *The Conservative Mind* and Richard Weaver's *Ideas Have Consequences*. But Weyrich saw cultural conservatives as the forgers of a revived conservative movement that embraced "Old Right intellectuals, New Right activists, neoconservative policy analysts, and liberals concerned with civility and serious literature."[55]

It was an ambitious concept but fated to fail because it was too ambitious; too many philosophical and cultural questions were left dangling. Its most serious flaw was its neutrality on divine will (which offended Christian conservatives) and natural law (which bothered many Catholics and other traditional conservatives). And without those important members of the conservative movement, cultural conservatism could have no meaningful political impact. Both Kirk and Weaver, of course, were anything but neutral about the need for a belief in God and an acknowledgment of natural law in politics.

Aside from the decline of the New Right, the 1980s were generally bountiful years for conservatives as all the elements of a successful political movement came together: a consistent philosophy, a national constituency, requisite financing, a solid organizational base, media support, and a charismatic, principled leader. At the center of the movement was that remarkable political fusionist Ronald Reagan, who brought in southerners, fundamentalist-evangelical Protestants, and ethnic Catholics while holding on to libertarians and midwesterners. He did so by appealing, as he put it in his final address, to their best hopes, not their worst fears. He did so by reiterating traditional American themes of duty, honor, and country. "In his evocation of our national memory and symbols of pride," said William J. Bennett, "in his summoning us to our national purpose and to national greatness, he performed the crucial task of political leadership."[56]

Reagan was faithful to conservative ideas at a time when Americans at last were ready to listen to them and act on them. He framed the debate, as analyst Peter J. Ferrara pointed out, forcing his adversaries to respond to his proposals on taxes and spending. He forced the debate "to take place on his terms and his choices," which were, wherever possible, to lower taxes, cut government programs, eliminate regulations, and reduce government handouts.[57]

He did not need focus groups and public polls to chart the path of his administration. He saw it as his duty to get government off the backs and out of the pockets of the people. Always, Ronald Reagan sought to restore power to the people rather than grab it for himself.

Chapter 13

The Reagan Doctrine

FOR THIRTY-FIVE YEARS, THROUGH SEVEN PRESIDENCIES, THE UNITED STATES and its allies labored unceasingly to contain communism around the world with a broad range of diplomatic, military, and economic initiatives that had cost tens of thousands of lives and hundreds of billions of dollars. They used economic programs like the Marshall Plan, military alliances like NATO and SEATO, direct conflicts like the Korean War and the Vietnam War, indirect engagements like the the Bay of Pigs, weapons treaties like SALT I, economic treaties like MFN (Most Favored Nation), and covert operations like the proposed assassination of Cuba's Fidel Castro. And yet, after three and a half decades, communism was not only alive and seemingly well in the Soviet Union, Eastern Europe, mainland China, Cuba, and North Korea but had spread to sub-Saharan Africa, Afghanistan, and Nicaragua.

Clearly, containment was not working, or at least it was not working fast enough. The time had come, Ronald Reagan decided, not merely to contain communism but to defeat it. He took his lead from fellow conservative Barry Goldwater, who had asked in his 1962 book of the same name, "Why not victory?" In his first news conference as president, Reagan bluntly denounced the Soviet leadership as still dedicated to "world revolution and a one-world Socialist-Communist state."[1]

As Reagan put it in his 1990 autobiography, "I decided we had to send as powerful a message as we could to the Russians that we weren't going to stand by anymore while they armed and financed terrorists and subverted democratic governments."[2]

242

To most liberals (and Republican realists like Henry Kissinger and Richard Nixon), any notion of victory over communism seemed quixotic, if not dangerous. Every sensible person knew that the Soviet Union was economically strong and militarily powerful; the West's only responsible option was negotiation and accommodation—in a word, détente. As liberal historian Arthur Schlesinger, Jr., declared after a 1982 visit to Moscow, "Those in the U.S. who think the Soviet Union is on the verge of economic and social collapse, ready with one small push to go over the brink, are . . . only kidding themselves."[3]

Two years later, the liberal establishment's favorite economist, John Kenneth Galbraith, published a glowing appraisal of Soviet economics, explaining that "the Russian system succeeds because, in contrast to the Western industrial economies, it makes full use of its manpower. . . . The Soviet economy has made great national progress in recent years."[4] The most glaringly faulty analysis of all was probably that of economist Lester Thurow, who wrote in his textbook, "Today [the Soviet Union] is a country whose economic achievements bear comparison with those of the United States."[5]

In truth, Mikhail Gorbachev took command in 1985 of an empire in deep trouble. Nearly seventy years after the Bolshevik Revolution, Soviet economic growth had stagnated, Soviet farms were unable to feed the people, most Soviet factories never met their quotas or inflated their figures, consumer lines in Moscow and other cities often stretched for blocks, and a distant war in Afghanistan dragged on with no end in sight to the fighting or the deaths of thousands of young Soviet men.

From intelligence reports and the insights accumulated over a lifetime of study and reading, Reagan concluded that communism was cracking, ready to crumble. He went public with his belief in a commencement address at his alma mater, Eureka College, in May 1982, declaring that the Soviet empire was "faltering because rigid centralized control has destroyed incentives for innovation, efficiency and individual achievement."[6]

In a prophetic address one month later to British members of Parliament at Westminster, Reagan said that the Soviet Union, "the home of Marxist-Leninism," was gripped by a "great revolutionary crisis" and that a "global campaign for freedom" would ultimately prevail. There would be "repeated explosions against repression" in Eastern Europe, he said, and continued: "The Soviet Union itself is not immune to this reality."[7]

Indeed, in one of the most memorable utterances of his presidency,

Reagan predicted that "the march of freedom and democracy . . . will leave Marxism-Leninism on the ash-heap of history as it has left other tyrannies which stifle the freedom and muzzle the self-expression of the people."[8]

It was bold, inspiring, and, according to most liberals and some conservatives, wishful thinking. The *New York Times* scorned the speech as an appeal for "flower power" and said that "curiously missing from his plan was any formula for using Western economic strength to promote political accommodation."[9] But Reagan did have a plan, although not the kind the *Times* had in mind.

Unwilling to continue the policy of containment and accommodation, which he viewed as strategically flawed, Reagan and his top foreign policy aides—CIA director William Casey, Defense Secretary Caspar Weinberger, national security adviser Richard V. Allen and his successor, William P. Clark—set out to end the cold war by winning it. "We adopted a comprehensive strategy," Weinberger later recalled, "that included economic warfare, to attack Soviet weaknesses."[10] It was an offensive strategy intended to shift "the focus of the superpower struggle" to the Soviet bloc and the Soviet Union itself.[11]

Reagan implemented his strategy despite strong criticism from both liberals and conservatives. During his first term, Reagan was unyielding toward Moscow, sparking sharp criticism from anxious doves. When asked why he had not yet met with any Soviet leader, Reagan quipped, "They keep dying on me"—a reference to the rapid successive deaths of Leonid Brezhnev, Yuri Andropov, and Konstantin Chernenko.[12] In his second term, Reagan was conciliatory with Gorbachev, eliciting strong opposition from suspicious hawks. William F. Buckley, Jr., wrote bluntly that to greet the Soviet Union "as if it were no longer evil is on the order of changing our entire position toward Adolf Hitler." In the end, however, through a remarkable combination of vision, tenacity, and improvisional skill, Reagan produced what Henry Kissinger termed "the greatest diplomatic feat of the modern era."[13]

Reagan and his aides implemented the president's vision through a series of top-secret national security decision directives (NSDDs). NSDD-32, approved in March 1982, declared that the United States would seek to "neutralize" Soviet control over Eastern Europe and authorized the use of covert action and other means to support anti-Soviet groups in the region. Conservatives had been urging such a policy since 1959, when an annual National Captive Nations Week had been authorized by Congress and signed into law by President Eisenhower. Even earlier, anticommunist writers like Eugene Lyons and Lev E. Dobriansky had referred to the people behind the iron curtain as "our secret allies."[14]

In November 1982, NSDD-66, drafted by National Security Council (NSC) aide Roger Robinson, stated that it would be U.S. policy to disrupt the Soviet economy by attacking a "strategic triad" of critical resources—financial credits, high technology, and natural gas—deemed essential to Soviet economic survival. NSDD-66 was tantamount, Robinson later explained, "to a secret declaration of economic war on the Soviet Union."[15]

The third directive was NSDD-75, written by the distinguished Harvard historian and Sovietologist Richard Pipes, who served on Reagan's NSC staff for two years. Issued in January 1983, it called for the United States no longer to coexist with the Soviet system but rather to seek to change it fundamentally. It "was a clear break from the past," said Pipes. "At its root was the belief that we had it in our power to alter the Soviet system through the use of external pressure." NSDD-75's language was unequivocal: America intended to roll back Soviet influence at every opportunity.[16]

From 1981 until 1987, the Reagan administration pursued a multifaceted foreign policy offensive that included covert and other support to the Solidarity movement in Poland, a psychological operation to engender indecision and fear among Soviet leaders, a global campaign to reduce Soviet access to Western high technology, and a drive to hurt the Soviet economy by driving down the price of oil and limiting natural gas exports to the West.

The Reagan Doctrine was the name given to Reagan's already functioning but top-secret foreign policy. Neoconservative columnist Charles Krauthammer came up with the phrase in an April 1985 column:

> The Reagan Doctrine proclaims overt and unashamed support for anticommunist revolution. . . . It is intended to establish a new, firmer—a doctrinal—foundation for such support by declaring equally worthy all armed resistance to communism whether foreign or indigenously imposed.[17]

Krauthammer had no way of knowing that Pipes, Robinson, and other members of the Reagan administration had already said much the same thing in NSDD-32, NSDD-66, and NSDD-75. In keeping with their boss's injunction not to worry who gets the credit so long as things get done, Reagan aides allowed Krauthammer to remain the man who "invented" the Reagan Doctrine. But none of the more than two hundred NSDDs that the president signed referred to a "Reagan Doctrine."[18] In truth, Reagan's strategy was far broader and more complex than Krauthammer's conception, which was essentially a policy of proxy warfare in four countries: Afghanistan, Nicaragua, Angola, and Cambodia.

No one should underestimate, however, the importance of the Reagan administration's decision to assist profreedom, anticommunist forces in each of these countries.

President Carter had begun helping the anti-Soviet *mujahideen* in Afghanistan during his final months in office. But American aid to what Reagan called "freedom fighters" increased significantly during his adminis-tration. A key decision was the White House approval of Stinger ground-to-air missiles, which the *mujahideen* desperately needed and promptly used to shoot down the Soviet Hind battle helicopters that had kept them on the de-fensive throughout the war.

Across the Atlantic Ocean, the Marxist Sandinistas were not only estab-lishing a Leninist state in Nicaragua but supporting communist guerrillas in El Salvador and elsewhere. Deeply worried about the spread of communism throughout the region, the Reagan administration directed the CIA to form an anti-Sandinista movement and then asked Congress to approve funds for the contras, as they were called, when ten thousand peasants joined them.

The president cared deeply about the future of Central America. When Tip O'Neill kept insisting that he and others in Congress would block the administration's program, Reagan privately exploded: "The Sandinistas have openly proclaimed Communism in their country and their support of Marx-ist revolutions throughout Central America . . . they're killing and torturing people! Now what the hell does Congress expect me to do about that?"[19]

Reagan, however, never contemplated sending U.S. troops to Nica-ragua. He believed that with sufficient military support and firm diplomatic negotiation, Nicaraguans could rid themselves of the Marxist regime. He was proved correct by the democratic elections in February 1990 when anti-Sandinista Violeta Chamorro decisively defeated commandante Daniel Or-tega for the presidency.

In another part of the world, when Soviet-backed forces formed a gov-ernment in Angola in sub-Saharan Africa, the United States promptly allied itself with the anticommunist Union for the Total National Independence of Angola (UNITA), led by Jonas Savimbi. Savimbi became a favorite of many conservatives; he was even dubbed the "George Washington" of southern Africa by Howard Phillips of the Conservative Caucus. Reagan began helping UNITA in 1985 when congressional proscriptions on assistance were lifted.[20]

And in Asia, after Pol Pot of the murderous Khmer Rouge had wiped out perhaps one-fourth of the Cambodian population in the mid-1970s, he was overthrown by a puppet regime installed by the communist government of Vietnam. A guerrilla movement then emerged in Cambodia, including elements of the old Sihanouk monarchy, some democrats, and the Khmer Rouge itself. In this constantly shifting situation, the Reagan administration supported the insurgents, while trying to minimize help to the Khmer Rouge faction.[21]

As applied in these four countries, the Reagan Doctrine was the most cost-effective of all the cold war doctrines, costing the United States only an estimated half-billion dollars a year and yet forcing the cash-strapped Soviets to spend several times that amount to deflect the impact. The doctrine was also one of the most successful in cold war history. It resulted in a Soviet pull-out from Afghanistan, the election of a democratic government in Nicaragua, and the removal of forty thousand Cuban troops from Angola and the holding of UN-monitored elections there. Only in Cambodia was the result less than satisfactory: former Khmer Rouge officials continued to dominate the government, although in 1997 Pol Pot was captured and scheduled to be tried for crimes against the Cambodian people before his death in 1998.

Some neoconservatives have boasted that "without the neoconservatives, there would not be a Reagan Doctrine."[22] But neoconservatives were more implementers than initiators of the doctrine developed by Reagan and other conservatives over the years. As Democrats who had worked for Hubert Humphrey in the 1960s and Henry "Scoop" Jackson in the 1970s, the neoconservatives had never been part of the political policy team that had worked to obtain the Republican presidential nomination for Ronald Reagan as early as 1968. To be sure, several neoconservatives served brilliantly in the Reagan administration: Jeane Kirkpatrick, the first female U.S. ambassador to the United Nations; Richard Perle, the Defense Department's canny arms control advocate; Max Kampelman, America's chief arms negotiator in Geneva; and Elliott Abrams, the assistant secretary of state for Latin America.

All four had been members of the Coalition for a Democractic Majority (CDM), founded in 1972 by centrist Democrats anxious to move the party away from "the isolationism of the New Left" and back to the muscular foreign policy of Roosevelt, Truman, Kennedy, and Johnson. CDM's manifesto was drafted by Norman Podhoretz, editor of the influential *Commentary* magazine; his wife and social critic, Midge Decter; and Ben Wattenberg, a political scientist who had written speeches for Lyndon Johnson.[23]

Most of CDM's members stayed loyal to the Democratic party through the 1970s, although their man, Jackson, lost the 1976 presidential nomination to Jimmy Carter. The Carter administration ignored all fifty-three of the coalition's recommendations for foreign policy positions with one slighting exception: the dispatching of a presidential envoy to the negotiations on the political status of Micronesia, an archipelago of tiny islands in the Pacific where the United States had once conducted nuclear tests. "They froze us out," remarked Elliott Abrams in disgust.[24]

Even with all of Carter's foreign missteps and mistakes, from SALT II to Iran to Afghanistan to Korea, CDM members could not bring themselves to leave the party they had supported for so long. The breaking point came in January 1980 when coalition leaders met with President Carter in the Roosevelt Room of the White House's West Wing. Slumping in the polls and challenged by Senator Edward Kennedy in the Democratic primaries, Carter needed all the support he could get from sympathetic Democrats. But when CDM's spokesman, political scientist Austin Ranney, began by making a distinction between Carter's foreign policy before and after the Soviet invasion of Afghanistan, the president's face flushed red, and he answered in his characteristically icy way:

> Your analysis is not true. There has been no change in my policy. I have always held a consistent view of the Soviet Union.
>
> For the record, I did not say that I have learned more about the Soviets since the invasion of Afghanistan, as is alleged in the press. My policy is my policy, and has been my policy. It has not changed, and will not change.[25]

The president's stubbornness stunned the group. There were similar nonresponses and non sequiturs from the president throughout the thirty-minute meeting. After Carter left for another meeting, Vice President Walter Mondale spent an hour with the visitors, stressing the hard-line attitude of the administration toward the Soviets' aggressive behavior and trying desperately, and without success, to erase the disastrous impression he knew the president had made.

The CDM delegation left the White House with almost everyone but Ranney and Wattenberg agreeing that their hopes for working with Carter had been "dashed." When Midge Decter asked Jeane Kirkpatrick for her reaction, Kirkpatrick replied in a firm voice, "I am not going to support *that* man."[26]

The following month, she was invited by Richard V. Allen (who had worked with Kirkpatrick on the launching of the bipartisan Committee on the Present Danger in 1976) to meet with Ronald Reagan and a group of foreign policy experts. The long-time Democrat was curious: she had received a highly flattering three-page letter from Reagan about her *Commentary* article "Dictatorships and Double Standards." At the policy meeting, Kirkpatrick was impressed by the serious questions Reagan asked and his "intuitive grasp" of the issues. That evening, she sat next to Reagan at a private dinner at the Chevy Chase home of columnist George Will. Afterward she told her husband, political scientist Evron Kirkpatrick, that Reagan was attractive and "very likable." And his view of foreign affairs, she stressed, was "generally correct and very realistic."[27]

A professor of government at Georgetown University and a senior fellow at the American Enterprise Institute, Jeane Kirkpatrick loved politics and was eager to make policy, not just write about it. She wanted to be a part of the action in 1980. But how could she, a lifelong Democrat, join the Republicans? She remembered how Reagan had teased her at the Will dinner, saying, "I was a Democrat once, you know," and then adding, after a pause, "I felt a little funny when I first started associating with Republicans."[28]

In May 1980, shortly before the Pennsylvania primary, a triumphant Richard Allen announced the establishment of a twelve-member policy council, supplemented by two groups of policy advisers—one on foreign affairs, the other on defense. Among the names was Jeane J. Kirkpatrick. When a *Washington Post* reporter asked her if she was supporting Reagan, Kirkpatrick mentioned the bad treatment by liberal Democrats and the friendly messages from conservative Republicans that she and other "Jackson Democrats" had been receiving. "After a certain time," she explained, "it begins to seem irresistible." And then she added, realistic as always, "Especially if the person seems likely to be the next president of the United States."[29]

R eagan's cold war strategy was later spelled out by Ed Meese, who, if not a member of the president's foreign policy inner circle, was in the immediate outer circle because of his White House position and his long association with the president. Meese listed several core elements of the president's offensive strategy that "never altered": Communism "was torn by fatal contradictions"—its overweening imperialist designs on the one hand and its crushing domestic problems on the other. Moscow could no longer afford guns and butter; it would have to choose one or the other. Therefore: It was incumbent on the United States and the rest of the West to take the initiative by refurbishing their defenses, assisting anticommunist forces around the world, and emphasizing their scientific-technological superiority. Finally: The West should "stop bailing the communists out of their technical and economic difficulties" through one-sided arms agreements, technology transfers, strategic trade, and economic credits.[30]

Most of these points Reagan had outlined when he challenged Gerald Ford in 1976 and in the years leading up to his successful run for the presidency in 1980. Reagan was convinced that if such a strategy were implemented firmly and consistently, the weak Soviet economy and the abandonment of ideology by the communists would lead to an end of the cold war on terms favorable to the forces of freedom.[31]

For President Reagan, 1983 was the pivotal year. In March, the president stated, without apology, that the West should recognize that the Soviets "are the focus of evil in this modern world" and the masters "of an evil empire."[32] In so doing, Reagan echoed the anticommunists who had preceded him, including Robert Taft, Whittaker Chambers, William F. Buckley, Jr., and Barry Goldwater.

Many conservatives consider Reagan's "evil empire" speech the most important of his presidency, a compelling example of what Czech president Vaclav Havel calls "the power of words to change history." When Reagan visited Poland and East Berlin after the collapse of Soviet communism, many former dissidents told him that when he called the Soviet Union an "evil empire," it gave them enormous hope. Finally, they said to each other, America had a leader who "understood the nature of communism."[33]

The president acted decisively whenever the Soviets tried to extend their empire. In October 1983, Reagan dispatched about two thousand American troops, along with units from six Caribbean states, to the island nation of Grenada to oust a Marxist regime that had recently seized power. It was the first time in nearly forty years of the cold war that America had acted to restore democracy to a communist country. The once-sacrosanct Brezhnev Doctrine—once a communist state, always a communist state—was successfully challenged.

As usual, the liberals did not get it. The *New York Times* complained editorially that the Grenada invasion was "a reverberating demonstration to the world that America has no more respect for laws and borders, for the codes of civilization, than the Soviet Union."[34] Reagan and his advisers shrugged off the rebuff, confident there was no moral equivalence between America and Soviet Russia.

A bipartisan congressional delegation visited Grenada shortly after the rescue, and almost every member, including critical Democrats, reported that after talking to the Grenadian people and inspecting the warehouses filled with Cuban weapons, they "agreed with the president" on his action.[35]

Subsequently, American troops uncovered a hoard of documents detailing the Marxist regime's secret arms pacts with other communist countries—three with the Soviet Union, one each with Cuba and North Korea—and "its plans to make the island a military base for Soviet bloc activities" throughout the Caribbean.[36] Moscow was clearly attempting to construct a revolutionary triangle in the region with Cuba, Nicaragua, and Grenada as its three points.

That fall, despite noisy protests in the streets of London, Rome, Paris, and other European cities, the Reagan administration calmly proceeded with the deployment of Pershing II and cruise missiles in Western Europe. They were deployed because the Soviets had installed several hundred SS-20s (intermediate-range nuclear missiles) aimed at key points in West Germany and other NATO countries.

The president had given Moscow a "zero option"—either to dismantle all the SS-20s or accept the deployment of American intermediate-range nuclear missiles directed at major Soviet targets. The Soviets had refused to dismantle, gambling that they could apply enough pressure through diplomatic maneuvers and through the nuclear freeze movement in Western Europe and the United States to force Reagan to cancel deployment. They had yet to take the full measure of the American president.

The stakes were high in Europe. Six Western European countries had scheduled elections for 1983—Great Britain, the Federal Republic of Germany, Italy, Belgium, Norway, and the Netherlands—and in each of these countries, political scientists Andrew E. Busch and Elizabeth Spalding wrote, "the leading liberal-left party had been captured by the peace movement and was opposing INF deployment."[37] Had voters turned against deployment, the NATO alliance would have been seriously weakened and might have collapsed. But backed by Western leadership, every one of the European parties that stood for military preparedness won that year.

Reagan directed American negotiators not to budge: It was the zero option or nothing. To the dismay and even despair of many in the U.S. foreign policy establishment and the State Department, the Soviets walked out of the arms control negotiations in Geneva. The president was immediately assailed in the press and by the disarmament movement; there were even warnings that nuclear war was imminent.[38]

But America's European allies concurred with Reagan that negotiations should come only after the establishment of Western strength and Soviet acknowledgment of that strength. As British prime minister Margaret Thatcher noted, Reagan "strengthened not only America's defenses, but also the will of America's allies."[39]

The calmest man during the negotiations was Reagan, who predicted that eventually the Soviets would return to the bargaining table. He was proved correct four years later, when the Intermediate-Range Nuclear Forces (INF) Treaty of 1987, in which both sides agreed to dismantle their "Euromissiles," was signed by Ronald Reagan and Mikhail Gorbachev. The zero option was formally ratified. Never before in the cold war had an entire category of nuclear weapons been eliminated.

Mikhail Gorbachev's signature on the treaty confirmed Reagan's shrewd judgment of him, which had been questioned by many hard-line anticommunists. Howard Phillips of the Conservative Caucus had gone so far as to declare that the president was "no longer in any way accountable to the millions who recognize that we are in a deadly, strategic end-game with the Soviet Union, militarily the most powerful regime in world history." "Rubbish," responded Secretary of State George Shultz, but even Senators Jesse Helms, Malcolm Wallop, and Dan Quayle—all solid conservatives— opposed the INF Treaty.[40]

Through it all, Reagan insisted that Gorbachev was "different" from previous Soviet leaders because he was willing "to take chances." The American president asserted that the Soviet president was "a remarkable force for change." Reagan's insightful evaluation was supported by another hard-nosed conservative, Margaret Thatcher, who pronounced after her first meeting with Gorbachev, "We can do business together."[41]

And then there was the most important initiative of all: the Strategic Defense Initiative (SDI). Reagan had long favored an alternative to the policy of mutual assured destruction (MAD), under which the United States and the Soviet Union each retained the nuclear capability to retaliate and destroy the other in the event of a nuclear attack. MAD was based on the assumption, as Caspar Weinberger put it, that in the area of nuclear strategy, the Soviet Union would act as the United States would act: "they would take no risks we would not." Proponents explained that mutual vulnerability was a vital precondition to MAD. That is, both sides would be safe because both were vulnerable. Weinberger was less diplomatic in his language; he called MAD a "mutual suicide pact."[42]

Reagan apparently first encountered the idea of missile defense in 1967 when he visited Edward Teller, the father of the hydrogen bomb, in the Lawrence Livermore National Laboratory in California. Teller briefed the new governor about the work being done to stop a missile attack on the United States. "It was a rather long presentation," Teller later recalled, "and I remember clearly that [Reagan] listened quite attentively." Some day, said Teller, space-based lasers might be used to destroy nuclear missiles fired at the United States. Reagan responded that history showed that "all offensive weapons eventually met their match through defense countermeasures."[43]

Caspar Weinberger, who served in Reagan's California cabinet, remembered that as governor, Reagan had expressed the view that America "would be better advised to rest [its] defenses on military strength" not only of an offensive character but "on means of protecting against the missiles of the other side." That was, as Weinberger states, very unconventional thinking in the late 1960s and early 1970s.[44]

In 1976, when he was challenging Gerald Ford for the Republican presidential nomination, Reagan often expressed his doubts about the MAD doctrine. Lieutenant General Daniel O. Graham, then a national security adviser to the conservative candidate, recalled that Reagan put it this way: "Our nuclear policy is like a Mexican stand-off—two men with pistols pointed at each other's head. If the man's finger flinches, you each blow the other's brains out. Can't you military people come up with something better than *that?*"[45]

The general had no answer in 1976, but Reagan kept looking for alternatives to MAD. In July 1979, he toured the headquarters of the North American Aerospace Defense Command (NORAD) in Colorado. According to Reagan biographer Lou Cannon, Reagan asked air force general James Hill what could be done if the Soviets fired a missile at an American city. Nothing, Hill replied. NORAD would track the incoming missile and then give city officials ten to fifteen minutes' warning before it hit. "That's all we can do," said Hill, "we can't stop it."[46]

The soon-to-be presidential candidate found it hard to believe that the United States had no defense whatever against Soviet missiles. "We have spent all that money and have all that equipment, and there is nothing we can do to prevent a nuclear missile from hitting us," he later remarked.[47] Reagan kept pushing for a better way, and it turned out to be the SDI, about which the normally modest president said flatly, "SDI was my idea."[48]

A number of people contributed the details, including General Daniel Graham, a former director of the Pentagon's Defense Intelligence Agency; Edward Teller; and George Keyworth, the president's science adviser. Keyworth's support was critical.

By his own admission, the science adviser had been skeptical about strategic defense since his days at Los Alamos in the late 1960s. But he came around after long talks with his mentor, Edward Teller, his own research, and interactions with General Graham and experts at the Heritage Foundation.

There was strong opposition to SDI throughout the Reagan administration, even at high levels of the Defense Department. Secretary of State George Shultz once called Keyworth "a lunatic" in front of the president for his advocacy of SDI, arguing that it would "destroy" NATO. But Reagan did not budge from his commitment, causing an admiring Keyworth to remark that Reagan "has this marvelous ability to work the whole thing while everybody else is working the parts."[49]

On March 23, 1983, President Reagan announced in a nationally televised address that development and deployment of a comprehensive antiballistic missile system would be his top defense priority—his "ultimate goal." "I call upon the scientific community in our country," he said, "those who gave us nuclear weapons, to turn their great talents now to the cause of mankind and world peace, to give us the means of rendering these nuclear weapons impotent and obsolete."[50]

Reagan called the system the Strategic Defense Initiative, but it was quickly ridiculed as "Star Wars" by liberal detractors, led by Senator Edward

Kennedy. The *New York Times* called SDI a "pipe dream, a projection of fantasy into policy."[51] One of its most enthusiastic congressional supporters was Newt Gingrich, who said of a space-based antimissile system: "Every citizen who is concerned about national survival and who wants the most effective defense possible for the least cost necessary should write their congressmen and senators and ask them to take a look at [it]."[52]

Even some conservatives, grown accustomed to a nuclear sword of Damocles, were uneasy over Reagan's proposal, particularly the suggestion that the goal should be to render nuclear missiles "obsolete." As Dr. Fred Schwarz had famously asserted, you can only trust the communists to be communists. America needed intercontinental ballistic missiles (ICBMs), argued hard-line conservatives, to protect itself against Soviet ICBMs. No other alternative seemed possible or safe.

Senate Democrats were so irrational in their opposition to SDI that they blocked a fourth star for Lieutenant General James Abrahamson simply because he was the director of the Strategic Defense Initiative Organization.[53] To those who said that the administration could not guarantee a 100 percent destruction of Soviet missiles, supporters of SDI responded that no military system in history ever had or ever could guarantee 100 percent efficiency. Defense Secretary Weinberger explained that SDI was not a strategic cure-all but would "strengthen our present deterrent capability" and help "curb" strategic arms competition.[54]

As Reagan put it, SDI was "vital insurance against Soviet cheating." By contrast, he said, MAD depended on "no slip-ups, no madmen, no unmanageable crisis, no mistakes—forever."[55]

Calling SDI a "strike weapon," the Soviets protested that the initiative was clearly a preparation for the launching of a U.S. nuclear attack inasmuch as it would nullify any Soviet response. They warned that SDI would force an expensive arms race in space, at the end of which the strategic balance would remain as it was at present despite the enormous expenditures.[56]

The intensity of Moscow's opposition to SDI showed that Soviet scientists and strategists regarded the initiative not as a pipe dream but as a technological feat they could not match. A decade later, General Makhmut Gareev, who headed the department of strategic analysis in the Soviet Ministry of Defense, told General Graham what he had told the Soviet general staff and the Politboro in 1983: "Not only could we not defeat SDI, SDI defeated all our possible countermeasures."[57]

More than any other strategic action he took, Reagan's unflinching commitment to SDI convinced the Kremlin it could not win, or afford, a continuing arms race and led Gorbachev and his communist colleagues to sue for peace and end the cold war. As Russian Nobel laureate Alexander Solzhenitsyn said, Gorbachev "had no choice but to disarm."[58]

Another application of Reagan's offensive strategy was the barrage of measures aimed at the Soviet-backed regime of General Jaruzelski in Poland. The administration worked closely with the AFL-CIO, headed by veteran anticommunist Lane Kirkland, and the Vatican to provide Solidarity with money, literature, and electronic and communications equipment. When Reagan and Pope John Paul II met in Rome in June 1982, they formed what investigative reporter Carl Bernstein called a "holy alliance" against communism in Eastern and Central Europe. Lech Walesa said later that the Solidarity movement in Poland would not have survived without American help, overt and covert. Asked, for example, how important Radio Free Europe had been, he replied, "Would there be earth without the sun?"[59]

The president applied pressure on the Soviet Union everywhere. He instructed Jeane Kirkpatrick to raise high the banner of democratic capitalism at the United Nations, challenging the prevailing socialist, anti-American orthodoxy. To do that, Kirkpatrick followed a course of what she called effective rather than quiet diplomacy. She unabashedly used America's vast power to influence UN conduct and policy, shunning process (unlike her predecessors) for content and outcome. Her aggressive conduct, Kirkpatrick later admitted, "took everyone by surprise."[60]

Meanwhile, Libya, under military dictator Muammar Qaddafi, had built up an arsenal of Soviet-made weapons and openly taunted the United States. Following a Libyan-inspired terrorist attack on a Berlin nightclub in which several Americans were killed, Reagan acted decisively: He ordered American planes to bomb Libya, calling Qaddafi the "mad dog of the Middle East." The American public overwhelmingly endorsed Reagan's action, which had the desired effect. The Libyan leader immediately muted his criticism of the United States and backed away from further terrorist actions.[61]

In the 1970s, America had retreated almost everywhere in the world: Vietnam, Laos, Cambodia, Angola, Ethiopia, Nicaragua, and in the face of the

OPEC oil cartel. It surrendered the Panama Canal, accepted Soviet violations of treaties like SALT I, encouraged the Soviets to invade Afghanistan by its indecisiveness and timidity, and allowed the overthrow of the shah of Iran, a good friend and vital ally.

In the 1980s, America once again became the leader of the free world. It did so because Reagan rebuilt America's arsenal, worked closely with Western allies on key security issues like the deployment of Euromissiles, and successfully challenged the Brezhnev Doctrine (no communist regime would be allowed to become anti-communist) in Grenada, Angola, Afghanistan, and Nicaragua. America demonstrated that once again it would fulfill its commitments to allies in Western Europe, Japan, Israel, and Southeast Asia.[62]

Reagan took his freedom offensive even into the heart of the disintegrating Soviet empire. Standing before Berlin's Brandenburg Gate in June 1987, Reagan directly challenged the Soviet leadership, proclaiming, "Mr. Gorbachev, tear down this wall!" His blunt words were a telling contrast to John F. Kennedy's emotional phrase a quarter of a century earlier, "*Ich bin ein Berliner,*" which thrilled the people of West Berlin but was ignored by the Kremlin.[63]

As Reagan said at the Brandenburg Gate, the Soviet Union faced a choice: make fundamental changes or become obsolete. "Gorbachev saw the handwriting on the Wall," Reagan wrote in his memoir, "and opted for change"—change that, although the Soviet leader did not realize it at the time, would bring about an end to Soviet communism.[64]

By introducing such populist concepts as *glasnost* and *perestroika,* Gorbachev made consideration of the people potentially as important as the traditional components of the Soviet state: the Communist party, the KGB, the Soviet army, and the *nomenklatura.* For his reforms to work, Gorbachev had to replace old ways with new ways of thinking, and that required diversity, debate, and even freedom. He gambled that he could control the virus of freedom he had let loose with *glasnost;* improve the economy and satisfy the consumer desires of the people through *perestroika;* reassure the military and the KGB he was not jeopardizing their role; persuade the *nomenklatura* to loosen its grip on the Soviet state; secure his own position as general secretary and president; and keep the Soviet Union socialist.

It was a formidable list, and Gorbachev probably had never read Alexis de Tocqueville, who once commented, "Experience teaches that the most critical moment for bad governments is the one which witnesses the first steps toward reform."[65] The Soviet Union in the mid-1980s was a very bad government attempting very radical reform.

The chances of Gorbachev's successfully implementing *glasnost* and *perestroika* were slim to none. He was trying to square a circle—democratize a totalitarian state—and manipulate an elemental human force, freedom, that has proved to be the downfall of every dictator sooner or later.

The following year, in May 1988, Reagan traveled to Moscow for what biographer Lou Cannon described as his premier presidential performance as "freedom's advocate."[66] Amid largely ceremonial events, the president delivered a moving speech beneath a gigantic white bust of Lenin at Moscow State University. His theme, drawn from his General Electric days and his 1964 television address for Goldwater, was the blessings of democracy, individual freedom, and free enterprise.

Reagan explained that "freedom is the right to question and change the established way of doing things." He lauded the "continuing revolution of the marketplace" and the right "to follow your dream or stick to your conscience, even if you're the only one in a sea of doubters." He declared that America had always sought to make friends of old antagonists and suggested that it was time for Americans and Russians to become friends:

> In this Moscow spring, this May 1988, we may be allowed [this] hope: that freedom, like the fresh green sapling planted over Tolstoy's grave, will blossom forth at last in the rich fertile soil of your people and culture. We may be allowed to hope that the marvelous sound of a new openness will keep rising, ringing through, leading to a new world of reconciliation, friendship and peace.[67]

The key word in his remarks was *freedom*—not *openness* or *reconciliation* or *friendship* or *peace* but *freedom*. In his remarks to some ninety-six dissidents at the U.S. embassy, Reagan stressed that his human rights agenda in Moscow was one of freedom of religion, freedom of speech, and freedom of travel for the Soviet people. Near the conclusion of his talk, Reagan quoted the poet Alexander Pushkin, revered above all others by the Russian people: "It's time, my friend, it's time."[68]

Democracy triumphed in the cold war, Reagan wrote in his autobiography, because it was a battle of ideas—"between one system that gave preeminence to the state and another that gave preeminence to the individual and freedom."[69]

The Iran-contra affair had its origins in two quite different but stereotypical impulses of Reagan. The first was humanitarian: to free the handful of American hostages held by terrorists in Lebanon. The second was ideological: to support the anticommunist resistance in Nicaragua, whose Marxist regime threatened stability in all of Central America.

But exchanging arms for hostages contradicted the administration's stated policy of not acquiescing to the demands of terrorists or dealing with Iran. Both Secretary of State Shultz and Defense Secretary Weinberger were adamantly opposed to any compromise with terrorists.

Nevertheless, as Reagan biographer Lou Cannon wrote, "Reagan was determined to get the hostages out, by whatever means possible." Indeed, the president became "so stubbornly committed to the trade of arms for hostages" that he could not be dissuaded from it even when new American hostages were taken.[70]

As Reagan put it in his memoir:

> What American trapped in such circumstances wouldn't have wanted me to do everything I possibly could to set them free. . . . It was the president's *duty* to get them home.[71]

And so the president decided at the end of 1985 to proceed with the Iranian initiative. His decision divided his top advisers, with Meese, Casey, and Poindexter in favor; Weinberger and Shultz were vehemently against it. A little more than a year later, the Reagan administration was struggling to contain a serious political crisis. In March 1987, a reluctant President Reagan conceded in a nationally televised address, "A few months ago, I told the American people I did not trade arms for hostages. My heart and my best intentions still tell me that's true, but the facts and the evidence tell me it is not."[72]

Conservatives were stunned by the admission. Commented one Reagan appointee, "It's like suddenly learning that John Wayne had secretly been selling liquor and firearms to the Indians."[73] Still, they did their best to defend their favorite president.

In his memoir, Ed Meese asserted that when it became clear that the U.S. initiative to build ties with Iranian "moderates" was not succeeding, "it should have been dropped and Congress should have been notified of what had happened." Meese, attorney general at the time, did not try to defend "the protracted failure to disclose" the administration's actions to Congress (as required by law) but argued that the sale of arms was "a policy error, not a crime."[74]

The American public was unequivocal in its rejection of any arms-for-hostages deal. A December 1986 *New York Times*/CBS News poll recorded a drop in Reagan's approval rating of twenty-one points, from 67 to 46 percent, the sharpest one-month drop in presidential surveys since such polling began in 1936.[75]

The contra half of the controversy erupted in March 1982 when Congress discovered that the CIA was involved in training anticommunist rebels in Nicaragua. Led by Democratic House Speaker Tip O'Neill, Congress passed, in the fall of 1982, the first Boland amendment, which prohibited funds "for the purpose of overthrowing the government of Nicaragua." The Reagan administration argued that the goal of contra funding was not to overthrow the Sandinista government but to persuade it to hold democratic elections (which it finally, though reluctantly, did in 1990).[76]

An always firm supporter of contra aid was Congressman Newt Gingrich. Once asked why the contras were not more successful, Gingrich replied sarcastically: "If you're on the pro-Soviet side, you get more equipment, more advisers, more money, more help, and when you're on the American side, you get more debates, more argument, more excuses and more evasion."[77]

Nicaragua was not a peripheral issue to either the administration or its critics. For Reagan, Nicaragua was "another Cuba"; for the Democratic leadership in Congress, it was "another Vietnam." Believing that the vital interests of the nation were at stake, each side dug in hard and prepared for political war.

American funding continued until December 1984, when Congress strengthened the Boland amendment by denying any U.S. support either "directly or indirectly" to the contras. Because the president wanted to keep helping what he called the Nicaraguan "freedom fighters," administration lawyers decided that although Boland prohibited American agencies "engaged in intelligence activities" from operating in Nicaragua, the National Security Council was not an intelligence agency. So the contra campaign was shifted from the CIA to the NSC under the direction of national security adviser John Poindexter and NSC staffer Oliver North.[78]

Apparently with CIA director William Casey's approval, North illegally diverted funds from the Iranian arms sales to the contras. Meese calls the fund diversion "a tremendous error that should never have been allowed to happen. That it did happen was a failure of the administration—for which it paid dearly."[79]

Ultimately, North, Poindexter, former national security adviser Robert McFarlane (who had succeeded William Clark), and General Richard Secord (who had bought weapons to trade for American hostages) were indicted and convicted on charges stemming from the Iran-contra affair. Many of the convictions were later overturned because independent counsel Lawrence Walsh had relied on information obtained by congressional investigators operating under grants of immunity to obtain the convictions.

Iran-contra was not Watergate reborn. Reagan did not try to cover up the affair but directed his attorney general to conduct an immediate inquiry, invited former senators John Tower and Edmund Muskie and Nixon's national security adviser, Brent Scowcroft, to undertake an independent investigation, and asked for the appointment of an independent prosecutor to determine if any laws had been broken.

Unlike Nixon, Reagan did not approve wiretaps, did not direct the IRS to examine people's tax returns, did not suggest that offices be broken into, and did not attempt to manipulate the FBI and the CIA in their investigations or compile an enemies' list. However flawed, Iran-contra was concerned with public policy; Watergate was always about electoral politics. Reagan approved the arms-for-hostages deal to save American lives; Nixon used Watergate to try to save himself.

Every official inquiry agreed that President Reagan had not personally authorized the diversion of money to the contras. The Tower Commission report found that the president had not even known of the diversion of funds. But it was highly critical of McFarlane and Poindexter, stating that the "National Security Adviser failed in his responsibility to see that an orderly process was observed."[80]

In November 1987, a select committee of the House and Senate released a seven-hundred-page report. Like the Tower Commission, the Democratic majority concluded that the president had been unaware of the funds diversion. It accepted Poindexter's testimony that "he shielded the president from knowledge of the diversion."[81] The Republican minority emphasized that the mistakes of the Iran-contra affair were just that: "mistakes in judgment and nothing more. There was no constitutional crisis, no systematic disrespect for the 'internal rule of law,' no grand conspiracy."[82] Indeed, Iran-contra soon faded from the American people's consciousness because they decided that it was an exception to rather than the rule of the Reagan Doctrine.

In his generally balanced biography, Lou Cannon concluded that "no president save FDR defined a decade as strikingly as Ronald Reagan defined the 1980s."[83] In fact, Reagan left an indelible mark on American politics starting in the mid-1960s, when he was governor of California, blossoming through the eight years of his presidency, and continuing to this day. Indeed, even as the first half of the twentieth century has been called the Age of Roosevelt by Arthur Schlesinger, Jr., and other historians, the last half of the twentieth century can be called the Age of Reagan.

Looking back, we can see that Ronald Reagan deliberately patterned his presidency after that of his favorite president, Franklin Delano Roosevelt. Just as FDR led America out of a great economic depression, Reagan sought to lift a traumatized country out of a great psychological depression, induced by the assassinations of John F. Kennedy and Martin Luther King, Jr., and sustained by the Vietnam War, Watergate, and the Carter malaise.

He used the same political instruments as Roosevelt—the major address to Congress and the fireside chat with the people—and the same optimistic, uplifting rhetoric. Although both Roosevelt and Reagan appealed to the best in America, there was a major philosophical difference between the two presidents: Roosevelt turned first to government to solve problems, while Reagan turned first to the people. "Trust the people" was Reagan's mantra.

Reagan persuaded Americans to believe in themselves and the future again. He led them to accept that they did not need the welfare state to solve all of their economic and social problems. And he looked the Soviets in the eye and concluded they were not ten feet tall after all.

He was right about the resilience of Americans and the weakness of the Soviets. It therefore came as no great surprise to anyone, including the Democrats, that Reagan was reelected in 1984 by a landslide. He received just under 59 percent of the popular vote and 525 electoral votes, carrying forty-nine states. With his overwhelming victory, summed up *Congressional Quarterly*, Reagan "ripped apart what was left of the once-dominant Democratic coalition," demonstrating that the GOP, at least at the presidential level, was the "real" umbrella party.[84] The only electoral cloud for Republicans was their disappointing showing in Congress, where they gained only fourteen seats in the House and lost two seats in the Senate, reducing their majority there to 53–47.

The 1984 election had never been in question, although a few doubts were raised following the president's poor performance in the first televised debate with Democratic candidate Walter Mondale. Reagan had repeated himself, sometimes sounded uncertain, and even looked old at times. No one had to tell Reagan what had happened; the old pro knew he had flopped.

There were some excuses about the president's being "overbriefed," but the truth, as campaign adviser Stuart Spencer later admitted, was that Reagan had not debated anyone for years, and his skill at political thrust and parry had grown rusty. The campaign staff had not helped by overly shielding Reagan from the press and the public. And so it was decided to let Reagan be Reagan. A tough, anti-Mondale speech was delivered with relish by the president. He revealed that he had become angry when Mondale kept distorting his record during their first debate and had thought of saying to Mondale, "You are taxing my patience." But then, said Reagan, "I caught myself. Why should I give him another idea? That's the only tax he hasn't thought of." The crowds loved it and chanted, "Four more years, four more years."[85]

When campaign consultant Roger Ailes warned the president that the age issue would probably be raised in the second debate, Reagan thought for a moment, smiled, and said, "I can handle that."[86] Thirty minutes into the debate, Henry Trewhitt of the *Baltimore Sun,* a member of the journalists' panel, stated that Reagan was the oldest president in U.S. history and noted that some members of the president's staff had said he was tired after the first debate in Louisville. "I recall," said Trewhitt, "that President Kennedy had to go for days on end with very little sleep during the Cuban missile crisis. Is there any doubt in your mind that you would be able to function in such circumstances?"

"Not at all, Mr. Trewhitt," replied Reagan calmly. "And I want you to know that also I will not make age an issue of this campaign." Absolutely deadpan, he added, "I am not going to exploit, for political purposes, my opponent's youth and inexperience."[87] Everyone laughed, including Mondale. For all practical purposes, the election was over.

Rather than lapsing into lame-duckism in his second term, as had many of his predecessors, Reagan achieved his greatest accomplishments in foreign policy and sustained an unprecedented economic expansion. It is little wonder, then, that by 1988, liberalism had all but disappeared from the national political landscape, replaced by conservatism as the new standard. A philosophical realignment, a turn to the Right, was clearly taking place in American politics.

Yet the conservative movement faced a dilemma in 1988: for the first time in forty years, it could not agree who should carry its banner. In 1948 and 1952, it had been Robert Taft. In 1960, it had been Richard Nixon, with scattered support for Goldwater. In 1964, it had been Barry Goldwater. In 1968, it had been Nixon, with some strongly preferring Reagan. In 1976, 1980, and 1984, it had been Ronald Reagan.

But in 1988 there was no consensus, even after Reagan had tacitly endorsed the man who had been at his side for eight years: Vice President George Bush. Bush was not conservative enough for either the New Right or the Old Right, and so conservatives went their separate ways, thereby ensuring Bush's nomination. *National Review* and *Human Events* endorsed Jack Kemp, with the latter arguing that "Kemp is part of the conservative movement."[88] Among Kemp's supporters were fellow congressmen Newt Gingrich and Trent Lott. Former Young Americans for Freedom chairman David Keene and Reaganaut Donald Devine went to work for Bob Dole, and the Christian Right backed televangelist Pat Robertson. Facing a divided opposition, Bush had only to win the right primaries to gain the presidential nomination.

As expected, midwesterner Dole won the Iowa caucuses with 37 percent, while Robertson unexpectedly finished second with 25 percent. Bush was third with 19 percent, while Kemp was a disappointing fourth with 11 percent.

Robertson's strong showing was evidence of his ability to mobilize and organize born-again Christians and other first-time conservative voters. Many voters said that moral issues were their primary concern, and Robertson addressed them more convincingly than anyone else. "Americans for Robertson," says Tom Atwood, who served as the organization's controller, "trained thousands of religious conservative activists who are still active today, showed the way for many other religious conservative candidates to follow, assembled a database of millions of religious conservatives, and was the precursor of the most powerful grassroots organization in the conservative movement, the Christian Coalition."[89]

By running a series of television ads that accused Dole of "straddling" on the issues and with a last-minute endorsement from conservative icon Barry Goldwater, Bush defeated Dole in New Hampshire by 38 percent to 28 percent. With Kemp a distant third and Robertson last in New Hampshire, the Republican contest was essentially reduced to a two-man race. Although Dole achieved solid victories in South Dakota and Minnesota, George Bush swept all sixteen Republican primaries on Super Tuesday, March 8, receiving 57 percent of the popular vote and 80 percent of the delegates. Reflecting the conflicted state of the conservative movement, Dole finished behind even Robertson in Louisiana and Texas.

Kemp bowed out of the race and also announced he would not seek reelection to Congress, where he had served for eighteen years. Conservatives attempted to sort out why the man who columnist Patrick Buchanan wrote "ought to be the Republican nominee" had done so poorly. There were references to the difficulty of running for president from the House of Representatives, Kemp's prounion stance, his constant outreach to non-Republican groups like blacks and Hispanics, and his failure to spend enough time in the South, "the stronghold of traditional conservatism."[90] In short, Jack Kemp neglected his political base and ran for president before he had even won the nomination.

Bob Dole formally withdrew on March 29, having won fewer than two hundred delegates to Bush's eight hundred. He had been badly managed, he spent money poorly, and he flubbed a pledge against taxes in a key New Hampshire speech. On May 16, Pat Robertson followed suit and endorsed Bush. He declared he would attend the Republican convention as "the true conservative voice" and would seek to influence the party's platform.

Robertson also revealed that he had filed papers to create a new political action committee, Americans for the Republic, to train and fund conservative Christian political candidates. The PAC quietly died, but a year later, Robertson formed the Christian Coalition and named as its executive director twenty-eight-year-old Ralph Reed, who had the face of a choir boy and the political instincts of a Green Beret.

George Bush was easily elected that fall because he gave the electorate, in effect, one more opportunity to vote for Reagan. American presidents are not always so successful in transferring their popularity, as even a widely admired president like Eisenhower learned in 1960. It helped Bush enormously that his Democratic candidate was the frozen-faced Michael Dukakis, who had a liberal record that only Americans for Democratic Action could love.

Dukakis had once led the legal fight against prayer in public schools; as governor of Massachusetts, he had vetoed a death penalty bill; he had invoked the First Amendment to justify killing a bill requiring that schoolchildren recite the Pledge of Allegiance; he supported gun control; and he had a "soft" record, as Bush biographer Herbert S. Parmet put it, on national defense.[91]

Bush campaign aides Lee Atwater and Roger Ailes determined to go on the attack early and stay there. With the help of Las Vegas advertising executive Sig Rogich, they produced and aired the most effective negative ads in presidential campaigning since the Democrats in 1964. One of Bush's attack ads panned across the littered, polluted waters of Boston Harbor, directly challenging Dukakis's reputation as an enlightened, efficient administrator. Another, filmed in black and white, showed a silent procession of men in prison garb moving through a prison gate, in and out, and right back into society. The announcer stressed that the governor had vetoed the death penalty and given furloughs to "first-degree murderers not eligible for parole."[92]

The latter ad made no reference to black Massachusetts convict Willie Horton because, as Rogich later explained, "We very carefully elected not to show him or mention his name because we knew we'd be hit for racism."[93] The controversial Willie Horton ad was, in fact, the work of Americans for Bush, an independent PAC headed by conservative activist Floyd Brown.

Although it was not a Reaganesque landslide, George Bush received 53.4 percent of the popular vote and carried forty states, giving him a decisive 426-to-112 triumph in the electoral college. He swept the South, the Rocky Mountains, much of the farm belt, and every large state except New York. There were some encouraging signs for Democrats. Dukakis came within five percentage points of carrying seven states with 125 electoral votes, including Illinois, California, and Pennsylvania. If a more attractive and moderate Democrat with appeal in the South came along, some experts speculated, he might do very well.

Democrats increased slightly their margins in Congress, picking up one seat in the Senate and two in the House. *Congressional Quarterly* suggested that election day ought to be renamed "incumbent appreciation day": 98 percent of the House members seeking reelection in 1988 got their wish.[94]

Most conservatives chose to stress the positive, accepting George Bush as a born-again conservative. After all, he had pledged "no new taxes" in his acceptance speech. He had emphasized in the campaign a conservative position on almost every issue that mattered—from abortion to school prayer to putting criminals behind bars. He had been Ronald Reagan's sturdy, reliable right-hand man for eight years.

In the initial flush of victory, most conservatives looked forward to the Bush years. *National Review* "heartily" congratulated Bush on "his ascendancy," noting his accomplishments and courage while reserving the right to "reproach as well as applaud."[95] And conservatives looked backward with fondness and appreciation on the Reagan years.

The conservative movement had generally flourished during the 1980s: *National Review* and *American Spectator,* for example, reached new circulation highs of 200,000 and more; the American Conservative Union drew 1,000 activists to its annual Conservative Political Action Conferences; and new organizations like the Family Research Council and the Competitive Enterprise Institute gathered strength. The Heritage Foundation doubled its annual budget during the 1980s to nearly $18 million, and the Cato Institute moved to Washington, D.C., in 1982 and laid plans for a national headquarters. Conservative think tanks sprang up in a dozen states.

Under Reagan, communism had been checked and then defeated. Conservatives now concentrated on the other great challenge of the late twentieth century: rolling back the federal government. They felt that just as the New Deal revolution of the 1930s laid the foundation for the Great Society of the 1960s, so the Reagan revolution of the 1980s prepared the way for a conservative, limited government in the 1990s and beyond. And they expected George Bush to lead the way.

Chapter 14

Contracts Made and Broken

EVERY NEW PRESIDENT WANTS TO MAKE HIS OWN MARK ON HISTORY, NO matter how much he owes his predecessor. Harry Truman, who praised FDR for creating the New Deal and winning World War II, did not hesitate to differ sharply with Roosevelt's foreign and domestic policies, adopting a strong anti-Soviet stance as early as 1946 and threatening to draft striking railway workers (a key element of the old Roosevelt coalition) into the army. Told that he was violating Roosevelt's stated wishes and policies, Truman replied that the buck now stopped with him.

Although personally picked by Theodore Roosevelt, William Howard Taft considered Roosevelt's ideas to be too "progressive" and steered a more conservative course as president. Roosevelt was so upset that he ran against Taft in 1912, a move that helped to put Democrat Woodrow Wilson in the White House. Asserting his independence in 1960, Richard Nixon waited until almost the last moment to seek President Eisenhower's campaign help—and lost one of the closest presidential contests in American history.

Even George Bush, who ran as a "no new taxes" conservative in 1988, had no sooner been sworn in as president than he declared that the purpose of America "is to make kinder the face of the nation and gentler the face of the world."[1] Conservatives wondered: Was he saying that America under Reagan had not been kind or gentle? Wouldn't liberals seize on his words and argue that they confirmed the 1980s as an unhappy, even desperate, time for many Americans?

No one expected George Bush to be a carbon copy of Ronald Reagan, but conservatives noted that the new president did not even mention the outgoing president's name in his inaugural address. Conservative unease increased when Bush named Louis W. Sullivan, known for his proabortion views, as secretary of health and human services and Richard Darman, a pro-tax moderate, as director of the Office of Management and Budget. Across the government, Reaganauts were informed that their services were no longer required.

And then there was the new president's heavy emphasis on ethics in government, as though the previous administration had been an ethical swamp. As Bush biographer Herbert S. Parmet put it, conservative ideology was out and Bush loyalty was in. The *New York Times* summed up the new mood neatly with the headline, "Reagan Doesn't Work Here Anymore."

New Right conservatives like Richard A. Viguerie nodded their heads and said, "We told you so." In a 1984 cover article, *Conservative Digest* had described George Bush as an "elitist" with "life-long ties to the liberal eastern Establishment." The populist magazine pointed out that as a congressman in the late 1960s, Bush had voted for foreign aid and Nixon's Family Assistance Plan. He was not a conservative and "will never be a conservative," declared *Conservative Digest*. After all, when Bush lost his 1964 bid for a U.S. Senate seat from Texas, he blamed his defeat on conservatives whom he called "nut fringe zealots."[2] Time would prove Viguerie's prediction about the Bush presidency to be accurate.

But for the conservative movement, the most important Washington events of 1989 came not from the Bush administration but from the House of Representatives, where Newt Gingrich engineered the forced resignation of Democratic Speaker Jim Wright and his own ascension to the number two Republican post, by just two votes.

Gingrich began attacking Wright's ethics in 1987, focusing on a sweetheart book deal that earned the Texas congressman a 55 percent royalty, about four times the most generous author's arrangement. Wright received $54,000 in "royalties" in 1985–1986 for a 117-page paperback, *Reflections of a Public Man,* a collection of his homilies and poems. It was sold, reportedly, only through a single Fort Worth bookstore. A child of the media age, Gingrich constantly worked the press on the assumption that "if enough newspapers said there should be an investigation, Common Cause [the liberal public interest group] would have to say so. Then members would say it. It would happen."[3]

As Gingrich foresaw, Common Cause president Fred Wertheimer soon asked the House Ethics Committee to appoint an outside counsel to investigate both Wright's book deal and his role in helping Texas savings and loan operators in financial trouble. Gingrich promptly filed his own complaint, citing the royalty arrangement and Wright's oil investments, thus forcing an investigation of the man he called "the least ethical Speaker in this century."[4]

By the spring of 1989, Wright's career was effectively over, following the release of an ethics committee report stating that the speaker was guilty of sixty-nine violations of House rules, in addition to excessive profits from bulk sales of his book.[5] Wright announced his resignation in May, brought down by his own wrongdoing and the take-no-prisoners tactics of a self-described conservative "revolutionary." Of the two factors, as conservative analyst M. Stanton Evans wrote, the more important was Wright's improper conduct, which was so blatant that it could not be ignored even by a House of Representatives that was 258–175 Democratic.[6]

At almost the same time, Gingrich took a decisive step toward his long-time goal of becoming House Speaker. It was obvious that Bob Michel of Illinois, a member of the World War II generation, was coming to the end of his long tenure as Republican House leader. But who would succeed him? Trent Lott of Mississippi had been the House Republican whip and Michel's likely successor, but he had left the House in 1988 and had run successfully for the Senate. Lott and Gingrich had worked closely in the House, with Lott strongly supporting the Conservative Opportunity Society (COS), a band of conservative backbenchers organized in 1983 by Gingrich. Gingrich often referred to Lott as "my mentor."[7]

Jack Kemp was another possible Republican leader (and COS supporter), but he too had left Congress after his unsuccessful run for the presidency in 1988. Kemp got a consolation prize from President Bush, the top spot at the Department of Housing and Urban Development.

Succeeding Lott as Republican whip was Dick Cheney of Wyoming, a solid 90 percent conservative (according to the American Conservative Union) and heir apparent to Michel. But when John Tower was rejected by the Democratic Senate as Bush's secretary of defense, the president nominated Cheney. The game of political chairs left the office of House Republican whip open. Although Michel's personal choice was the mildly conservative Edward Madigan of Illinois, Gingrich quickly announced his own candidacy. Veteran GOP strategist Eddie Mahe summed up the

Gingrich–Madigan contest: "Newt's conception of the job is figuring out how to become a majority. Madigan's concept of the job is figuring out how to get along with Democrats."[8]

Gingrich was the underdog, but that was nothing new. He declared that the choice was activism versus passivism. Gingrich and his COS associates—Robert S. Walker of Pennsylvania, Vin Weber of Minnesota, Judd Gregg of New Hampshire, Dan Coats of Indiana, Connie Mack of Florida, and Dan Lungren and Duncan Hunter of California—worked all weekend before the vote on March 13. (It is a measure of Gingrich's ability to pick winners that Gregg, Coats, and Mack all become U.S. senators, and Lungren California's attorney general.) The Gingrich team reached out to all elements of the party, Left and Right, stressing Gingrich's vision of a Republican majority. "By Monday morning," recalled Walker, "we had 60 people committed to vote for Newt for whip. . . . The last 30 or 35 votes came real hard."[9]

Among the first members that Gingrich telephoned personally, according to political reporter Dan Balz, were two moderate House Republicans, Nancy L. Johnson of Connecticut and Steve Gunderson of Wisconsin. Johnson and Gunderson committed to Gingrich and began lining up other moderates. Johnson told her colleagues: "This is a leader who has the vision to build a majority party and the strength and charisma to do it."[10]

No one knew whether Gingrich could actually do so, but anything was better than the Republicans' current status as a seemingly permanent minority in the people's branch of government. As one observer put it, "The Democrats ran over them; the Republican White House ignored them; Senate Republicans often belittled them. . . . it was a miserable existence."[11]

Even so, Gingrich was a tough sell. Although he quoted conservative heroes like Ronald Reagan and Barry Goldwater, he also cited spacey non-conservatives like futurist Alvin Toffler, who preferred direct to representative democracy regardless of what the Constitution said. Gingrich, moreover, was controversial and egotistical. Undeniably brilliant, he was almost willfully unorganized. By his own admission, he was an idea man, not a vote counter, which was one of the whip's primary responsibilities. But he had high energy, a burning desire to succeed, and a surprising willingness, when he wanted to, to listen to others—"a part of his personality that is least understood by his critics," according to the *Washington Post*.[12]

Gingrich received help that critical weekend not only from moderate Republicans but from the New Right. Paul Weyrich, who had met Gingrich in 1979 when he first came to Washington, spent an hour and a half with Congressman Phil Crane convincing him to back Gingrich rather than Madigan, his colleague from Illinois. "He's not one of us," Weyrich freely conceded to his fellow movement conservative, "but he will do business differently. He is an opportunity to break out of the box we've been in."[13] Reluctantly, Crane agreed to support Gingrich.

Every vote was critical, and Gingrich finally squeezed out a narrow victory by just two votes, 87 to 85. His election as House Republican whip was a pivotal event in the history of the conservative movement. If Gingrich had not become the number two Republican in 1989, he would not have been in a position to succeed Bob Michel when he retired. When Michel announced in 1993 that he would leave at the end of that Congress, Gingrich garnered the support of a majority of House Republicans to be the new party leader within a week—and began preparing the way for a historic document, the Contract with America.

History was also being made across the Atlantic Ocean, with the disintegration of the iron curtain from Berlin to Warsaw to Prague to Bucharest. The collapse of communism in Eastern and Central Europe came from decades of political tyranny and economic backwardness—and initiatives launched by farsighted Western leaders like Ronald Reagan and John Paul II.

While the West basked in remarkable prosperity and personal freedom, the East slipped further and further into an economic and political morass from which escape seemed impossible. With no incentives to compete or modernize, Eastern Europe's industrial sector became a monument to bureaucratic inefficiency and waste, a musty museum of the early industrial age.

As the *New York Times* pointed out, Singapore, an Asian city-state of only 2 million people, exported 20 percent more machinery to the West in 1987 than all of Eastern Europe.[14] Life expectancy declined dramatically in the Soviet bloc, and infant mortality rose. The only groups exempted from social and economic hardship were Communist party members, upper-level military officers, and the managerial elite.

Increasingly, the once-impenetrable iron curtain was breached by modern communications and technology, allowing the peoples of Eastern Europe to see how the other half of Europe lived. Increasingly, Poles, Hungarians, Czechs, and East Germans demanded change and reform, not only in the marketplace but in the realm of human rights and liberties.

The miraculous year began in February 1989 with talks in Poland, after months of strikes, between leaders of the still-outlawed Solidarity union and the communist government. In March, seventy-five thousand demonstrated in Budapest on the anniversary of the 1848 revolution in Hungary, demanding a withdrawal of Soviet troops and free elections.

In April, Solidarity and the Polish government agreed to the first open elections since World War II, and the union's legal status was restored. In July, Soviet leader Gorbachev reminded the Council of Europe meeting in Strasbourg that he rejected the Brezhnev Doctrine, stating that "any interference in the domestic affairs and any attempts to restrict the sovereignty of states, both friends and allies or any others, are inadmissible."[15] His public abandonment of the Brezhnev Doctrine speeded up powerful forces of change already in motion.

In September, an exodus began when Hungary opened its borders with Austria and allowed thousands of East Germans to cross its borders to defect to the West. On November 9, a tidal wave of East Germans poured across the border as travel restrictions were lifted, and the Berlin Wall fell after nearly four decades. Only that summer, East German communist boss Erich Honecker had declared defiantly that the wall would stand for at least another hundred years. Millions of Czechs and Slavs walked off their jo bs and onto the streets, and the communist government of Czechoslovakia resigned.

The year of miracles ended in December with the execution of Romanian despot Nicolae Ceauşescu and the election of Vaclav Havel, who had begun the year in jail, as president of Czechoslovakia. The sudden collapse of communism like a house of cards confirmed what Walter Judd had often said: "Tyrants have almost always looked invincible until the last five minutes, and then all of a sudden they fall apart."[16]

Meanwhile, in America, Newt Gingrich was trying to loosen the tight and sometimes tyrannical hold that Democrats had on the House of Representatives. Many political observers said it was a hopeless task; some even wondered whether the Democrats would control Congress for another hundred years. But Gingrich was no Don Quixote on a glorious and unrealistic quest. He was at last well organized, well financed, and focused on his primary goal: to create a conservative governing majority. In many ways, he was not that different from the three "misters" who had dominated conservatism since the 1940s. Like Bob Taft—Mr. Republican—Gingrich was intensely ambitious and an unapologetic partisan. Like Barry Goldwater—Mr. Conservative—he was fiery in his speech and thrived on controversy. Like Ronald Reagan—Mr. President—he was a charismatic leader and passionately in love with ideas.

With a nod to Mao Zedong, he declared, let a thousand ideas bloom, although not all did. At the National Republican Congressional Committee, which he visited often in the early 1980s, a bemused staff changed the labels of three filing cabinets to read "Newt Ideas" and labeled one last drawer: "Newt Good Ideas."[17]

From his teen years on, Gingrich had been a fountainhead of ideas, seeing himself as a "transformational figure" who would devote his life to saving America from its enemies, within and without. He became a Republican in 1952 at the age of nine, under the influence of his aunt and uncle. He read voraciously—histories, biographies, science fiction, and even the *Encyclopedia Americana,* which his stepfather, Bob Gingrich, a career officer in the infantry, gave him at eleven.

A pivotal experience was a family visit in 1958 to the World War I battlefield of Verdun. The fourteen-year-old boy surveyed the shell-scarred, mine-pocked land and peered through the windows of the ossuary, a receptacle of the bones of more than 100,000 unidentified bodies. A sense of horror and reality pervaded the impressionable young American. As he wrote in his 1984 book, *Window of Opportunity,* "I left that battlefield convinced that men do horrible things to each other, that great nations can spend their lifeblood and their treasure on efforts to coerce and subjugate their fellow man."[18] Gingrich thereafter dedicated his life to trying to prevent a recurrence of such a devastating war through military strength and moral preparedness.[19]

The family later moved to Fort Benning, Georgia, where Gingrich was active in high school politics, managing the campaign of a friend, Jimmy Tilton, who was running for senior class president. Tilton won, and Gingrich got his first sweet taste of winning politics.

On the defining issue of southern politics, race, Gingrich was always an integrationist, rejecting the segregation that characterized most of Georgia. He embraced the 1960 Nixon-Lodge ticket as a "progressive reform ticket" while what he called "the forces of corruption, racism and one-party rule" aligned themselves with the Georgia Democratic party.[20] And he became a Republican for pragmatic reasons as well; with so few Republicans in heavily Democratic Georgia, he was assured, as biographers Judith Warner and Max Berley put it, of "rapid recognition and instant exposure."[21]

At Emory University in Atlanta, he founded a Young Republican club and managed an unsuccessful Republican congressional campaign. In his sophomore year, he told his fellow YRs that the Republican party believed in five things: "personal freedom, limited government, the federal system, the law, and capitalism."[22] Few other twenty-year-olds could have offered a more succinct and accurate summary of Republican philosophy.

Graduating from Emory in 1965 with a degree in history, Gingrich entered graduate school at Tulane University in New Orleans. He received a draft deferment because of his wife (his former high school geometry teacher) and their two small daughters. It would have been "irrational," he later argued, for him to volunteer and leave his young family behind (although other young fathers did).[23]

He became active in the 1968 Louisiana presidential primary campaign of Nelson Rockefeller, who was challenging, albeit ineffectively, Richard Nixon. Gingrich actually favored Ronald Reagan as the GOP's 1968 presidential candidate. He had seen Reagan "annihilate" Robert F. Kennedy in a nationally televised debate in 1967 and realized that the California governor was not "some shallow Hollywood actor."[24]

Convinced that Nixon could not win, Gingrich went to work for Rockefeller when Reagan insisted he was not a candidate. Gingrich admired Rockefeller for his support of a strong national defense and his outspoken commitment to civil rights, always a defining issue for Gingrich.

Receiving his doctorate in history, the activist-scholar spent the next decade in Carrollton, Georgia, thirty-five miles west of Atlanta, teaching history at West Georgia College and trying to get elected to Congress from the Sixth Congressional District, which stretched from Atlanta's suburbs to distant rural communities. He ran against the incumbent Democrat, John J. Flynt, a segregationist and symbol of Old South courthouse politics, in 1974 and again in 1976. He lost both times, but only by a couple of points. Each time, Gingrich portrayed himself as a "moderate conservative," even declining to take sides in the heated 1976 primary battle between Ford and Reagan.

By word and action, Gingrich disavowed his former liberal Republican connections. He was convincing enough to be endorsed by Paul Weyrich's Committee for the Survival of a Free Congress in 1974 and again in 1976. He promised if elected to close tax loopholes "which allow the very rich like

Nelson Rockefeller" to avoid taxes, and sent a telegram to President Ford in 1974 "stating his objections" to the appointment of the New York liberal as vice president.[25] He even omitted from his official biography the fact that he had once worked for Rockefeller. Although he was endorsed by the League of Conservation Voters and the Sierra Club, Gingrich was clearly moving to the right.

Almost broke but undaunted after his 1976 loss, Gingrich resolved to run for Congress a third time. At an Atlanta fund-raising dinner in the fall of 1977, the thirty-four-year-old Gingrich announced that he believed "deeply in the need for a conservative majority government."[26] At the time, just three years after the Watergate scandal and one year after the defeat of President Ford by an obscure southern governor, most Republicans were worried about the political survival of their party, let alone achieving a majority.

Undeterred, Gingrich uttered a battle cry a few months later that shaped his congressional campaign and the next two decades of his career. He castigated the Republican leadership, blaming Ford's pardon of Nixon for his 1974 congressional defeat and calling both former presidents "pathetic."[27] And he described what the GOP needed to become a majority party:

This party does not need another generation of cautious, prudent, careful, bland, irrelevant, quasi leaders who are willing to drift into positions because nobody else is available. What we really need are people who are tough, hard-working, energetic, willing to take risks, willing to stand up in a slug fest and match it out with their opponent.

You're fighting a war. It is a war for power . . . to build a majority capable of sustaining itself.[28]

It all came together for Gingrich in 1978. He was able to raise seed money from a group of wealthy supporters of his previous campaigns. He was highlighted by political reporter David Broder of the *Washington Post* as one of several rising Republicans who were challenging Democratic incumbents. And he met in Washington with Eddie Mahe, one of the GOP's top operatives and a former political director of the Republican National Committee. "It took me three-and-a-half minutes," Mahe recalled, "to find out he was smarter than I was and I should listen to him."[29]

Gingrich campaigned and won in 1978 as what can be called a New South conservative: economically and socially conservative, strongly anti-communist, pro–civil rights, and environmentally liberal. He received one-third of the black vote, an impressive showing given the nearly all-white composition of the Republican party in the South. Gingrich easily beat his Democratic opponent, state senator Virginia Shapard, by fifty thousand votes, although Shapard was endorsed by the powerful *Atlanta Constitution,* which criticized Gingrich for allowing his imagination to "run away with him in this election year" (a reference to his attack ads).[30]

The congressman-elect barely took time to thank his campaign support-ers for all their hard work before traveling to Washington to talk to anyone who would listen about his plans to make Republicans the majority in America. He spent three hours with Congressman Guy Vander Jagt of Michigan, chairman of the Republican Congressional Committee. Vander Jagt, who had kept in touch with Gingrich for five years, later appointed him head of a task force to plan a Republican majority. "I skipped him over about 155 sitting Republicans," he admitted.[31]

Gingrich talked openly about radically changing the balance of power in government. "The Congress in the long run," he told *Congressional Quarterly,* "can change the country more dramatically than the president. I think that's healthy. One of my goals is to make the House the co-equal of the White House."[32]

It was an audacious statement and an impossible goal. Congress can change the country, and has done so throughout modern American history, from rejecting the Treaty of Versailles in 1920 to resisting U.S. involvement in World War II in the late 1930s to the passage of the Taft-Hartley Act in 1947 over President Truman's veto. But because of its multiple membership and divided leadership, Congress's impact is necessarily limited and usually short-lived. The president can focus like a laser on an issue while Congress is debating which issues to focus on. And certainly Gingrich's omission of the Senate is significant.

Nixonian in his ability to seek out centers of political power, Gingrich called on New Right leader Paul Weyrich in his office just a few blocks from the U.S. Capitol. He told Weyrich that although he did not consider himself to be part of the New Right, "I identify with you. We can be strategic allies as we work together to gain power."[33] Antiestablishment from his first days in Washington, Weyrich admired the freshman congressman for his willingness to "take on the entrenched interests of either party," whether it was House Speaker Tip O'Neill or Republican leader Bob Michel.[34]

For the next few years, Gingrich and conservatives worked together.

The transformation of Newt Gingrich into a movement conservative seemed complete. Gingrich often co-chaired the weekly luncheon meetings of the Kingston Group (one of Weyrich's coalition groups). Ed Feulner recalls Gingrich's attending several of the Heritage Foundation's brown bag luncheons. "He was very bright," said Feulner; "very."[35] Heritage was sufficiently impressed to include Gingrich in a special 1983 discussion of the "future of conservatism." The other participants were conservative heavyweights Russell Kirk, Irving Kristol, and editor Robert Bartley of the *Wall Street Journal*.

As he did wherever he went, Gingrich would spout a new idea or propose a new study, and conservatives would dutifully carry out the research. But the alliance began to fray as conservatives wearied of receiving, in return for all their efforts, little more than new ideas and more new policies that were never implemented. Gingrich, aware of the growing disaffection, asked Weyrich what he should do, and Weyrich, never at a loss for advice, told the two-term congressman that he would remain a backbencher until he targeted some powerful figure and "went after him." If you succeed in bringing him down, predicted Weyrich, "you'll become a force to be reckoned with in this town."[36] Weyrich was not certain that Gingrich could do it, but he was sure the young congressman would one day be a "very important conservative leader."[37]

Conservative publisher Richard Viguerie, for his part, openly admired the Georgia congressman and put him on the May 1982 cover of *Conservative Digest* with the headline, "A New Conservative Leader for the '80s." The magazine described Gingrich as "a prototype conservative populist" and quoted Congressman Jack Kemp as calling him "a key intellectual figure within the Republican Party."[38]

The article revealed a politician who knew where he was going and seemed utterly confident he would get there. He was for dismantling the Great Society but keeping the New Deal in order "to meet all the underlying desires to protect the needy and elderly."[39] He expressed a fervent interest in technology, particularly outer space, and explained that the exploration of space was the modern-day equivalent of the building of the Panama Canal or the transcontinental railroads.

That January, in a Washington speech to conservative leaders, Gingrich had outlined what he called a "conservative opportunity society." Among its seven principles were the need for American military strength (Gingrich

called himself a hawk, "but a cheap hawk"); an emphasis on local governments, volunteer agencies, and the private sector rather than centralized government; and "workfare" rather than welfare. He called for a coalition
among "economic conservatives, national defense conservatives, and social
conservatives," all committed to "traditional American values."[40]

In the *Conservative Digest* interview, he argued that the conservative
movement had to go beyond political action committees like NCPAC and
the Committee for the Survival of a Free Congress and encourage a prolifer-
ation of special interest groups. Among his suggestions: Americans for Jobs
and Prosperity Through Space, Victims United Against Violent Crime, and
Americans for Strong Local and State Government. "The very basis of
American society," Gingrich told *Conservative Digest,* borrowing from Alexis
de Tocqueville, "is the right of individuals to be involved in voluntary associ-
ations."[41]

At about this time, Gingrich talked candidly with the *Washington Post's*
David Broder about the future of his party and the nation:

> I am a Republican, but I think the greatest failure of the last 20 years has
> been the Republican Party, not the Democratic Party. The Democratic
> Party has attempted to do what the governing party should do—govern.
> But it failed. And when it failed, there was nobody there to take up the bur-
> den. And I think that in order for this civilization to survive, at least as a free
> society, we've got to have a more rigorous and cohesive sense of an alterna-
> tive party.[42]

Gingrich was looking everywhere for ways to lead the GOP to a rebirth
of what he saw as its heyday: from the 1850s through the first decade of the
twentieth century, during all of which it was the party of economic growth
and individual opportunity. In his first year in the House, he led a Republican drive to expel Democratic congressman Charles C. Diggs of Michigan,
who had been convicted for diverting money from his congressional payroll
to his personal use. In his second year, he brought House and Senate candidates to the Capitol steps, where they posed with presidential candidate
Ronald Reagan and asked voters to elect a Republican majority in Congress. It almost worked: Republicans won a majority in the Senate in 1980
and picked up thirty-three seats in the House.[43]

In 1983, Gingrich took the first of several steps that would transform him in just six years from a relatively obscure House member into a formidable conservative force. And during those years, he voted right nearly all the time: his 1984 rating from the American Conservative Union was 91 percent.

Gingrich decided that he needed his own political organization to carry out his revolutionary agenda. Following the disappointing 1982 midterm elections in which House Republicans lost twenty-six seats, Richard Nixon told Gingrich, "You can't change the House yourself. You have to go back and form a group," one centered on ideas. The former president warned that this task would not be easy. House Republicans, he said, "are not used to having ideas and they're not used to thinking that ideas matter." That had to change, Nixon argued. Republicans had to become more interesting, more energetic, and more idea-oriented.[44] Gingrich emphatically agreed, and soon created the Conservative Opportunity Society, a House caucus of like-minded young conservative activists.

Gingrich's political strategy, wrote political reporters Dan Balz and Charles R. Babcock, was simple: Erode the people's confidence in the "corrupt" Democrats who had controlled Congress for thirty years and develop a set of Republican ideas and programs that would appeal to a majority of voters.[45] Reagan had already laid the foundation for the positive side of the strategy with his 1980 campaign theme of "family, work, neighborhood, peace and freedom" and his specific proposals to cut taxes and limit government.

Gingrich's critical contribution was on the negative side: to attack and keep attacking the Democrats. Democratic leaders like Jim Wright called Gingrich "a nihilist."[46] But, in truth, Gingrich was a political revolutionary in the American tradition, a Sam Adams or a Patrick Henry, determined to wrest power from the Democrats who had grown accustomed to dealing with go-along, accommodationist Republicans like Bob Michel and Gerald Ford. The always genial Michel was well known for sparring with House Speaker Tip O'Neill on the House floor and later playing golf with him.

Gingrich, Vin Weber, Bob Walker, and several dozen other House Republicans began meeting once a week. "Trent Lott was the godfather," Gingrich recalled. "He hosted a weekly luncheon."[47] They described themselves as direct descendants of the founding fathers, fighting for freedom and against a too-powerful government.

COS's undisputed enemy was the liberal welfare state, a primary target of conservatives from Bob Taft through Barry Goldwater and Ronald Reagan to the present. Gingrich stressed that although President Reagan unquestionably had "slowed down" the liberal welfare state, he had not fundamentally changed its character or its size. Advocates of the welfare state still wielded considerable power and influence. COS members therefore sought "wedge" issues, like abortion, school prayer, and anticommunism, that would split the Democratic coalition by forcing Democrats to choose between their base constituencies—organized labor, blacks, liberal special interest groups—and the majority of Americans. COS members also developed magnet issues, calculated to draw voters to the Republican vision for America—issues like tax reform, crime, and immigration.

Gingrich and his colleagues drew from a rich reserve of conservative ideas, including Reagan's prepresidential speeches, William F. Buckley's early writings, and Barry Goldwater's *The Conscience of a Conservative*. Dick Armey would later remark that Goldwater's "eloquent defense of freedom has altered our country forever."[48] In a December 1983 memo to Weber, Hugh Gregg proposed nine core issues for the COS to champion, including a line-item veto, a balanced budget amendment, tougher penalties for crime, welfare reform, High Frontier (Reagan's SDI), House rules reform, and voluntary school prayer.

With his political organization firmly in hand, Gingrich next considered how best to communicate his revolutionary message. He decided that, unlike Lenin, he did not have to create his own newspaper—particularly given the in-House television network, C-SPAN, launched in 1979.

Actually, it was Bob Walker, the Republicans' official point man during floor debate, who learned from the telephone messages he kept getting that lots of people were watching C-SPAN's coverage of the House. In early 1984, COS members began using the period set aside for special orders at the end of each day's regular session to talk about conservative issues. Few House members were present, but C-SPAN's cameras were, and they daily piped COS's presentations to the 17 million Americans with access to C-SPAN. In short order, Gingrich and his fellow Young Turks became television celebrities, and other news media began paying increasing attention to them.

It was time to step up the attack. In May 1984, COS members took command of an almost empty House floor and condemned the Democrats, including majority leader Jim Wright, for writing a "Dear Comandante" letter to Nicaragua's Sandinista leader Daniel Ortega. Gingrich labeled "appeasers" the Democrats who had a "pessimistic, defeatist and skeptical view toward the American role in the world." Dramatically, he challenged them to respond to his charges. Naturally, no one did, since he was addressing a chamber devoid of Democrats.[49]

The COS indictment stung the Democrats—particularly because there was so much truth in it—and several days later, a still angry O'Neill took the House floor. Shaking his finger at Gingrich, he shouted, "You deliberately stood in the well before an empty House and challenged these people and you challenged their Americanism! It's un-American! It's the lowest thing I've ever heard in my 32 years here!"[50]

O'Neill had overreacted; personal attacks are against the rules of the House. He was formally reprimanded for his emotional outburst, and his words were stricken from the *Congressional Record,* an almost unprecedented rebuff of a Speaker. Earlier, O'Neill had tried to nullify the speeches of COS members by ordering the C-SPAN cameras to pan the empty chamber when they spoke. But the old Democrat did not understand the new media. COS's target had always been the living room, not the House floor. From the beginning, Weber later explained, COS was trying to build "a cadre" among C-SPAN viewers.[51]

Some senior Republicans—and even a few COS members—were uncomfortable over Gingrich's harsh rhetoric and confrontational tactics. Michel counseled his younger colleague to be "gentlemanly," and backbencher Dan Coats suggested that "Newt's belief" that "you almost had to destroy the system so that you could rebuild it" was "kind of scary stuff." Still, Coats admitted, "We wouldn't have gotten to where we are today had Newt not kept pushing it as hard as he did."[52]

But leading conservatives like Trent Lott, Jack Kemp, and Dick Cheney encouraged Gingrich and other COS members to keep pushing. They understood that there was only one way they were ever going to capture the House: They had to stay on the offensive. President Reagan too appreciated the importance of the COS, using the phrase "an opportunity society for all" in his 1984 State of the Union address.[53]

The president also paid personal tribute to Gingrich, thanking him for organizing a rally on the Capitol steps to support the administration's prayer-in-school amendment. Supporters and opponents alike wondered whether Gingrich ever slept. He would regularly call one Reagan White House official at 6:30 A.M., believing that he could influence the official's thinking for the whole day "if he got to him early enough."[54]

Having created his own political caucus (which would never have occurred to Barry Goldwater) and with free access to a national television network (which Robert Taft would have disdained), Gingrich now proceeded to establish his own tax-exempt think tank, the American Opportunity Foundation. For Newt Gingrich, ideas had true political power. Eddie Mahe, one of the organizers, explained that the foundation was supposed to generate funding for "the research and education that all of Newt's projects tend to need. . . . He just sucks up information."[55]

Gingrich added another important political tool to his arsenal in 1986 when former Delaware governor Pete DuPont offered to hand his political action committee, GOPAC, over to him. DuPont was preparing to run for president and did not want GOPAC, which he had started back in 1979, to be compromised by his presidential candidacy. A delighted Gingrich accepted DuPont's generous offer and proceeded to transform GOPAC from a fund-raising committee for state and local candidates into a hard-hitting, national political organization. In short order, GOPAC was sending training tapes to thousands of GOP candidates running for federal as well as state and local office. Among other things, the tapes suggested "contrast words" to use against opponents, including "decay, failure, shallow, traitors, pathetic, corrupt, incompetent, sick."[56]

With GOPAC funds, Gingrich traveled across the country to recruit, train, and campaign for candidates. Barry Goldwater had done much the same thing, but always within the framework of official party organizations like the Republican Senatorial Campaign Committee, which he had headed. Reflecting the emerging new politics, Ronald Reagan had formed his own PAC, Citizens for the Republic, following his 1976 presidential bid. Gingrich proudly referred to GOPAC, which spent an estimated $8 million between 1991 and 1994, as "the Bell Labs of GOP politics."[57] The head of the Republican "labs," however, was not the chairman of the Republican National Committee but Gingrich himself.

The PAC and the foundation were components of the "far-flung network of political and philosophical organizations" that Gingrich used, with purpose and passion, to spread his new conservative message across the country.[58]

A disputed congressional election in Indiana gave Gingrich one more major opportunity to demonstrate his political muscle before taking on

Speaker Jim Wright. Democratic incumbent Frank McCloskey narrowly defeated Republican challenger Richard D. McIntyre on election night 1984 but was declared the loser—by just thirty-four votes—by Indiana's Republican secretary of state. At issue were a number of contested ballots. House Democrats, who constituted a majority, refused to seat McIntyre in January 1985.

After a drawn-out legal battle, a House task force composed of two Democrats and one Republican voted to seat Democrat McCloskey. Furious Republicans were convinced that Democrats had stolen a congressional seat from their would-be colleague, Richard McIntyre. On May 1, 1985, McCloskey took his seat, and within minutes the entire Republican membership—old bulls and young turks—marched out of the House and down the steps of the U.S. Capitol in protest, the first House walkout in ninety years.

Vin Weber is convinced that the walkout, conceived by COS, was crucial to Gingrich's emergence as a political leader of the House and future Speaker. The McCloskey "steal" was all the proof the Republicans needed that the Democrats were indeed corrupt and that politics as usual could no longer be tolerated. "I don't think," said Weber, "that Republicans ever looked upon the Democrats the same."[59] They were even ready to think the unthinkable—like forcing a House Speaker to resign.

Hell hath no fury like a conservative betrayed. President Bush had campaigned and won easily in 1988 as a read-my-lips, no-new-taxes conservative. But in the second year of his presidency, his lips were saying something else. All through 1989 and 1990, technocrats in the White House, led by OMB director Richard Darman, and liberal Democrats on Capitol Hill pressured the president to do something about the stagnant economy, growing by barely 2 percent, and the rising federal deficits, estimated at some $160 billion. For them, the solution was obvious: raise taxes.

Conservatives argued that such a move would be bad policy and worse politics. In May 1990, the Heritage Foundation's Daniel J. Mitchell warned that new taxes would "slow economic growth and could lead to a recession." He stated that the primary cause of the deficit was not lack of tax revenue but "runaway government spending." Citing the Congressional Budget Office, Mitchell pointed out that federal tax receipts had doubled over the past decade, from $517 billion in 1980 to an estimated $1.067 trillion in 1990. A panel of conservative economists insisted that the budget deficit problem was being "hyped" to stampede voters into accepting an unnecessary tax hike. There was no *deficit* crisis, they asserted, only a *political* crisis for big spenders seeking more funds for their grandiose programs.[60]

Bush, however, caved in and agreed to make a deficit-cutting deal with the Democratic Congress, which included "tax revenue increases"—in other words, new taxes. "If George Bush had pardoned Willie Horton or burned Old Glory on the lawn of the White House," reacted Daniel Mitchell caustically, "it would hardly have rivaled the flip-flop he has committed on taxes."[61] An ABC News/*Washington Post* survey agreed; it showed public disapproval of the Bush administration's tax flip-flop by 54 to 45 percent.

Although present at the bipartisan budget negotiations, Gingrich did not attempt to conceal his disinterest, spending much of his time reading novels and making notes. But he did send a two-page memo to the White House in late July assailing the administration's surrender strategy. He suggested that the Democrats were borrowing from one of their heroes, Woodrow Wilson, who had once commented, "You should never kill someone who is in the process of committing suicide."[62]

On Sunday, September 29, 1990, the leadership of both parties met with President Bush before a Rose Garden signing ceremony. Gingrich, the number two House Republican, astounded everyone, especially White House aides, by announcing that he did not believe the plan would pass Congress and that "he wouldn't support it."[63] He was speaking not just for himself but for conservatives in and out of the administration.

The plan was neatly summed up by conservative analyst Charles Kolb, who wrote that the Bush administration "had just agreed to raising taxes, renouncing Reaganomics, and acquiescing in major domestic spending increases, while simultaneously castigating GOP members of Congress who were willing to stand up for real spending cuts, economic growth and lower taxes!" A glum Vice President Dan Quayle would later concede that all Bush got was "four months of agony and a broken promise that would haunt him for the rest of his presidency."[64]

Conservatives were outraged by the compromise. "The issue," wrote *National Review*, "is whether the decade of Reaganism meant anything, or whether Mr. Bush merely thought his promises were a vehicle to the Oval Office, to be discarded at his convenience."[65] *Human Events* reared back and fired a high, fast one at Bush's head, calling the budget deficit reduction deal "one of the worst political and economic blunders ever made by a sitting Republican president." According to the conservative weekly, Bush did not just retreat before the Democrats, "he surrendered. Unconditionally."[66]

Heritage senior vice president Burton Yale Pines later remarked that George Bush could have been conservatism's Harry Truman, codifying the Reagan legacy as Truman had FDR's New Deal. Instead, said Pines, Bush did almost "everything he could in the most crass and oedipal way to undermine the Reagan Revolution."[67] Columnist Patrick J. Buchanan declared that the Bush administration stood for "continued growth in social spending—paid for by cuts in defense—and higher taxes on working folks." It also stood for "owls against loggers, feminists against Virginia Military Institute" and a "New World Order where our wealth is spread around the globe through foreign aid and institutions like the United Nations and the World Bank." If George Bush were renominated for president in 1992, asserted Buchanan, "the Reagan Revolution would be over."[68]

Buchanan's harsh assessment of the administration's domestic policies was essentially correct, except in one critical area, the federal judiciary, where Bush expanded conservative influence, particularly with one brilliant but explosive nomination.

"My name is Clarence Thomas," the strong, vibrant voice said, "and I like what you have to say!" It was the morning of Christmas Eve 1979, and J. A. (Jay) Parker, the black editor and founder of the conservative *Lincoln Review*, was sitting in his downtown Washington office when he picked up the phone. For the next forty minutes, Parker mostly listened as Thomas, a legislative assistant to Senator John Danforth (R–Missouri), talked about politics, black-white relations, and how much he had enjoyed reading the quarterly journal's views on free enterprise, limited government, and traditional moral values. "I thought I was the only one out there," Thomas said several times.[69] It was the beginning of a close and enduring friendship between the young black lawyer on Capitol Hill and the founding father of the contemporary black conservative movement in America.

Jay Parker was one of the few blacks active for Barry Goldwater in the early 1960s, the first black to sit on the national board of Young Americans for Freedom, the first black conservative to start his own public affairs firm in Washington. Over the years, he developed a national network of black conservative writers and thinkers that included Thomas Sowell of the Hoover

Institution and Walter Williams of George Mason University. It was not a large network. Sowell and Williams recall joking in 1971, "If we wanted to have a pinochle game among black conservatives, we couldn't."[70]

But by the late 1970s, black conservatives were a growing force in the conservative movement. It was not surprising, then, that following Reagan's 1980 presidential victory, transition coordinator Edwin Meese III asked Parker to head the effort at the Equal Employment Opportunity Commission (EEOC). Parker invited his young protégé, Thomas, to join the transition team. The hardworking Thomas wound up coauthoring the EEOC report. It was the beginning of a rapid rise in Washington for the Georgia-born black lawyer.

During the Reagan years, Thomas served in the civil rights division of the Department of Education, as EEOC chairman, and as a judge on the U.S. Court of Appeals for the District of Columbia. He was an eloquent defender of equal opportunity but a blunt opponent of equal results through affirmative action and other government edicts. He once remarked at a "black alternatives" conference that the worst experience of his life was attending college and law school with whites who believed he was there only because of racial quotas. "You had to prove yourself every day," he said, "because the presumption was that you were dumb and didn't deserve to be there on merit."[71]

He staked out a legal and philosophical position that was part traditional conservative and part libertarian. He praised natural law—the idea that there are governing principles higher than any written law—pointing out that the Declaration of Independence is a classic American statement of natural law with its proclamation that persons are "endowed by their Creator with certain inalienable rights."[72]

His 1991 nomination to the Supreme Court became a cause célèbre when Anita Hill, a former colleague at the Education Department and the EEOC, accused him of sexual harassment. Hill's testimony, despite sharp questioning by skeptical Republicans on the Senate Judiciary Committee, persuaded many watching the televised hearings that Thomas had harassed her in some fashion. Judge Thomas returned to the committee to deny categorically all of Hill's charges and to compare the proceedings to "a lynch mob." Subsequent female witnesses, black and white, who had worked with Thomas testified they had never been misused or harassed by their boss.

The Senate Judiciary Committee voted, largely along party lines, to confirm Thomas's nomination. Following an often sharp debate in the Senate, Judge Thomas won confirmation by a vote of 52 to 48, becoming (at age forty-three) the youngest member of the Supreme Court. Since then, Justice Thomas has become an increasingly influential conservative voice on the Court.

He once told a college audience how much he admired Thomas Sowell and Jay Parker for refusing to give in to "the cult mentality" that "hypnotizes" so many black Americans. "I only hope," Thomas said, "I can have a fraction of their courage and strength."[73] Justice Thomas has demonstrated both traits as he continues to insist that blacks, like any other group in America, should be free to think for themselves and not be obliged to follow racially prescribed lines. "We have no hope of stopping drive-by shootings in the streets," he declared, "until we can stop drive-by . . . character assassination."[74]

The Persian Gulf War was most Americans' idea of a perfect war: short, almost bloodless, victorious, and in prime time. Iraq invaded Kuwait on August 2, 1990. Over the next six months, President Bush carefully secured UN and then congressional approval to use force against Iraq if its troops did not leave Kuwait. Bush authorized the start of Operation Desert Storm on January 15, 1991, and on February 24, 1991, after five weeks of punishing air and missile strikes, General H. Norman Schwarzkopf launched a two-front ground attack. Most of the Iraqi army was quickly routed. Just one hundred hours after coalition forces attacked, Bush ordered a cease-fire. Despite many predictions of massive U.S. casualties, only 148 Americans were killed in action. Kuwait was a sovereign nation once again, and oil reserves essential to the West were safe.

General Schwarzkopf and General Colin Powell, chairman of the Joint Chiefs of Staff, became overnight heroes, returning soldiers were hailed in a series of victory parades, the ghost of the Vietnam War was finally laid to rest, and President Bush enjoyed public approval ratings of some 90 percent.

Then, more rapidly than ever before in modern politics, a president seeking reelection went from prohibitive favorite to unpopular underdog. In less than eighteen months, Bush's approval plummeted nearly sixty points to the mid-thirties just before the Republican convention in July 1992.

The central reason was smoldering public dissatisfaction with a dipping economy. Median household income in 1991 fell 3.5 percent. Only 1 million new jobs were created during the first three and a half years of the Bush presidency—the worst record of any administration since World War II. And unemployment hit 7.7 percent, the highest since the 1982–1983 recession.

The public was quick to assign blame. When the federal government failed to provide emergency relief quickly in the wake of Hurricane Andrew in August 1992, a Gallup Poll showed that Americans, by 57 to 35 percent, thought that President Bush cared more for the suffering of victims in Kuwait and Bosnia than for the suffering of Americans in Florida and Louisiana. It was a devastating judgment that Bush could not overcome.

The president was also a victim of what has been called the Churchill syndrome, a term political scientists coined to describe the surprise defeat of British prime minister Winston Churchill in the 1945 elections after he had guided his country to victory over the Nazis in World War II. Like Churchill, Bush was being told by an inward-looking electorate, "You're a wonderful global leader, but you don't understand our problems here at home."

Confronted by a superb campaigner in Arkansas governor Bill Clinton, a united Democratic party, and a well-financed third-party nominee—billionaire Ross Perot—Bush went down to defeat in November 1992. He received only 37.4 percent of the popular vote, less than Barry Goldwater did in his humiliating 1964 loss to Lyndon Johnson. Clinton carried thirty-two states and the District of Columbia, and won 370 of the 538 electoral votes. Another mark of the public's widespread discontent was the 19 million votes cast for Ross Perot, whose 18.9 percent of the vote total was the highest for an independent presidential candidate since Theodore Roosevelt in 1912.

Clinton won a plurality among independents, who had last supported a Democrat in 1964, and prevailed among suburbanites, who for the first time constituted a majority of voters. According to political analyst William Schneider, the suburban voters of 1992 were quite different from the silent majority of the 1970s and the Reagan Democrats of the 1980s. They were young, well educated, moderate, independent, and "very unhappy" with the nation's economic performance in the past four years.[75]

Some Bush partisans persisted in blaming conservative Patrick J. Buchanan for the president's defeat, arguing that the sharp-tongued television commentator's primary challenge had divided and weakened the Republican party. But Buchanan's strong showing in New Hampshire (where he received 37 percent of the primary vote and nine of twenty-three delegates) forced Bush to begin stressing traditional GOP themes and to move to the right of center, where the majority of American voters are to be found (as the elections of 1980, 1984, and 1988 demonstrated).

Human Events drew an apt parallel between Buchanan and Congressman John Ashbrook of Ohio, who "paved the way for the Buchanan challenge" when in 1972 he became the first modern-era conservative to battle an incumbent Republican president.[76] Buchanan, however, was unable to mount a sustained challenge to the better-organized and better-financed Bush, who made much of a personal endorsement by Ronald Reagan.

There was also the liberal argument that the Republican National Convention in Houston was a profile in extremism that badly damaged the GOP's reputation and Bush's chances. In truth, the Republican convention boosted President Bush's standing in the polls. Before Houston, he trailed Clinton by anywhere from sixteen to twenty-one points in the polls. The day after forceful speeches by "right-wingers" Buchanan and Pat Robertson, a survey showed that Bush had closed to within six points of the Arkansas governor.[77] And after his effective acceptance speech, filled with conservative rhetoric and themes, Bush was only two points behind Clinton. He never got that close again.

In the Senate that fall, Democrats retained their 57–43 margin; in the House, Republicans picked up only a modest ten seats. Democrats still enjoyed a solid 258–176 majority. Vic Fazio, chairman of the Democratic Congressional Campaign Committee, gloated that the Republicans "had a major failure."[78]

And they almost had heart failure when Newt Gingrich retained his seat by a microscopic margin of 980 votes out of more than seventy thousand cast in a Republican primary. How could so prominent a Republican leader, who outspent his opponent by ten to one, almost lose? Because he had been relocated to an entirely new congressional district where he had never helped anyone get a social security check; because his opponent, Herman S. Clark, also was conservative and a strong conservationist; because Gingrich had twenty-two overdrafts at the House bank and a taxpayer-supported car with a $60,000-a-year driver; and because a liberal coalition, including the United Steelworkers of America and the League of Conservation Voters, had targeted him for defeat. Cross-over voting is allowed in Georgia, and thousands of Democrats voted in the GOP primary. "Newt presented a very inviting target," wrote political columnist Dick Williams.[79] If five hundred more Democrats had crossed over, Newt Gingrich would not have become the Speaker of the House of Representatives two years later.

Conservative reaction to President Bush's defeat in 1992 ranged from sarcastic to frustrated. The president "inherited an impregnable fortress from Mr. Reagan," wrote *National Review* editor John O'Sullivan, "and set assiduously about undermining the ramparts. All that Mr. Clinton did was lean on it." To make sure that no one missed the point, the magazine added, in an unsigned editorial, that "firm, principled leadership, rooted in an accurate understanding of the nation's problems (too much government, and a governing class that maintains its power by enlarging the government), is the best way to create [a] majority—the essence *both* of governing well *and* of winning elections."[80]

"Who would ever have thought," asked one prominent conservative, "that a Republican president closely identified with the Reagan revolution would be defeated by a Democratic challenger campaigning against him from the right?"[81]

Sorting through the results, political consultant Donald Devine suggested that in the wake of Bush's defeat, there were now four major schools of Republicanism: the deficit cutters, represented by Bob Dole; the opportunity society/supply-siders, led by Newt Gingrich and Jack Kemp; the social conservatives, epitomized by Pat Buchanan and Pat Robertson; and the federalists, as defined by Ronald Reagan, who argued that the conservative purpose was to reestablish American government "on the terms originally intended by the founders."[82] Devine did not or could not suggest any successor to Reagan.

Heritage president Ed Feulner insisted that America, and the conservative movement, owed George Bush a "great debt of gratitude" for his lifetime of service to the country, for bringing dignity to the White House, for standing firm on judicial appointments like Clarence Thomas, and for steering the Persian Gulf War so skillfully. But on the twin issues most important to the majority of Americans, taxes and spending, he had "stumbled badly." And during his campaign, Bush had failed to convince the electorate that he knew what he wanted to do in a second term. Bush proved, said Feulner, that "a 'leader' without a cause is a leader without a following."[83]

For his part, Clinton knew precisely the image he wanted to project: he was a "different kind of Democrat," a founder of the moderate Democratic

Leadership Council, not the successor to ultraliberal George McGovern. While campaigning, Clinton said he favored a balanced budget amendment, federal deregulation, free trade with Mexico, the line-item veto (which he had had as Arkansas governor), the death penalty, getting tough with China over its brutal violations of human rights, and intervening in the war in former Yugoslavia. All these were issues that, in the words of COS member Vin Weber, "Ronald Reagan would probably have been running on if he ran in 1992."[84]

President-elect Clinton insisted that he was a New Democrat who sought a "third way" between the Big Government of liberal Democrats and the No Government of conservative Republicans. His third way, he said, would foster community, encourage opportunity, and demand responsibility. One of Clinton's most applauded lines during the fall campaign was his pledge to "end welfare as we know it."[85]

Whatever his intentions, however, the new president quickly surrendered to Democratic liberals in Congress, who had their own ideas about the best balance between government and society. The end result, particularly Clinton's proposed top-to-bottom overhaul of the nation's health care system, so alarmed the American people that they were ready to listen to a Republican alternative called the Contract with America.

Chapter 15

Newt! Newt! Newt!

BEFORE THERE WAS THE CONTRACT WITH AMERICA, THERE WAS A 1990 LEC-
ture by Newt Gingrich at the Heritage Foundation listing five goals for the
United States. And before Heritage, there was an eighteen-day retreat in the
Colorado Rockies during which Gingrich declared that the welfare state
had to "be blown up to be replaced." And before the Crested Butte, Colorado, retreat, there was a 1986 series of Gingrich speeches suggesting six
points for America's future. And before the 1986 speeches, there was a 1983
memorandum by Judd Gregg outlining nine conservative programs. And before the Gregg memo, there was a 1981 meeting in Racine, Wisconsin, at
which Gingrich set forth a twelve-year plan for a conservative majority in
America. And before Racine, there was the October 1980 rally on the steps
of the U.S. Capitol where Republican members of the House and Senate
stood proudly behind their presidential candiate, Ronald Reagan, and
pledged to support his conservative presidential platform.

But that is only the tip of the giant conservative iceberg that in November 1994 tore into the seemingly impregnable Democratic majority in Congress and sank it faster than the *Titanic*.

Before there was a Contract with America, there were seminal works
like Russell Kirk's *The Conservative Mind* and Whittaker Chambers's *Witness*
and Richard Weaver's *Ideas Have Consequences* and F. A. Hayek's *The Road to
Serfdom*. There were political manifestos like Barry Goldwater's *The Conscience of a Conservative* and Robert Taft's *A Foreign Policy for Americans*.

There were best-sellers like Bill Buckley's *Up from Liberalism* and Milton

Friedman's *Free to Choose* and Irving Kristol's *Reflections of a Neoconservative*. There were policy exposés like Charles Murray's *Losing Ground* and moral lessons like William Bennett's *The Book of Virtues*.

There were grassroots political organizations like the Committee of One Million and Young Americans for Freedom and the American Conservative Union and the Christian Coalition. There were single-minded, single-interest groups like the National Right to Work Committee and the National Right to Life Committee and the Family Research Council. There were authoritative think tanks like the Heritage Foundation and the Cato Institute and the American Enterprise Institute and the Hoover Institution.

There were creative fund raisers like Richard A. Viguerie and Steven Winchell and Bruce Eberle and the Heritage Foundation's John von Kannon. There were farsighted donors like Roger Milliken and Joseph Coors and Richard Scaife and William Simon. There were risk-taking foundations like Olin and Bradley and Noble and Earhart and Carthage.

There were forthright conservative journals like *Human Events* and *National Review* and *The American Spectator*. There were trenchant neoconservative magazines like *Commentary* and the *Public Interest* and the *New Criterion*. There were influential mainstream publications like the *Wall Street Journal* and *Reader's Digest* and the *Washington Times*.

There were prescient anticommunists like Sidney Hook and Max Eastman and Isaac Don Levine and Walter Judd. There were nationally known columnists like George Sokolsky and John Chamberlain and William F. Buckley, Jr., and George Will and Patrick Buchanan. There were powerful broadcasters like Fulton Lewis, Jr., and Paul Harvey and Rush Limbaugh.

There were budget-slashing congressmen and senators like Clare Hoffman of Michigan and H. R. Gross of Iowa and Harry Byrd of Virginia. There were naysaying senators like Jesse Helms and Strom Thurmond and penitent isolationists like Arthur Vandenberg and Everett Dirksen. There were skilled political operatives like F. Clifton White and David Keene and Lee Atwater. There were shrewd publicists like Lyn Nofziger and Vic Gold and Hugh Newton. There were successful entrepreneurs like Amway founders Rich DeVos and Jay Van Andel and publisher Tom Phillips.

And most important of all, there were the three political leaders— Robert Taft, Barry Goldwater, and Ronald Reagan—on whose shoulders Newt Gingrich and all the other revolutionary conservatives stood as they prepared to seize what had been a Democratic citadel for forty years.

In his 1990 Heritage lecture (delivered to young conservatives who composed conservatism's Third Generation), Gingrich quoted from Goldwater's *Conscience of a Conservative*, Reagan's 1964 television address for Goldwater, Bill Buckley's *National Review,* and two articles by Irving Kristol in the *Wall Street Journal.* After seventeen months as House Republican whip, he had come to a somber conclusion: Congress was a broken, corrupt, and sick institution "in an imperial capital that wallows in the American people's tax money."[1]

Rejecting the old Republican vision of balancing the budget above all, Gingrich declared that America faced "a real turning point" in its history, and he offered five goals that, if realized, would create "a prosperous, free country offering hope and opportunity to all": (1) integrity in government, (2) physical safety for all citizens, (3) a growing economy, (4) a replacement for the collapsing presence of the bureaucratic state in education, welfare, health, and the environment, and (5) priority of the family budget over the government budget.[2]

He emphasized that these five tasks—integrity, safety, jobs, new model government, and a profamily tax policy—were a monumental challenge that could not be met by politicians alone. "Only a citizens movement," Gingrich said, "can force Washington, the state capitals, the county courthouses, and city halls to change their ways. Only a citizens movement can force a decade of creativity to launch a successful twenty-first-century America."[3]

The address was characteristic, in tone and content, of the thousands of political speeches that Gingrich gave between 1979, his first year in Congress, and 1994, when he led an eager Republican army up Capitol Hill. Gingrich kept working and reworking his rhetoric (much as Ronald Reagan had in the years leading up to his first bid for public office) until he was convinced that he had the right message to inspire the country and achieve a Republican majority in the people's branch of government.

Gingrich also took care of important political business in early 1993 by inviting two potential conservative rivals—Congressmen Dick Armey and Tom DeLay, both of Texas—to dinner on Capitol Hill. How could a small gang of conservatives, he asked them seductively, take over the Republican party and win back Congress?[4] In ensuing weeks, the three conservatives, along with Bob Walker of Pennsylvania and Bill Paxon of New York, discussed with increasing excitement how such a historic goal could indeed be accomplished. Everyone agreed that Gingrich should become the Republican leader in place of the too accommodating Michel, as well as Speaker of the House.

The Democrats still controlled Congress in 1993–1994, but they were acting more and more like a worn-out bull ready for pasture. Congressional scandals continued to plague the majority party. Dan Rostenkowski, chairman of the powerful House Ways and Means Committee, was indicted on charges of embezzlement, fraud, and cover-up. The Baltimore *Sun* referred to a "dysfunctional Congress," while the *Washington Post* speculated that the 103rd Congress might be "the worst" ever. Public support for term limits soared.

President Clinton did little to help the Democratic cause. He endorsed gays in the military, alarming not only members of the armed forces but millions of veterans and middle-class Americans. He promised to revolutionize U.S. health care, arousing the great majority of citizens who wanted reform, not revolution. He radically expanded the U.S. mission in Somalia, adopting a UN-endorsed "nation-building" policy that alienated prudent conservatives as well as neoisolationists. In so acting, Clinton defined himself not as a New Democrat but as an old-fashioned, spend-tax-intervene Democrat.

There were early indications that the 1994 elections spelled trouble for the Democrats when Republicans won two special House elections in May, in Oklahoma and Kentucky. In the latter contest, Ron Lewis, who ran a small Christian bookstore, easily won a seat that had not been held by a Republican for more than a century. He defeated Joseph Prather, majority leader of the Kentucky state senate and former chairman of the state Democratic party, who tried but failed to portray Lewis as a captive of the "religious right." Lewis, for his part, constantly linked Prather and President Clinton, declaring in his television ads that "if you like Bill Clinton, you'll *love* Joe Prather. . . . [But] Kentucky doesn't need another professional politician."[5]

These House Republican victories followed Kay Bailey Hutchison's pickup of a U.S. Senate seat in a special Texas election in 1993 and a GOP sweep of gubernatorial contests in New Jersey and Virginia the same year. Republicans were on an electoral roll.

As they prepared for the fall campaign, Gingrich and his colleagues were determined to present "a clear blueprint" for the future and to avoid any "mudslinging," which would turn off the supporters of Ross Perot—a key voting bloc. Back in January, about half the members of the House Republican Conference had participated in a weekend retreat in Salisbury on Maryland's Eastern Shore. They had heard Frank Luntz, a brash young pollster who had worked for Perot in 1992, argue that "we had to stake out a strong case for reform if we wanted to get the country's attention." The conferees took Luntz's advice and wrote the Salisbury Statement, which became the first draft of the Contract with America.[6]

By June, House Republicans had agreed to gather on the steps of the Capitol in late September to announce a united party platform. Gingrich asked Dick Armey, chairman of the House Republican Conference, to assemble ten task forces of House Republicans and nonincumbent candidates to develop platform items. Content and language were refined in the succeeding weeks with the advice of sympathetic public policy groups like the Heritage Foundation and extensive polling coordinated by Luntz. Armey credits his chief of staff, Kerry Knott, with coining the contract's name.

Social issues like abortion and school prayer, which were so vital to the Religious Right, were purposely omitted from the Contract because they would have polarized public reaction and support. But the Christian Coalition, largest of the social conservative groups, still endorsed the Contract with America, particularly its $500 tax credit for children. "We were very supportive," says Marshall Wittmann, then the Christian Coalition's legislative director, who recalls wearing a button that read "Pass America's Contract."[7]

The coalition's approval was a sign of its political maturation and the prudent leadership of its shrewd young executive director, Ralph Reed. In one of the most important political statements by a social conservative in the early 1990s, Reed wrote in the summer 1993 issue of Heritage's *Policy Review* that "the most urgent challenge for pro-family conservatives is to develop a broader issues agenda." While not discounting "vital" issues like abortion and homosexuality, Reed argued that to win at the ballot box and in the court of public opinion, social conservatives had to "speak to the concerns of average voters in the areas of taxes, crime, government waste, health care, and financial security."[8]

Some social conservatives, however, qualified their support of the Contract. While acknowledging that the document would help move Perot voters back into the Republican column, Paul Weyrich of the Free Congress Foundation complained that it was "primarily an economic document" that did not take into account issues like school prayer, parental choice, and the "reestablishment of values in our culture."[9] That prompted other conservatives to quote columnist Cal Thomas, former communications director for Jerry Falwell's Moral Majority, who wrote that "neither princes, nor kings, nor Presidents" have the power to restore America's values—"only God does."[10] The question of government's proper role in helping to reverse America's undeniable moral decline would be fiercely debated by economic and social conservatives throughout the 1990s.

The formal signing of the Contract with America on the steps of the U.S. Capitol on September 27 was a calculated media event with fervent prayers, a solemn Pledge of Allegiance, a spirited marching band, fluttering American flags, and bright red, white, and blue bunting. Gingrich's dramatic words matched the crusading spirit of the occasion: "Today on these steps we offer this contract as a first step toward renewing American civilization."[11]

House Republicans expected the politically astute White House to ignore the Contract with America. When they learned that President Clinton intended to launch an all-out attack, they were delighted. The president's counterattack, Gingrich later commented, "turned a potential inside-page photo opportunity into the centerpiece of the campaign."[12]

Gingrich, Armey, and the others were confident that if Americans read the Contract, they would endorse each item, and the candidates pledged to implement them. By now, they knew they had a winner; every poll confirmed it. The first item—applying all the laws of the nation to Congress itself—was supported by 90 percent of the people (and loved by Perot voters). The balanced budget amendment, the line-item veto, welfare reform, term limits, the $500 tax credit for children, and an enforceable death penalty had 80 percent support. Even the less favored items—regulatory reform, litigation reform, and social security reform—had 60 percent public backing. Although many voters did not know all the details of the Contract, they realized they were being given a choice between politics as usual and a new, more open, and more responsive way.

The Contract, like all other good political documents, balanced what the public wanted with what the public needed. It was a commonsense platform that at the same time represented a radical change from the way things had been done in the nation's capital since the 1930s: A balanced budget mocked Keynes, welfare reform threatened the New Deal, and a tough death penalty challenged the criminal rights decisions of countless liberal courts. But regardless of public opinion, the Washington establishment would not surrender power quietly. Gingrich warned his colleagues that "they will do anything to stop us. . . . There is no grotesquerie, no distortion, no dishonesty too great for them to come after us."[13]

And come after them the Democrats did. In a major campaign speech in Michigan, President Clinton called the GOP document a "contract *on* America" that would take the nation back to the terrible "trickle-down economics" of the 1980s. He suggested a simple answer to the Contract: "We've been there. We've seen that. We've tried it. And we will not be fooled again." But ominously for the president and Democrats, the crowd's reaction to his fiery rhetoric was "lackluster," according to the *New York Times.*

House Democrats, led by majority leader Richard Gephardt, charged that the Contract "would blow a hole in the federal budget." Democratic National Committee chairman David Wilhelm dismissed the document "as voodoo part two, the son of Reaganomics."[14] Democrats chortled reflexively, but more reflective analysts saw something different and important in the Republican initiative.

The point of the Contract, neoconservative columnist Charles Krauthammer explained, was to "limit the power, resources, and reach of government (except for national defense and policing) as the beginning of a radical ideological project, the dismantling of the welfare state." It was a renunciation of President Bush's attempt to manage Big Government and a return to President Reagan's vision of "re-limiting and, in some areas, de-legitimizing government."[15]

Distraught over the possibility of being the first Democratic president since Harry Truman to face a Republican Congress, Clinton became increasingly shrill in his attacks. At a White House news conference, the president called the Contract "a trillion dollars of unfunded promises" that would hurl America back to "the 80s when we lost jobs and weakened our country."[16] Even for a political leader desperate to prevent a historic defeat by his party, the assertion was absurd: during the 1980s, America *gained* over 19 million new jobs and ended the forty-year-long cold war through a fixed policy of military strength.

Republicans running for the House and the Senate, for governor and even lieutenant governor, took full advantage of the White House's anti-

Contract strategy and ran against Clinton day and night. Any association by a Democratic candidate with the president, however casual, sparked a sharp Republican response. In North Carolina, a Republican television ad showed an incumbent Democratic congressman jogging with Clinton and commented, "In Washington, they're a team." In New Mexico, a GOP commercial featured the incumbent Democratic senator shaking hands with Clinton. "No one owns Colin McMillan [the Republican challenger]," stated the ad, "especially Bill Clinton."[17]

A Tennessee Democrat summed up his party's panic about the man in the White House: "I'd rather kiss [a Republican] on the lips in front of the courthouse than have to campaign with Clinton now."[18]

Once, in a moment of pique, Gingrich had referred to Bob Dole as "the tax collector for the welfare state." Now, in the fall of 1994, the two Republican leaders campaigned together across the country. The crowds were large and enthusiastic, and the money—always a sure political indicator—poured in. Gingrich himself raised an estimated $3 million meeting and eating with the Republican faithful. By mid-October, it was clear (even to the White House) that Republicans were going to make enormous gains in Congress.

The National Republican Congressional Committee reported that not one Republican House member trailed his Democratic challenger, anywhere. The big question was whether the GOP would win the forty seats needed to rule the House for the first time since 1953–1954. Republicans, in fact, had held a majority in the House in only four of the past sixty-four years. Because there were so many open-seat elections in the Senate and the Republican candidates were so attractive, the odds were excellent that the GOP would pick up the seven seats needed to retake the upper chamber.

On November 8, 1994, a day that will live in conservative history, Republicans gained fifty-two seats and assumed a majority in the U.S. House of Representatives for the first time since Dwight Eisenhower was president. It was a Republican triumph and a Democratic debacle with "a long-term significance," in the words of the nonpartisan *Congressional Quarterly*, well beyond that of other recent congressional landslides.[19] The *New York Times* called it a "political upheaval of historic proportions."[20]

Republicans, whose national vote for House seats had never totaled more than 28 million in a midterm election, won 36.6 million votes in 1994.

The 9-million-vote rise represented the largest midterm-to-midterm increase in one party's vote total in the nation's history. The 1994 election was not just an anti-Clinton vote (although it certainly was that) but a positive landslide because of the enormous surge in votes for the Republican party—and the conservative Contract with America.

Republicans won and Democrats lost almost everywhere. Democrats were outpolled in every region of the country except the East and in every state with at least ten congressional districts except Massachusetts.

The returns were especially bleak for Democrats in the South, once the cornerstone of their party. Republican House candidates received more votes than Democrats in every southern state but Mississippi, where the Democratic candidates "were so conservative" that they should have run on the Republican ticket, according to the *New York Times*.[21] In fact, five southern House Democrats did switch in 1995 to the GOP. Altogether, Democrats lost nineteen House seats in the South, more than in any other region. Newt Gingrich became the first Republican Speaker of the House from the South.

After eight years as the minority in the Senate, Republicans recaptured the upper house by 52–48, sweeping all nine open-seat elections and defeating two Democratic incumbents. In every case, the more conservative candidate topped the more liberal candidate. The day after the election, Senator Richard C. Shelby of Alabama, a Democrat, announced he was switching parties, giving the GOP a 53-to-47 margin. "I thought there was room in the Democratic Party for a conservative like myself," Shelby explained. "But I can tell you there's not." Quipped a delighted Bob Dole, the forthcoming Senate majority leader, "We'll be happy to accept other applications."[22] In March, after Democratic votes killed the balanced budget amendment, Ben Nighthorse Campbell of Colorado also became a Republican, increasing the Republican edge to 54–46.

The Republican tide swept over the states as well. Republicans increased their number of governorships to thirty (their first majority since 1970) and reached "near parity in state legislatures," gaining a total of 482 seats. The GOP controlled the governor's mansion in eight of the nine most populous states and in states representing more than 70 percent of the population.[23] Particularly painful for the Democrats were the defeats of two of their brightest stars: Governor Mario Cuomo of New York by George Pataki and Governor Ann Richards of Texas by George W. Bush, son of the former president.

As conservative activist Grover Norquist wrote, the election of sheriffs, county commissioners, and school board officials, along with the gain of nearly five hundred state legislative seats, gave Republicans "a strong farm team for future statewide and national elections." And it meant the loss of thousands of patronage jobs to the Democrats. In New York state alone, Republicans would now be able to fill twelve thousand patronage positions. Nationwide, Norquist estimated that Democrats lost "more than 50,000 political patronage jobs" on that fateful November day in 1994.[24]

"Conservatism's long march," declared columnist George Will, "began thirty years ago with Barry Goldwater's capture of the Republican Party."[25] Will did not go back far enough. The transformation of the GOP from a minority to a majority party actually began in 1946 with the first major conservative victory of the postwar period: the election of the Republican Eightieth Congress and the emergence of Robert Taft as its leader.

In the White House, a stunned President Clinton contemplated the horror of it all and considered his options. The media were calling him a lame duck and wondering how relevant he was in a brave new Republican world. "Is he Hoover, Carter or Truman?" *Newsweek* asked. Clinton "is in doodoo so deep," the magazine decided, that it hardly mattered.[26]

The Friday morning following the election, Newt Gingrich and his wife, Marianne, bumped into Supreme Court justice Clarence Thomas and his wife, Ginni, in front of the Capitol, each of them on his or her way to work. "Here we are," Gingrich recalled saying. "You're on the court over here, and I'm going to be Speaker over there. Do you think that is what they mean when they talk about a revolution?"[27]

The House of Representatives proved that it was a different kind of House by staying in continuous session for fourteen and a half hours on its first day of business, January 4, 1995, the longest opening day in history. When the final gavel sounded, the House had adopted a comprehensive set of new rules calculated to produce a more efficient and democratic national legislature.

The reforms included requiring a supermajority for tax increases; cutting committee staff by one-third and eliminating three full committees and twenty-five subcommittees; limiting the terms of committee chairmen and the Speaker; and opening all committee meetings (unless classified) to the public and the media. Many observers had compared the House committee structure under the Democrats to "a feudal system." Creating a Congress in which there were "few hiding places" and even fewer excuses for failing to "advance an advertised agenda," suggested congressional analyst David Mason, might be the Contract's most important reform.[28]

Over the next one hundred days, with Speaker Gingrich as chief executive officer and chairman of the board and majority leader Dick Armey as chief operating officer, Republicans pushed through the Contract, item by item, bill by bill. With a majority of only twelve votes (FDR had a Democratic majority of over three hundred in his first hundred days back in 1933), there was little margin for error and no place for second thoughts.

Key to their success was what House whip Tom DeLay of Texas called "growing the vote." DeLay listened carefully to each member and determined what would make him more likely to vote for a bill. He brought together grassroots activists and committed congressmen to support a bill as it came to the floor for a vote. DeLay was also a frequent participant in the coalition meetings of Paul Weyrich and Grover Norquist, head of Americans for Tax Reform, an influential new conservative group in Washington. Other supportive groups included the National Federation of Independent Business (NFIB), National Taxpayers Union, and Christian Coalition. None of these organizations, with the exception of NFIB, had existed before the early 1970s.[29]

Radio talk show hosts, like Rush Limbaugh, G. Gordon Liddy, Oliver North, and Michael Reagan, son of the former president, were invaluable allies. Republican leaders not only appeared on their programs during the hundred days, but invited the hosts of national and local talk shows to broadcast their programs from Washington. During the last week of implementing the Contract, over forty talk shows originated from the U.S. Capitol. It became so crowded in and around the Speaker's office, Gingrich remembered, that "every time my stomach growled, I felt it was broadcast on national radio."[30]

House Republicans were also fortunate to have adroit committee chairmen—like Gerald Solomon of the Rules Committee, Henry Hyde of the Judiciary Committee, and William Archer of the Ways and Means Committee—who performed political miracles in just thirteen weeks, the time a congressional committee normally takes to decide its agenda for the next two years. Judiciary chairman Hyde led the way by producing two constitutional amendments (balanced budget and term limits), three litigation reform bills, and five crime bills. Hyde's efforts were all the more re-markable because he personally opposed the term limits amendment and publicly said so.

House Republicans were sustained by the widespread support of the electorate. Archer's Ways and Means Committee wrote welfare reform legis-lation that included work requirements, strengthened the family, reestab-lished male responsibility for children, and discouraged young girls from getting pregnant outside marriage. By the time the bill passed the House, noted Gingrich, one poll showed that 96 percent of Americans favored re-placing the present welfare system—"a unanimity virtually unknown on any other issue."[31]

On April 5, 1995, the House passed a $187 billion tax cut (the final item on the agenda). Republicans kept their promise about the Contract with America in only ninety-one days, bringing every item to the House floor for a vote. There had been some disappointments, particularly the failure of the term limits amendment to receive the necessary two-thirds vote, the tally falling sixty-one votes short. But House Republicans had wrested the agenda-setting role from the White House and forced Clinton and the Demo-crats to accept major GOP goals, most notably balancing the budget in seven years.

Throughout, the Republican National Committee ran advertisements on national cable television with the tag line, "The new Republican Con-gress: Making Washington work, for a change."[32]

But the year that began with such shining promise ended in deep disap-pointment. The Republican House watched its public approval sink from a high of 52 percent in December 1994, shortly before it took office, to 41 percent in June 1995, and down to the high 20s in January 1996, right after the two shutdowns of the federal government. Speaker Gingrich, who had been the man of the hour in January, now had a personal approval rating of only 27 percent and an ominous disapproval rating of 51 percent.[33]

Only five of the twenty-one legislative priorities in the Contract with America were enacted by Congress, because of President Clinton's skillful opposition and use of the veto, the Republican House's failure to pay suffi-cient attention to the Democrats' propaganda war, and the Republican Sen-ate's far more measured pace.

Republicans, syndicated columnist Mona Charen pointed out, had made several major "tactical errors" that cost them dearly. First, they failed to use their majority status to educate the public. They assumed, erroneously, that "the case for cutting government did not need to be made—again." Congressional hearings detailing "government waste and duplication" would have helped the electorate understand what Congress was attempting to do.[34]

Second, Republicans did not concentrate on one or two critical reforms (after passing the Contract with America) that would have delineated the differences between the two political parties. They acted more like impulsive revolutionaries than thoughtful legislators. "Step by step," said political scientist Steven S. Smith, "they came to be viewed as radical."[35]

But the House's radicalism did have at least one favorable outcome: It inspired the Senate to come up with its own aggressive agenda. "We don't want to fall behind," explained Senate majority leader Bob Dole.[36] The Senate focused on fewer items, including a balanced budget amendment, national defense, crime, middle-class tax cuts, welfare reform, and relaxation of the earnings test for social security recipients.

Third, wrote Charen, Republican leaders became "too wrapped up in their own egos."[37] Gingrich revealed in November that he had forced the first government shutdown in part because he felt that Clinton had snubbed him by seating him in the rear of *Air Force One*. "CRY BABY," headlined the *New York Daily News,* next to a caricature of Gingrich in a diaper.[38] And many had not forgotten that two weeks before he was sworn in as Speaker, Gingrich had received a $4.5 million book advance from publisher Harper-Collins. Gingrich later renounced the multimillion-dollar advance, but the damage had been done: the Speaker looked like just another politician trying to cash in on his prestige.

Finally, Republicans underestimated President Clinton's ability to seize the offensive and win the debate over budget showdowns and two government shutdowns. The president, for example, was able to convince the public that Republicans wanted to "cut" rather than reform Medicare. Still, argued Charen, Clinton was obliged to adopt important GOP proposals, from a balanced budget to ending automatic benefits for welfare mothers, proving that most Republican issues were winners rather than losers.[39]

But Republicans lost the information battle, and badly. A crucial misstep was their failure to respond to the multimillion-dollar advertising campaign of the AFL-CIO, which convinced many Americans, especially senior citizens, that the GOP was out to slash their Medicare benefits; the fact was that the Republicans sought to scale back the *growth* of Medicare and turn Medicaid (the health care program for the poor) over to the states. These were certainly major reforms and required sophisticated, sustained marketing to the public. Instead, GOP silence created a vacuum that Clinton and congressional Democrats quickly filled. Along with outside allies like organized labor, Democrats got away with depicting Republicans as hard-hearted extremists who wanted to cut popular programs like Medicare to finance generous tax breaks for upper-income Americans.

Gingrich and his House colleagues had mistakenly assumed from the beginning that Clinton had no real choice but to accept deep cuts in the budget to avoid shutting down the government. As the Speaker put it, "It's their government, not ours."[40]

Republicans also recalled that President Reagan, not Congress, had been blamed by the media and then the public for the last government shutdowns in the 1980s. But then Clinton began vetoing and some congressional Republicans began revealing their lack of enthusiasm for truly changing the way Washington worked. Gingrich and the other House revolutionaries underestimated Clinton's grit—and overestimated the public's taste for rapid change.

Republicans "mistook public dissatisfaction with excesses in government," said Democratic congressman Barney Frank of Massachusetts, "for hatred of government. People are not ready for a radical repudiation of a governmental role in society."[41]

The parallels between the Gingrich 104th Congress and the Taft 80th Congress are revealing.

The Republican majorities in both Congresses were ruled by hubris. Following the 1946 election, Republican leaders referred to America as "Republican country"; forty-eight years later, Gingrich declared that the 1994 election "signaled the end of the New Deal and Great Society eras."[42] As one conservative leader put it, Gingrich failed to make a critical distinction between winning a battle and winning a war.[43]

Emblematic of the pride was Speaker-to-be Gingrich's address on December 5, 1994, to the House Republican Conference, including seventy-three newcomers, in the majestic Cannon Caucus Room on Capitol Hill. A beaming Gingrich was greeted by ecstatic chants of "Newt! Newt! Newt!" A wiser leader would have quieted the triumphant assembly, but Gingrich thirstily drank in every last "Newt!"

Republicans in both Congresses also were often more ideological than prudential. Taft was eager to eliminate much of the New Deal, while Gingrich argued that "we have the opportunity . . . to begin decisively changing the shape of the government."[44] But the liberal welfare state had not been built overnight, and it could not be dismantled overnight.

Republicans in both Congresses sorely misjudged the political skills of the president they faced. As a result, Truman and Clinton ran against Congress in the next election and were returned to office.

And the GOP majorities of the 80th and 104th Congresses took the people for granted. Having won what they considered to be mandates, Republicans did not think they had to bother with communicating what they were doing, and why, to the public. Truman took advantage of GOP obtuseness to portray the 80th Congress as a "do-nothing" Congress, while Clinton painted the 104th Congress as a "repeal everything" Congress.

Republicans in the 1940s and again in the 1990s, moreover, had been out of power so long that they did not know how to govern consistently. After decades of saying either "no" or "me too," they had to come up with conservative alternatives to programs and policies that had been closely woven into the fabric of America. Sometimes they succeeded, as with the Taft-Hartley Act or approval of a balanced budget; sometimes they failed, as with the reduction of farm subsidies in 1948 or Medicare reform in 1996.

The two Congresses also suffered from Caesarization: they rose and fell along with the reputations of their leaders, Bob Taft and Newt Gingrich. Both men had enormous assets and liabilities. The media transformed Gingrich into such an unsympathetic figure (with help from the conservative leader himself) that the public's fear of the GOP Medicare plan was exceeded only by "its animosity toward the Speaker," in the words of *National Review*'s Rich Lowry.[45]

At the root of the problem for both the 80th Congress and the 104th Congress was the political reality that governing from Congress is almost impossible, particularly in the modern media age. Presidential power is too great and congressional power too diffuse for Congress to prevail over the president for more than a limited time, like a hundred days.

In the second session of the 104th Congress, both the president and Congress moved toward the center. Clinton, the artful dodger, made the more dramatic shift with his statement in his 1996 State of the Union address that "the era of big government is over." But, he immediately added, "We cannot go back to the time when our citizens were left to fend for themselves."[46]

A chastened Gingrich dropped *revolution* from his vocabulary and admitted that he had mishandled himself and the legislative struggle with Clinton. "We kept thinking it was a series of tactical problems that we could solve," he said, "when in fact we were in a different world and we didn't understand that."[47] It was not a brave new world but a traditional world of checks and balances, of shared power and responsibility, of frequent cooperation and only occasional confrontation. It was the reality of American government, circa 1995, divided between a charismatic, infinitely flexible president and a conservative and often inflexible Congress. It was not pretty, but divided government was apparently what a majority of Americans wanted.

Throughout 1996, Clinton clung to the ideological middle of the road while Republicans from Bob Dole to Steve Forbes to Pat Buchanan to Newt Gingrich tried unsuccessfuly to dislodge him.

The president agreed to the GOP fashioning of a balanced budget in seven years but resisted Republican attempts to dismantle Democratic social programs. He allowed two-thirds of the states to experiment with welfare reform but fought proposals to give states blanket authority over core programs like Medicare. Initially uncomfortable as commander in chief, Clinton now eagerly played the peacemaker in hot spots from Haiti to Northern Ireland to the Balkans. Then, too, according to one estimate, the president embraced a dozen GOP reforms that he had originally vetoed, opposed, or ignored during his first three years in office.[48] Clinton was Reagan-morphing before the nation's eyes.

Meantime, although the media did not underscore it and the public did not fully appreciate it, the 104th Congress, under conservative leadership, accomplished several significant shifts in national policy, including what George Will called "one of the most momentous legislative acts of the last six decades"—the first-ever elimination of a major entitlement program, Aid to Families with Dependent Children (AFDC).[49] As summarized by *Congressional Quarterly,* Congress:

- Did away with New Deal–era farm subsidy programs.
- Gave the president the line-item veto, allowing him to strike specific items from spending bills.

- Rewrote the ground rules for the nation's telecommunications industry, wiping out barriers to competition among developing technologies.
- Replaced six decades of federal welfare policy by giving states broad new authority to run their own welfare programs.
- Ended AFDC. Henceforth, federal funds for low-income mothers and their children would be sent to the states in block grants, giving states almost complete control over eligibility and benefits.[50]

Encouraged, however, by the raucous Republican primaries, during which conservatives criticized each other rather than the Democrats and dismissed ideas like the flat tax as "nonsense," Democrats decided they had a winner in President Clinton. The Clinton campaign raised more money sooner than any other presidential campaign in history: $26 million (with matching federal funds of $14 million) for the primary season alone. At the same point in 1992, President Bush had collected less than $10 million. The nation later learned that the Clinton-Gore campaign had illegal fund-raising help from foreign contributors.

Still, Clinton's reelection was far from certain. Although the nation was in the sixth year of an economic recovery, there were some signs of a slowdown. There was the Whitewater real estate development in Arkansas, a still unresolved question mark about the president's financial ethics. And there was the peacekeeping mission in the Balkans, opposed by many members of Congress (conservatives as well as liberals) and by most Americans. Clinton's approval ratings hovered around 50 percent.

Because he could no longer depend on the South, as previous Democrats had, Bill Clinton had a smaller political base than any other president since World War II. He had won in 1992 because George Bush ran an ineffective, visionless campaign; Ross Perot siphoned off millions of Republican votes; Democrats carried such unlikely states as Georgia, Louisiana, and Kentucky; and he campaigned as an outsider and a New Democrat. Almost none of those factors would be present in 1996.

Normally a presidential election is a referendum on the president's conduct of domestic policy, particularly taxes and spending, and of foreign and national security policy, particularly his handling of conflicts, large and small. But 1996 was not a normal year, for it offered a second national referendum—on the Republican "revolution" in government. By their votes for president and Congress, Americans would indicate their approval of the

GOP's proposed downsizing (materially reducing both spending and taxes) and devolution (transferring significant power from the federal to the state level of government).

In the Republican primaries, Bob Dole had proved that he was broadly acceptable to rank-and-file Republicans, winning 59 percent of all primary voters. A critical endorsement was that of the Christian Coalition in the South Carolina primary. Dole's closest competitor was conservative commentator Pat Buchanan, who received 21 percent of the total primary vote but only 141 delegates. Buchanan's America First brand of protectionism and neoisolationism polarized voters, attracting support in northern blue-collar strongholds but alienating New South conservatives. In 1992, Buchanan had received 22 percent of the GOP primary vote, suggesting that there was a low ceiling to his support.

Although he won only two primaries (in Delaware and Arizona), publisher Steve Forbes attracted national attention—and almost 1.4 million votes—with his calls for lower taxes and less government. He might have done better if he had addressed social issues like abortion and the decline of public morality. No Republican can win the presidential nomination without the support of social conservatives.

In the absence of a unifying candidate, wrote political analyst Ramesh Ponnuru in *National Review,* the Reagan coalition split, with economic conservatives backing Forbes and social conservatives going to Buchanan. *National Review* itself endorsed Senator Phil Gramm, who started late and finished almost last. Conservatives, stated Ponnuru, badly "overestimated their power in the nominating process"; they failed to comprehend that the conservative majority in America "has to be continually converted, recruited, and given rousing song sheets." Regardless of the outcome in the fall of 1996, Ponnuru argued that conservatives had simultaneously to "hold the conservative coalition together," keep the GOP anchored within "a conservative, anti-statist consensus," and resolve both "cultural and economic anxieties."[51]

In the fall of 1996, Dole ran an aggressive but unfocused campaign, failing, for example, to embrace the idea of an across-the-board tax cut of 15 percent until it was too late. He also neglected to work closely with many elements of the conservative coalition that had produced the Reagan and Bush victories of the 1980s.

Conservative leader Morton Blackwell recounted that on September

21, 1996, only six weeks before election day, he took part in a meeting with vice presidential nominee Jack Kemp and leaders of about twenty-five other national conservative organizations. Kemp asked for advice that top Dole aides could have had as early as March.

A curious Blackwell asked his fellow conservatives, "How many of you personally feel that your organization's people are as fully integrated as they should be in the Dole-Kemp campaign at the national and local levels?" Only two of twenty-five raised their hands.[52] Asked why Clinton won, a disappointed Blackwell responded, "The better man lost to the better candidate."[53]

And to the far better campaign. The social issues—above all, partial-birth abortion—which especially concerned Catholics and Reagan Democrats were never seriously addressed. In the final weeks, Dole belatedly adopted a "California strategy," campaigning against affirmative action quotas and immigration overload.[54] But the effort was too late and too calculated: Voters were skeptical about the Republican commitment. The California Civil Rights Initiative (against affirmative action) won by two to one, but Clinton carried the state.

Bill Clinton was the first Democratic president since Franklin D. Roosevelt to win reelection and the first Democrat ever to be elected with an opposition Congress. The president defeated Dole by 49 percent to 41 percent, carrying thirty-three states with 379 electoral votes, including the golden prize of California. His 1996 victory was remarkably similar to his first presidential win in 1992, when he carried thirty-two states and received 370 electoral votes. Ross Perot was again on the ballot, this time as the Reform party candidate, but gained only 7.9 million votes, less than half his 1992 total. He got no electoral votes. The sucking sound heard was Perot's diminishing impact on electoral politics.

Despite the most virulent anti-Congress rhetoric since 1948, Republicans retained control of the House, albeit narrowly, and increased their margin in the Senate. The new line-up in the House was 227 Republicans, 207 Democrats, and 1 independent, who generally voted with the Democrats. The GOP had had 235 seats in the old House. Once again, Republicans were bolstered by their solid base in the South, where they achieved a net gain of seats.

The breakdown in the new Senate was 55 Republicans and 45 Democrats—a pickup of one for the GOP. Here as in the House, Republicans continued to transform the South into the foundation of their national constituency.

The elections left intact the enormous Republican majority among governors, thirty-two to seventeen, with one independent in Maine. Clinton had no coattails in the state capitals. When he was first sworn in as president in 1993, Democrats had held thirty governorships.[55]

Narrowly reelected Speaker of the House (the first Republican in sixty-eight years to be so honored), Gingrich avoided inflammatory rhetoric, talking instead of forging "a broad, center-right coalition" and finding "common ground" with President Clinton. He portrayed himself as "a cross between victor and survivor," a "wiser" leader who would not repeat his mistakes. Gingrich no longer described Clinton as "a counterculture Mc-Governik" as he had following the 1994 election.[56]

Some observers noted, and not for the first time, the many similarities between the two baby boomer politicians. As political reporter Dale Russakoff pointed out, both had adoring mothers, complex relationships with adoptive fathers, early and "voracious" appetites for learning, and "obsessive, decades-long quests for political power." Neither had fought in the Vietnam War (although Gingrich had obtained a legitimate deferment), and both owned 1967 Ford Mustangs, the classic middle-class muscle car.[57]

Gingrich had good reason to be in a chastened mood. After several months of investigation, the House Ethics Committee had determined that Gingrich's use of tax-deductible money for political purposes and the inaccurate information that he had supplied to investigators represented "intentional or . . . reckless" disregard of House rules. The Speaker admitted violating House rules and accepted the committee's findings. The House subsequently voted to reprimand Gingrich and ordered him to pay $300,000 to defray the cost of the inquiry, making him the first Speaker ever to be cited for his conduct.[58]

It is impossible to imagine Bob Taft showing the same disregard for Senate rules.

On the other side of the Capitol, Senate majority leader Trent Lott was feeling good, sustained by the Republican gain of one seat and the knowledge that almost every one of the nine new Republican senators was more conservative than his predecessor.

The Senate agenda, as drawn up by Lott, Senate majority whip Don

Nickles of Oklahoma, and other Republican leaders, addressed pressing concerns of the American people but gave them a conservative twist. Emphasized were education choice, missile defense (conservatives kept trying to implement some form of Reagan's SDI), a tax relief package including a $500-per-child tax credit, a reduction in the capital gains tax, and reform of the unpopular estate tax—the so-called death tax. And Lott promised once again to offer a ban on partial-birth abortion, which Clinton had vetoed.

In his 1997 State of the Union address, President Clinton positioned himself right of center, promising a balanced budget by 2002 and urging citizen volunteerism in a wide variety of fields. He offered a "new kind of government—not to solve all of our problems for us, but to give all our people the tools to make the most of their own lives."[59] It sounded so reasonable that some may not have noticed that the president once again had taken one conservative step forward and then two liberal steps backward.

Columnist George Will was unrestrained in his scorn, accusing Clinton of "pandering" to the people with a $51 billion education plan. He noted that there already were more college students than high school students, "a majority of whom will never get a degree." Clinton's plan to increase the number of community colleges, the columnist continued ruthlessly, will "churn out graduates unequipped to guffaw when a president utters solemnities at the expense of the education system."[60]

But there was only a muted response from House Republican leaders because Gingrich's ethics case had consumed their attention for months and prevented them from drafting an agenda for the next two years. Gingrich's reelection as Speaker only papered over the wide dissatisfaction among many House Republicans with his mishandling of the government shutdowns in late 1995 and his ethical lapses. GOP unhappiness shot up when Gingrich stumbled through the first half of 1997, trying to govern with a razor-thin margin and a popular Democratic president.[61] Revolution, it seemed, had been replaced by compromise. For some die-hard House conservatives, it seemed as though the Contract with America had never been written and Bob Michel had never retired.

Tensions among the conservative troika that ruled the House—Gingrich, Armey, and DeLay—finally exploded in July when DeLay, along with Bill Paxon of New York, attempted a coup against the Speaker. But the plot failed when Armey made it clear that he would not be a member of the conspiracy. Like his fellow baby boomer in the White House, Gingrich survived another political crisis. In the coup's wake, Gingrich fired Paxon as GOP leadership chairman and almost replaced DeLay as House whip.

Along with Senate majority leader Lott, Gingrich moved on to make a historic deal in the summer of 1997 with the Clinton administration to achieve a balanced budget by 2002. The five-year plan cut taxes by $95 billion, trimmed spending by $263 billion, and sought to control entitlement expenditures. It was made possible in large measure by Republican fears of causing another government shutdown and being blamed for it, and by last-minute projections that, in *Congressional Quarterly's* words, "the booming U.S. economy would produce a tax revenue windfall of $225 billion over the five years."[62] Whatever the contributing factors, it was a balanced budget, a perennial conservative objective, and applause if not a standing ovation was in order. Or was it?

Human Events declared that the deal would "guarantee" that the size, power, and cost of the federal government would "continue to grow for at least another decade." And the Cato Institute's Stephen Moore pronounced it a "monumental" setback for the conservative movement.[63] The 1994 Contract with America, Moore pointed out, had asked for the elimination of three hundred federal programs, but the 1997 budget agreement gave "almost all of these programs a new lease on life."[64]

Moore's blunt criticism, which caused more than a few congressional conservatives to wince, typified the increasingly confident tone of the libertarian Cato Institute. Founded in 1977 by financial analyst Edward Crane and California businessman Joseph Shell, Cato moved from San Francisco to Washington, D.C., in 1982. The institute's uncompromising free-market prescriptions, like the privatization of Social Security, had been coolly received on Capitol Hill during most of the 1980s. But with the end of the Cold War and the admission by even liberals that big government had had its day, more and more Washington policymakers paid closer attention to Cato. It helped that the organization's chairman was the widely respected William Niskanen, who had served as chairman of President Reagan's Council of Economic Advisers.

Although best known for its economic analyses, Cato also acknowledged the importance of moral standards in a good society. "We believe," Ed Crane told *Human Events,* "that people and society are most moral when they are given freedom and themselves develop the will to choose to make ethical decisions and not have a government coercing them to do so."[65]

One undeniable victory for Republicans in the 1997 budget agreement was the inclusion of a $500-per-child tax credit for families, a major provision of the Contract with America. But there was little else in the agreement that excited the Right. Gingrich, Lott, and other GOP negotiators insisted that it was the best they could do, given the power of the president and the narrow Republican margins in the House and Senate. But as one disgruntled conservative commented, "Give me $1.7 trillion, and I'll balance the budget too."[66]

Steve Forbes, the once and future presidential candidate, likened Clinton versus the GOP to Cortes versus the Aztecs—a swift wipeout of a proud but unprepared people. Paul Gigot of the *Wall Street Journal* sarcastically wrote that Republicans were "afraid to fight about anything, even taxes. So they are left drawing a new line in the sand every week, after Democrats walk over the old one."[67]

But Democrats, particularly President Clinton, were undeniably dealing from a position of considerable strength. The nation was in the midst of an economic golden age.

Unemployment was the lowest in a quarter of a century, inflation was under 3 percent, and the gross domestic product was growing at a robust 3 percent plus per annum. The Dow Jones Industrial Average kept climbing despite Asian shocks and European stagnation.

America was at peace. Although American forces had been dispatched to Bosnia and Haiti during Clinton's watch, not a single American had died in a combat-related incident in the past five years. The world was enjoying, or at least accepting, a Pax Americana.

Most people did not seem to care much about the serious questions that had been raised concerning the Clinton campaign's fund-raising practices or the new allegations of sexual misconduct between the president and a twenty-one-year-old White House intern that burst onto the scene. Nor did they seem to be impressed by Hillary Rodham Clinton's declaration (on national television) that the real culprit was "a vast right-wing conspiracy that has been conspiring against my husband since the day he announced for president."[68]

Undoubtedly the first lady had in mind a 332-page White House "report," first released in the fall of 1995, that charged there was a right-wing "conspiracy" behind the way that news stories flowed from ideological publications to talk radio to the mainstream media. The notion that *Human*

Events, National Review, Rush Limbaugh, Ollie North, the *New York Times,* and the *Washington Post* were working together to bring down the Clinton administration was so absurd that the White House quickly backed off from the word *conspiracy.*

Hillary Clinton's charge of a right-wing conspiracy against her husband was, of course, nothing new in liberal politics. The same false accusation had been made against Robert Taft by Eisenhower forces in 1952, against Barry Goldwater by Nelson Rockefeller and then Lyndon Johnson in 1964, and against Ronald Reagan by Pat Brown in 1966 and by Jimmy Carter in 1980.

B ill Clinton challenged his critics with an optimistic State of the Union address in January 1998. The president presented a glowing report of a nation prosperous and peaceful because of his policies and went on to offer the most expansive domestic agenda since Republicans gained control of Congress in 1995. "With barely 700 days left in the 20th century," he declared, "this is not a time to rest."[69]

A week later, Clinton again borrowed from conservatives and formally submitted the first balanced budget in thirty years. "This budget," said Clinton, undoubtedly relishing the irony, "marks an end to decades of deficits that have shackled our economy, paralyzed our politics and held our people back."[70]

Gingrich retorted that the $1.7 trillion budget was a "far cry from the 'leaner, more flexible' government" touted in the State of the Union address. Columnist James K. Glassman had a more astringent reaction, accusing Clinton of "big, brazen and undeniable lies." It was not true, as the president claimed, that "we have the smallest government in 35 years." In fact, Glassman pointed out, "we don't even have the smallest government in *five* years." Federal spending in 1992, when Clinton took office, was $1.4 trillion. In 1998, it would be $1.7 trillion, a 21 percent increase when inflation had increased less than 14 percent.[71]

Clinton had also claimed that the deficit was brought down from $390 billion in 1992 to a negligible $22 billion in 1997 because of the "truly historic bipartisan balanced budget agreement." In truth, Glassman rebutted, the deficit plummeted because of the reduction in defense spending (which began under President Reagan) and because American businesses "became leaner, smarter and more imaginative." The result was a private sector renaissance and a flood of new tax revenues that inundated a happy White House.[72]

Gingrich too was enjoying something of a rebirth. In a speech at the first International Conservative Congress the preceding September, he had offered a conservative strategy for the future based on (1) tax reform so thorough "that we can abolish the IRS as we know it"; (2) an end to race-based quotas and set-asides; (3) educational reform, including moving 90 percent of all federal funding to "the local community"; (4) a commitment to defend freedom around the world along with "the best [national] defense that science and technology can create"; (5) the establishment of "a sound personal pension system" for the baby boomers and their children; (6) an insistence that "the law be enforced and that lawbreakers be found and be punished"; and (7) true campaign reform, including no political action committees, no "soft" money, and no labor union money.[73] Clearly, the idea man was back.

The week of Clinton's address to Congress, Gingrich offered four major legislative goals for Republicans in 1998 and beyond: the creation of "a drug-free, safe America"; the empowerment of "local parents, teachers and schools"; a system that will provide "retirement security for all Americans"; and a national consensus on how much government at all levels should take through taxes. He personally favored a taxation limit of no more than 25 percent—"a far cry from the roughly forty percent we pay today."[74] The goals were not only politically popular but philosophically consistent—evidence that Gingrich had recovered from the attempted coup, the government shutdowns, and other miseries of the past year. Indeed, he was even rising in the polls: by February 1998, his job approval ratings, while not as high as the president's, were pushing 40 percent. Those of Congress approached 60 percent, higher than they had been in many years.

And yet the Gingrich revival was short-lived. The legislative agenda for 1998 was soon eclipsed by the burgeoning scandal over the president's sexual relationship with a twenty-one-year-old White House intern and the accompanying allegations of perjury and obstruction of justice. In September the independent counsel, Kenneth W. Starr, sent his report to Congress, detailing a host of possibly impeachable offenses, and a month later the House of Representatives authorized an open-ended impeachment inquiry. As the Judiciary Committee prepared to hold hearings, Gingrich made the fateful decision to use the Clinton scandal to galvanize Republican support in some thirty congressional races, mostly in the South. Incredibly, Gingrich and his associates believed that they could run a series of local television ads attacking the president, at a cost of $25 million, without attracting national notice.

The anti-Clinton commercials were seized upon by the Democrats to turn out their core constituencies, particularly Southern blacks, with the result that Republicans went down to defeat in North Carolina, South Carolina, Alabama, and other states once considered solid for the GOP. Nationwide, the Republicans posted a net loss of five seats in the House (and no gain in the Senate), making them the first party since before the Civil War to lose seats to the party of a president in his second term.

The recriminations among conservatives began the day after the election, as Gingrich was pilloried by his fellow Republicans for failing to deliver the gain of twenty to thirty seats that he had predicted. Representative Robert L. Livingston of Louisiana then announced that he would challenge Gingrich for the speakership, and within seventy-two hours it was over. On the evening of Friday, November 6, 1998, Newt Gingrich announced that laudably, he was stepping down as Speaker and resigning his seat in the House as well. He had decided that his party would be better served by his departure than by a bitter and divisive battle to retain power. Five weeks later, Livingston arrived at the same decision (after admitting his marital infidelity) and declared he would not seek the speakership and would, in fact, resign his congressional seat in six months. The new Speaker was Dennis Hastert of Illinois, a low-key but staunch conservative who promised to seek political consensus, but not at the sacrifice of principle.

In many ways, Gingrich had never recovered from the decision to shut down the federal government during the Christmas holidays of 1995. Even three years later, the president, the press, and the public blamed Congress— and particularly Gingrich—for the shutdown, and this put the speaker and Senate majority leader Trent Lott on the defensive whenever they had to negotiate with Clinton. The 1998 budget negotiations, which concluded just three weeks before election day, saw Gingrich compromising with the Democrats on core conservative issues like tax cuts and federal spending, making it harder for Republican congressional candidates to run on a single national theme as they had in 1994. All this helped to contribute to a sense of disillusionment toward the Speaker within the ranks of the conservative movement. Where they had repected Taft, loved Goldwater, and idolized Reagan, conservatives by the fall of 1998 barely tolerated Gingrich. In the critical days following the election, not one major conservative leader, publication, or organization (with the exception of the Speaker's most loyal ally,

Grover Norquist) came forward to argue that Newt Gingrich should remain as Speaker.

Nevertheless, his place in political history is secure. The Contract with America was brilliant politics and led directly to the historic capture of the House of Representatives in 1994. Gingrich's leadership, with all its flaws, produced three straight Republican Houses in 1994, 1996, and 1998—the first such string of GOP victories in seventy years. His reforms reshaped the House of Representatives, strengthening the Speaker's authority, reducing the power of the committee chairmen, empowering backbenchers. He recruited dozens of candidates and raised millions of dollars, vitalizing the party and the movement. He spawned countless conservative ideas, issues, and programs that will be happily used by his successors.

And yet older conservatives have not disguised their disappointment with and even suspicion of Gingrich. "In no way, shape or form is Gingrich a conservative," Phyllis Schlafly says flatly. "Note that Taft, Goldwater and Reagan retained the loyalty of their followers despite mistakes and defeats, but the antagonism against Gingrich is intense."[75]

While Taft, Goldwater, and Reagan all had personal character of "an unquestioned high order," states Richard Ware, who ran the quietly effective Earhart Foundation for many years, Gingrich is "not in the same class." He "has exposed himself unnecessarily to personal attacks."[76]

He is "a flash in the pan," suggests right-to-work leader Reed Larson, "mercurial and inconsistent."[77] While Gingrich is undeniably principled, says *National Review* senior editor Richard Brookhiser, "half his principles are crazy."[78] Publicist Peter Hannaford, who worked closely with Reagan throughout the 1970s, echoes Schlafly's point about loyalty: "Goldwater and Reagan had charisma, and both had corps of friends who would stick with them throughout anything. Gingrich doesn't inspire such loyalty."[79]

For Catholic libertarian Leonard Liggio and many other conservatives, Gingrich's most serious flaw is his inability to stay within any "boundary of ideas." In fact, "Gingrich has so many ideas," says Liggio, "that he trips over them." In contrast, Reagan repeated the same basic principles over and over and then tried to encourage his listeners to apply those principles to policy issues. Reagan was "the great communicator," asserts Liggio, because his ideas were founded on solid economic and moral principles.[80]

The conservative revolution "floundered" following the historic 1994 triumph, political consultant Donald Devine asserts, because Gingrich tried to do the impossible: "rule from Congress." And he gave Clinton "a reason to be reelected—to stop GOP extremism." Moreover, "unlike Goldwater and Reagan (especially the latter)," adds Devine, Gingrich "did not understand his circumstances."[81]

Historian Alvin S. Felzenberg, who as a congressional staffer has observed Gingrich firsthand, sees parallels between Reagan and the former House leader, particularly in their commitment to a "long march." It took Reagan sixteen years—between 1964 and 1980—to win the presidency. It also took Gingrich sixteen years—between his first congressional victory in 1978 and the Contract with America in 1994—to win the House of Representatives. "This showed," says Felzenberg, "courage, discipline, and being willing to be the only one to believe one can succeed."[82]

David Keene of the American Conservative Union offers a different historical perspective about Gingrich, comparing him to Samuel Adams, the fiery Boston radical who led the Boston Tea Party, rather than John Adams, the Harvard lawyer who served as our second president. "After all," asks Keene, "what did Sam Adams do *after* the Revolution?"[83]

Younger conservatives are more tolerant of Gingrich's personal flaws and appreciative of his political contributions. Grover Norquist, who worked closely with the ex-Speaker, argues that Gingrich "taught the [House] GOP how to fight" and absorbed "the full force of the establishment Left's anger and attempt to drive conservatism from Washington." He has moved congressional Republicans so far to the right, argues Norquist, that "if Richard Nixon came to life and was elected to Congress he would be the most liberal member of the GOP caucus."[84]

As befits a publisher, Alfred Regnery takes the long view. Taft, he says, was "a foundation builder," Goldwater a rallier of the troops, and Reagan "the master politician who pulled it all together and explained [conservatism] to the American people." Although Gingrich did "a masterful job" of orchestrating the 1994 election of a Republican Congress, he subsequently lost his way, "not understanding that he was no longer a revolutionary but had to be a consensus-building politician."[85] Consensus is not easy, of course, when the mass media are firing at you from every side and your colleagues are seeking all available cover.

Heritage's Ed Feulner insists that although some conservatives are unhappy with the 1997 budget deal, they should remember that Congress has passed and the president has signed an agreement that balances the budget and cuts taxes. "It has long been argued by the liberal establishment," reminds Feulner, "that you can't have both at the same time. We did it!"[86]

The ambivalent attitude of many conservatives about Newt Gingrich is perhaps captured best by William Rusher, catalyst for the Draft Goldwater movement, a longtime Ronald Reagan confidant, and a movement conservative since the mid–1950s:

> Gingrich is a remarkable, but flawed, man. He combines enormous tenacity and drive (qualities that enabled him, almost singlehandedly, to engineer the Republican conquest of Congress) with a temperament more intellectual than political—more suited to a college campus than to the halls of Congress. This leads him to commit gaffes that any ordinary politician would instinctively avoid.
>
> I also question whether he is a "movement conservative," in the way that Reagan was. He is a conservative on most subjects, certainly, but his mind is too restless to seek—or find—comfort in simply cleaving to certain bedrock principles.[87]

Conservatives believe that cleaving to principle and even being willing to lose on principle—not always but sometimes—are what conservatism is all about. Sometimes, as Taft, Goldwater, and Reagan all demonstrated, you win by losing.

Chapter 16

Can Conservatives Govern?

FOR MORE THAN TWO HUNDRED YEARS, SINCE THE FOUNDING OF THE Republic, Americans have debated, often fiercely, the central question of American politics: How much government do we need? There has been no serious dispute, except from radical antifederalists in the beginning and radical libertarians in the modern era, that we require at least some government to ensure life, liberty, and the pursuit of happiness.

"If men were angels," James Madison wrote in Federalist No. 51, "no government would be necessary."[1] But the founders recognized the darker side of human nature and attempted in the Constitution to forge a balance between liberty, for which they had fought a revolution, and order, which would protect the rights of all, not just the most powerful. They sought to create what had never before existed: a government, as Abraham Lincoln later phrased it, of the people, by the people, and for the people.

The essential problem confronting the founders, political scientist James Q. Wilson has written, was "how to devise a government strong enough to preserve order but not so strong that it would threaten liberty."[2] Their solution was a complex system of checks and balances among the three branches of the national government and between the national government and the states. The Constitution was a blueprint for a never-ending struggle among all these parties to determine the domestic and foreign policies of our government. But how do you prevent the concentration of power in the hands of any one "faction," to use Madison's term? The answer, for the delegates to the Constitutional Convention of 1787, lay in neither democracy nor aristocracy but a "federal republic."

Accepting human nature as it was and not as they wished it to be, the founders decided to set ambition against ambition and interest against interest. In this protracted conflict, "the private interest of every individual," Madison argued, "may be a sentinel over the public rights."[3] And with power divided between the states and the national government, "the different governments will control each other, at the same time that each will be controlled by itself."[4]

It was not intended that the American government should be neat or efficient or predictable. It was intended that it should be a republic—in modern terms, a representative democracy—in which the government would be as good and fair and honest as the representatives chosen by the people could make it.

This was all uncharted territory. There were no historical precedents for a government that derived its powers from the consent of the governed. Even the founders, as Wilson points out, came away from the 1787 convention with conflicting views of what was meant by a federal republic.

Alexander Hamilton thought that the national government was "the superior and leading force in political affairs" and that its powers therefore should be broadly defined and liberally construed. Thomas Jefferson, on the other hand, felt that the central government, although undoubtedly important, was the product of an agreement among the states that, through *the people,* were "the ultimate sovereigns."[5]

Madison was in the middle, supporting a strong national government at the 1787 convention (alarmed by the turmoil and uncertainty generated by the ineffective Articles of Confederation) but later becoming a champion of states' rights. However, even when trying to win ratification of the Constitution, he wrote in Federalist No. 45: "The powers delegated by the proposed Constitution to the federal government are few and defined. Those which are to remain in the State governments are numerous and indefinite."[6]

Was there a "true" conservative among the founders? Russell Kirk suggested that it was John Adams, who taught the value of "good and practical laws, transcending the passions of the hour," and who kept the American government "one of laws, not of men."[7] No less important to Adams than the rule of law was the practice of virtue. Indeed, our second president wrote:

> Public virtue is the only foundation of republics. There must be a positive passion for the public good, the public interest, honor, power and glory, established in the minds of the people, or there can be no republican government, *nor any real liberty*.[8]

But public virtue depends on private character. And for the best definition of American character, we must turn to the historic embodiment of America, George Washington. Throughout his public career, our *pater patria* maintained that the inalienable rights that Americans enjoyed required a commitment to moral duty and civic virtue.

Washington always sought, as political historian Matthew Spalding has written, to inculcate balance and moderation in the conduct of America's domestic and international affairs. In his Farewell Address, Washington expressed the hope that his prudential advice would be remembered so as to "moderate the fury of party spirit, to warn against the mischiefs of foreign intrigue, [and] to guard against the impostures of pretended patriotism."[9]

Today, however, no matter what their differences at the time may have been, almost all of the founders would call themselves conservatives, not liberals. Some would be traditional conservatives, others libertarians; but none, not even Hamilton, would have endorsed Franklin Roosevelt's call for a national government that intervened directly in the economy, created giant social welfare programs, and helped specific groups (like organized labor) to obtain greater economic and political power.

Limited government, individual responsibility, equal opportunity, a careful balance between liberty and law, a belief in God, a commitment to public virtue: these are the core beliefs, bounded by the Constitution, on which American conservatism rests and by which its leaders like Robert Taft, Barry Goldwater, Ronald Reagan, and Newt Gingrich have strived to govern and politick. They did not always succeed, being human, but their failures were usually because they failed conservatism, not because conservatism failed them.

Can conservatives govern? Of course they can, as the solid accomplishments of the 80th Congress under Robert Taft, of the Reagan presidency, and of the 104th Congress under Newt Gingrich demonstrated. In 1946 and 1947, Congress passed the Taft-Hartley Act, cut government spending, reduced income taxes, and supported the Truman Doctrine and the Marshall Plan, building blocks of the bipartisan policy of containment. From 1981 through 1989, Ronald Reagan presided over the longest economic expansion in peacetime by defying Keynesian economics and cutting taxes and limiting the growth of government. In 1995 and 1996, Congress did away with New Deal–era farm subsidies, passed a presidential line-item veto, transformed federal welfare policy by giving states broad authority to run welfare programs, and ended, for the first time, a federal entitlement program, Aid to Families with Dependent Children.

Sometimes, to be sure, conservatives have failed, as with the narrow defeat of the Bricker Amendment in the 1950s, the doubling of the national debt in the 1980s, and the failure to pass a balanced budget amendment in the 1990s, but they never gave up.

As the minority in Congress throughout most of the post–World War II period, conservatives usually played the role of the loyal opposition. They prevented repeal of section 14(b) of the Taft-Hartley Act in the 1950s, warned that the Civil Rights Act of 1964 would lead to affirmative action, blocked President Nixon's Family Assistance Plan in the 1970s, and forced President Clinton in the 1990s to concede that the era of big government was over. But when they had the majority in the Senate, as during most of the 1980s, they helped President Reagan produce a remarkable record: historic tax reform, unprecedented economic growth, and a peaceful end to a cold war that had brought the world close to a hot war many times.

Along the way, congressional conservatives learned that sometimes the best way to govern is to govern as little as possible. After winning control of Congress in 1994, they adopted the first rule of Democrats who had retained power in Washington for forty years: "Get home early and often and never stop campaigning." To some hard-core grassroots conservatives, columnist Donald Lambro wrote, "this strategy seems like a cynical abdication of principle and responsibility."[10]

But for those who think (as the founders did) that the less Congress does the better and that building political power for a stronger offense in the near future against big government is shrewd tactics, the Gingrich-Lott strategy was sensible strategy. Of all people, conservatives should be willing to applaud, when appropriate, a passive rather than an activist congress.

Conservatives have also demonstrated impressively that they can govern at the state level. As Governor John Engler of Michigan has pointed out, Republican governors and legislatures have been balancing budgets, cutting taxes, and making government "more responsive to the people" for the last decade. That explains why more Americans are represented by Republican governors than ever before in America's history: some 70 percent of the population.[11]

Governor John Rowland of Connecticut turned a $174 million deficit into a $74 million surplus in just one year. Governor John V. Voinovich of Ohio held state spending to its lowest rate of growth in four decades. Governor Arne Carlson of Minnesota erased a deficit of $1.8 billion, and Engler transformed a similar $1.8 billion deficit into a surplus of over $1 billion. And while they were holding down spending, they were also cutting taxes. Since 1991, Michigan has cut taxes more often than any other state— twenty-one times, a modern record. The average family of four, estimates Engler, "has been able to keep $2,000 more in their wallets every year."[12]

Indeed, the Michigan governor argues convincingly that Clinton owes his 1996 reelection and his persistent high approval ratings to the prosperity generated by the conservative spending and tax policies of the nation's Republican governors. They have also led the way in the area of welfare reform. No other GOP governor has received more attention, and justifiably, than Tommy Thompson of Wisconsin and his "Work Not Welfare" program. The program requires welfare recipients to participate in job training to receive benefits. Since Wisconsin implemented the Thompson reforms in 1987, its welfare caseload has decreased by 49.2 percent. Michigan's caseload has declined by 22 percent over the same period.[13]

The message that Engler, Thompson, and other conservative governors are sending to the federal government is pointed: "Free the states! Unshackle us from overweening federal control. Let us in the states govern as the U.S. Constitution meant us to govern."[14] It is a powerful message, backed by the unquestioned political success of its messengers, that Washington dares not ignore. And it provides an unequivocal answer of *yes* to the question: Can conservatives govern?

But modern liberals have shown that they cannot govern wisely, wed as they are to the socialist ideal. So convinced were they in the 1930s that government, and only government, could save the nation that they proposed a radical break with American tradition—nothing less than a new contract between the government and the governed. Their model was not the American Revolution, rational and grounded in the law, but the French Revolution, utopian and guided by the impulse of the moment. The New Deal, presidential candidate Franklin D. Roosevelt explained in October 1932, was not a political slogan but "a changed *concept* of the duty and responsibility of Government." Government, FDR declared, now "has a final responsibility for the well-being of its citizens."[15]

With those fateful words, "a final responsibility," and Roosevelt's subsequent election, America began a fifty-year experiment in ever larger government and ever less individual responsibility that produced a swarm of executive agencies, a thicket of federal statutes and bureaucratic regulations, and a 90 percent solution to almost everything, from taxes to subsidies. The liberal experiment was not just any old failure—it was a multi-trillion-dollar failure. In the thirty years following the birth of the Great Society in 1965, the federal government spent $5.4 trillion trying to eliminate poverty in America.

"For $5.4 trillion," Heritage analyst Robert Rector pointed out, "one could purchase every factory, all the manufacturing equipment, and every office building in the United States." That is not all: "With the leftover funds, one could go on to purchase every airline, every railroad, every trucking firm, the entire commercial maritime fleet, every telephone, television, and radio company, every power company, every hotel, and every retail and wholesale store in the entire nation."[16] And all the while, low-income families disintegrated, illegitimacy soared, and crime in the inner city multiplied.

Given such a horrendous record, conservatism's remedy was simple and obvious: Roll back the liberal welfare state. Conservative politicians preached unceasingly that government was not the solution but the problem. Libertarian thinkers argued that government had no business underwriting public housing, controlling social security, and running national parks. Popularizers asserted that Americans should stop propping up the "manifestly failed" public school system.[17]

But "life in this target-rich environment," George Will wrote, turned out to be "too easy" for conservatives, who did not always consider the extended impact of their efforts.[18] There were unintended consequences of conservatism's antigovernment crusade. Some Americans began to believe that government was always the problem. Antipathy and then antagonism spread, affecting everything from voter turnout to respect for government as an institution. Conservatives were obliged to explain that they were for limiting, not eliminating, government.

Some Americans concluded that conservatives, in their rush to wipe out fifty years of welfarism, apparently did not care what happened to people who were dependent on welfare. One prominent conservative urged his colleagues to reassure the people that conservatives did not just know how to balance the budget or quote from the *Federalist Papers* but also cared deeply about the future of every American.[19]

Editor William Kristol of the *Weekly Standard* and his colleague David Brooks would ask a pertinent question: "How can Americans love their nation if they hate its government?" Government does have its great and legitimate purposes, they argued, and we should be guided not just by anger but by "a love of country and informed patriotism." They urged a revival of "national greatness" conservatism, modeled on the example of Theodore Roosevelt: a debatable choice because, as political historian Matthew Spalding has pointed out, TR's New Nationalism called for "an activist state with strong regulatory powers," a goal at cross purposes with modern conservatism. While conservatives might find Roosevelt's "brand of vigorous leadership refreshing," conceded Spalding, a better and more recent statesman to emulate was Ronald Reagan.[20]

Starting in 1989, traditional conservatives, libertarians, neoconservatives, and social conservatives began fussing and feuding like so many Hatfields and McCoys. They missed the soothing presence of Ronald Reagan and the unifying threat of communism. As soon as the Berlin Wall came down, conservatives immediately began building walls between one another. Just four years after Reagan's departure, there was open talk of a "conservative crackup." Editor-columnist R. Emmett Tyrrell wrote scathingly about organizations multiplying by the dozens to promote "The Supply Side! Our Judeo-Christian Heritage! The Black Tie Fund-Raising Banquet!"[21]

Often violent disagreements erupted between conservatives about trade, immigration, and the direction of U.S. foreign policy. One outspoken offshoot was the paleoconservatives, who took particular delight in savaging neoconservatives. The paleoconservatives, who included political activist Llewelyn Rockwell of the Mises Institute and one-time *National Review* editor Joseph Sobran among their leadership, spawned the John Randolph Club and the America First Committee. They attempted to forge an alliance with paleolibertarians like Murray Rothbard, who had once argued that even a city's traffic lights should be privately owned. Casting about for a political leader, Rothbard declared at a 1992 meeting of the John Randolph Club, "With Pat Buchanan as our leader, we shall break the clock of social democracy. . . . We *shall* repeal the twentieth century."[22]

But with Buchanan's failure to win even one Republican primary in 1992 or 1996 and Rothbard's death in 1995, the paleoconservatives became no more than a small political offshoot. They were reduced to arguing, as historian Paul Gottfried did, that President Reagan "had handed over his administration to global Democrats and Eastern Republicans."[23] Most conservatives, and Americans, noting the sustained prosperity of the 1980s and the collapse of communism, would shake their heads in bewilderment at such rhetoric. Equally strained was the paleoconservative charge that a "neoconservative empire" controlled the conservative movement from New York to Washington and beyond.[24] In truth, conservatism's fundamental political problem, following the end of the cold war and the departure of President Reagan, was that no one was in charge of the movement.

Slowly conservatives began reconstructing what political strategist Ralph Reed called the three-legged coalition of "economic free-marketeers, antigovernment Perot supporters, and believers in conservative family values."[25] The last group turned out to be in many ways the most important. Despite the three straight presidential triumphs of 1980, 1984, and 1988, conservatives discovered yet again that man does not live by politics alone. They looked around and saw Robert Mapplethorpe's homoerotic photographs in museums, heard Snoop Doggy Dogg's pornographic lyrics on radio, noticed Calvin Klein's sexually provocative ads in magazines, watched "Ellen" coming out on television, and found themselves agreeing with Robert Bork that "American popular culture is in a free fall, with the bottom not yet in sight."[26]

Conservatives had been right about communism (it was evil) and the welfare state (it was a chimera), but they had neglected what T. S. Eliot had written to his friend Russell Kirk: "A decline in private morality is certain to be followed in the long run by a decline in public and political morality also."[27]

In the wake of the 1964 Goldwater defeat, conservatives had resolved to concentrate most of their energy, attention, and money on national politics, reasoning that political success could be achieved by winning the presidency, the preeminent American political symbol. They did not have the resources to fight both a political and a cultural war, and they gambled that American culture would resist Sodom and Gomorrah successfully with the support of mediating institutions like the family, the church, and the community. Believing as the founders did in the fallen nature of man, they should have known better.

At the 1992 Republican National Convention, Pat Buchanan demanded that attention be paid to the degraded state of American culture. "There is a religious war going on in this country," he thundered, "for the soul of America. It is a cultural war as critical to the kind of nation we shall be as the Cold War itself."[28] Buchanan was attacked in much of the mass media for fostering an atmosphere of "hate and fear" (a *Newsweek* headline), but conservatives agreed with him that while America had been winning the war against communism, it had been losing the war for American culture.[29] A week later, *Newsweek* reported that its own national survey revealed that two-thirds of the population believed something was "morally wrong" with the country.[30]

The conservatives enthusiastically entered the lists of the cultural war. The Family Research Council (FRC), founded in 1981 by family advocate James Dobson, became an influential Washington presence in the early 1990s under the leadership of Gary Bauer. Bauer had learned the way Washington works as director of the White House Office of Policy Development under President Reagan. In 1991, he chaired the Citizens Committee to Confirm Clarence Thomas, which played a major role in preventing the black nominee for the Supreme Court from being "Borked" by liberals. The FRC (and its 200,000 members), explained Bauer, focuses on "the sanctity of human life, the quality of our schools, and the role of government and how it impacts families."[31]

Another powerful voice of the profamily movement is James Dobson's weekly radio program, *Focus on the Family*, heard by 3 to 5 million listeners in fifty-eight countries around the world. Although it concentrates on helping families with "practical solutions to everyday problems," *Focus on the Family* has become more active politically out of necessity. "We could really be facing cultural meltdown," says Dobson, "if we don't change."[32]

In 1994, therefore, when the 103rd Democratic Congress was considering a federal education bill containing a provision that would have invited government regulation of home schoolers (representing about 15 percent of *Focus on the Family*'s audience), Dobson warned his listeners. Within seventy-two hours, about 800,000 calls opposing the home-schooling provision were received by Congress. A week later, the House voted 421 to 1 to strip home schooling from the legislation.[33]

The largest women's organization in America today is not the liberal National Organization for Women but the conservative Concerned Women for America, founded by Beverly LaHaye. With 600,000 members and an annual budget of $10 million, Concerned Women has materially affected public attitudes about pornography and partial-birth abortion. While conceding the proportions of the job ahead, LaHaye is optimistic and feels that American women "are coming over to our conception of feminism—an appreciation of marriage and families."[34]

A major part of the work of the Media Research Center (MRC), headed by L. Brent Bozell III, is devoted to America's culture war. Through publications like *MediaWatch* and *TV, etc.* and projects like the Parents Television Council, the center tracks the mass media's treatment of social and cultural issues. In 1993, for example, MRC archives revealed that of eighteen thousand stories on the nightly news programs, only 212 (a little over 1 percent) dealt with religion. In the same year, there were 150 stories on violence in front of abortion clinics but only one unfavorable mention of the violent nature of abortion itself—in a story about Bosnia. With an annual budget of just under $5 million and more than 120,000 hours of programming in its video archive, MRC has become in barely a decade one of the most important media watchdogs in America. "We are not asking the media to be biased in conservatives' favor," explains Bozell, "but we do demand that they bring balance to political reporting and work to restore traditional values to Hollywood."[35]

The MRC's newest attempt to achieve that balance is the Conservative News Service, an on-line, full-time news operation intended to fill the vacuum left by the establishment media's pursuit of the sensational at the expense of important stories. Launched in June 1998, CNS has an annual budget of about $1.8 million and aims to provide an Internet alternative to the Cable News Network.[36]

Profamily organizations create a climate in which politicians are willing to speak out. Vice President Dan Quayle, for example, roundly criticized the counterculture in a May 1992 speech, linking recent riots in Los Angeles to "the breakdown of family structure, personal responsibility and social order in too many areas of our society." He singled out Murphy Brown, a character in a highly popular television situation comedy, for "mocking the importance of fathers, by bearing a child alone, and calling it just another 'life style choice.'" At the time, liberals uniformly mocked Quayle's critique of Murphy Brown, some seeing it as an attack on single mothers and working mothers, others calling it a "far-fetched attempt" to place blame for the ills of American society on Hollywood.[37]

But just a year later, the *Atlantic Monthly,* whose liberal credentials are impeccable, published a cover article entitled "Dan Quayle Was Right." Sociologist Barbara Dafoe Whitehead discussed two social science findings that affirmed Quayle's thesis: The dissolution of two-parent families was "harmful" to large numbers of children, and the increasing number of single-parent and stepparent families "dramatically" weakened and undermined society.[38]

Presidential hopeful Steve Forbes now spends as much time courting the Christian Coalition as he does the Cato Institute. And the Religious Right likes what it hears: The millionaire publisher was interrupted seven times by standing ovations at the Christian Coalition's annual convention in September 1997. Forbes brought the delegates to their feet by calling for a flat tax, a ban on partial-birth abortions, resistance to assisted suicide, and no legalization of drugs. He ended by quoting President Calvin Coolidge on the importance of moral foundations to America:

> We do not need more material development, we need more spiritual development.
> We do not need more intellectual power, we need more moral power.
> We do not need more knowledge, we need more character.
> We do not need more government, we need more culture.
> We do not need more law, we need more religion.
> We do not need more of the things that are seen, we need more of the things that are unseen.[39]

When describing his vision of a contract for 2000, Newt Gingrich invariably included three social goals: "a country which is virtually drug-free, where every child is learning at their best rate, and where practically all children are born into families that can nurture and raise them." Gingrich was hopeful that he and other Republican leaders could persuade every GOP candidate in 2000, from the person running for the White House down to the courthouse, to sign a new contract that moves America toward "a faith-based, healthier, economically faster-growing, more decentralized, less-governmental society."[40]

House majority leader Dick Armey has also seen the light. He urged House Republicans, in a January 1998 memorandum, to help America "recover [its] moral emphasis." Often described as the apostle of the flat tax, Armey surprised many political observers by saying flatly: "I believe the issues of values and morality will be the dominant issues of 1998 and 2000." The Republican leader pointed to a recent poll of the Republican National Committee in which 71 percent of the respondents said there was a "moral crisis" in America.[41] What the former professor of economics did not reveal was that not long ago he had become a born-again Christian.

Armey suggested a six-point legislative agenda that included tax cuts to strengthen the family, expansion of charter schools, more effective drug rehabilitation, a ban on partial-birth abortion, and making an end of religious persecution "a high priority of our foreign policy." Acknowledging that on many issues there was no place for a direct federal role, Armey nevertheless called for "[appropriate] legislation, good oversight, and proper use of our bully pulpit" to refocus public attention on the moral problems in America.[42]

Just as conservatives have always opposed centralized economic planning, so do they oppose centralized political planning. The conservative movement is and always has been a loosely bound movement made up of, in Morton Blackwell's words, "activists, scholars, donors and organizational entrepreneurs held together by . . . shared philosophy, shared enemies, and shared experiences."[43] The often spirited debate about the future of conservatism between the different kinds of conservatives is a sign of the movement's vitality. Debate and even disagreement can strengthen a movement as long as they are based on principle and not driven by a desire for political power. The political goal of conservatives is, as it always has been, the forging and maintaining of a winning national coalition broad-minded enough, as Phyllis Schlafly says, "to allow people to vote for *our* candidates for the reason of *their* choice."[44]

Will conservatives succeed, or is the conservative revolution over? Where is conservatism headed: for the mountaintop or the ash heap?

Certain elements are necessary for any successful political movement. First, it must have a clearly defined, consistent philosophy. And it is a given

that conservatives of all stripes honor the Constitution and its carefully established system of checks and balances. They agree that government should be
limited, that individuals should be free, and that there can be no lasting liberty without virtue—public and private. Although there are differences between traditionalists and libertarians—for example, over how much to
reduce the size of the federal government—there is no quarrel that it has become a Leviathan that must be significantly reduced. In this respect, congressional leaders Dennis Hastert and Trent Lott are in willing tandem with
presidential hopefuls George W. Bush, Steve Forbes, and Lamar Alexander.

Second, a political movement must have a broad-based and broad-
minded national constituency. Conservatives are independent, individualistic, a naturally contentious lot. They like to argue about ideas and
institutions with their friends as well as their adversaries. They are uncomfortable with compromise and usually scorn accommodation. But they have
come together and stayed together when the times demanded it and the
right leadership encouraged it—like Robert Taft in the 1950s, Barry Goldwater in the 1960s, Ronald Reagan in the 1980s, and Newt Gingrich in the
1990s.

The conservative movement includes, as activist Grover Norquist puts
it, the "Leave Us Alone Coalition": small businessmen harassed by multiplying government regulations and taxes; home owners threatened by rising
property taxes; parents who oppose the distribution of condoms in their
children's schools; home schoolers who want to teach their children without
government interference; gun owners who are angered by violations of their
Second Amendment rights; evangelical Protestants, traditional Catholics,
and Orthodox Jews who believe in the right to life; workers who are punished by affirmative action; young Americans who resent their earnings
being siphoned off to bolster a tottering social security system; and veterans
who love their country but wonder whether liberals do.[45]

Third, a movement must have a sound financial base. Thanks to technical proficiency and political success, the number of identifiable conservative
donors has grown and grown and grown, from a few thousand in the 1950s
to at least 5 million in the 1990s. The fiscal strength of conservative organizations, including the Heritage Foundation (annual budget of over $25 mil-
lion), the Christian Coalition ($20 million), Concerned Women for
America ($10 million), the Cato Institute ($10 million), and the Media Research Center (almost $5 million), is impressive. If you include frequent allies

like the National Federation of Independent Business ($70 million), the National Rifle Association ($125 million), and the U.S. Chamber of Commerce ($70 million), the conservative movement would be rated "triple A" by Moody's.

Fourth, a political movement must be media savvy, knowing how to communicate effectively with the public through its own media as well as the mainstream media. Here there is a paradox: Conservatives have displayed distrust, anger, and contempt toward the mass media for decades. Yet the number one columnist in America (measured by the number of newspapers that carry his column) is conservative George Will, who appears in more than 500 daily papers and is also a prominent television commentator and best-selling author. The number two syndicated columnist is also a conservative: Cal Thomas, with 450 daily newspapers.

The number one radio talk show host is conservative Rush Limbaugh, heard by approximately 20 million Americans each week. Nearly tied with Limbaugh is Dr. Laura Schlessinger, whose advice on social and cultural problems is firmly right of center. Other conservatives in the top ten talk shows are G. Gordon Liddy, Michael Reagan, and Ollie North. The host of the longest-running public affairs program on PBS (almost a quarter of a century) is William F. Buckley, Jr. *National Review* (175,000) and the *American Spectator* (186,000) continue to vie for the largest circulation among journals of public opinion. The magazine with the largest circulation in the world (27 million) is *Reader's Digest*. Weekly television talk shows like *The McLaughlin Group*, hosted by John McLaughlin, a former Washington editor of *National Review,* and *The Capital Gang*, created by political columnist Robert Novak, consistently receive high ratings and have no difficulty in obtaining *Fortune* 500 corporate sponsors.

Only on the evening television newscasts and nightly television magazine programs (*60 Minutes, 20/20, Dateline*) do liberals predominate, but their share of the viewing audience has dropped dramatically over the past thirty years—from close to 90 percent to barely 50 percent—because of competition from CNN, C-SPAN, local news programs, and other cable programs.

C-SPAN is a unique medium with a relatively small but highly sophisticated, activist audience. Under the scrupulously fair direction of founder Brian Lamb, C-SPAN helped Newt Gingrich and the Conservative Opportunity Society become nationally known and has given conservative groups and causes equal access, in contrast to mainstream television, still run by a liberal media elite.

Which brings us to the fifth and last element of a political movement: experienced, effective, principled leadership. For the first time in fifty years, there is no undisputed conservative leader—no Robert Taft, no Barry Goldwater, no Ronald Reagan—and no designated successor like George Bush or Bob Dole. For the new millennium, there will be a new generation of conservative leaders.

There are almost as many contenders for the Republican presidential nomination in 2000 as there are primaries, but they all have one thing in common (beside their desire to be president): they are conservative. Gone are the days when Bob Taft or Barry Goldwater was the only conservative candidate confronted by a phalanx of liberal competitors. The possibilities for 2000 include Governor George W. Bush of Texas, millionaire magazine publisher Steve Forbes, Senator John Ashcroft of Missouri, and possibly ex-House Speaker Newt Gingrich. It is a sign of our media-dominated times that three contenders—Forbes, Patrick J. Buchanan, and Gary Bauer—have never been elected to any public office. But many conservatives argue that given the poor showing of the last two Republican nominees, both of them veteran officeholders, it is time for a citizen-politician.

Once one of these aspirants rises to the top, most of the frustration and uncertainty that characterize the conservative movement will fade away, as they did when Robert Taft, Barry Goldwater, and Ronald Reagan became the acknowledged leaders of American conservatives.

Conservatives in and out of Washington are generally optimistic about the future of the movement and the nation, qualified as always by an acceptance of man's nonangelic side. They see conservatism as intellectually dominant, as well as politically dominant.[46] They argue that conservative ideas have been proved correct by the failures of the welfare state in America and the collapse of communism in the Soviet Union and Eastern Europe.[47]

It is hard not to be optimistic about America, argues television and film producer Neal B. Freeman, "when even a modestly equipped American seems to have a fifty-fifty shot to succeed wildly—and a thousand foreigners would pay handsomely to take his place, no questions asked."[48] One pessimist, at least in the near term, is national security expert Frank Gaffney, who laments the lack of a successor to Ronald Reagan who "exemplifies his personal courage and subscribes to his political vision."[49]

Some conservatives even question whether a conservative movement exists. They argue that in the process of defeating communism, the Constitution was destroyed through the creation of a military-industrial complex and the whole character of the nation was changed. America, they say, is no longer a nation but a vast archipelago of disconnected human beings.[50]

But most conservatives are more sanguine, pointing to the success of conservative policies since 1981, the failure of liberal social programs, and the large conservative infrastructure that has been put in place since the late 1970s.[51] In 1997 alone, as columnist Charles Krauthammer pointed out, AFDC, a sixty-year-old welfare entitlement, was abolished; California outlawed affirmative action; and the Supreme Court unanimously overturned lower courts' attempts to legalize physician–assisted suicide.[52] Phyllis Schlafly, who supported Taft in 1952, Goldwater in 1964, and Reagan in 1976, who stopped the equal rights amendment when everyone said its ratification was inevitable, and under whose auspices the first profamily rally was held in April 1976, says simply, "The conservative movement is tremendous today!"[53]

Such optimism is based on the remarkable political triumphs of the 1980s and the 1990s and the bright constellation of philosophers, popularizers, and politicians who today lead the conservative movement. Conservatives have always known that in politics, there are no permanent victories and no permanent defeats, only permanent things like wisdom, courage, prudence, justice, and, overarching them all, liberty. Liberals used to say that conservatism was out of date, but that is like saying that the Ten Commandments, the Golden Rule, and the United States Constitution are out of date. It never made much sense, and in the wake of the defeat of communism and the continuing rollback of the welfare state, it now makes no sense at all. The conservative revolution is here to stay.

Acknowledgments

I HAVE BEEN WRITING ABOUT AMERICAN CONSERVATISM SINCE 1961 WHEN I was the first editor of *The New Guard*, the magazine of Young Americans for Freedom. For this history, I have drawn freely on my books, articles, and columns, especially my biographies of Ronald Reagan and Barry Goldwater, but have extensively revised the material.

The conservative literature about the politics of the conservative movement is surprisingly limited (conservatives are all too American in their lack of interest in political history), but what is there is "cherce"—as Spencer Tracy once remarked about Katharine Hepburn. Leading the list are George H. Nash's seminal work *The Conservative Intellectual Movement in America Since 1945*, William A. Rusher's autobiographical history *The Rise of the Right*, F. Clifton White's comprehensive *Suite 3505*, Martin Anderson's revealing *Revolution*, paleoconservative Paul Gottfried's *The Conservative Movement*, James C. Roberts's excellent *The Conservative Decade*, Richard A. Viguerie's feisty *The New Right: We're Ready to Lead*, Russell Kirk's and James McClellan's insightful *The Political Thought of Robert Taft*, and M. Stanton Evans's early books, especially *Revolt on the Campus*.

The liberal literature on conservative politics is wildly uneven. *Washington Post* reporter Lou Cannon's two biographies of Ronald Reagan are must reading, as is John B. Judis's biography of William F. Buckley, Jr. (remarkably, the only biography so far of this major conservative figure). Useful histories include William Manchester's *The Glory and the Dream* and James T. Patterson's *Grand Expectations* (Patterson's biography of Robert A. Taft—*Mr. Republican*—is by far the best), and Paul Johnson's magisterial *A History of the American People*, although Johnson is too laudatory about Richard Nixon. Godfrey Hodgson's *The World Turned Upside Down: A History of the Conserva-*

tive Ascendancy in America is good about earlier conservatives but flawed in its analysis of the Reagan presidency.

One person alone cannot research or write a political history of modern American conservatism. As always, I have depended on my wife, Anne, for major research and editorial assistance. Her trips took her to the John M. Ashbrook Center for Public Affairs at Ashland University in Ohio (where David Roepke was especially helpful); the Herbert Hoover Presidential Library in West Branch, Iowa; the Sterling Library at Yale (where Bill Buckley's papers are located); and the Library of Congress in Washington, D.C., repository of the William Rusher and Robert A. Taft papers. Together we examined the John Tower Papers at Southwestern University in Georgetown, Texas, and Reagan material at the Ronald Reagan Presidential Library in Simi Valley, California. I spent several days at the Hoover Institution at Stanford University going through the Peter Hannaford and Michael Deaver papers and Martin Anderson's personal files.

Over seventy prominent conservatives responded to my questionnaire about the past, present, and future of conservatism. I particularly enjoyed the note at the bottom of President George Bush's response: "Lee, I am rather pleased that you have written to me as 'one of the . . . leading conservatives.' Better not tell Howie Phillips or Ron Paul."

The personal reflections of the following were especially helpful: Leonard Liggio, David R. Jones, William A. Rusher, William F. Buckley, Jr., Neal B. Freeman, and George Nash.

I am indebted to Seth Becker, Jason Boffetti, Daniel Barnes, and John Nixon for their research help and to William S. Connery for his organizational skills and unfailing serenity.

Patricia Bozell and William T. Poole carefully read an often raw manuscript and patiently pointed out my many violations of the Chicago style book.

Grants from the Earhart Foundation, the Atlas Economic Research Foundation, the Historical Research Foundation, the Fund for American Studies, the Roe Foundation, and the Wilbur Foundation enabled Anne and me to make our many library visits and conduct our research. And all the while, I had a spacious office, PC, telephone, fax, access to NEXIS-LEXIS, and all the other modern research accoutrements, courtesy of the Heritage Foundation and its generous president, Dr. Edwin J. Feulner, Jr.

Because Leona Schecter is my literary agent, because the Free Press is my publisher, and because Paul Golob is my editor, this history is far better than it would have been if I had my own way.

I pay special tribute to my father, the late Willard Edwards, a Washington reporter and columnist for the *Chicago Tribune,* who covered American politics from 1935 until 1972. I miss him very much.

In writing this book, I have been struck once again by the reality that writing history is a constant process of selection—of deciding what to include and what to exclude, whom to highlight and whom to leave in the shadows. Because it is impossible to include everything (even in the Age of the CD-ROM), a historian is forever being forced to make choices between what is important and what is only interesting, what is significant and what is merely arresting. My choices have been influenced by the undeniable fact that I am a conservative. Indeed I have been a conservative activist, particularly in the 1960s and 1970s, as well as a conservative writer over the past forty years.

Those seeking absolute objectivity will not find it here. But then they will not find it in Arthur Schlesinger, Jr.'s history of Franklin D. Roosevelt's presidency or William Manchester's biography of John F. Kennedy either. Indeed, objectivity is impossible; we all have our biases, prejudices, and beliefs, and we carry them with us wherever we go or whatever we do. This history is a work of scholarship, selection, and yes, praise for a movement that has made a profound difference in the life of every American for half a century.

Notes

Introduction

1. "Dr. Fell's Election," *New York Times,* November 10, 1994; "The Sea Change," *Washington Post National Weekly Edition,* November 14–20, 1994.
2. See, for example, John Lewis Gaddis, *Strategies of Containment: A Critical Appraisal of Post-War American National Security Policy* (New York: Oxford University Press, 1982); Daniel Yergin, *The Shattered Peace: The Origins of the Cold War and the National Security State* (Boston: Houghton Mifflin, 1977); and Strobe Talbott, *Deadly Gambits: The Reagan Administration and the Stalemate in Nuclear Arms Control* (New York: Knopf, 1984).
3. Among many negative studies of the Reagan years, see Sidney Blumenthal, *Our Long National Daydream: A Political Pageant of the Reagan Era* (New York: Harper & Row, 1988), and Haynes B. Johnson, *Sleepwalking Through History: America in the Reagan Years* (New York: Norton, 1991).

Chapter 1: "Had Enough?"

1. *Congress and the Great Issues 1945–1995,* ed. Ronald D. Elving (Washington, D.C: Congressional Quarterly, 1996), p. xi.
2. Ibid., p. x.
3. James T. Patterson, *Grand Expectations: The United States, 1945–1974* (New York: Oxford University Press, 1996), p. 62.
4. Ibid., p. 43.
5. Joseph Stalin, "New Five Year Plan for Russia," address delivered over Radio Moscow, February 9, 1946, *Vital Speeches of the Day,* March 1, 1946.
6. Walter LaFeber, *America, Russia and the Cold War, 1945–1980,* 4th ed. (New York: Knopf, 1980), p. 39; John L. Gaddis, *The United States and the Origins of the Cold War, 1941–1947* (New York: Columbia University Press, 1972), pp. 299–302.
7. Arthur H. Vandenberg, Jr., ed., with the collaboration of Joe Alex Morris, *The Private Papers of Senator Vandenberg* (Boston: Houghton Mifflin, 1952), pp. 246–248.
8. Ibid., p. 250.
9. William Manchester, *The Glory and the Dream: A Narrative History of America, 1932–1972* (Boston: Little, Brown, 1973), 1:488.
10. Robert W. Merry, "Robert A. Taft: A Study in the Accumulation of Legislative Power," in *First Among Equals: Outstanding Senate Leaders of the Twentieth Century,* ed.

Richard A. Baker and Roger H. Davidson (Washington, D.C.: Congressional Quarterly, 1991), p. 172.

11. Manchester, *The Glory and the Dream,* 1:505.
12. Patterson, *Grand Expectations,* p. 139.
13. Ibid., p. 182.
14. Merry, "Robert A. Taft," p. 164.
15. Caroline Thomas Harnsberger, *A Man of Courage: Robert A. Taft* (Chicago: Wilcox and Follett, 1952), p. 7.
16. Robert A. Taft, speech before the Young Republican Club of Lawrence County, Ohio, April 4, 1936, Robert A. Taft Papers, Library of Congress.
17. Russell Kirk and James McClellan, *The Political Principles of Robert A. Taft* (New York: Fleet Press, 1967), p. 62.
18. James T. Patterson, *Mr. Republican: A Biography of Robert A. Taft* (Boston: Houghton Mifflin, 1972), p. 332.
19. Kirk and McClellan, *The Political Principles of Robert A. Taft,* pp. 68, 100, 133, 135.
20. Robert A. Taft speech to the Maine Republican Convention, March 31, 1950, reprinted in *Congressional Record,* April 4, 1950, p. A2532.
21. Kirk and McClellan, *The Political Principles of Robert A. Taft,* p. 194.
22. Patterson, *Mr. Republican,* p. 330.
23. The following description is based in large part on Caroline Thomas Harsberger's frequently insightful biography, *A Man of Courage: Robert A. Taft.*
24. Patterson, *Mr. Republican,* p. 306; Manchester, *The Glory and the Dream,* 1:493.
25. Patterson, *Mr. Republican,* p. 307; see also Merry, "Robert A. Taft," p. 176.
26. Patterson, *Mr. Republican,* p. 307.
27. Merry, "Robert A. Taft," p. 176.
28. Ibid.
29. Patterson, *Mr. Republican,* p. 312.
30. Ibid., p. 313.
31. Joseph C. Goulden, *The Best Years, 1945–1950* (New York: Atheneum, 1976), p. 226.
32. Ibid.
33. Ralph B. Levering, *The Public and American Foreign Policy, 1918–1978* (New York: Morrow, 1978), pp. 95–96.
34. Goulden, *The Best Years,* p. 227.
35. Ibid., pp. 228–229.
36. Ibid., pp. 231–232.
37. Manchester, *The Glory and the Dream,* 1:509.
38. Willard Edwards, "G.O.P. Vows Aid to Truman in a 'U.S. Policy,'" *Chicago Tribune,* November 12, 1946.
39. R. M. Hartwell, *A History of the Mont Pelerin Society* (Indianapolis: Liberty Fund, 1995), pp. 26–51. The Friedman quote is found in George H. Nash, *The Conservative Intellectual Movement in America Since 1945* (New York: Basic Books, 1976), p. 21.
40. *Human Events,* statement of purpose signed by Felix Morley, William Henry Chamberlin, and Frank C. Hanighen, January 15, 1944, Post-Presidential Papers—Felix Morley, Herbert Hoover Presidential Library, West Branch, Iowa.
41. Felix Morley, "The Fifth of November," *Human Events,* October 30, 1946; Felix Morley, "Our Own Iron Curtain," *Human Events,* November 13, 1946.
42. Booton Herndon, *Stormy Petrel: The Story of Fulton Lewis, Jr.* (New York: Duell, Sloan and Pearce, 1954), p. 107.

43. Russell Kirk, "The Books of Conservatism," *Books on Trial* (November 1954).
44. Russell Kirk, *The Politics of Prudence* (Bryn Mawr, Pa.: Intercollegiate Studies Institute, 1993), p. 16.
45. Friedrich A. Hayek, *The Road to Serfdom* (Chicago: University of Chicago Press, 1944), pp. xx, 70.
46. Nash, *The Conservative Intellectual Movement in America Since 1945,* pp. 91–93; Whittaker Chambers, *Witness* (New York: Random House, 1952), pp. 741–742.

Chapter 2: An Extraordinary Congress

1. William Manchester, *The Glory and the Dream* (Boston: Little, Brown, 1973), 1:546–547.
2. James T. Patterson, *Mr. Republican: A Biography of Robert A. Taft* (Boston: Houghton Mifflin, 1972), p. 372.
3. Ibid., p. 373.
4. Ibid.
5. Ibid., p. 374.
6. Ibid., pp. 66–67.
7. Ibid., p. 75.
8. Edna Lonigan, "Labor and Collectivism," *Human Events,* July 2, 1947, p. 3.
9. *The Private Papers of Senator Vandenberg,* ed. Arthur H. Vandenberg, Jr., with the collaboration of Joe Alex Harris (Boston: Houghton Mifflin, 1952), pp. 318–319.
10. Robert A. Taft to Arthur Vandenberg, October 20, 1946, Vandenberg Papers, Bentley Historical Library, University of Michigan.
11. Justus D. Doenecke, *Not to the Swift: The Old Isolationists in the Cold War Era* (Lewisburg, Pa.: Bucknell University Press, 1979), p. 10.
12. Robert Donovan, *Conflict and Crisis: The Presidency of Harry S. Truman, 1945–1948* (New York: Norton, 1977), p. 278.
13. Harry S. Truman, *Memoirs,* Vol. 2: *Years of Trial and Hope* (Garden City, N.Y.: Doubleday, 1956), pp. 99–101.
14. Felix Morley, "Europe's Coronary Thrombosis," *Human Events,* May 21, 1947, p. 4.
15. Patterson, *Mr. Republican,* p. 371.
16. Walter Lippmann, "Cassandra Speaking," *New York Herald Tribune,* April 5, 1947.
17. *Private Papers of Senator Vandenberg,* pp. 373–374.
18. Memorandum of William L. Clayton to the President, May 25, 1947, Papers of William L. Clayton, Harry S. Truman Library, Independence, Missouri.
19. Oral history interview with George M. Elsey, July 7, 1970, Harry S. Truman Library. Also see oral history interview with Clark Clifford, April 19, 1971, Truman Library.
20. Frank C. Hanighen, "Not Merely Gossip," *Human Events,* July 30, 1947, p. 5.
21. Ibid.
22. Ibid.
23. Frank C. Hanighen, "Not Merely Gossip," *Human Events,* November 20, 1946, p. 5.
24. Statement by Herbert Hoover for the Senate Foreign Relations Committee, January 18, 1948, Post-Presidential Individual File, Arthur H. Vandenberg, Herbert Hoover Presidential Library, West Branch, Iowa.
25. Ibid.
26. Ibid.
27. Ibid.
28. Ibid.

29. Richard Norton Smith, Introduction to *Herbert Hoover and Harry S. Truman: A Documentary History*, ed. with commentary by Timothy Walch and Dwight M. Miller (Worland, Wyo.: High Plains Publishing, 1992), p. 13.
30. Statement by Robert A. Taft during debate on the European Recovery Plan, *Congressional Record*, March 8, 1948, p. 2641.
31. Statement by Robert A. Taft, *Congressional Record*, March 4, 1948, pp. 2642–2643.
32. Patterson, *Mr. Republican*, p. 392.
33. Willard Edwards, "3,181 Federal Aides Disloyal, U.S. Estimates," *Chicago Tribune*, July 19, 1947.
34. Willard Edwards, "Orders Issued from Moscow, Probers Told," *Chicago Tribune*, October 21, 1947.
35. Ibid.
36. Willard Edwards, "Cooper Tells of Rejecting 'Pinko' Scripts," *Chicago Tribune*, October 24, 1947.
37. Ibid.
38. Ibid.
39. Ibid.
40. Willard Edwards, "Joined Reds, Actor Says; Names Leaders in Party," *Chicago Tribune*, April 11, 1951.
41. Willard Edwards, "Orders Issued from Moscow."
42. David McCullough, *Truman* (New York: Simon & Schuster, 1992), pp. 551, 553.
43. Ibid.
44. Willard Edwards, "Kept on Jobs for 9 Years, Inquiry Told," *Chicago Tribune*, August 4, 1948.
45. Michael Barone, *Our Country: The Shaping of America from Roosevelt to Reagan* (New York: Free Press, 1990), p. 216.
46. Manchester, *The Glory and the Dream*, 1:549.
47. Patterson, *Mr. Republican*, p. 416.
48. Ibid., p. 404.
49. McCullough, *Truman*, pp. 627, 629; Patterson, *Mr. Republican*, p. 379.
50. All of these quotations are from McCullough, *Truman*: Dewey, p. 700; Taft, p. 661; Hoover, p. 681; Republicans, p. 658; the Eightieth Congress, p. 663.
51. Willard Edwards, "Implies Dewey Is a 'Front Man' Like Hitler," *Chicago Tribune*, October 26, 1948; "Truman Warns of 'Weak U.S.' If G.O.P. Wins," *Chicago Tribune*, October 27, 1948.
52. Willard Edwards, "Truman Lashes at Dewey for 'Following Me,'" *Chicago Tribune*, October 29, 1948; Willard Edwards, "Truman Tells East Coasters He Hates Reds," *Chicago Tribune*, October 28, 1948.
53. McCullough, *Truman*, p. 696.
54. Irwin Ross, "What Happened in 1948," in *Harry S. Truman and the Fair Deal*, ed. Alonzo L. Hamby (Lexington, Mass.: D. C. Heath, 1974), p. 105.
55. Frank C. Hanighen, "Not Merely Gossip," *Human Events*, November 24, 1948, p. 5.
56. John Redding, *Inside the Democratic Party* (Indianapolis: Bobbs-Merrill, 1958), p. 44.
57. Harold Ickes, "Taft Minus Hartley," *New Republic*, July 18, 1949, p. 16.
58. Patterson, *Mr. Republican*, p. 425.
59. Ross, "What Happened in 1948," p. 117.
60. Ronald Reagan, *An American Life* (New York: Simon & Schuster, 1990), p. 133.

61. George H. Nash, *The Conservative Intellectual Movement in America Since 1945* (Wilmington, Del.: Intercollegiate Studies Institute, 1996), pp. 34–35.
62. Lionel Trilling, *The Liberal Imagination* (New York: Viking Press, 1950), p. ix.

Chapter 3: We Like Ike

1. Alonzo L. Hamby, *Man of the People: A Life of Harry S. Truman* (New York: Oxford University Press, 1995), pp. 493–494.
2. Richard C. Cornuelle, *Reclaiming the American Dream* (New York: Random House, 1965), p. 24.
3. See pp. 161–169 in my *Missionary for Freedom: The Life and Times of Walter Judd* (New York: Paragon House, 1990) for a more detailed analysis of the fall of China to the communists in 1949.
4. William F. Buckley, Jr., and L. Brent Bozell, *McCarthy and His Enemies: The Record and Its Meaning* (Chicago: Regnery, 1954), p. 3.
5. Ibid.
6. Frank C. Hanighen, "Not Merely Gossip," *Human Events,* June 22, 1949, p. 5.
7. I am indebted for this analysis to conservative author and journalist M. Stanton Evans, who has been collecting material for a book about McCarthy for many years.
8. Buckley and Bozell, *McCarthy and His Enemies,* p. 62.
9. Ibid., p. 189.
10. Roy Cohn, *McCarthy: The Answer to "Tail Gunner Joe"* (New York: Manor Books, 1977), p. 275.
11. Ibid., p. 279.
12. Nicholas von Hoffman, "Was McCarthy Right About the Left? The Reds Were Under the Bed While the Liberals Looked Away," *Washington Post,* April 14, 1996.
13. Ibid.
14. M. Stanton Evans, "McCarthyism: Waging the Cold War in America," *Human Events,* May 30, 1997, p. S5.
15. Ibid.
16. Ibid., p. S8.
17. Ibid., p. S7.
18. In *No Wonder We Are Losing* (Plano, Tex.: University of Plano Press, 1961), Robert Morris writes, "Just as China fell because of activities by men in Washington, so did the people of Cuba become enchained because of what was done in our nation's capital" (Foreword).
19. Statement by President Harry S. Truman, June 27, 1950, Walter H. Judd Papers, Hoover Library, Stanford University.
20. Statement by Walter H. Judd, June 29, 1950, *Congressional Record,* p. A4893; Walter H. Judd to D. D. Streator, July 1, 1950, Walter H. Judd Papers, Hoover Library, Stanford University.
21. Hsiang Chi-pei, "Will Communism Capture Asia?" *Human Events,* May 17, 1950, p. 3.
22. Robert A. Taft to Samuel Lamm, September 12, 1950, Post-Presidential Individual File—Robert A. Taft, Herbert Hoover Presidential Library, West Branch, Iowa.
23. Felix Morley, "Alliance or Union?" *Human Events,* April 20, 1949, p. 1.
24. Ibid., p. 96.
25. James T. Patterson, *Mr. Republican: A Biography of Robert A. Taft* (Boston: Houghton Mifflin, 1972), p. 464.

26. Ibid., pp. 97–98.
27. Ibid., p. 103; Robert A. Taft to Herbert Hoover, Post-Presidential Individual File—Robert A. Taft, Herbert Hoover Presidential Library.
28. Patterson, *Mr. Republican,* pp. 472–473.
29. Willard Edwards, "Nation Fights a 'Useless War' in Korea: Taft," September 21, 1951, "Taft Tells His Plan to Meet Soviet Threat," September 22, 1951, *Chicago Tribune.* Quote about Indochina, Patterson, *Mr. Republican,* p. 529.
30. Patterson, *Mr. Republican,* pp. 103–104.
31. Robert Taft handwritten thoughts, Box 415, Robert Taft Papers, Library of Congress.
32. "GOP Leaders Give Taft Wide Margin in Poll," *Evening Star,* January 17, 1952; Patterson, *Mr. Republican,* p. 514.
33. Phyllis Schlafly, *A Choice Not an Echo* (Alton, Ill.: Pere Marquette Press, 1964), p. 56.
34. Ibid., p. 526.
35. Ibid., p. 546.
36. Richard Rovere, *Affairs of State: The Eisenhower Years* (New York: Farrar, Straus, 1956), p. 25.
37. William Manchester, *The Glory and the Dream: A Narrative History of America, 1932–1972* (Boston: Little, Brown, 1973), 1:754; Patterson, *Mr. Republican,* pp. 548–549; statement by Herbert Hoover, July 9, 1952, Post-Presidential Papers, Box 103, Herbert Hoover Presidential Library.
38. Schlafly, *A Choice Not an Echo,* p. 57.
39. Ibid., p. 58.
40. Manchester, *The Glory and the Dream,* 1:755.
41. Ibid.
42. Gallup Poll cited in "Taft Has Edge in Delegates; Ike Leads in Popular Polls," *Newsweek,* June 23, 1952; Manchester, *The Glory and the Dream,* 1:756.
43. Manchester, *The Glory and the Dream,* 1:756.
44. Willard Edwards, "Wild Disorder Hits Climax as Dirksen Raps New Yorker," *Chicago Tribune,* July 10, 1952.
45. "The Problem of Taft," *Human Events,* November 7, 1951, p. 399.
46. "The I-S-I," *Human Events,* May 14, 1952, p. 3.
47. Patterson, *Mr. Republican,* p. 560.
48. "Famous Victory," *Human Events,* July 16, 1952, p. 1.
49. William S. White, *The Taft Story* (New York: Harper & Brothers, 1954), pp. 180–181.
50. Patterson, *Mr. Republican,* pp. 563–564.
51. Ibid., p. 570; "GOP Split," *Human Events,* July 30, 1952, p. 1.
52. Patterson, *Mr. Republican,* p. 574.
53. Ibid., pp. 576–577.
54. White, *The Taft Story,* p. 188; *New York Times,* September 14, 1952, p. 1.
55. White, *The Taft Story,* p. 191.
56. Ibid., p. 193.
57. Schlafly, *A Choice Not an Echo,* pp. 64–65.
58. Patterson, *Mr. Republican,* p. 579.
59. Paul F. Boller Jr., *Presidential Campaigns* (New York: Oxford University Press, 1984), p. 284.
60. Thomas C. Reeves, *The Life and Times of Joe McCarthy: A Biography* (New York: Stein and Day, 1982), pp. 432–433.

61. Ibid., p. 439.

62. James T. Patterson, *Grand Expectations: The United States, 1945–1974* (New York: Oxford University Press, 1996), p. 255.

63. "Our Vote," *Human Events,* October 29, 1952, p. 1.

64. Arthur Krock, *New York Times,* November 5, 1952.

65. Manchester, *The Glory and the Dream,* 1:783.

66. Kathleen Hall Jamieson, *Packaging the Presidency: A History and Criticism of Presidential Campaign Advertising,* 2d ed. (New York: Oxford University Press, 1992), p. 85.

67. Willard Edwards, "Visual-Sound Methods Bring Votes to G.O.P.," *Chicago Tribune,* October 13, 1950.

68. Ibid.

69. Robert A. Taft, "Results of Election," Box 428; Taft to Edward W. Allen, November 13, 1952, Box 404, Taft Papers, Library of Congress.

70. "Lubell on 1956," *Human Events,* November 5, 1955, p. 1; Patterson, *Mr. Republican,* p. 580.

71. Robert Taft to Lou Guylay, December 1, 1952, Box 978, Taft Papers.

Chapter 4: Profiles in Courage

1. James T. Patterson, *Grand Expectations: The United States, 1945–1974* (New York; Oxford University Press, 1996), p. 279.

2. Ibid.

3. Ibid.

4. William Manchester, *The Glory and the Dream: A Narrative History of America, 1932–1972* (Boston: Little, Brown, 1973), 1:811.

5. Ibid., p. 812.

6. Ibid.

7. Robert W. Merry, "Robert A. Taft: A Study in the Accumulation of Legislative Power," in *First Among Equals,* ed. Richard A. Baker and Roger H. Davison (Washington, D.C.: CQ Press, 1991), p. 190.

8. In his virulently anti-McCarthy biography, liberal journalist Richard Rovere quotes Taft as saying with some satisfaction, "We've got McCarthy where he can't do any harm." See *Senator Joe McCarthy* (New York: Harcourt, Brace, 1959), p. 188. But there is good reason to question this quotation, which appeared for the first time six years after Taft's death. In his review of Rovere's biography, Willard Edwards of the *Chicago Tribune* wrote that the author attributed to Taft "statements incredible to those who knew Taft." See "Rovere on McCarthy," *Human Events,* July 29, 1959, p. 4. Taft often expressed his support of McCarthy's militant anticommunism and recognized his strong appeal to the Republican rank and file. Would Taft have voted to censure McCarthy? Not if in so doing, he would have damaged the Republican party and aided the Democrats.

9. William S. White, *The Taft Story* (New York: Harper & Brothers, 1954), pp. 221–222.

10. Dwight D. Eisenhower, *Mandate for Change, 1953–1956* (New York: Doubleday, 1963), pp. 194–195; White, *The Taft Story,* p. 218.

11. White, *The Taft Story,* p. 251.

12. Merry, "Robert A. Taft," p. 193; White, *The Taft Story,* pp. 224, 227.

13. White, *The Taft Story,* pp. 230–241; James T. Patterson, *Mr. Republican: A Biography of Robert A.* Taft (Boston: Houghton Mifflin, 1972), pp. 595–596.

14. Patterson, *Mr. Republican,* p. 596.

15. "Yalta," *Human Events,* February 25, 1953, p. 1.
16. White, *The Taft Story,* p. 245.
17. Merry, "Robert A. Taft," p. 193.
18. Manchester, *The Glory and the Dream,* 1:813.
19. Ibid.
20. White, *The Taft Story,* p. 257.
21. Ibid., pp. 253–261; Patterson, *Mr. Republican,* p. 607.
22. Patterson, *Mr. Republican,* pp. 608–609; Herbert Hoover quote, "Hoover on Taft," *Human Events,* April 22, 1959, p. 4.
23. Patterson, *Mr. Republican,* p. 611.
24. Russell Kirk and James McClellan, *The Political Principles of Robert A. Taft* (New York: Fleet Press, 1967), p. 195.
25. Patterson, *Mr. Republican,* pp. 614–615.
26. Francis Cardinal Spellman, August 4, 1953, Post-Presidential Individual File—Joseph R. McCarthy, Herbert Hoover Presidential Library, West Branch, Iowa.
27. Richard Gid Powers, *Not Without Honor: The History of American Anticommunism* (New York: Free Press, 1995), p. 260.
28. George Nash, *The Conservative Intellectual Movement in America Since 1945* (New York: Basic Books, 1976), pp. 114–115.
29. Lee Edwards, *Goldwater: The Man Who Made a Revolution* (Washington, D.C.: Regnery, 1995), pp. 58–59.
30. Thomas C. Reeves, *The Life and Times of Joe McCarthy* (New York: Stein and Day, 1982), p. 547.
31. Ibid., p. 534; Edwards, *Goldwater,* p. 59.
32. Roy Cohn, *McCarthy: The Answer to "Tail Gunner Joe"* (New York: Manor Books, 1977), p. 208.
33. Willard Edwards, "Joe Began His Climb in 1950," *Chicago Tribune,* May 4, 1957.
34. Jack Bell, *Mr. Conservative* (Garden City, N.Y.: Doubleday, 1962), pp. 100–101; Barry Goldwater, *With No Apologies* (New York: Morrow, 1979), p. 61.
35. Ibid.
36. Bell, *Mr. Conservative,* pp. 96–98.
37. Willard Edwards, "Report Calls for Perjury Indictments," *Chicago Tribune,* July 3, 1952. Also see M. Stanton Evans, "History's Vindication of Joe McCarthy," *Human Events,* May 16, 1987, reprinted in *The Best of Human Events: Fifty Years of Conservative Thought and Action,* ed. James C. Roberts (Lafayette, La.: Huntington House Publishers, 1995), p. 270.
38. Evans, "History's Vindication of Joe McCarthy," p. 271.
39. Ibid., p. 274.
40. Willard Edwards, "McCarthy's Record," *Chicago Tribune,* November 7, 1954, reprinted in *Human Events,* November 10, 1954.
41. Ibid.
42. Nash, *The Conservative Intellectual Movement,* p. 122.
43. "The Irrepressible Conflict I," *Human Events,* May 4, 1957, p. 1.
44. William S. Schlamm, "Across McCarthy's Grave," *National Review,* May 18, 1957, p. 470.
45. Willard Edwards, *Human Events,* April 14, 1973, p. 117.
46. Congressional Quarterly, *Powers of the Presidency* (Washington, D.C.: CQ Press, 1989), p. 121.
47. Manchester, *The Glory and the Dream,* 1:824–825.

48. Edwin McDowell provides an excellent analysis of the Bricker Amendment in *Barry Goldwater: Portrait of an Arizonan* (Chicago: Regnery, 1964), pp. 99–101.

49. Manchester, *The Glory and the Dream,* 1:827.

Chapter 5: "Let's Grow Up, Conservatives!"

1. Prominently displayed in the Goldwater campaign plane in the fall of 1964 was a bumper sticker that read: "Better Brinksmanship Than Chickenship." See my *Goldwater: The Man Who Made a Revolution* (Washington, D.C.: Regnery, 1995), p. 324.

2. Phyllis Schlafly, *A Choice Not an Echo* (Alton, Ill.: Pere Marquette Press, 1964), p. 69.

3. "Mike Wallace Interviews Fulton Lewis Jr.," February 1, 1958, Post-Presidential Individual File—Fulton Lewis, Jr., Herbert Hoover Presidential Library, West Branch, Iowa.

4. "Generation to Generation," *Time,* July 6, 1953; George Nash, *The Conservative Intellectual Movement in America Since 1945* (New York: Basic Books, 1976), pp. 73–74.

5. William A. Rusher, "Death of a Giant," *University Bookman* 34 (1994): 16.

6. "Anniversary," *Human Events,* February 3, 1954, p. 4.

7. For a brief history of this remarkable organization, see "The 'China Lobby'" in my *Missionary for Freedom: The Life and Times of Walter Judd* (New York: Paragon House, 1990), pp. 204–215.

8. "Realignment," *Human Events,* May 12, 1954, p. 1.

9. Nash, *The Conservative Intellectual Movement,* pp. 140–141.

10. See John Chamberlain's autobiography, *A Life with the Printed Word* (Washington, D.C.: Regnery Gateway, 1962), for a personal account of the early days of the *Freeman.*

11. Nash, *The Conservative Intellectual Movement,* p. 133.

12. Ibid., p. 136.

13. William F. Buckley, Jr., to Frank Hanighen, September 25, 1954, William F. Buckley, Jr., Papers, Sterling Library, Yale University; John B. Judis, *William F. Buckley, Jr.: Patron Saint of the Conservatives* (New York: Simon & Schuster, 1988), p. 114.

14. Judis, *William F. Buckley, Jr.,* p. 119.

15. Ibid., p. 120.

16. William F. Buckley, Jr., to Herbert Hoover, March 1, 1955, Buckley Papers, Sterling Library, Yale University.

17. Morrie Ryskind to William F. Buckley, Jr., September 19, 1955, Buckley Papers, Sterling Library, Yale University.

18. Regarding Roger Milliken's support of *National Review,* see memorandum of A. W. D. Harris to William F. Buckley, Jr., November 10, 1955, Buckley Papers, Sterling Library, Yale University; Judis, *William F. Buckley, Jr.,* p. 129.

19. Nash, *Conservative Intellectual Movement,* p. 148.

20. "Enigma of Nixon," *Human Events,* November 5, 1955, p. 1.

21. "The Magazine's Credenda," *National Review,* November 19, 1955, p. 6.

22. Ibid., p. 5.

23. William Rusher, *The Rise of the Right* (New York: Morrow, 1984), pp. 72–73.

24. Patrick J. Buchanan in Judis, *William F. Buckley Jr.,* p. 140.

25. Jameson Campaigne, Jr., to the author, March 23, 1998.

26. "Ninety-Six Senators Rated," *Human Events,* September 29, 1956, Article Section I.

27. House ad for the January 1961 Political Action Conference, *Human Events,* November 17, 1960.

28. Edwin McDowell, *Barry Goldwater: Portrait of an Arizonan* (Chicago: Regnery, 1984), pp. 137–138.

29. "What Happened in the Election—Congress," *Human Events*, November 10, 1956, p. 1.

30. *Congressional Record*, April 8, 1957, pp. 5258–5265.

31. President's News Conference, April 10, 1957, in *Public Papers of the Presidents: Dwight D. Eisenhower* (Washington, D.C.: Government Printing Office, 1958), pp. 270–272.

32. Rob Wood and Dean Smith, *Barry Goldwater* (New York: Avon Books, 1961), p. 111.

33. Robert Welch, *The Politician* (Belmont, Mass.: privately printed, 1963), pp. 276–279. G. Edward Griffin, Welch's official biographer, says that in the original manuscript of *The Politician*, Welch wrote that Eisenhower was either (1) an opportunist who collaborated with communists for "personal political advantage," (2) "too dumb to realize" what he was doing, or (3) "a dedicated, conscious agent of the Communist Conspiracy." According to Griffin, Welch made it clear that he believed in the last explanation. See G. Edward Griffin, *The Life and Words of Robert Welch* (Thousand Oaks, Calif.: American Media, 1975), p. 226.

34. Russell Kirk, "Conservatives and Fantastics," *America* (February 1962).

35. Rusher, *Rise of the Right*, p. 63.

36. Barry M. Goldwater with Jack Casserly, *Goldwater* (New York: Doubleday, 1988), p. 126.

37. Ibid., p. 127.

38. Memorandum of William F. Buckley, Jr., January 21, 1957, Buckley Papers, Sterling Library, Yale University.

39. Ibid.

40. "Young GOP," *Human Events*, June 29, 1957, p. 1.

41. "The New Trend on Campus: Conservatism," *Human Events*, September 14, 1957, Article Section I.

42. Ibid.

43. Wood and Smith, *Barry Goldwater*, p. 118.

44. Clarence Manion, "Confidential Memorandum," May 15, 1959, Clarence Manion Papers, Chicago Historical Society.

45. Ibid.

46. Clarence Manion to D. B. Lewis, May 27, 1959, Manion Papers, Chicago Historical Society.

47. "Goldwater to the Fore," *Human Events*, July 1, 1959, p. 1.

48. Author's interview with L. Brent Bozell, January 10, 1992.

49. Goldwater, *Goldwater*, p. 120.

50. McDowell, *Barry Goldwater*, p. 43.

51. Rusher, *Rise of the Right*, p. 78.

52. Barry Goldwater, *The Conscience of a Conservative* (Shepherdsville, Ky.: Victor Publishing, 1960), p. 55.

53. Ibid., p. 112.

54. Ibid., p. 111.

55. George Morgenstern, "Harsh Facts, Hard Sense on the Perils to Liberty," *Chicago Sunday Tribune Magazine of Books*, April 17, 1960; "Old Guard's New Spokesman," *Time*, May 2, 1960; "The Conscience of a Conservative," Westbrook Pegler, *New York Journal American*, April 29, 1960.

56. *Human Events*, May 19, 1960, p. 2. Goldwater called the health care plan proposed by Arthur Fleming, secretary of health, education, and welfare, "socialized medicine."

57. Schlafly, *A Choice Not an Echo,* p. 74.

58. Barry Goldwater, *With No Apologies* (New York: Morrow, 1979), pp. 110–111.

59. Ibid.

60. Ibid., p. 112.

61. Author's interview with Robert Croll, October 2, 1993.

62. Jack Bell, *Mr. Conservative* (Garden City, N.Y.: Doubleday, 1962), p. 23.

63. Goldwater, *With No Apologies,* p. 115.

64. Bell, *Mr. Conservative,* p. 14.

65. Ibid., p. 15.

66. Ibid.

67. Ibid.

68. Ibid.

69. Stephen Shadegg, *Barry Goldwater: Freedom Is His Flight Plan* (New York: Fleet Publishing, 1962), p. 270.

70. Dan Smoot to Paul H. Talbert, August 25, 1960, Manion Papers, Chicago Historical Society; author's interview with Barry Goldwater, December 17, 1991.

71. Frank S. Meyer to William F. Buckley and other senior *NR* editors, May 10, 1960, Buckley Papers, Sterling Library, Yale University.

72. Ibid.

73. Bill Rusher to Bill Buckley, October 10, 1960, Buckley Papers, Sterling Library, Yale University.

74. James Burnham to Bill Buckley, October 9, 1960; Priscilla L. Buckley to Bill Buckley, October 1960, Buckley Papers, Sterling Library, Yale University.

75. Bill Buckley to Jim Burnham, October 11, 1960, Buckley Papers, Sterling Library, Yale University.

76. "National Review and the 1960 Elections," *National Review,* October 22, 1960, p. 234.

77. Barry Goldwater, "Conservatives Should Support Nixon," *Human Events,* August 4, 1960, sect. IV.

78. John Chamberlain, "Rising Campus Conservatism," *Human Events,* November 17, 1960.

79. Herbert Hoover to Ben Morrell, April 2, 1960, Post-Presidential Subject File, ACA, Herbert Hoover Presidential Library, West Branch, Iowa.

80. See John J. Synon, "The ACA-Index: How to Trap a Demagog," *Human Events,* May 26, 1960, sect. III.

81. See M. Stanton Evans, *Revolt on the Campus* (Chicago: Regnery, 1961).

82. Lee Edwards, *You Can Make the Difference* (New Rochelle, N.Y.: Arlington House, 1980), pp. 241–242.

83. Goldwater, *With No Apologies,* p. 125; Schlafly, *A Choice Not an Echo,* p. 76.

84. "Salesman for a Cause," *Time,* June 23, 1961, p. 16.

Chapter 6: The Reluctant Champion

1. F. Clifton White with William J. Gill, *Suite 3505: The Story of the Draft Goldwater Movement* (New Rochelle, N.Y.: Arlington House, 1967), p. 35.

2. William Rusher, *The Rise of the Right* (New York: Morrow, 1984), p. 99.

3. White, *Suite 3505,* p. 32.

4. Although Herbert Hoover was a major player in the building of the modern conservative movement, helping to launch *Human Events* and Americans for Constitutional Action in the 1940s and 1950s, he campaigned and won the presidency in 1928 as an

"activist" Republican as contrasted to Calvin Coolidge, who favored a more minimal-ist approach to government. See George Nash, "'The Great Enigma' and 'The Great Engineer': The Political Relationship of Calvin Coolidge and Herbert Hoover," *Calvin Coolidge and the Coolidge Era: Essays on the History of the 1920s,* John Haynes, ed. (Washington, D.C.: Library of Congress/University Press of New England, 1998).

5. Stewart Alsop, "Can Goldwater Win in 1964?" *Saturday Evening Post,* August 24, 1963, p. 21.

6. White, *Suite 3505,* p. 41.

7. Ibid., pp. 45–46; Rusher, *Rise of the Right,* p. 108.

8. William A. Rusher, "Reflections on the Rise of the Right" (keynote address at a conference on American conservatism, Princeton University, May 3, 1996, reprinted by the Claremont Institute, Claremont, California).

9. White, *Suite 3505,* pp. 61, 75.

10. Ibid., pp. 73–74.

11. Ibid.

12. Whittaker Chambers, "Big Sister Is Watching You," *National Review,* December 28, 1957, pp. 594–596.

13. George H. Nash, *The Conservative Intellectual Movement in America Since 1945* (New York: Basic Books, 1976), p. 144; Garry Wills, "But Is Ayn Rand Conservative?" *National Review,* February 27, 1960, p. 139.

14. Ibid., p. 145.

15. Rusher, *Rise of the Right,* p. 117.

16. Ibid., pp. 121–123.

17. "Thunder Against the Right," *Time,* November 24, 1961, p. 11; Alan Barth, "Report on the Rampageous Right," *New York Times Magazine,* November 26, 1961, pp. 25, 130–131.

18. "The Question of Robert Welch," *National Review,* February 13, 1962, pp. 83–88.

19. Ibid.

20. John B. Judis, *William F. Buckley, Jr.: Patron Saint of the Conservatives* (New York: Simon & Schuster, 1988), p. 199.

21. Ibid., p. 199; Barry M. Goldwater with Jack Casserly, *Goldwater* (New York: Double-day, 1988), p. 127.

22. Nash, *Conservative Intellectual Movement,* pp. 157–158.

23. Ibid., p. 161.

24. Goldwater, *Goldwater,* p. 135.

25. Ibid.

26. Graham Allison, *Essence of Decision: Explaining the Cuban Missile Crisis* (Boston: Little, Brown, 1971), pp. 188–189.

27. Robert Kennedy, *Thirteen Days: A Memoir of the Cuban Missile Crisis* (New York: Norton, 1969), pp. 202–203.

28. White, *Suite 3505,* p. 78.

29. Ibid., pp. 97–99.

30. J. William Middendorf II Notes, Part I, December 1963, Middendorf Archives, Washington, D.C.

31. White, *Suite 3505,* p. 117.

32. Ibid., p. 118.

33. Ibid., p. 123.

34. Ibid., p. 126.

35. "The President Thing," *Time,* June 14, 1963, pp. 26–31.

36. White, *Suite 3505,* pp. 176–177.

37. Lawrence E. Davies, "Young G.O.P. Group Hails Goldwater," *New York Times,* July 15, 1963.

38. Howard Norton, "6,000 at D.C. Rally Launch Draft-Goldwater Drive," *Baltimore Sun,* July 5, 1963.

39. Remarks by Barry Goldwater, Young Republican rally, Dodger Stadium, Los Angeles, September 16, 1963, *Human Events* Library, Washington, D.C.

40. *Time,* October 3, 1963, pp. 34–35.

41. Ibid.

42. Richard Reeves, *President Kennedy: Profile of Power* (New York: Simon & Schuster, 1993), pp. 655–656.

43. William Manchester, *The Death of a President: November 20–25, 1963* (New York: Harper & Row, 1967), p. 243–244.

44. Walter Cronkite, comment over CBS News, November 22, 1963.

45. Eugene Methvin, telephone interview with the author, September 12, 1997.

46. Francis J. McNamara to John R. Tunheim, June 3, 1996, Private Papers of Francis J. McNamara.

47. Methvin interview.

48. Ibid.

49. Robert Alan Goldberg, *Barry Goldwater* (New Haven, Conn.: Yale University Press, 1995), pp. 178–179.

50. Richard N. Goodwin, *Remembering America: A Voice from the Sixties* (Boston: Little, Brown, 1988), p. 302; Goldwater, *Goldwater,* pp. 150–151.

51. Goldwater, *Goldwater,* pp. 151–152; author's telephone interview with John Grenier, May 31, 1994.

52. Author's interview with Barry Goldwater, December 6, 1991.

53. Goldwater, *Goldwater,* pp. 153–154.

54. "Transcript of Goldwater's News Conference on His Entry into Presidential Race," *New York Times,* January 4, 1964.

55. Theodore White, *The Making of the President—1964* (New York: Signet Books, 1965), p. 131.

56. Ibid., pp. 135–137.

57. William F. Buckley, Jr., "The One and Only Barry Goldwater," *Family Weekly,* December 30, 1984, p. 5.

58. White, *Suite 3505,* p. 298.

59. "The Dialogue Begins," *National Review,* January 28, 1964, p. 51.

60. Stephen Shadegg, *What Happened to Goldwater?* (New York: Holt, Rinehart and Winston, 1965), p. 116.

61. Author's telephone interview with Stuart Spencer, July 15, 1993.

62. Author's telephone interview with Phyllis Schlafly, May 17, 1994.

63. Goldberg, *Barry Goldwater,* p. 189; White, *Suite 3505,* p. 341.

64. "Goldwater Poses New Asian Tactic," *New York Times,* May 25, 1964.

65. White, *Making of the President,* p. 143.

66. Author's interview with R. L. "Dick" Herman, April 26, 1993; Shadegg, *What Happened to Goldwater?* p. 125; Wallace Turner, "University Bars Rockefeller Talk," *New York Times,* May 28, 1964.

67. Edwin McDowell, *Barry Goldwater: Portrait of an Arizonan* (Chicago: Regnery, 1964), p. 170.

68. Ibid., p. 178.

69. Thomas Sowell, *Civil Rights: Rhetoric or Reality?* (New York: Morrow, 1984), pp. 39–40.

70. Ibid., p. 41.
71. Goldwater, *Goldwater,* p. 173; Barry Goldwater, "Civil Rights," *Congressional Record,* June 18, 1964, p. 14319.
72. Goldwater, "Civil Rights."
73. Ibid.
74. Goldwater, *Goldwater,* p. 173.
75. Earl Mazo, "Gov. Scranton's Call to Battle," *New York Herald Tribune,* June 13, 1964.
76. Walter Lippmann, "A Choice But a Bad One," *New York Herald Tribune,* June 30, 1964.
77. White, *Suite 3505,* p. 350.
78. William Scranton to Barry Goldwater, July 12, 1964, Scranton Papers, Pattee Library, Pennsylvania State University.
79. White, *Making of the President,* p. 239.
80. Goldwater, *Goldwater,* pp. 185–186.
81. Honorable Everett McKinley Dirksen Nominating Honorable Barry Goldwater for President, *Official Proceedings of the Twenty-Eighth Republican Convention* (Washington, D.C.: Republican National Committee, 1964), pp. 301–305.
82. Ibid., p. 415.
83. Ibid., pp. 416–418.
84. Ibid., pp. 418–419.
85. White, *Making of the President,* p. 228.

Chapter 7: Landslide

1. Doris Kearns, *Lyndon Johnson and the American Dream* (New York: Harper & Row, 1976), p. 206.
2. Anthony Lewis, "The Issues: Civil Rights, Extremism and Nuclear Policy Are the Major Themes Now," *New York Times,* August 30, 1964.
3. Kathleen Hall Jamieson, *Packaging the Presidency: A History and Criticism of Presidential Campaign Advertising* (New York: Oxford University Press, 1992), p. 186.
4. Ibid., pp. 198–199.
5. Ibid., p. 200; Edwin Diamond and Stephen Bates, *The Spot: The Rise of Political Advertising on Television* (Cambridge, Mass.: MIT Press, 1988), p. 129.
6. Jamieson, *Packaging the Presidency,* p. 200.
7. Ibid., p. 201.
8. Victor Lasky, *It Didn't Start with Watergate* (New York: Dial Press, 1977), p. 181.
9. Diamond and Bates, *The Spot,* p. 137.
10. Jamieson, *Packaging the Presidency,* p. 192; Lasky, *It Didn't Start with Watergate,* p. 180.
11. Milton Cummings, ed., *The National Election of 1964* (Washington, D.C.: The Brookings Institution, 1966), p. 68; Goldwater speech before the American Political Science Association, Chicago, September 11, 1964, William J. Middendorf II Archives, Washington, D.C.
12. Theodore White, *The Making of the President 1964* (New York: Signet Books, 1965), p. 389.
13. Goldwater speech at East St. Louis, Illinois, October 28, 1964, Middendorf Archives, Washington, D.C.
14. Ibid.
15. John Chamberlain, "Barry Won't Play the Demagogue," *Human Events,* October 17, 1964, p. 8; Charles Mohr, "Goldwater Says 'We Are at War,'" *New York Times,* September 20, 1964.

16. Author's interview with Robert Mardian, December 19, 1991.

17. John B. Judis, *William F. Buckley, Jr.: Patron Saint of the Conservatives* (New York: Simon & Schuster, 1988), pp. 230–231.

18. Ibid., p. 232.

19. Ronald Reagan, *An American Life* (New York: Simon & Schuster, 1990), p. 140; Lee Edwards, *Goldwater: The Man Who Made a Revolution* (Washington, D.C.: Regnery, 1995), p. 334.

20. Reagan, *An American Life,* pp. 140–141.

21. Lee Edwards, *Ronald Reagan: A Political Biography* (Houston, Texas: Nordland Publishing, 1981), pp. 69–70.

22. Ronald Reagan, "A Time for Choosing," *Human Events,* November 28, 1964, pp. 8–9.

23. Stephen Hess and David Broder, *The Republican Establishment: The Present and the Future of the G.O.P.* (New York: Harper & Row, 1967), pp. 253–254; author's interview with Henry Salvatori, December 21, 1991.

24. Author's interview with William F. Buckley, Jr., April 13, 1992.

25. Robert Alan Goldberg, *Barry Goldwater* (New Haven, Conn.: Yale University Press, 1995), p. 234.

26. Walter Lippmann, *Washington Post,* November 5, 1964; Tom Wicker on Faber, *The Road to the White House,* p. ix; "The Elections," *Time,* November 13, 1964, p. 5; Chet Huntley, quoted in Gene Shalit and Lawrence K. Grossman, eds., *Somehow It Works* (Garden City, N.Y.: Doubleday, 1965), p. 215; James Reston, *The Road to the White House* (London: Faber & Faber), p. 273.

27. Knowland quote in Robert J. Donovan, *The Future of the Republican Party* (New York: Signet Books, 1964), p. 66; Ronald Reagan, *National Review,* November 17, 1964, p. 1001; George Bush, p. 1053.

28. Buckley and Burnham, *National Review,* November 17, 1964, p. 1000; Meyer, *National Review,* December 1, 1964, p. 1057.

29. "From the Phoenix Ashes," *Human Events,* November 14, 1964, p. 4.

30. *Quotations from Chairman Bill: The Best of William F. Buckley, Jr.,* comp. David Franke (New Rochelle, N.Y.: Arlington House, 1970), p. 96.

31. Author's interview with Anne Edwards, July 20, 1997.

32. Edwards, *Goldwater,* p. 342.

33. See Charles Murray, *Losing Ground: American Social Policy 1950–1980* (New York: Basic Books, 1984). Also numerous studies by the Heritage Foundation such as Robert Rector, "The Poverty Paradox" (The Heritage Foundation, October 1993), which found that after the nation had spent $1.5 trillion on welfare, there were still 30 million "poor" Americans.

34. White, *Making of the President 1964,* page 409.

35. Edwards, *Barry Goldwater,* p. 346; Goldberg, *Barry Goldwater,* p. 219.

36. Author's interview with David Franke, May 28, 1992.

37. Author's interview with William E. Brock, October 28, 1992.

38. Goldberg, *Barry Goldwater,* p. 236.

39. Irving Kristol, "A Letter from Irving Kristol," *National Review,* March 16, 1992, p. S-17.

40. Author's interview with John Sears, June 9, 1992.

41. M. Stanton Evans, *The Future of Conservatism* (New York: Holt, Rinehart and Winston, 1968), p. 135.

42. Ibid., p. 137.

43. Richard A. Ware to James A. Kennedy, November 6, 1964, Private Files of the Earhart Foundation, Ann Arbor, Michigan.

44. Stephen J. Tonsor, "The Foundation and the Academy," *National Review*, May 14, 1982, p. 548.

45. Thomas Sowell to Richard A. Ware, January 9, 1985, Private Files of the Earhart Foundation, Ann Arbor, Michigan.

46. Goldberg, *Barry Goldwater*, p. 237.

47. The September–October issue of *Fact* magazine published a cover article entitled "1, 189 Psychiatrists Say Goldwater Is Psychologically Unfit to Be President." Although the senator dismissed most of the smears of the 1964 campaign, he filed a libel suit against publisher Ralph Ginsburg and his magazine. A libel judgment of $1 in compensatory damages and $75,000 in punitive damages was awarded by a U.S. district court jury in southern New York in 1968 and was upheld when the U.S. Supreme Court denied review in 1970.

48. Author's interview with Mark Rhoads, June 17, 1993.

49. Edwards, *Goldwater*, p. 456.

Chapter 8: The Citizen Politician

1. K. L. Billingsley, "Is California Still the American Dream?" *The World and I* (September 1993): 57.

2. Bill Boyarsky, *The Rise of Ronald Reagan* (New York: Random House, 1968), p. 8.

3. Lee Edwards, *Ronald Reagan: A Political Biography* (Houston: Nordland Publishing, 1981), p. 107.

4. Ibid., p. 75.

5. Ronald Reagan, *An American Life* (New York: Simon & Schuster, 1990), p. 145.

6. Edwards, *Reagan*, p. 76.

7. Ibid., p. 76.

8. William F. Buckley, Jr., *The Unmaking of a Mayor* (New York: Viking Press, 1966), pp. 6–7.

9. Ibid., pp. 91–93.

10. Ibid., p. 93.

11. William A. Rusher, interview with the author, August 20, 1997; Buckley, *Unmaking of a Mayor*, p. 94.

12. "What Makes Buckley Run?" *New York Times*, June 25, 1965; William F. Buckley, Jr., letter to the editor of the *Times*, June 28, 1965, Buckley Papers, Sterling Library, Yale University.

13. Ibid.

14. Buckley, *Unmaking of a Mayor*, p. 120.

15. "As New York Goes . . . ," *National Review*, October 5, 1965, p. 859; "Mr. Buckley Answers Lindsay Charges on Goldwater," news release, Buckley for Mayor, October 25, 1965.

16. Buckley, *Unmaking of a Mayor*, pp. 293–294.

17. Ibid., p. 281.

18. J. Daniel Mahoney, "Where We've Been and Where We're Going," *National Review*, November 2, 1965, p. 977.

19. William F. Buckley, Jr., "Harlem Is in New York City," *National Review*, November 2, 1965, pp. 978–979.

20. Kevin Phillips, *The Emerging Republican Majority* (New Rochelle, N.Y.: Arlington House, 1969), p. 168; John B. Judis, *William F. Buckley, Jr.: Patron Saint of the Conservatives* (New York: Simon & Schuster, 1988), p. 256.

21. Buckley, *Unmaking of a Mayor*, pp. 307–308.

22. Author's telephone interview with Reed Larson, September 11, 1997.
23. Lee Edwards and Anne Edwards, *You Can Make the Difference* (New Rochelle, N.Y.: Arlington House, 1968), p. 80.
24. Ibid.
25. Ibid., p. 81.
26. Ibid.
27. Interview with Larson.
28. Richard A. Viguerie, *The New Right: We're Ready to Lead* (Washington, D.C.: Viguerie, 1980), p. 20.
29. Ibid., p. 21.
30. Ibid., p. 25.
31. Ibid, p. 27.
32. Ibid., p. 29.
33. Ibid., p. 19.
34. Boyarsky, *Rise of Ronald Reagan,* p. 143.
35. Edwards, *Reagan,* p. 79.
36. Reagan, *An American Life,* p. 147.
37. Ibid., p. 148.
38. Edwards, *Reagan,* p. 81.
39. Lou Cannon, *Reagan* (New York: Putnam, 1982), p. 115.
40. Lyn Nofziger, *Nofziger* (Washington, D.C.: Regnery Gateway, 1992), p. 50; Edwards, *Ronald Reagan,* pp. 83–84.
41. Edwards, *Ronald Reagan,* p. 90.
42. Cannon, *Reagan,* p. 111.
43. Nofziger, *Nofziger,* p. 39.
44. Edwards, *Ronald Reagan,* p. 104.
45. Ibid.
46. Cannon, *Reagan,* pp. 108–109.
47. Edwards, *Ronald Reagan,* pp. 116–117.
48. Cannon, *Reagan,* p. 116.
49. Ibid., p. 117.
50. "The Making of a Candidate: A Look at the Reagan Boom," *U.S. News and World Report,* July 24, 1967, p. 53.

Chapter 9: The Real Nixon

1. William Rusher, *The Rise of the Right* (New York: Morrow, 1984), p. 195.
2. Ibid., p. 197.
3. Lee Edwards, *Ronald Reagan: A Political Biography* (Houston: Nordland Publishing, 1981), p. 177.
4. M. Stanton Evans, *The Future of Conservatism* (New York: Holt, Rinehart and Winston, 1968), pp. 286–287.
5. Rusher, *Rise of the Right,* p. 206.
6. The author attended both the Washington and Newport meetings.
7. John B. Judis, *William F. Buckley, Jr.: Patron Saint of the Conservatives* (New York: Simon & Schuster, 1988), p. 280.
8. Ibid.
9. Judis, *William F. Buckley, Jr.,* p. 282.
10. Richard Scammon and Ben Wattenberg, *The Real Majority* (New York: Primus, 1992), p. 2.

11. James T. Patterson, *Grand Expectations: The United States, 1945–1974* (New York: Oxford University Press, 1996), p. 702.

12. Rusher, *Rise of the Right,* p. 213.

13. Barry Goldwater, *With No Apologies* (New York: Morrow, 1979), p. 207.

14. Richard Nixon, *RN: The Memoirs of Richard Nixon* (New York: Grosset & Dunlap, 1978), p. 309.

15. Richard Nixon letter to the author, November 4, 1992.

16. Richard Nixon, *Nixon on the Issues* (New York: Nixon-Agnew Campaign Committee, October 1968), pp. 8, 15, 98, 128.

17. Richard Nixon, *Nixon Speaks Out* (New York: Nixon-Agnew Campaign Committee, 1968), pp. 2, 15–16.

18. Willard Edwards, "Revealing Nixon Speech Devoid of Political Phrases," *Chicago Tribune,* October 9, 1968.

19. Ibid.

20. Patterson, *Grand Expectations,* p. 699.

21. Rusher, *Rise of the Right,* p. 221.

22. Kevin Phillips, *The Emerging Republican Majority* (New Rochelle, N.Y.: Arlington House, 1969), p. 474.

23. Ibid.

24. *Congress and the Nation 1969–1972* (Washington, D.C.: Congressional Quarterly Service, 1973), p. vi.

25. Herbert Stein, "On Nixon's Economics," *Wall Street Journal,* April 27, 1994.

26. Rusher, *Rise of the Right,* pp. 231–232.

27. Ibid.

28. Stein, "On Nixon's Economics"; Milton Friedman quote, Robert Schuettinger and Eamonn Butler, *Forty Centuries of Wage and Price Controls: How Not to Fight Inflation* (Washington, D.C.: The Heritage Foundation, 1979). p. 150.

29. Stanley D. Bachrack, *The Committee of One Million: "China Lobby" Politics* (New York: Columbia University Press, 1976), p. 269.

30. Lee Edwards, *Missionary for Freedom: The Life and Times of Walter Judd* (New York: Paragon House, 1990), p. 300.

31. Nixon, *RN,* p. 552.

32. Theodore H. White, *The Making of the President 1972* (New York: Atheneum, 1973), p. 59.

33. "A Declaration," *National Review,* August 10, 1971, p. 842.

34. Ibid.

35. See pp. 302–304 of Judis, *William F. Buckley, Jr.,* for details of Kissinger's ardent and effective courtship of Buckley.

36. Ibid., p. 332.

37. Ibid., pp. 332–333; Allan Ryskind, interview with the author, June 8, 1997; H. R. Haldeman, *The Haldeman Diaries: Inside the Nixon White House* (New York: Putnam, 1994), pp. 356–357, 444–445. According to Haldeman, Nixon thought that John Connally was "the only man who could be President" (p. 445).

38. Tom Winter recalled that while "there were a lot of conservatives out there . . . they weren't going to take on the President of the United States." See interview with Thomas S. Winter by Mary Ann Buschka, "Right Rebellion: The Conservative Movement and John Ashbrook's 1972 Campaign," University of Delaware, May 1993.

39. "Nixon Vow of Change Unfulfilled—Ashbrook," *Manchester (N.H.) Union-Leader,* February 17, 1972; press release, United Republicans of California, May 1972,

Human Events Archives, Washington, D.C.; "Abortion, Pot Studied by G.O.P." *Chicago Tribune,* August 15, 1972.

40. Jack Rosenthal, "Ashbrook, Nixon's Rival on the Right, Finding Florida Campaign Trail Rough," *New York Times,* February 15, 1972.

41. Ibid.

42. Charles Moser, *Promise and Hope* (Washington, D.C.: Free Congress Foundation, 1974), p. 8.

43. Edwin McDowell, *Barry Goldwater: Portrait of an Arizonan* (Chicago: Regnery, 1964), p. 137.

44. Edwards, *Goldwater: The Man Who Made a Revolution* (Washington, D.C.: Regnery, 1995), pp. 82–84.

45. Richard A. Viguerie, *The New Right: We're Ready to Lead* (Washington, D.C.: Viguerie, 1980), p. 32.

46. Rusher, *Rise of the Right,* p. 245; "Lead-Off Primary: Nixon Faces Test Within Party," *U.S. News and World Report,* February 14, 1972, p. 36.

47. Don Oberdorfer, "Has Nixon Muzzled the Right?" *Arizona Republic,* June 21, 1972.

48. Moser, *Promise and Hope,* p. 36.

49. "Sisyphus and Mr. Ashbrook," *Richmond News Leader,* January 4, 1972.

50. *Congress and the Nation 1969–1972* (Washington, D.C.: Congressional Quarterly Service, 1973), p. 22.

51. Rusher, *Rise of the Right,* p. 251; Nixon, *RN,* p. 717.

52. Godfrey Hodgson, *The World Turned Right Side Up* (Boston: Houghton Mifflin, 1996), pp. 124–127.

53. Haldeman, *Diaries,* p. 444.

54. Paul Gottfried, *The Conservative Movement,* rev. ed. (New York: Twayne, 1993), p. 78. Also see page 97 for a brief discussion of some similarities between the New Right and neoconservatism.

Chapter 10: New Right and Old Left

1. H. R. Haldeman, *The Haldeman Diaries: Inside the Nixon White House* (New York: Putnam, 1994), pp. 506–507; Barry Goldwater, *With No Apologies* (New York: Morrow, 1979), p. 249.

2. Goldwater, *With No Apologies.*

3. Ibid., p. 251.

4. "Watergate or Waterloo?" *Right Report,* April 9, 1973, p. 1.

5. Clark R. Mollenhoff, *Game Plan for Disaster: An Ombudsman's Report on the Nixon Years* (New York: Norton, 1976), p. 342.

6. "Is There a Conservative Consensus on Watergate?" *Right Report,* July 9, 1973, p. 1.

7. Goldwater, *With No Apologies,* p. 264.

8. Ibid.

9. Barry Goldwater with Jack Casserly, *Goldwater* (New York: Doubleday, 1988), p. 265.

10. Ibid., p. 272.

11. "Will Nixon Survive?" *Right Report,* April 8, 1994, p. 1.

12. *Congress and the Nation,* vol. 4 (Washington, D.C.: Congressional Quarterly Service, 1995), p. 938.

13. Ibid.

14. Ibid., pp. 942–944.

15. Ibid., p. 959.

16. Lee Edwards, *Goldwater: The Man Who Made a Revolution* (Washington, D.C.: Regnery, 1995), p. 380.

17. Ibid., p. 381.

18. Ibid., p. 400.

19. *1974 CQ Almanac,* p. 892.

20. Robert Goldberg, *Barry Goldwater* (New Haven, Conn.: Yale University Press, 1995), p. 282.

21. Goldwater, *Goldwater,* p. 280.

22. Jon Utley, interview with the author, October 5, 1997, San Antonio, Texas.

23. Gerald Ford, *A Time to Heal* (New York: Harper & Row, 1979), pp. 142–143.

24. Richard A. Viguerie, *The New Right: We're Ready to Lead* (Falls Church, Va.: Viguerie, 1980), p. 51.

25. Ibid., p. 52.

26. Ibid., p. 54.

27. Ibid., pp. 54–55.

28. Kevin P. Phillips, "Notes on the New Right," *Baltimore News-American,* June 25, 1976; "The Growing Importance of the New Right," *New York Daily Press,* October 13, 1978.

29. Richard A. Viguerie and Lee Edwards, "Goldwater: Leader or Legend?" *Conservative Digest* (January 1976): 6–10.

30. Ibid.

31. Viguerie, *The New Right,* p. 57.

32. Ibid., p. 60.

33. William J. Lanouette, "The New Right—'Revolutionaries' Out After the 'Lunch-Pail' Vote," *National Journal,* January 21, 1978, p. 88.

34. Viguerie, *The New Right,* p. 60.

35. Myra MacPherson, "The New Right Brigade: John Terry Dolan's NCPAC Targets Liberals and the Federal Election Commission," *Washington Post,* August 10, 1980.

36. Ibid.

37. Viguerie, *The New Right,* p. 63.

38. Ibid.

39. John Fialka, "Arch-Conservative's Crusade: Abolish the Republican Party," *Washington Star,* June 24, 1975.

40. Robert W. Merry, "Kingmaker with a Cause," *National Observer,* February 21, 1976; Viguerie, *The New Right,* pp. 32–33.

41. Viguerie, *The New Right,* p. 33.

42. Nick Thimmesch, "The Grass-Roots Dollar Chase—Ready on the Right," *New York,* June 9, 1975, p. 59.

43. William A. Rusher, *The Rise of the Right* (New York: Morrow, 1984), p. 268.

44. Lou Cannon, *President Reagan: The Role of a Lifetime* (New York: Simon & Schuster, 1991), p. 185.

45. Rusher, *Rise of the Right,* p. 270.

46. "Is It Time for a New Party?" interview with Ronald Reagan, *Conservative Digest,* May 1975, pp. 4–8.

47. Stephen Isaacs, "Newcomers' Hopes Are Scuttled at 3rd-Party Session," *Washington Post,* August 28, 1976.

48. Ibid.

49. Ibid.

50. Lee Edwards, *You Can Make the Difference* (New Rochelle, N.Y.: Arlington House, 1980), p. 198.

51. Ibid., p. 201.

52. Ibid., p. 202.

53. Ibid., p. 203.

54. Ibid., p. 286.

55. William Manchester, *The Glory and the Dream: A Narrative History of America 1932–1972* (Boston: Little, Brown, 1973), 2:1430.

56. Robert H. Bork, *Slouching Towards Gomorrah: Modern Liberalism and American Decline* (New York: ReganBooks, 1996), p. 1.

57. Nathan Glazer, "On Being Deradicalized," *Commentary* (October 1970): 74–80.

58. George Nash, *The Conservative Intellectual Movement in America Since 1945* (Wilmington, Del.: Intercollegiate Studies Institute, 1996), pp. 314–315.

59. Ibid., p. 314.

60. Ibid., p. 309; Peter Steinfels, *The Neoconservatives: The Men Who Are Changing America's Politics* (New York: Simon & Schuster, 1979), pp. 47–48.

61. Nash, *Conservative Intellectual Movement*, p. 312.

62. Theodore H. White, "The Action Intellectuals," *Life*, June 15, 1967, p. 35; Steinfels, *Neoconservatives*, p. 9.

63. "Is America Turning Right?" *Newsweek*, November 7, 1977, p. 34.

64. William E. Simon, "A Tribute to Irving Kristol," in Christopher Demuth and William Kristol, eds., *The Neoconservative Imagination: Essays in Honor of Irving Kristol* (Washington, D.C.: AEI Press, 1995), p. 86.

65. Sidney Blumenthal, *The Rise of the Counter-Establishment: From Conservative Ideology to Political Power* (New York: Times Books, 1986), p. 148.

66. Godfrey Hodgson, *The World Turned Right Side Up* (Boston: Houghton Mifflin, 1996), p. 177.

67. Ibid., p. 178.

68. Ibid., p. 180.

69. Ed McAteer, telephone interview with the author, May 3, 1994.

70. Hodgson, *World Turned Right Side Up*, p. 181; Ed McAteer, interview, May 3, 1994.

Chapter 11: Winning Conservative

1. Austin Ranney, *The American Elections of 1980* (Washington, D.C.: American Enterprise Institute, 1981), p. 31.

2. *Human Events*, August 25, 1979, p. 1.

3. Rowland Evans and Robert Novak, *The Reagan Revolution* (New York: Dutton, 1981), p. 48.

4. Lee Edwards, *Ronald Reagan: A Political Biography* (Houston: Nordland Publishing, 1981), p. 165.

5. Charles D. Hobbs, "How Ronald Reagan Governed California," *National Review*, January 17, 1975, p. 39.

6. Lyn Nofziger, *Nofziger* (Washington, D.C.: Regnery Gateway, 1992), p. 179.

7. Lou Cannon, "Reagan's Victories Bust Ford Strategy," *Washington Post*, May 9, 1976.

8. M. Stanton Evans, conversation with the author, May 10, 1996.

9. "Republican Rumble," *Time*, May 17, 1976, p. 11.

10. Ibid., p. 11.

11. "A President 'in Jeopardy,'" *Newsweek*, May 17, 1976, p. 22.

12. Edwards, *Ronald Reagan*, p. 181.

13. Lee Edwards, *Goldwater: The Man Who Made a Revolution* (Washington, D.C.: Regnery Publishing, 1995), p. 416.

14. Ibid.

15. Frank van der Linden, *The Real Reagan* (New York: Morrow, 1981), p. 144.

16. Ibid.

17. "Reagan: Leading Contender, But Age Looms," *U.S. News and World Report,* May 7, 1979, pp. 54–56.

18. Edwards, *Ronald Reagan,* p. 188.

19. Ibid.; Tom Goff, "Legacy for State: Footprints, But No Permanent Monuments or Scars," *Los Angeles Times,* September 29, 1974.

20. "Reagan: GOP's Front-Runner Starts to Run," *U.S. News and World Report,* November 26, 1979, p. 48.

21. Van der Linden, *The Real Reagan,* p. 171.

22. Jeff Greenfield, *The Real Campaign* (New York: Summit Books, 1982), p. 48.

23. Ibid.

24. "Reagan Regains Front-Runner Role," *Human Events,* March 8, 1980, pp. 1, 19; "George Bush Slipped Here," *Nation,* March 8, 1980, pp. 260-261.

25. "Reagan's Rousing Return," *Time,* March 10, 1980, pp. 12-16.

26. Greenfield, *The Real Campaign,* p. 48.

27. "Anderson Tiptoes in as Independent," *Human Events,* May 3, 1980, p. 3.

28. Greenfield, *The Real Campaign,* p. 159.

29. Ibid., p. 160.

30. "Ford on His Quandary," *Newsweek,* July 28, 1980, p. 25.

31. "Inside the Jerry Ford Drama," *Time,* July 28, 1980; van der Linden, *The Real Reagan,* p. 213.

32. "Hour by Hour, the Deal That Got Away," U.S. *News and World Report,* July 28, 1980, pp. 22-23.

33. Van der Linden, *The Real Reagan,* p. 217.

34. Ibid.

35. Ibid.

36. "Inside the Jerry Ford Drama," pp. 16–19.

37. Greenfield, *The Real Campaign,* p. 164.

38. "Ford on His Quandary."

39. "George Bush on His Role as No. 2," *U.S. News and World Report,* July 28, 1980, pp. 23–24.

40. Lee Edwards, *You Can Make the Difference* (New Rochelle, N.Y.: Arlington House, 1980), p. 288.

41. Ibid., p. 289.

42. Ibid., p. 292.

43. Lou Cannon, *President Reagan: The Role of a Lifetime* (New York: Simon & Schuster, 1991), p. 280.

44. Edwards, *Ronald Reagan,* p. 220.

45. "Oh, I'll Take the Low Road," *Newsweek,* September 29, 1980, pp. 22–23.

46. "Two for the Show," *Time,* September 22, 1980, pp. 8–9; William F. Buckley, Jr., "Reagan vs. Anderson," *National Review,* October 17, 1980, pp. 1286–1287.

47. "Why Anderson Narrowly Won the Debate," *Human Events,* October 4, 1980, pp. 3–4; Edwards, *Ronald Reagan,* p. 222.

48. Robert Nagle, *American Conservatism: An Illustrated History* (New York: Philosophical Library, 1989), p. 278.

49. Greenfield, *The Real Campaign,* pp. 235–241. Greenfield's almost minute-by-minute analysis of the Reagan-Carter debate is required reading.

50. Ibid., p. 241.

51. "Time to Pull Together" (excerpts from transcript of presidential debate), *U.S. News and World Report,* November 10, 1980, pp. 100 ff.

52. Ibid.

53. Edwards, *Ronald Reagan,* p. 232; Greenfield, *The Real Campaign,* pp. 244–245.

54. Cannon, *President Reagan,* p. 300.

55. "Start of a New Era," *U.S. News and World Report,* November 17, 1980, pp. 21–66, 90–110; "That Winning Smile," *Time,* November 17, 1980, pp. 20–24 ff.; "Election Special," *Newsweek,* November 17, 1980, pp. 27–34 ff.

56. Peter Hannaford, ed., *Recollections of Reagan: A Portrait of Ronald Reagan* (New York: Morrow, 1997), p. 45.

57. "Victory at Last!" *Human Events,* November 15, 1980, p. 23.

Chapter 12: Golden Years

1. Edwin Meese III, *With Reagan* (Washington, D.C.: Regnery Gateway, 1992), p. 73.

2. Martin Anderson, *Revolution* (San Diego: Harcourt Brace Jovanovich, 1988), p. 139.

3. "A Modest Program," *Wall Street Journal,* September 22, 1980.

4. Anderson, *Revolution,* p. 232.

5. "A Time for Choosing," in *A Time for Choosing: The Speeches of Ronald Reagan 1961–1982* (Chicago: Regnery Gateway, 1983), pp. 41–57; Meese, *With Reagan,* p. 121.

6. Lou Cannon, *President Reagan: The Role of a Lifetime* (New York: Simon & Schuster, 1991), p. 236.

7. "RWR's Own New Deal," *Newsweek,* March 2, 1981.

8. Cannon, *President Reagan,* p. 176.

9. Ibid., p. 177.

10. David Frum, *Dead Right* (New York: Basic Books, 1994), p. 42.

11. "President Reagan Inaugural Address," *New York Times,* January 21, 1981.

12. Ronald Reagan, *An American Life* (New York: Simon & Schuster, 1990), pp. 196–197.

13. Ibid., p. 316.

14. Peter J. Ferrara, "Welfare," in *Issues '94: The Candidates' Briefing Book* (Washington, D.C.: Heritage Foundation, 1994), pp. 121–122.

15. Kevin R. Hopkins, "Social Welfare Policy: A Failure of Vision," in David Boaz, ed., *Assessing the Reagan Years* (Washington, D.C.: Cato Institute, 1989), p. 211.

16. Donald Devine, *Reagan's Terrible Swift Sword: An Insider's Story of Abuse and Reform Within the Federal Bureaucracy* (Ottawa, Ill.: Jameson Books, 1991), p. 1.

17. Ron Haskin and Representative Hank Brown, "A Billion Here, a Billion There," *Policy Review* (Summer 1989): 22–28.

18. Ronald F. Docksai, "Health," in Charles L. Heatherly and Burton Yale Pines, eds., *Mandate for Leadership III: Policy Strategies for the 1990s* (Washington, D.C.: Heritage Foundation, 1989), p. 236.

19. Lee Edwards, *Ronald Reagan: A Political Biography* (Houston: Nordland Publishing, 1981), p. 69.

20. Cannon, *President Reagan,* p. 247.

21. Ibid., p. 179.

22. Reagan, *An American Life,* p. 335.

23. Stephen Moore, "Who Really Balanced the Budget?" *American Enterprise* (November–December 1997): p. 52.

24. Dinesh D'Souza, *Ronald Reagan: How an Ordinary Man Became an Extraordinary Leader* (New York: Free Press, 1997), p. 104.

25. Ibid., p. 126.

26. Laurence I. Barrett, *Gambling with History: Ronald Reagan in the White House* (Garden City, N.Y.: Doubleday, 1983), pp. 80–93.

27. D'Souza, *Ronald Reagan,* p. 89; Lee Edwards, *The Power of Ideas: The Heritage Foundation at 25 Years* (Ottawa, Ill.: Jameson Books, 1997), p. 55.

28. Paul E. Peterson and Mark Rom, "Lower Taxes, More Spending and Budget Deficits," in Charles O. Jones, ed., *The Reagan Legacy: Promise and Performance* (Chatham, N.J.: Chatham House Publishers, 1988), pp. 219–220.

29. Peter Hannaford, ed., *Recollections of Reagan: A Portrait of Ronald Reagan* (New York: Morrow, 1997), p. xiii.

30. Meese, *With Reagan,* p. 147.

31. Lyn Nofziger, *Nofziger* (Washington, D.C.: Regnery Gateway, 1992), p. 285.

32. "Reagan's State of the Union Address," in *Reagan: The Next Four Years* (Washington, D.C.: Congressional Quarterly, 1985), p. 153.

33. "Congress Enacts Sweeping Overhaul of Tax Law," in *1986 CQ Almanac* (Washington, D.C.: Congressional Quarterly Press, 1989), p. 491.

34. John B. Judis, "Pop-Con Politics: Conservatives in the GOP," *New Republic,* September 3, 1984, p. 18.

35. Stuart M. Butler, Michael Sanera, and W. Bruce Weinrod, eds., *Mandate for Leadership II: Continuing the Conservative Revolution* (Washington, D.C.: Heritage Foundation, 1984), p. 3.

36. Robert Rector and Michael Sanera, eds., *Steering the Elephant: How Washington Works* (New York: Universe Books, 1987).

37. Peter J. Ferrara, "What Really Happened in the 1980s?" in Issues '94: *The Candidates' Briefing Book* (Washington, D.C.: Heritage Foundation, 1994), pp. 16–17; Richard B. McKenzie, *What Went Right in the 1980s* (San Francisco: Pacific Research Institute for Public Policy, 1994), p. 1.

38. David M. O'Brien, "The Reagan Judges: His Most Enduring Legacy?" in *Reagan Legacy,* pp. 60–61.

39. Ibid., p. 89.

40. Ibid., p. 62.

41. Ibid., p. 74.

42. Suzanne Garment, "The War Against Robert H. Bork," *Commentary* (January 1988): 17–26.

43. "Reagan Picks Bork, Sparks Liberal Uproar," *Washington Times,* July 2, 1987.

44. Cannon, *President Reagan,* p. 807.

45. O'Brien, "Reagan Judges," p. 94.

46. Cannon, *President Reagan,* p. 802.

47. Paul Gottfried, *The Conservative Movement,* rev. ed. (New York: Twayne, 1993), p. 104.

48. "Ronald Reagan, Kremlin Dupe?" *Chicago Tribune,* December 9, 1987.

49. Ibid.

50. Howard Phillips to the author, August 13, 1997.

51. Richard A. Viguerie, *The Establishment vs. The People: Is a New Populist Revolt on the Way?* (Chicago: Regnery Gateway, 1983), pp. 10–11.

52. Gottfried, *Conservative Movement,* p. 114.

53. Lee Edwards, "Paul Weyrich: Conscience of New Right Fighting for Conservative Victory in '82," *Conservative Digest* (July 1981): 2.

54. Ibid.

55. Gottfried, *Conservative Movement,* pp. 114–115.

56. William J. Bennett to the author, September 3, 1997.

57. Peter J. Ferrara, "The Politics of Substance," in *Issues '94* (Washington, D.C.: Heritage Foundation, 1994), p. 1.

Chapter 13: The Reagan Doctrine

1. "Start of the Reagan Era," *U.S. News and World Report,* January 26, 1981, pp. 18–20.

2. Ronald Reagan, *An American Life* (New York: Simon & Schuster, 1990), p. 267.

3. Peter Schweizer, *Victory: The Reagan Administration's Secret Strategy That Hastened the Collapse of the Soviet Union* (New York: Atlantic Monthly Press, 1994), p. xiv.

4. Ibid.

5. Ibid., p. xv.

6. Dinesh D'Souza, *Ronald Reagan: How an Ordinary Man Became an Extraordinary Leader* (New York: Free Press, 1997), p. 140.

7. Lou Cannon, *President Reagan: The Role of a Lifetime* (New York: Simon & Schuster, 1991), pp. 314–315.

8. Ibid.

9. "Ronald Reagan's Flower Power," *New York Times,* June 9, 1982.

10. Schweizer, *Victory,* p. xv.

11. Ibid.

12. D'Souza, *Ronald Reagan,* p. 180.

13. William F. Buckley, Jr., "So Long, Evil Empire," *National Review,* July 8, 1988; D'Souza, *Ronald Reagan,* p. 134.

14. See Eugene Lyons, *Our Secret Allies: The Peoples of Russia* (New York: Duell, Sloan and Pearce, 1953).

15. Schweizer, *Victory,* p. 126.

16. Ibid., p. 131.

17. Charles Krauthammer, "The Reagan Doctrine," *Time,* April 1, 1985, p. 54.

18. Cannon, *President Reagan,* p. 372.

19. Reagan, *An American Life,* p. 479.

20. Mark P. Lagon, *The Reagan Doctrine: Sources of American Conduct in the Cold War's Last Chapter* (Westport, Conn.: Praeger, 1994), p. 4.

21. Ibid.

22. Ibid., p. 93.

23. Jay Winik, *On the Brink: The Dramatic, Behind-the-Scenes Saga of the Reagan Era and the Men and Women Who Won the Cold War* (New York: Simon & Schuster, 1996), pp. 80–81.

24. Ibid., pp. 83–84.

25. Ibid., p. 100.

26. Ibid., p. 102.

27. Ibid., pp. 105–106.

28. Ibid., p. 108.

29. Ibid., p. 114.

30. Edwin Meese III, *With Reagan* (Washington, D.C.: Regnery Gateway, 1992), pp. 169–170.

31. Ibid., p. 170.

32. See Reagan, *An American Life,* pp. 568–571, for Reagan's discussion of the phrase.

33. Vaclav Havel, "Words on Words," *New York Review of Books,* January 18, 1990, p. 58; D'Souza, *Ronald Reagan,* p. 135.

34. "Goliath in Grenada," *New York Times,* October 30, 1983.
35. Constantine Menges, *Inside the National Security Council* (New York: Simon & Schuster, 1988), p. 89.
36. Ibid., p. 158.
37. Andrew E. Busch and Elizabeth Edwards Spalding, "1983," *Policy Review* (Fall 1993): 72.
38. D'Souza, *Ronald Reagan,* p. 148.
39. Busch and Spalding, "1983," p. 72.
40. Howard Phillips, *New York Times,* December 11, 1987; George Shultz, *Turmoil and Triumph* (New York: Scribners, 1993), p. 1006.
41. Cannon, *President Reagan,* p. 739; Geoffrey Smith, *Reagan and Thatcher* (New York: Norton, 1991), p. 146.
42. Caspar W. Weinberger, *Fighting for Peace* (New York: Warner Books, 1990), pp. 293–294; Caspar Weinberger, "U.S. Defense Strategy," in *The Reagan Foreign Policy,* ed. William G. Hyland (New York: New American Library, 1987), p. 185.
43. Edward Teller in *Recollections of Reagan,* ed. Peter Hannaford (New York: Morrow, 1997), p. 169; D'Souza, *Ronald Reagan,* p. 174.
44. Weinberger, *Fighting for Peace,* p. 296.
45. Daniel O. Graham, *Confessions of a Cold Warrior* (Fairfax, Va.: Preview Press, 1995), p. 103.
46. Cannon, *President Reagan,* p. 319.
47. Ibid.
48. Ibid., p. 320.
49. George A. Keyworth, interview, September 28, 1987, Oral History Project, Ronald Reagan Presidential Library, Simi Valley, California.
50. Cannon, *President Reagan,* p. 332.
51. *New York Times,* March 27, 1983.
52. "High Frontier Launched," *Human Events,* May 22, 1982, p. 15.
53. Weinberger, *Fighting for Peace,* p. 316.
54. Ibid., p. 327.
55. Ibid.
56. Graham, *Confessions of a Cold Warrior,* p. 165.
57. Ibid., p. 153.
58. Richard Gid Powers, *Not Without Honor: The History of American Anti-Communism* (New York: Free Press, 1995), p. 429.
59. Carl Bernstein, "The Holy Alliance," *Time,* February 24, 1992, pp. 28–35; Lech Walesa, *Proceedings* of "The Failure of Communism: the Western Response," an international conference sponsored by Radio Free Europe/Radio Liberty, November 15, 1989, p. 47.
60. Winik, *On the Brink,* p. 227; D'Souza, *Ronald Reagan,* p. 167.
61. Peter B. Levy, *Encyclopedia of the Reagan-Bush Years* (Westport, Conn.: Greenwood Press, 1996), p. 234.
62. See Burton Yale Pines, "The Ten Legacies of Ronald Reagan," *Policy Review* (Spring 1989): 16–20.
63. See Reagan, *An American Life,* pp. 680–683.
64. Ibid., p. 708.
65. Alexis de Tocqueville, *The Old Regime and the Revolution* (New York: Harper, 1856), p. 214.
66. Cannon, *President Reagan,* p. 786.

67. Reagan, *An American Life,* pp. 713–714.
68. Cannon, *President Reagan,* p. 786.
69. Reagan, *An American Life,* p. 715.
70. Cannon, *President Reagan,* pp. 656, 661.
71. Reagan, *An American Life,* p. 513.
72. Cannon, *President Reagan,* p. 653.
73. Quoted in James Schlesinger, "Reykjavik and Revelations: A Turn of the Tide?" in *America and the World 1986,* ed. William G. Hyland (New York: Council on Foreign Relations, 1987), p. 441.
74. Meese, *With Reagan,* p. 271.
75. Cannon, *President Reagan,* p. 704.
76. Powers, *Not Without Honor,* p. 411.
77. "Contras Can Win," *Human Events,* March 22, 1986, p. 17.
78. Powers, *Not Without Honor,* p. 411.
79. Meese, *With Reagan,* p. 286.
80. Menges, *Inside the National Security Council,* p. 317.
81. Select Committee of the House and Senate, *Report of the Congressional Committees Investigating the Iran-Contra Affair* (Washington, D.C.: Government Printing Office, 1987), p. 21.
82. Ibid., pp. 437–438.
83. Cannon, *President Reagan,* p. 831.
84. *Reagan: The Next Four Years* (Washington, D.C.: Congressional Quarterly Press, 1984), p. 15.
85. Cannon, *President Reagan,* p. 549.
86. Ibid., p. 548.
87. Ibid., p. 550.
88. "Why Conservatives Should Rally Around Jack Kemp," *Human Events,* January 23, 1988, p. 1.
89. Thomas Atwood to the author, August 12, 1997.
90. Patrick J. Buchanan, "Jack Kemp and the Conservatives," *Human Events,* January 2, 1988, p. 8.
91. Herbert S. Parmet, *George Bush: The Life of a Lone Star Yankee* (New York: Scribner, 1997), p. 335.
92. Ibid., p. 350.
93. Ibid.
94. *1988 CQ Almanac* (Washington, D.C.: Congressional Quarterly, 1989), pp. 9A–10A.
95. "The Week," *National Review,* December 9, 1988, p. 10.

Chapter 14: Contracts Made and Broken

1. Herbert S. Parmet, *George Bush: The Life of a Lone Star Yankee* (New York: Scribner, 1997), p. 364.
2. "Do We Need Another Establishment President?" *Conservative Digest* (January 1984): 6–7.
3. Dan Balz and Charles R. Babcock, "Gingrich, Allies Made Waves and Impression; Conservative Rebels Harassed the House," *Washington Post,* December 20, 1994.
4. Dick Williams, *Newt! Leader of the Second American Revolution* (Marietta, Ga.: Longstreet Press, 1995), p. 109.
5. Ibid.

6. M. Stanton Evans, "Democrats Did in Wright, Smeared Foley," *Human Events,* p. 8.

7. Dan Balz and Serge F. Kovaleski, "Gingrich Divided GOP, Conquered the Agenda; Revolt Gave Party a Glimpse of the Future," *Washington Post,* December 21, 1994.

8. "Capital Brief," *Human Events,* April 1, 1989, p. 2.

9. Ibid.

10. Balz and Kovaleski, "Gingrich Divided GOP."

11. Ibid.

12. Ibid.

13. Paul Weyrich, interview with the author, December 2, 1997.

14. "Survey of East European Economies," *New York Times,* December 20, 1987.

15. Ivo Banc, ed., *Eastern Europe in Revolution* (Ithaca, N.Y.: Cornell University Press, 1992), p. 3.

16. Lee Edwards, *Missionary for Freedom: The Life and Times of Walter Judd* (New York: Paragon House, 1990), p. 323.

17. Dale Russakoff and Dan Balz, "After Political Victory, A Personal Revolution," *Washington Post,* December 19, 1994.

18. Newt Gingrich, with David Drake and Marianne Gingrich, *Window of Opportunity: A Blueprint for the Future* (New York: T. Doherty Associates in association with Baen Enterprises, 1984), p. 219.

19. Ibid.

20. Newt Gingrich, *To Renew America* (New York: HarperCollins, 1995), p. 23.

21. Judith Warner and Max Berley, *Newt Gingrich: Speaker to America* (New York: Signet, 1995), p. 30.

22. Ibid. p. 31.

23. Williams, *Newt!* p. 79.

24. Newt Gingrich, interview with the author, February 13, 1998.

25. Warner and Berley, *Newt Gingrich,* p. 53.

26. Ibid., p. 62.

27. Ibid.

28. Ibid., pp. 62–63.

29. Williams, *Newt!,* p. 84; Dale Russakoff, "He Knew What He Wanted," *Washington Post,* December 18, 1994.

30. Warner and Berley, *Newt Gingrich,* p. 67.

31. Ibid., p. 82.

32. Ibid.

33. Paul Weyrich, interview with the author, December 2, 1997.

34. Ibid.

35. Edwin J. Feulner, Jr., interview with the author, June 11, 1996.

36. Weyrich interview.

37. Steven K. Beckner, "Rep. Newt Gingrich: A New Conservative Leader for the '80s," *Conservative Digest* (May 1982): 11.

38. Ibid., p. 6.

39. Ibid., p. 8.

40. Ibid., p. 9.

41. Ibid., p. 10.

42. David Broder, *Changing of the Guard: Power and Leadership in America* (New York: Simon & Schuster, 1980), p. 461.

43. Gingrich, *To Renew America,* p. 119.

44. Williams, *Newt!,* pp. 98–99; Balz and Babcock, "Gingrich, Allies Made Waves."

45. Balz and Babcock, "Gingrich, Allies Made Waves."

46. Ibid.

47. Williams, *Newt!* p. 99.

48. Richard Armey, fax to the author, December 19, 1994.

49. Ibid.

50. Balz and Babcock, "Gingrich, Allies Made Waves."

51. Ibid.

52. Ibid.

53. Ronald Reagan, "Our Noble Vision: An Opportunity Society for All," *Human Events,* March 17, 1984, p. 214.

54. Balz and Babcock, "Gingrich, Allies Made Waves."

55. Ibid.

56. Eleanor Clift, "Now, a Whole Newt World," *Newsweek,* November 21, 1994, p. 40.

57. Balz and Kovaleski, "Gingrich Divided GOP."

58. Ibid.

59. Ibid.

60. M. Stanton Evans, "Gingrich, Conservatives Can Stop a Tax Hike," *Human Events,* August 4, 1990; "New Taxes Threaten Recession, Could Lead to Higher Spending, Study Says," Heritage Foundation news release, May 17, 1990; "Economics Panel Labels Tax Hike Unnecessary," Heritage Foundation news release, May 30, 1990.

61. Daniel F. Mitchell, "Bush's Deplorable Flip-Flop on Taxes," Heritage Foundation Executive Memorandum, June 29, 1990.

62. "Inside Washington," *Human Events,* August 11, 1990, p. 3.

63. Williams, *Newt!,* p. 126.

64. Ibid., pp. 126–127.

65. "Read My Hips?" *National Review,* November 5, 1990, p. 18.

66. "President Bush's Budget Debacle," *Human Events,* October 13, 1990, p. 1.

67. Burton Yale Pines, interview with the author, May 9, 1996.

68. Patrick J. Buchanan, "The End of the Reagan Revolution," *Human Events,* October 13, 1990, p. 5.

69. J. A. Parker, interview with the author, January 13, 1998.

70. Allan C. Brownfeld, "Black Conservatives: A Growing Force," *Human Events,* September 21, 1991.

71. Allan C. Brownfeld, "Black Conservatives Emerge as Major Force," *Human Events,* January 3, 1981, p. 5.

72. "Supreme Mystery," *Newsweek,* September 16, 1991, p. 31.

73. Herb Boyd, "Clarence Thomas and His Right-Wing Bedfellows," *New York Amsterdam News,* August 31, 1991.

74. Allan Brownfeld, "The Tumultuous Journey of Clarence Thomas," *Campus Report,* February–March 1997, p. 7.

75. Lee Edwards, "The All-Important Suburban Vote," *The World & I,* November 1992, p. 29.

76. "Buchanan's Splendid Showing in New Hampshire," *Human Events,* February 29, 1992, p. 1.

77. Lee Edwards, "Why Bush Lost," *The World & I,* February 1993, pp. 27–28.

78. "Wave of Diversity Spared Many Incumbents," *Congressional Quarterly Almanac* 68 (1992): 15-A.

79. "Why Gingrich Nearly Lost," *Human Events,* August 8, 1992, p. 4.

80. John O'Sullivan, "ITYS, Number 453," *National Review,* November 30, 1992, p. 6; "Not with a Bang, . . ." *National Review,* November 30, 1992, p. 18.

81. "Capital Briefs," *Human Events,* November 28, 1992, p. 2; Edwin J. Feulne, Jr., "A New 'Mandate' for Limited Government," the Heritage Foundation, January 4, 1993.

82. Donald Devine, "Major Schools of Republicanism," *The World & I,* February 1993, p. 45.

83. Feulner, "New 'Mandate' for Limited Government."

84. Lee Edwards, "Why Bush Lost—and What It Means," *The World & I,* February 1992, pp. 28–29.

85. See Bill Clinton interview on CNN, April 20, 1992.

Chapter 15: Newt! Newt! Newt!

1. Newt Gingrich, "The Washington Establishment vs. the American People," August 22, 1990, Heritage Foundation.

2. Ibid.

3. Ibid.

4. Juliet Eilperin and Jim Vande Hei, *Roll Call,* October 6, 1997, p. 20.

5. "Democrats Reeling from Big Kentucky Defeat," *Human Events,* June 3, 1994, p. 1.

6. Newt Gingrich, *To Renew America* (New York: HarperCollins, 1995), p. 124.

7. Marshall Wittmann, interview with the author, January 5, 1998.

8. Ralph Reed, Jr., "Casting a Wider Net," *Policy Review* (Summer 1993): 31.

9. "GOP 'Contract with America' a Good Start on Needed Reform," *Human Events,* October 7, 1994, p. 16.

10. Cal Thomas, "Politicians Cannot Restore Values," *Human Events,* October 7, 1994, p. 11.

11. Judith Warner and Max Berley, *Newt Gingrich: Speaker to America* (New York: Signet, 1995), pp. 182–183.

12. Gingrich, *To Renew America,* p. 126.

13. Dick Williams, *Newt! Leader of the Second American Revolution* (Marietta, Ga.: Longstreet Press, 1995), p. 151.

14. Warner and Berley, *Newt Gingrich,* p. 185.

15. Charles Krauthammer, "Republican Mandate," *Washington Post,* November 11, 1994.

16. Dick Armey, "Democrats Falsely Assail 'Contract with America,'" *Human Events,* October 28, 1994, p. 3.

17. "Clinton Remains a Political Pariah," *Human Events,* October 28, 1994.

18. John Gizzi, "A GOP House in '94?" *Human Events,* October 28, 1994, p. 12.

19. *Congressional Quarterly Almanac, 103rd Congress, 2nd Session* (Washington, D.C.: Congressional Quarterly, 1995), p. 561. I have relied on the authoritative *CQ Almanac* for much of my analysis of the 1994 elections.

20. "Dr. Fell's Election," *New York Times,* November 10, 1994.

21. *CQ Almanac* (103rd Congress, 2nd session) *1995,* p. 563.

22. Ibid., p. 565.

23. Ibid., p. 578.

24. Grover G. Norquist, *Rock the House* (Ft. Lauderdale, Fla.: VYTIS Press, 1995), pp. 9–10.

25. George Will, "Reagan's Third Victory," *Washington Post,* November 10, 1994.

26. "Conventional Wisdom Watch," *Newsweek,* November 21, 1994, p. 10.

27. Howard Fineman, "Revenge of the Right," *Newsweek,* November 21, 1994, p. 41.

28. David Mason, "A Real Revolution," *The World & I,* April 1995, p. 31.

29. Gingrich, *To Renew America,* p. 139.

30. Ibid., p. 232.

31. Ibid., p. 141.

32. *CQ Almanac* (104th Congress, 1st session) *1995,* pp. 1–6.

33. Kevin Phillips, "The Rise and Folly of the GOP: As Voter Disgust Rises, So Do Clinton's Chances," *Washington Post,* August 6, 1995; Morton Kondracke, "Debate That Tilted to Gingrich," *Washington Times,* October 7, 1996.

34. Mona Charen, "Can the Revolution Recover?" *Washington Times,* May 17, 1996.

35. *Congressional Quarterly Almanac, 104th Congress, 1st Session, 1995* (Washington, D.C.: Congressional Quarterly, 1996), pp. 1–11.

36. Ibid., pp. 1–4.

37. Charen, "Can the Revolution Recover?"

38. David Maraniss and Michael Weisskopf, *"Tell Newt to Shut Up!"* (New York: Touchstone, 1996), p. 152; *CQ Almanac 1996,* pp. 1–23.

39. Charen, "Can the Revolution Recover?"

40. Stephen Moore, "The Little Engine That Couldn't," *National Review,* September 25, 1995, p. 27.

41. *CQ Almanac* (104th Congress, 1st session) *1995,* pp. 1–11.

42. Ralph Hallow, "Supports a Line Item Veto Even If It Benefits Clinton," *Washington Times,* November 10, 1994.

43. David Keene, interview with the author, April 28, 1998.

44. Ceci Connolly, *Gainsville (Ga.) Times,* February 16, 1997.

45. Rich Lowry, "Who's Shrinking Whom?" *National Review,* December 25, 1995, pp. 34–35.

46. Alison Mitchell, "Clinton Offers Challenge to Nation, Declaring 'Era of Big Government Is Over,'" *New York Times,* January 24, 1996.

47. Maraniss and Weisskopf, *"Tell Newt to Shut Up!"* p. 205.

48. Lee Edwards, "The Winner—and Still President," *The World & I,* k.iNovember 1996, p. 25.

49. George Will, *The Woven Figure: Conservatism and America's Fabric* (New York: Scribner, 1997), p. 246.

50. *1996 CQ Almanac* (104th Congress), pp. 1-12–1-13.

51. Ramesh Ponnuru, "Reagan's Spoiled Children," *National Review,* May 6, 1996, pp. 36–38.

52. Morton C. Blackwell, "Why Clinton Won," *The World & I,* January 1997, p. 78.

53. Ibid., p. 76.

54. "Theirs to Lose," *National Review,* November 25, 1996, pp. 12, 14.

55. *1996 CQ Almanac* (104th Congress), pp. 11–34.

56. Kevin Merida, "Gingrich Pledges to Find 'Common Ground' with Clinton," *Washington Post,* November 7, 1996.

57. Dale Russakoff, "He Knew What He Wanted," *Washington Post,* December 18, 1994.

58. John E. Yang and Helen Dewar, "Ethics Panel Supports Reprimand of Gingrich, $300,000 Sanction for House Rules Violations," *Washington Post,* January 18, 1997.

59. James Bennett, "President, Citing Education as Top Priority of 2nd Term, Asks for a 'Call to Action,'" *New York Times,* February 5, 1997.

60. George F. Will, "Infantile Spectacle," *Washington Post,* February 6, 1997.

61. Elperin and Hei, *Roll Call,* p. 23.

62. "With Tone, Tenor First Session, It Seemed Like Old Times," *CQ,* December 6, 1997, p. 2975.

63. "Bad Deal, Worse Leadership," *Human Events,* May 16, 1997, p. 1; Stephen Moore, "This Is Biggest-Spending Congress Ever," *Human Events,* October 10, 1997, p. 8.

64. Moore, "Biggest-Spending Congress."

65. "The Cato Institute," *Human Events,* July 8, 1994, p. 14.

66. Overheard by the author at a meeting of the Grover Norquist coalition, June 20, 1997.

67. Paul Gigot, "Coup de GOP: Off with Our Own Heads!" *Wall Street Journal,* July 18, 1997.

68. "Some Folks Are Going to Have a Lot to Answer For," excerpts from Hillary Rodham Clinton's interview with Matt Lauer on NBC's *Today* show, January 27, 1998, *Washington Post,* January 28, 1998.

69. John F. Harris, "Clinton Pledges Activist Agenda," *Washington Post,* January 28, 1998.

70. Eric Pianin, "First Balanced Federal Budget in 30 Years Offered by Clinton," *Washington Post,* February 3, 1998.

71. Clay Chandler, "President's Balancing Act Has Wide Political Appeal," *Washington Post,* February 3, 1998; John Godfrey, "Clinton Proposes $1.7 Trillion Budget," *Washington Times,* February 3, 1998; James K. Glassman, "Budget Whoppers," *Washington Post,* February 3, 1998.

72. Glassman, "Budget Whoppers."

73. Newt Gingrich, "Conservatism Now," *National Review,* December 22, 1997, pp. 42–45.

74. Newt Gingrich, "Setting New Legislative Goals for 1998," *The Hill,* January 28, 1998.

75. Phyllis Schlafly to the author, August 10, 1997.

76. Richard A. Ware to the author, September 2, 1997.

77. Reed Larson to the author, August 13, 1997.

78. Richard Brookhiser to the author, August 4, 1997.

79. Forrest McDonald to the author, July 29, 1997; Peter D. Hannaford to the author, August 11, 1997.

80. Leonard P. Liggio to the author, July 29, 1997.

81. Donald Devine to the author, July 28, 1997.

82. Alvin S. Felzenberg to the author, January 1, 1998.

83. David Keene, interview with the author, April 28, 1998.

84. Grover G. Norquist to the author, August 26, 1997.

85. Alfred S. Regnery to the author, September 3, 1997.

86. Edwin J. Feulner, Jr., to the author, August 11, 1997.

87. William A. Rusher to the author, August 19, 1997.

Chapter 16: Can Conservatives Govern?

1. Alexander Hamilton, James Madison, and John Jay, *The Federalist Papers* (New York: Mentor Books, 1961), No. 51, pp. 320–325.

2. James Q. Wilson, *American Government: Institutions and Policies,* 4th ed. (Lexington, Mass.: D. C. Heath, 1989), p. 25.

3. Madison, Federalist No. 51.

4. Ibid.

5. Wilson, *American Government,* p. 53.

6. Federalist No. 45, pp. 288–294.

7. Russell Kirk, *The Conservative Mind* (Chicago: Regnery, 1953), p. 63.

8. John Adams to Mercy Warren, quoted in Forrest McDonald, *Novus Ordo Seclorum:*

The Intellectual Origins of the Constitution (Lawrence: University of Kansas Press, 1985), p. 72.

9. Matthew Spalding and Patrick J. Garrity, *A Sacred Union of Citizens: George Washington's Farewell Address and the American Character* (Lanham, Md.: Rowman and Littlefield, 1996), p. 187.

10. Donald Lambro, "Somnolent Strategy," *Washington Times,* March 20, 1998.

11. John Engler, "The Liberal Rout," *Policy Review* (January–February 1997): 44–45.

12. Ibid., p. 46.

13. Robert Rector, "Wisconsin's Welfare Miracle," *Policy Review* (March–April 1997): 25.

14. Engler, "The Liberal Rout," p. 48.

15. George F. Will, *The Woven Figure: Conservatism and America's Fabric* (New York: Scribner, 1997), p. 108.

16. Robert Rector and William F. Lauber, *America's Failed $5.4 Trillion War on Poverty* (Washington, D.C.: Heritage Foundation, 1995), p. 2.

17. Rush Limbaugh, *See, I Told You So* (New York: Pocket Books, 1993), p. 349.

18. Will, *The Woven Figure,* p. 110.

19. Edwin J. Feulner, Jr., "The Conservative March: A Long View," March 3, 1997, distributed by the Heritage Foundation.

20. Matthew Spalding, "The Trouble with TR," *National Review,* February 23, 1998, pp. 31–34.

21. R. Emmett Tyrrell, Jr., *The Conservative Crack-Up* (New York: Simon & Schuster, 1992), p. 238.

22. Paul Gottfried, *The Conservative Movement* (New York: Twayne, 1993), p. 161.

23. Ibid., p. 162.

24. Ibid., pp. 165–166.

25. Judith Warner and Max Berley, *Newt Gingrich: Speaker to America* (New York: Signet, 1995), p. 194.

26. Robert H. Bork, *Slouching Toward Gomorrah* (New York: ReganBooks, 1995), p. 139.

27. T. S. Eliot to Russell Kirk, quoted in Russell Kirk, *The Sword of Imagination: Memoirs of a Half Century of Literary Conflict* (Grand Rapids, Mich.: William B. Erdmans Publishing, 1995), p. 214.

28. Patrick J. Buchanan, "America Deserves Better Than '70s Liberalism," *Human Events,* August 29, 1992, p. 11.

29. "Media Bias More Blatant Than Ever," *Human Events,* September 5, 1992, p. 3.

30. "Did Stress on Social Issues Undermine Bush?" *Human Events,* September 5, 1992, p. 3.

31. Michael J. Catanzaro, "Family Research Council," *Human Events,* October 10, 1997, p. 18.

32. "Focus on the Family," *Human Events,* February 23, 1996, p. 18.

33. Ibid.

34. "Beverley LaHaye and Concerned Women for America," *Human Events,* February 18, 1994, p. 10.

35. L. Brent Bozell, "A Move in the Right Direction," *Media Research Center 10 Year Report,* October 1997, p. 1.

36. "The Right News Right Now," news release, Media Research Center, June 16, 1998.

37. Andrew Rosenthal, "Quayle Says Riots Arose from Burst of Social Anarchy," *New York Times,* May 20, 1992; Barbara Vobejda, "Can a Sitcom Change Society?" *Washington Post,* May 21, 1992.

38. Barbara Defoe Whitehead, "Dan Quayle Was Right," *Atlantic Monthly* (April 1993): 1–21.
39. Steve Forbes, "The Things That Are Unseen" (address to Christian Coalition Conference, September 13, 1997, Atlanta, Georgia, Internet/MCI ID: 376-5414).
40. "Gingrich Envisions a New 'Contract' Emerging in 2000," interview of Newt Gingrich with editors and reporters of the *Washington Times,* June 9, 1997.
41. Memo of Dick Armey to Republican Members of the House of Representatives, January 16, 1998.
42. Ibid.
43. Morton C. Blackwell, "Thoughts on the Conservative Movement Now" (paper prepared for the Frank Meyer Society, Washington, D.C., November 18, 1992).
44. Ibid.
45. Grover G. Norquist, *Rock the House* (Ft. Lauderdale, Fla.: VYTIS Press, 1995), p. 34; also see Grover G. Norquist, "The New Majority: The 'Leave Us Alone' Coalition," *Imprimis,* May 1996.
46. William J. Bennett to the author, October 3, 1997.
47. Edwin J. Feulner, Jr., to the author, August 11, 1997.
48. Neal B. Freeman to the author, November 27, 1997.
49. Frank Gaffney to the author, September 6, 1997.
50. James McClellan to the author, August 14, 1997.
51. James Piereson to the author, July 28, 1997.
52. Charles Krauthammer, "Conservative Malaise," *Washington Post,* October 3, 1997.
53. Phyllis Schlafly to the author, August 10, 1997.

Index

Index

Index